CONTRACT LAW IN PERSPECTIVE

Fourth Edition

Cavendish
Publishing
Limited

London • Sydney • Portland, Oregon

CONTRACT LAW IN PERSPECTIVE

Fourth Edition

Linda Mulcahy, LLB, LLM, PhD
Anniversary Professor of Law and Society,
Birkbeck, University of London

John Tillotson, BA, LLM, PGCE
formerly Faculty of Law, University of Manchester

Cavendish
Publishing
Limited

London • Sydney • Portland, Oregon

Fourth edition first published in Great Britain 2004 by
Cavendish Publishing Limited, The Glass House,
Wharton Street, London WC1X 9PX, United Kingdom
Telephone: + 44 (0)20 7278 8000   Facsimile: + 44 (0)20 7278 8080
Email: info@cavendishpublishing.com
Website: www.cavendishpublishing.com

Published in the United States by Cavendish Publishing
c/o International Specialized Book Services,
5824 NE Hassalo Street, Portland,
Oregon 97213-3644, USA

Published in Australia by Cavendish Publishing (Australia) Pty Ltd
45 Beach Street, Coogee, NSW 2034, Australia
Telephone: + 61 (2)9664 0909   Facsimile: +61 (2)9664 5420

© Mulcahy, L and Tillotson, J   2004
Third Edition   1995
Fourth Edition   2004

The first two editions of this book were published by Butterworths Ltd.

British Library Cataloguing in Publication Data
Mulcahy, Linda 1962–
Contract law in perspective – 4th ed
1 Contracts – England 2 Contracts – Wales
I Title II Tillotson, John
346.4'2'02

Library of Congress Cataloguing in Publication Data
Data available

ISBN 1-85941-771-X
ISBN 978-1-859-41771-3

1 3 5 7 9 10 8 6 4 2

Typeset by Phoenix Photosetting, Chatham, Kent
Printed and bound in Great Britain by
Biddles Ltd, Kings Lynn, Norfolk

PREFACE

In 1981, when Tillotson's first edition of *Contract Law in Perspective* was published, I was in my first year at university studying for my LLB. I spent a considerable amount of time in the library trying to understand the intricacies of the 15 or so contract cases which we were asked to read each week. The weighty 'black letter' texts my lecturers directed me to in order to help me understand the cases failed to stimulate and were insufficiently critical of formal rules for my liking. They dealt with the detail at the expense of the big ideas. I stopped going to seminars and spent some time in bookshops looking for an approach to contract law that would inspire me to return to the cases. I was saved by the publication of Tillotson which moved away from doctrinal intricacies to reflect on the function of contract law, its relevance to my life and the reasons why it was an important and relevant field of scholarship. At the time it was first published, Tillotson's *Contract Law in Perspective* was a breath of fresh air for those of us who wanted to place what we were learning within a historical, political and sociological context. I gave up all thought of abandoning the law and stuck to it.

Twenty-three years later as a law professor I am able to direct my students to a burgeoning number of socio-legal and critical texts on the subject. Within academic circles we talk more readily of the importance of understanding contracts from a range of different perspectives. A host of empirical studies now inform our understanding of how contract law works in practice and its relevance to those who use it on a regular basis. At one level, the message of these studies is depressing. We have had to accept that the law of contract is frequently ignored and that it often lacks legitimacy within the business community. But at another level, there is a growing sense of the challenge this poses to contract scholars; we are undoubtedly beginning to have the debates which allow us to make closer links between everyday understanding of obligations and the law. As I have grappled with relational contract theory, feminist perspectives on the subject and notions of good faith and inequality, I have been made patently aware of what an exciting time it is to study the subject. It goes without saying that I feel extremely honoured to follow in the steps of John Tillotson in introducing students to law in its everyday setting and looking at it from a range of different perspectives.

In this fourth edition, I have sought to take account of recent developments within the subjects covered as well as rewriting and reorganising many topics within the book. The growth of the literature on contract in context has justified a new chapter on contemporary critiques of contract. The post-Woolf world of litigation also requires that more time be devoted to mediation and self-help remedies. I have also included a case study near the beginning of the book which I hope will encourage students to see contracts and litigation as a complex web of relationships rather than as discrete impersonal exchanges.

I am extremely grateful to a number of people who have helped with the gestation of this project. John Tillotson has been supportive throughout and has done me the honour of trusting my instincts even if the detail of our approaches may have sometimes differed. Carol Mulcahy, a partner at Berwin Leighton Paisner, has so long told me that academics know very little about the real world of negotiations and contracts that I thought it appropriate to invite her to take responsibility for drafting the chapters on remedies and dispute resolution. She has written with such a level of insight that I must concede that she may occasionally be right. Those of you with older siblings will appreciate how difficult it is for me to admit this! I am also indebted to Steve Banks who has provided support as my research assistant, Marie Selwood who has overseen production and copy-editing and Jenny Spiegal who has helped with some of the typing. Ruth Massey and Jon Lloyd at Cavendish Publishing have also been very supportive and extremely patient.

Finally, I am grateful to those who know so much more about contract than me but with whom I have been privileged to work. I was fortunate to take up my first academic job as Hugh Beale's research assistant to whom I owe a more informed love of the subject. Whilst at the Centre for Socio-Legal Studies in Oxford, I was fortunate to continue learning about the real world of contract under the guidance of Don Harris, Dave Campbell and Sally Wheeler. Martha-Marie Kleinhans also allowed me to use her as a sounding board for many of the new issues raised in this edition. Finally, I would like to thank Richard, Connor and Sam for their tolerance of my many faults when writing.

Linda Mulcahy
Anniversary Professor of Law and Society
Birkbeck College
September 2004

CONTENTS

PART THREE: MAKING A DEAL

PART FIVE: THE CONTRACT

TABLE OF CASES

TABLE OF STATUTES

TABLE OF STATUTORY INSTRUMENTS

PART ONE:

INTRODUCTION

CHAPTER 1

INTRODUCTION, AIMS AND GENERAL PRINCIPLES

INTRODUCTION AND AIMS

... the student is, or should be encouraged to study the principles of the law in their context, and to consider critically whether they are apt to meet the needs of society today ... those who are responsible for schools of law have to decide how to find the balance between these three elements, knowledge, analysis and the social context. *Sir Robert Goff*

If I am faced with the alternative of forcing commercial circles to fall in with a legal doctrine which has nothing but precedent to commend it or altering the doctrine so as to conform with what commercial experience has worked out, I know where my choice lies. The law should be responsive as well as, at times, enunciatory, and good doctrine can seldom be divorced from sound practice. *Lord Wilberforce*

In a lecture given some years ago Lord Scarman expressed the view that the law of contract 'if studied in abstraction ... is no more than a generalised theory about the nature and consequences of agreement coupled with rules ... as to the meaning of words and phrases'. This remark quite clearly carries with it criticism of approaches to the study of contract law which place undue emphasis on abstract principles. In this book we argue that a study of contract law is dangerously abstract if it concentrates on legal analysis and technicalities at the expense of how contract functions in everyday life – particularly business life.

The lawyer's view of contract tends to focus on the legal implications of contractual breakdown; on rights, obligations and the consequences of litigation. There are other views. The lawyer's preoccupations by no means occupy the forefront of the businessperson's mind. For someone in business the contract is primarily a facilitative device within an economic cycle which turns on such processes as the acquisition of materials, the production of finished goods, marketing and sales, finance and payment. Business people and economists are also frequently concerned with the cost of contracting. For example, standard form contracts are less expensive to produce than 'tailor-made' documents. It is often the case that, for them, insistence on precise contractual performance is expensive in terms of both money and business relationships.

Lord Scarman's message is quite clear. The person, and that includes the lawyer, who only knows the law of contract, and little or nothing of how contracts are performed, has only a small, incomplete, view. Anthropologists, economists, historians, philosophers, sociologists and others also have much to say about the subject. It would appear that contract law can only acquire a full or true meaning if studied and evaluated in the light of findings from other disciplines and insights from practice.

By the time you finish reading this book you will probably have made tens, if not hundreds, of contracts. Each time you buy a newspaper, get on a bus, rent a DVD, order a book from Amazon or register for your latest course, you are entering into a contract. Few people in a modern society could survive without exchanging their labour for money and their money for goods and services. Moreover, each exchange you make is probably only possible because of earlier exchanges between, for instance, your newsagent and a newspaper owner, the newspaper owner and their paper supplier, the paper supplier and a paper maker. It should soon become clear to you that the law of contract is not a remote and archaic body of rules but a living area of law with which you engage on a daily basis.

The main aim of this book is to present a broader view of the basic features of contract law than that found in the traditional 'black letter' treatments of the subject. The idea of putting the law into its social, political or economic context is not new. However, the aim of looking not only at, but also beyond, legal rules has been pursued more vigorously in some areas than in others. Most expositions of contract law do not venture beyond the rules. They tell us little or nothing of the social or economic significance of those rules, or how they relate to the practices of the business community. The result is an unhealthy division between the study of formal law and an evaluation of the needs of the wider community it should be designed to serve. At a level suitable for student readers, this books starts to remedy those defects.

Debate and argument regarding the state of the health of contract law continue more energetically than ever before. In fact, numerous critiques and suggested theories of contract law have been produced over the last 50 years or so. Many of them point to a 'transformation' of contract law. Writers in this vein argue that there has been a movement, observable in the case law and statutory interventions from 'principles to pragmatism', from 'doctrine to discretion' or from 'market-individualism to consumer-welfarism'. Indeed, as will be seen from the cases, the 19th century foundations of contract law, built on the concepts of promise and agreement, have been to some extent shifted and overlaid by an increased emphasis on such open-ended notions as reliance, reasonableness, good faith and fairness. This can lead to situations where it may be said that the 'old' view of the courts would give rise to a certain result but the 'new' approach would produce a different decision. This sounds like a simple transformation but a closer examination of cases reveals that a mixture of old and new approaches is apparent.

This has led some commentators to conclude that the modern law of contract is in a muddle and lacks a set of clear principles to underpin it. For a growing group of academics this crisis relates to the absence of a clear theoretical framework. But the inadequacies of existing doctrine are also made apparent in the work of a number of researchers who have found that the business community often ignores or circumvents contractual rules because they fail to facilitate flexible enough working agreements. These charges are serious because they suggest that the law lacks legitimacy within the very community it emerged to serve. Looking at contract law in perspective allows us to interrogate these claims in ways which are not possible in books which focus on doctrine and rules. On a modest scale, discussion of such changes and debate are built in to this examination of contract law, together with consideration of the likely influences operating on the law which have led to such changes. Here, an essential factor is the changing nature of the relationship between contract itself, the individual and the government.

GENERAL PRINCIPLES: THE NATURE AND CONTENT OF CONTRACT LAW

In a society where the exchange of goods and services is central to its economic order, as in a developing capitalist society based on free enterprise, a means of supporting the process of exchange needs to be found. It is in this context that the foundations of modern contract law were established. It was argued at the time that contract was the juristic form for the distribution and utilisation of the goods and personal abilities that are in existence in society. By the third quarter of the 19th century, British society had experienced accelerating industrialisation, generated by scientific innovation, economic entrepreneurship and increasing access to both capital and labour. This gave rise to an unprecedented boom in trade, both at home and in expanding markets overseas. This boom had been accompanied by a similarly massive development of those areas of the law which were designed to facilitate and regulate business relationships. In particular, there was a considerable expansion of contract, commercial and company law.

At the time that the classical model emerged, it was more accurate than it is today to refer to a general law of contract. Even then, there were specialist rules which related to certain types of contract but the tendency to develop special rules has increased, especially in the field of labour law and contracts involving customers. Despite this development, it is still possible to state that there are general principles which apply to *all* contracts irrespective of the type of subject matter or parties involved. Many contractual problems, however, involve a consideration of both general principles *and* particular rules. Let us consider, for example, the question of breach of contract. In a legal action, it might well be necessary to take account of the *general* principle that a serious breach gives the injured party a right to terminate the contract. However, if the breach has been committed by a seller of goods, it may also be necessary to bring into play further *particular* rules which apply to sales to consumers. These can be found in specific legislation, such as the Sale of Goods Act, first passed in 1893 in order to protect those in weaker bargaining positions in a contract.

The general principles of contract law are still, for the most part, of a judge-made character. Some of them are centuries old but many date from the time of the industrial revolution. However, since the late 19th century, principles and rules, both old and new, have tended to become incorporated into statutes concerning particular transactions. Statutes of this kind have for some time marked out most of the ground rules for what is called commercial or consumer law, and they govern, for example, the sale and hire purchase of goods and many aspects of transport and insurance. A similar process has seen the later emergence, by means of acts such as the Restrictive Trade Practices Act 1956 and the Fair Trading Act 1973, of competition law and a correspondingly radical decline in the applicability of judge-made rules in this field. As regards contracts of employment, a mass of modern legislation and voluntary codes and practices has virtually removed the general principles of contract law from the employment arena. In broad terms, the general principles of contract law may be regarded today as foundations which are necessary in some areas, such as commercial law, but have become largely irrelevant in others, such as labour law. In another sense they can be regarded as a *residue*; those rules that remain untouched by, or are merely amended by, statutory interventions into the judge-made law of transactions.

There is another sense in which it is important to look at contract law in an abstract way. The theoretical assumptions underpinning the classical model of contract were heavily influenced by prevailing economic theories of the 19th century which treated contracting parties as economic units assumed to have equal bargaining strength and endowed with complete freedom of decision. Indeed, the key theme underpinning contract law during this period was the idea of *freedom of contract*. According to this view, it was in the best interests of individual enterprise and a free market economy for the courts to uphold the terms of contracts agreed by the parties wherever possible. The premise behind this was that when the parties are allowed to determine the basis on which they exchange goods, services and money, they are more likely to be happy with the outcome. It has been argued that free exchange of this kind allows the members of a society to determine supply and demand of goods and services. If they are free to make their own choices about the goods and services they need and suppliers are free to respond to consumer demand then it is argued that the market will in the long run supply consumers with what they want at a price they are willing to pay. It followed that the judges saw their role as a minimalist one. The purpose of the law was not to control the terms on which parties might contract, nor would it readily give relief if agreed terms turned out to be harsh or unfair to one party. It is these principles to which lawyers have recourse when analysing and unravelling contractual problems and to which many judges still aspire in setting disputes brought to court for resolution.

It can be seen from this that the notion of freedom of contract is closely associated with a belief in the free market:

> If there is one thing more than another which public policy requires, it is that men of full age and competent understanding shall have the utmost liberty in contracting, and that their contracts, when entered into freely and voluntarily, shall be held sacred and shall be enforced by Courts of Justice.

However, much of the history of contract law since these words were spoken by Sir George Jessel in 1875 concerns the decline in influence of the idea of freedom of contract. In part, this has come about as a result of social change. Almost 130 years on, it is no longer the individual entrepreneur but the government which is primarily concerned with the allocation of resources in the British economy. The facts of economic life have also revealed the myth of equality of bargaining power presumed to exist between contracting parties and upon which the idea of freedom of contract rests. But it is also argued that there was as little equality of bargaining strength between employer and employee in the 19th century as there is today between a large-scale supplier of goods and individual consumers. In this sense, many modern commentators have argued that the notion of freedom of contract was never an adequate social tool through which to understand the market.

The general principles of contract and doctrines associated with them are by now immense. Treatment of them usually takes the form, in lawyers' books, of a seemingly timeless catalogue of rules, sub-rules and exceptions. We have tried to avoid this approach. As we have already argued, the changing nature of the relationships between contract law, its political and economic environment, and business practice is at the heart of a proper understanding of this field of study. We will return to these broad themes later in the book. But before doing so, we think it important to sketch out a general picture of the common structure for the study of contract. The aim of the section which follows is to provide an overview of the general principles and 'rules' governing the law of contract. Having touched on some of the premises underlining this area of the law, the remainder of this chapter will map out the treatment of these themes in this book.

AGREEMENT, PROMISES AND BARGAIN

The key to understanding the law of contract is an appreciation of the continued importance of the related ideas of agreement, promise and bargain. It follows on from the idea of freedom of contract that a contract is taken to result from an agreement between the parties to it. Agreement has traditionally been seen as coming about through the interlocking mechanism of a precise offer from one party unequivocally accepted by the other. The idea of promise is essential here for when the parties reach agreement they are making promises about something they are going to do. If you buy a compact disc (CD) from an internet site using a credit card, the company you are buying the disc from is, at the moment of agreement, promising to send the CD to you. In exchange, you are promising to allow them access to a certain amount of money in your account. At the moment of agreement, when the company accepts your offer to buy the CD, the law requires that the two promises must be fulfilled.

There are two important issues about agreement that must be fully understood. In recent years the law has been much concerned with the reality of agreement between parties possessing unequal bargaining strength. The legislature and judiciary have been particularly concerned about the marked tendency for economically powerful parties, such as large-scale suppliers of goods or services, to impose their terms and conditions of contract on economically weak parties such as consumers. Where necessity or absence of choice in these circumstances gives the weaker party no real option but to 'agree', the law has moved in several ways to redress the balance of power. This first point can lead us to our second.

Although agreement has been used to establish the existence of contract, it does not necessarily clearly determine the full range of rights and obligations created. For example, agreement is reached between Powermotors and Connor over the sale of a motor car for £12,000. The contract is in writing and is made up of a number of what are known as *express terms*. These relate to such matters as the price to be paid, the fact that the car is new and the terms of delivery. However, as well as express terms, binding on the parties as a result of their agreement, other *implied terms* may well be added to the express terms by statutes. The Sale of Goods Act 1979 lays down, for instance, that in most instances goods shall be of an acceptable commercial standard. This rule takes the form of a term which is imposed on the parties and becomes just as much an integral part of the contract as the other, express, terms. In this way, the legislature has intervened to regulate the contract in the interests of protecting the weaker party.

CONSIDERATION

Agreement about what is to be done is not enough to form a contract: there must also be an exchange of something of material value. If Connor agrees with Itay that he will give him his new car if Itay promises to be at his house at 10 am on Wednesday, there is agreement but no 'consideration'. This transaction would be viewed by the law as a gift, as Itay has not traded anything for the car. For the agreement to be legally enforceable as a contract, there has to be *exchange*. Each of the parties has to lose something and gain something else. Because of the importance of forward planning in the business sector, promises to exchange something in the future can be treated as consideration. So, for instance, there would be a valid contract if Itay agreed with Connor that in exchange for the car he would give him £15,000 from his bank account once he had transferred funds from a trust fund. The agreement would be considered to be supported by 'executory' or future consideration and Itay would be in breach of contract if he failed to give Connor £15,000. If he did provide the money, this would be treated as 'executed' consideration. Either way, the importance of the example for present purposes is that the agreement supported by consideration would be enforceable even if the car and money had not yet changed hands. The astute among you may have noticed that Connor would do rather well from this sale as when he purchased the car from Powermotors it only cost him £12,000. In the absence of duress or statutory protection, this would not be a ground for setting aside the contract which would be valid even if Itay paid £1 million for two wing mirrors. This is because the principle of freedom of contract requires that it is for the parties themselves to determine what constitutes a good bargain, not the courts. However, we shall see in Chapter 8 how these basic tenets of the doctrine of consideration have been challenged.

BREACH

None of the cases you will read about in this book would have come before the courts unless something had gone wrong. It follows that the law reports you will study involve an action for breach. This happens where a party defectively performs or fails to perform the whole or part of their contractual obligations. It may be an action for breach of express terms or for breach of implied terms. It is also worth noting at this stage that not all contractual breaches are of the same significance. The remedies for breach provided for the injured party by the law of contract reflect this distinction, wider remedies being available in the case of serious breaches. However, the basic common law remedy for any breach of contract is damages, which are available to compensate the injured party for the loss they have suffered as a result of the breach.

STRUCTURE OF THE BOOK

In the remainder of this first section we introduce you to the sad tale of Angie and Georgie. The characters in this case study have become involved in a number of contracts which raise important legal problems. The aim of the chapter is to put these problems within the context of their broader life, needs, desires and networks of relationships. As with all legal problems these contexts are as likely to determine the outcome of a dispute as formal legal rules. Examples from this case study appear in all the subsequent chapters.

Part Two of this book carries on from the introductory section by establishing some 'views' about the notion of contract. Legal and business perspectives are introduced, as are some sociological and economic ideas and influences. These 'views' of contract are set within the framework of a shift from what is generally described as a *laissez-faire* economy to a mixed economy. This shift broadly coincides with the rise and fall of the idea of freedom of contract, and hence with a transformation of contract's function and substance. The aim of the section is to introduce students to this historical account of contract in order that they can understand the environments in which different visions of contract have emerged. Students are also introduced to contemporary critiques of contracts. The literature on relational contract theory, feminist perspectives and empirical understandings of the subject provides students with a range of tools with which to critique and interrogate traditional models. These various themes and perspectives are pursued throughout the remainder of the book by reference to specific doctrines and practices.

Part Three focuses on how contracts are formed. It looks at the process by which a contract emerges from negotiations which may be lengthy and protracted. It is in this section above all that students will become aware of the formalistic and 'rule-bound' tendencies of the English common law. We will discuss these tendencies with reference to alternative views of the formation process which draw on ideas about the expectations of the parties, their respect of and need for formality, and understanding of obligation.

The fourth Part is rather loosely labelled 'Bargaining naughtiness and formation problems'. Where Part Three introduces the reader to ideas around what ought to happen before a binding contract can be recognised or enforced, Part Four focuses on the various ways in which contract may be set aside because of behaviour considered to be inappropriate. The next section moves on to look at what is contained within a contract and particular emphasis is placed on the trend towards judicial and legislative interference with content. Here, the stress is on the ways in which welfarist approaches to the law of contract have mitigated against the harshness of the market. The tensions which are played out in case law and commentaries about the appropriate rule of the judiciary and legislature in the regulation of 'private' contracts remains significant and many examples of these tensions emerge from this section. Moreover, they will undoubtedly remain a subject for discussion in many years to come.

In the final substantive section, we look at what happens when things go wrong in the performance of the contract. The focus here is on what constitutes breach of contract, the remedies which are available for breach and the ways in which disputing parties are most likely to resolve their dispute.

The vast majority of cases to be found in this book are of modern origin and therefore illustrate contemporary business situations. Discussion of many of them is, however, on a modest scale as is inevitable in a work of this nature. Ultimately, there is no substitute for the law reports or a cases and materials book. At the end of each chapter is a bibliography drawn from a wide range of materials and a series of questions designed to test and expand on the subject matter of preceding pages. It is also important to pursue further reading from these references. The choice of questions aims to keep links between the various topics in the book firmly in the forefront of the student's mind so that a co-ordinated view of contract will eventually emerge.

CONCLUDING REMARKS

A large and important part of the general law of contract is concerned with the issues outlined in this chapter and lawyers specialising in this field of law will spend a considerable amount of time considering whether there is a binding agreement, the scope of the agreement, the significance of breach and the remedies available. There are, however, other important issues which need discussion which have lately found their way into lawyers' treatments of contract. For example, should it be reliance on the undertakings of another, rather than a promise supported by consideration which signals the start of a contract? How relevant are the old rules on agreement and promises to modern standard form contracts prepared by an economically stronger party and presented to a weaker on a 'take-it-or-leave-it' basis? Does it make a difference if the economically powerful party is a private sector enterprise, such as a motor vehicle manufacturer, or the provider of a service such as gas, electricity or rail transport? How relevant are the traditional rules of contract law to the contracts entered into by government departments such as the Ministry of Defence or the Department of Health? The vast majority of contractual disputes are not decided by the courts, so who decides or settles them and how? These are important questions to be considered by today's students and tomorrow's practitioners. All these issues are related and it is social, economic and political changes that have thrown many of them up. Mass production, globalisation, standardisation, imperfect competition and increased governmental regulation have all created strains upon and the need for a broader view of contract and contract law if they are to remain legitimate in the eyes of those who use them.

REFERENCES AND FURTHER READING

Adams, J and Brownsword, R (2000) *Understanding Contract Law*, 3rd edn, London: Sweet & Maxwell.

Atiyah, P (1989) *An Introduction to the Law of Contract*, 4th edn, 'Part 1: The development of the modern law of contract', Oxford: Clarendon.

Collins, H (2002) *Regulating Contracts*, Oxford: OUP.

Friedman, L (1965) *Contract Law in the USA*, 'Introduction', Madison, WI: University of Wisconsin Press.

Tillotson, J 'Anyone for contract?' (1976) JALT 135.

Wightman, J (1996) *Contract – A Critical Commentary*, London: Pluto Press.

For a good summary of how the law of contract can be studied from a rule-based perspective, see Upex, R (1999) *Davies on Contract*, 8th edn, London: Sweet & Maxwell.

QUESTIONS

(1) 'In principle it is not easy to see why the law relating to the sale of goods should be different from the law relating to the performance of other contractual obligations, whether charterparties or other types of contract. Sale of goods law is but one branch of the general law of contract. It is desirable that the same legal

principle should apply to the law of contract as a whole and that a different legal principle should not apply to different branches of the law': Roskill LJ in *Cehave NV v Bremer Handelsgesellschaft mbH* (1976). Do you agree with this statement? Can you think of any reasons why specialist rules might be needed in certain areas? Give reasons for your response supported by examples.

(2) What restrictions or qualifications of freedom of contract are to be found in Sir George Jessel's statement about the subject reproduced above?

(3) In *Lochner v New York* (1905), a majority of the US Supreme Court declared a New York statute imposing maximum hours for work in bakeries to be unconstitutional on the basis that no legislature should pass any law impairing the obligations of contract.

Justice Holmes expressed the following view in his dissenting judgment:

> This case is decided upon an economic theory which a large part of the country does not entertain. If it were a question whether I agreed with that theory, I should desire to study it further and long before making up my mind. But I do not conceive that to be my duty, because I strongly believe that my agreement or disagreement has nothing to do with the right of a majority to embody their opinions in law. It is settled by various decisions of this court that state constitutions and state laws may regulate life in many ways which we as legislators might think as injudicious or if you like as tyrannical as this, and which equally with this interfere with the liberty to contract ... The liberty of the citizen to do as he likes so long as he does not interfere with the liberty of others to do the same, which has been a shibboleth for some well-known writers, is interfered with by school laws, by the Post Office, by every state or municipal institution which takes his money for purposes thought desirable, whether he likes it or not.

Do you think it is appropriate for people to be left alone to make a contract on the terms they see fit without interference by the state? Compile a list of reasons for and against Justice Holmes' argument.

CHAPTER 2

THE SAD TALE OF ANGIE AND GEORGIE

INTRODUCTION

Short problem questions dealing with a particular legal doctrine are regularly used in university law schools to encourage students to take the concepts and rules they have learnt about and apply them to new fact patterns. One of the main aims of such exercises is to encourage students to apply the abstract to the specific and to test the limits of a doctrine or judgment. The disputes which contracting parties bring before the court will each have unique elements. What we ask students to do in applying doctrine to new cases is to establish whether the fact pattern before them is sufficient to bring it within a particular doctrine or judicial line of reasoning or not. Exam papers up and down the country are full of problem questions which attempt to stretch the application of the contractual canon to its limits.

In a book which aims to study contract law in perspective, it is difficult to justify presenting students with small discrete fact patterns which are concerned with just one doctrine. In real life, lawyers are presented with long stories by their clients and part of their task is to sift through these accounts of the harm that has been done to people and determine what is legally relevant or irrelevant. Moreover, a particular set of facts may raise questions about a host of doctrines which could be argued in the alternative if the case were ever to reach a court. Finally, you will soon realise that most disputes about contract never get to court. This may be because of extra-legal considerations to do with the relationship between the contracting parties, because there is insufficient evidence to support a claimant's case, or because they do not have the financial resources necessary to pursue litigation. These factors will influence the lawyer and client considerably when they are deciding what to do. The case study which follows tells a story in which there are networks based on personal relationships, trust and commercial interests. In addition to the usual array of facts which can be matched to a range of doctrines, there are evidential problems, financial constraints and emotional entanglements which should all have a part to play in the advice which is given to the parties. We suggest that you read the case study through and respond to the questions at the end before turning to any of the other chapters in the book.

LOVE AT FIRST SIGHT

Angie and Georgie are lovers and have been together for 10 years. They met in the early 1990s when they were both working in the international marketing department at the head office of Emmotts, a national supermarket chain. Georgie is a rather moody type while Angie is very lively and gregarious. Despite these differences they were immediately attracted to each other and found that they had a lot of other things in common. Most notably, both of them were disenchanted working for a large impersonal organisation whose only interest was making money.

Angie and Georgie dated for three months after which they decided that they wanted to be together for the rest of their lives. They were both opposed to marriage but at a candlelit dinner, witnessed by their friend Kirsteen (an international vegetable buyer for Emmotts) and their parents, they vowed to love, honour and respect each other whatever happened and to support each other financially and emotionally in sickness and in health. Georgie later embroidered the vows in a tapestry which they hung in the entrance hall of their studio flat for everyone to see. In 1992, Angie and Georgie adopted Zen and five years later in 1997 they adopted Dylan.

A NEW BEGINNING

A year after meeting they decided to give up their jobs as marketing executives. They sold their flat in London, moved to St Ives and set up a health food store called Earth2Earth! which specialised in selling a wide range of organic root crops at low cost. They bought a rare but reliable vintage Dormobile at an auction for use as a mobile shop in remote villages and for making deliveries. Fortunately, the Dormobile was also big enough for them to live in while they looked for more permanent accommodation. Angie used some of her savings to purchase a computer and printed out some handbills and posters which she left around St Ives.

After looking around at a number of premises they rented a shop in St Ives High Street from a retiring electrician and part-time musician called Mister C who was going to live next door, rent free, with his sister Missy J. The premises consisted of a shop downstairs, a storeroom in the garden and a self-contained flat above the shop. They decided to employ a delivery assistant and were delighted when Chelsea, Mister C's granddaughter, applied for the job. Because of their political ideals, Angie and Georgie paid her a wage which was much higher than the average for the area.

A group of organic farmers known locally as Orange Peril plc agreed to supply Angie and Georgie with five tons of their top of the range root crops every week at a reasonable price as long as they did not sell to anyone outside St Ives or in competition with the other stores in the area supplied by Orange Peril plc. Angie and Georgie were delighted to become involved with this established group and were particularly pleased when they were able to negotiate a further discount because they did not require Orange Peril plc to clean the vegetables and were prepared to collect the order. This meant that they could fulfil their mission of selling the stock on at a low price and promote the crops as being 'straight from the earth' on their publicity materials.

Their new venture was not well-received by local farmers producing non-organic crops. One local farmer called Max was particularly opposed to the scheme. Like others in the area he ran his own farm shops and was worried that the low prices at which Angie and Georgie intended to sell their stock would mean that he would lose a lot of custom.

THE BUSINESS THRIVES

Despite the hostility from local farmers, their business thrived and they soon had a healthy turnover and modest profit. Much of this was due to Missy J who quickly became a great supporter of their enterprise. She spread the word in St Ives amongst her pensioner friends at the local reggae club that the store sold and delivered cheap, good quality food. Angie and Georgie were overjoyed when, as a result of the publicity, *Organic Weekly* ran a very complimentary feature on them. This led to them securing a contract with the Monkish Soup Company to supply them with washed and sliced carrots for their 'Winter Warmer Root Soup'. In order to fulfil the contract they made an agreement with a local student called Marcus that he would deliver the carrots to the Monkish Soup Company in London three times a week on his way to attending classes at the Chelsea College of Art. In exchange he was paid £400 a week, plus petrol expenses. On the strength of Monkish Soup Company's assurances that they were likely to place regular weekly orders, Angie and Georgie hired an expensive carrot cleaning and slicing machine for £7,000 from the Wacky Machine Company which speeded up the process of preparing the order. In addition, they converted the storeroom into an office and work area dedicated to this project and took on more casual staff.

Although no paperwork was produced, the agreement ran successfully for seven years. During that time they build up a particularly good relationship with Ned, the buyer for Monkish, and came to trust him completely. Ned came to visit them at the beginning of every season and talked through the orders for the months ahead. He talked through their business plans with them and often made useful suggestions as to how they might increase their profit. Two years ago he told them that Monkish were expanding their business into pesto sauce and Angie and Georgie started to grow basil under Ned's guidance with a view to supplying Monkish with ingredients for pesto sauce in the future.

On Missy J's recommendation Dipti, an eccentric amateur cook who lives in the local manor house, also started to place large orders for carrots, potatoes and other provisions with Earth2Earth! Because of her mobility problems she placed a monthly order in advance by email and had her vegetables delivered by Chelsea. In time, Angie and Georgie became very fond of Dipti and often invited her around for a meal. When they discovered that Dipti was almost bankrupt and had recently had her telephone disconnected because she couldn't pay the bill, they suggested that she no longer had to pay for her weekly order. Dipti was overjoyed but said that she could not take charity. She accepted their offer but only if they would agree to her giving them a dish of her home made Hepworth risotto every week. In reality the risotto was not to Angie and Georgie's taste and they often threw it away.

THINGS START TO GO WRONG

One sunny September morning at 7 am, some weeks later, Dipti phoned Chelsea to say that she was having a special dinner party that evening for some representatives of a national grocery store chain who were interested in buying her secret recipe for Hepworth risotto. Dipti asked whether she could add artichokes to the order she was due to have delivered that morning. Chelsea said that posed no problem and wrote down the list of additional items on one of Earth2Earth!'s order forms. Unfortunately, Chelsea became distracted while on the phone. She had just had an argument with Marcus, whom she had started dating, and Dylan was pulling at her combat trousers. She handed him a raw carrot to chew on which he proceeded to jam down an uncovered vent in the cooler fan of the carrot cleaning machine. Instead of writing down 'artichokes' Chelsea wrote down 'lots of cokes' before dashing off to attend to a large gash in Dylan's hand.

When the order was delivered at the close of business, Dipti immediately noticed the mistake on the order form placed on the top of the delivery basket. Still in a bad mood after her argument with Marcus, Chelsea said it was not possible to change the cokes at short notice and that Dipti should not be so fussy. Irritated by Dipti's high-handed manner, Chelsea also suggested that Dipti should not have been stupid enough to 'phone at such a busy time in the morning as mistakes are bound to happen'. Dipti refuses to pay for the order.

The next morning Dipti phoned at 7 am in a rage. She claimed that the batch of carrots delivered to her the previous day were infected with 'Spotty Greenfingeritis', an unsightly fungal disease, and that her guests had been vomiting all night. Distraught by the whole experience and shaken by the fear that the supermarket representatives would now shun her, Dipti was hampered with her new plan to start to market and sell her risotto to supermarket chains for three months.

ATTEMPTS TO GET THEMSELVES OUT OF THE MESS

Angie and Georgie phoned up Orange Peril plc to complain about the infected carrots. The company confirmed that there had been an outbreak of this rare disease across the nation and that the British government had just put a complete ban on the sale of carrots for the foreseeable future. In an attempt to avert any further problems, Angie contacted the Monkish Soup Company to warn them that they would be unable to deliver any carrots for a while. She was put through to the company's legal director, Ms Meanlean, who was sympathetic to their problems but pointed out that Monkish's market share was falling and the director of the company was likely to want to sue if Angie and Georgie delivered no carrots. She told them that their Winter Warmer Root Soup was outselling all their other soups by 500% and it was vital to the success of the whole venture that they get a regular supply of clean organic sliced carrots.

Distraught that the situation could ruin their business, Angie and Georgie contacted Kirsteen and begged her to help them find another supplier from the continent where the carrots did not seem to be affected. Kirsteen suggested that they meet her at the Place de Gourmet, a well-known vegetable market on the North Bank of the Seine. Chelsea managed to find a Turkish website which sold cheap ferry tickets and purchased one for Angie and the Dormobile with her credit card. Angie set off, leaving Georgie to look after Dylan, Zen and the shop. But when she got to the ferry port she discovered that the next three ferries had been cancelled because of bad weather, a strike and a shortage of fuel. Angie wanted to complain but had no documentation about the company, her ticket details or the customer service department.

Eventually, she got to Paris and met Kirsteen. They went directly to the Place de Gourmet where there were hundreds of exhibits and stalls but very little produce left. Kirsteen seemed to know her way around and she introduced Angie to Claude, who worked for Gourmond, a large established farm in Normandy. Angie made it clear that she was only interested in good quality organic carrots to make soup and that anything purchased would have to comply with their charter of standards. Claude was adamant that his carrots were far superior to anything Angie could buy in England and claimed that no other carrots in France sold so quickly.

Claude showed Angie some baskets of carrots which were more expensive than those supplied by Orange Peril plc and would reduce their profits considerably. However, they looked very big and healthy and were a lovely bright orange. Angie talked the deal over with Kirsteen and they agreed that Angie really had no choice but to buy them as the market was closing and they had to get back to England that night. Angie bought enough of the carrots to satisfy that month's order, signed the documents that Claude pushed her way, left a cheque and Earth2Earth! charter of standards and dragged Kirsteen away from the paperwork so that they would not miss the last ferry home. Claude told Angie not to worry about loading the carrots in the Dormobile as he would deliver them to her free within 12 hours.

On the way back Angie made clear to Kirsteen how grateful she was to her for helping out at such short notice. She asked her how much commission she owed Kirsteen for helping to arrange the sale. At first Kirsteen said she would take nothing, as Angie and Georgie had been really helpful to her when she was a trainee at Emmotts, but Angie persisted and in the end they decided that Earth2Earth! would pay Kirsteen £500 in 10 £50 instalments. Angie dropped Kirsteen off at her home and drove back to St Ives with a lighter heart. But her good mood did not last long. When she returned home she found a note to say that Claude Gaumont had called. The carrots had been loaded in their truck but would not arrive in St Ives for another day as the truck was travelling via Sheffield to deliver an order to a large supermarket chain and rain was holding them up. When the carrots did arrive most of them had rotted because of inadequate storage and the remainder could not be sent to Monkish as the carrot washer and slicer would not work. In a fury, Georgie was quick to point out that they were also tasteless and too large to be organic carrots. The final straw came when they found that Claude had also delivered a consignment of turnips that they had not ordered and had charged them for delivering all the produce.

Angie and Georgie sat up long into the night deciding what to do. In the end, Georgie declared 'There is only one thing we can do. Sell the crop on as though it is organic. If we don't sell these then we will go bust – the Monkish Soup Company deal is just too big to lose'. Despite her objections that selling the carrots on as organic might be dishonest, Angie eventually agreed to Georgie's plan as the only one which allowed them to continue the business. With sad hearts, they loaded up the delivery boxes for the next day and went to bed.

THINGS GET REALLY SERIOUS

While Angie had been away, Chelsea had been trying to placate Dipti, but to no avail. She had sent her a box of chocolates but not only did Dipti send them back, she also drove down to the offices of the *St Ives Times* in her new Jaguar to complain about Earth2Earth! Unfortunately for Angie and Georgie, the paper was owned by Max Trax and he encouraged the editor to write a damning feature article about the business. As a result of the article, less and less people shopped at Earth2Earth! and the business was soon facing financial ruin.

The financial problems created a lot of friction between Angie and Georgie and they began to argue a lot. Reluctantly, they agreed that they needed another source of income. Neither of them wanted to go back to working for someone else so they decided that they would both retrain as horticulturists and set up a plant section in the shop to supplement falling profits. Georgie suggested that Angie go to college full-time for a year to study for the *Royal Horticultural Certificate in Plant Care* while Georgie looked after the store. They agreed that when Angie graduated they should reverse roles. In an attempt to help the young couple, Angie's mother Grace, who was an accountant, offered to help with the accounts and process the order forms while Angie was at college. Later that month, Angie enrolled for the horticulture course at the St Ives Further Education College.

FRIENDS COME TO THE RESCUE

In the meantime, Angie and Georgie had fallen behind with the rent and servicing of machinery. They were also being pressed for payment by Orange Peril plc who had recently started legal proceedings against them for their failure to pay for the infected vegetables and by Claude who claims their cheque has 'bounced'. Orange Peril plc claimed that there was no way they could have discovered about the Greenfingeritis and that it was up to Angie and Georgie to check deliveries. Angie and Georgie confided in Mister C and he agreed that while he was able to live rent-free at Missy J's he was happy to reduce their rent by 25%. However, they still didn't have enough money to pay off their bills or to buy in new stock. When Chelsea heard of the problems they were facing from her grandfather she was concerned that she would lose her job. She offered to have her wage reduced on the basis that it had always been much higher than was sensible for a new business and she was keen to keep her job as Marcus, with whom she was now in love, worked next door. Chelsea also knew that many of the local farmers would refuse to employ her now that she had worked at Earth2Earth! and she was concerned that she would not find alternative employment. Angie and Georgie accepted the offer rather than sack Chelsea, as she was a good worker. They were also aware that she had already brought in a number of new customers from surrounding towns because of her lively personality and knowledge of local surfing conditions. When Chelsea told Marcus what she had done he was furious as they had been using Chelsea's salary to subsidise his college fees. Marcus asserted that he could only continue to deliver produce for Angie and Georgie if they paid him more for his trouble.

ANGIE AND GEORGIE SEEK HELP

Financial ruin still loomed and, one day, while Angie was at college, Georgie decided to approach St Ives Bank for a loan so that they could buy some new kinds of stock and relaunch the business. The bank was managed by Max's son Nigel who said the bank would only lend Georgie the money if the loan was secured by a charge on the vintage Dormobile and they started making more effort to sell their produce at farmers' markets around the county and in the North of Brittany. Later that same day, when Angie got home, Georgie explained what had happened at the bank. Angie said she was reluctant to sink more money into the business but, secretly, she was increasingly losing confidence in Georgie's ability to make sound business decisions. She tried to persuade Georgie to at least approach some other larger banks, but Georgie would not hear of it and became furious when Angie would not immediately agree to the loan. Georgie claimed that the bank would never repossess the Dormobile and that, if Angie didn't give in, she could pack her bags and go.

They went to the bank and Nigel asked to see Angie alone. The bank had prepared the necessary documents which included a requirement that the charge over the Dormobile be signed by Angie and Georgie. Nigel advised Angie to take her time before she signed but also pointed out that if she did not sign by the close of business that day, there was likely to be some delay in processing the claim as the bank was closing for a week. The document Angie was given to sign suggested that independent advice should be sought but Angie was too upset to read it properly or think straight and signed it through a blur of tears.

Angie and Georgie decided that their next goal should be to get Monkish Soup Company to drop their claim against Earth2Earth! With this in mind, Georgie made an appointment with Ms Meanlean for the next day hoping to persuade her to negotiate a settlement or agree to refer the dispute to mediation. Georgie set off in the Dormobile and arrived at the offices of Monkish Soup Company with time to spare. However, there were no free parking spaces to be found in the surrounding streets and Georgie was eventually forced to go into a nearby multi-storey car park which was known to be expensive. Georgie went through the automatic barrier and parked the Dormobile in the underground section of the car park. It was rather dark but Georgie managed to locate and purchase a ticket from the 'pay and display' machine on that level. Narrowly avoiding a signpost positioned close to a barrier, Georgie put £5 in the machine as requested and received a long yellow ticket covered with lots of unsightly coloured writing. Georgie put the ticket behind the sun visor, anticipating that it would be necessary to show it to an attendant on the way out.

William, a security guard, had recently started work at the car park and was in charge of collecting the supermarket trolleys which customers tended to leave scattered about in there. He was rather ambitious about the number of trolleys he could control at any one time and as he attempted to return the trolleys to the area reserved for them, he lost control of them. They sped off down the dark car park which was built on a slight slope. As Georgie was locking the Dormobile the trolleys slid towards the vehicle at a high speed. Georgie did not have enough time to get out of the way and suffered substantial injuries before the trolleys moved on to damage the side panel of the Dormobile. Georgie was rushed off to hospital but telephoned Ms Meanlean from the Accident & Emergency Department to explain what had happened. Ms Meanlean dismissed Georgie out of hand, offered to see Earth2Earth! in court and informed her that henceforth, they will be getting their stock from another supplier in the next town!

The following day, Angie phoned Ned who informed her that the Board at Monkish feel they have been placing too much trust in Earth2Earth! and have decided to put future orders out to tender. Angie asks if they will be invited to make a bid and is encouraged to do so. However, at a subsequent board meeting it was decided that as Angie and Georgie had let them down, they would not consider dealing with them again.

THE END OF ONE BEAUTIFUL RELATIONSHIP AND THE START OF ANOTHER ...

Georgie became severely depressed whilst in hospital. She became moody and introverted and things did not get much better when she was taken home. As the ambulance pulled up at the shop, Angie was having a heated argument with Marcus who was refusing to deliver their vegetables. Her mood deteriorated even further when Missy J died. The son to whom Missy J had left her house evicted Mister C who came to live with Angie and Georgie instead. A couple of weeks later a debt collector hired by Orange Peril plc turned up and warned them that unless they paid the contract price for goods received, the interest which had accumulated and the debt collection fees incurred, they would proceed with their court action and Angie and Georgie would end up paying legal fees as well. In the end, Angie reluctantly agreed to pay the bill from their final reserves. She did not believe that Orange Peril plc had a good claim, but agreed in order that their reputation as a reliable commercial enterprise did not suffer any further.

The same week Mister C reluctantly told Angie that he did not think the flat share was working out. He complained he was kept awake by Dylan and Zen who played on their Gameboys all night and felt that at his age he deserved some peace and quiet. He suggested that they move out to live in the Dormobile in the garden at the back of the shop until they could find somewhere more suitable to live.

Unable to bear the tension and misery any longer, Angie has declared that she had had enough and is leaving with the children. She told Georgie that she and Ned have fallen in love and, once she has graduated, they would like to use the knowledge of basil they have gained and set up a smallholding. She wants to sell up her share in Earth2Earth! and sever her links with Georgie who no longer makes her happy. Georgie sinks into clinical depression and wants nothing more to do with Dipti, Mister C or Chelsea. Unable to work, she has to rely for financial support on a medical insurance policy she took out when working at Emmotts.

The financial situation has become so grave that Grace comes to you for advice. She is concerned that Georgie is so depressed and Angie so lovestruck that neither is in a position to manage their affairs competently. She brings along the documents reproduced below which she has found in the office which may be relevant.

Handbill and Poster

Earth2Earth! – Charter of Standards

You Should Know What You Are Buying

We purchase all our produce from *Orange Peril plc*, an internationally renowned organic food grower. *Orange Peril plc* has won the *Soil Association Company of the Year Award* for the last five years and has been described by *Organics Weekly* as being 'almost single-handedly responsible for a revolution in the market place'.

Orange Peril plc grow all their vegetables on extensive farmland in rural Cornwall. The vegetables are grown free from chemicals and pesticides in the way that Nature intended and are free from blemishes. *Orange Peril plc* has been an active opponent to GM crops and has successfully fought off attempts by the government to pilot GM crops within a 10 mile radius of their farm.

Our produce comes straight from the earth! Please don't worry if there is soil on our vegetables. You may not think that it makes them as attractive as pre-packed products from supermarkets but we believe that it keeps them fresh. It also means that we can sell them to you at a much cheaper price because we do not have to pay someone to clean them. The dirt will be brushed off our produce when they are weighed so that you are paying for tasty organic produce and not mud!

Our Pledge To You

An important part of the *Earth2Earth!* philosophy is that our customers deserve reasonably priced good quality vegetables. It is also important to us that the service is brought to you with a smile. We promise to be polite and good natured towards our customers at all times. In the unlikely event that we ever fail in this then do feel free to come and tell us. We will give a free basket of fruit to any customer who feels that we have been less than polite to them.

At *Earth2Earth!* we only sell you what you want. We do not engage in aggressive marketing of our products. Neither do we add produce to your orders which you have not requested.

All contracts made by *Earth2Earth!* are subject to the following terms and conditions:

All deliveries are free within a 10 mile radius of the store. Property in goods supplied shall pass on their acceptance by the customer. Goods found to be inferior in quality, defective or not in accordance with the order cannot be changed after the order has been accepted. The right is reserved to cancel the whole or part of an order within a week before the delivery date. An invoice will be rendered for each order. The invoice will be sent immediately after the delivery is made. *Earth2Earth!* cannot accept any responsibility for damages or losses of any description whatsoever. No goods will be supplied, or services rendered, without an official order. No alteration is to be made to an order without confirmation in writing. An order may be cancelled or suspended in the event of strikes, lock-outs, accidents, actions of the Queen's enemies or acts of God. *Earth2Earth!* shall be entitled, without prejudice to its other rights and remedies, either to terminate, wholly or in part, any or every contract between itself and the customer or to suspend further deliveries under any such contract if a debt remains unpaid or the customer becomes insolvent. Any contract arising from this quotation shall in all respects be construed and operate as an English contract and in conformity with English law and the English court shall have jurisdiction.

Gaumont Associates purchase and delivery contract

Present document witnesseth as follows:

OF THE ONE PART: The entity known as Gaumont Associates hereinafter called the *Vendor* and of the other part the entity known as Angie in the City of St Ives Republic of Cornwall hereinafter called the *Purchaser*. Both parties recognising their respective capacities enter into the present contract on the terms and conditions following:

Clause one:

The Vendor hereby sells and the Purchaser hereby purchases/reimburses the Vendor for the following:

(1) ...*3*... tons of fresh:

Carrots	[X]
Turnips	[X]
Broccoli	[ ]
Onions	[ ]
Kale	[ ]
Tomatoes	[ ]

in compliance with the French Farmers' Association code of practice, copies of which are available on request.

(2) Six wooden containers used to transport the produce.

(3) All cargo costs necessary to get the produce to its destination to include shipping, petrol for land transportation and insurance.

Clause two:

The Purchaser agrees that any contract formed by the Vendor's acceptance of this offer shall be governed by their terms and conditions of sale and that this order form shall represent the agreed contract between the Purchaser and the Vendor. The Purchaser certifies that the details and description of the produce given in clause one above are true and accurate in all respects.

Clause three:

The Purchaser undertakes to pay to the Vendor in Euros in Paris the total price of the products mentioned in clause one of this Contract. In times of commercial pressure the Vendor shall reserve the right to vary the terms of payment to reflect their additional costs.

Clause four:

The Vendor undertakes to notify the Purchaser within forty-eight hours (48 hours) following the departure of each vessel of the following: number of boxes shipped and volume of each of the same.

Clause five:

The Vendor warrants the Purchaser against any defect which might arise in the vegetables the subject matter of this contract on the following conditions:

(a) For the term of three hours from delivery.

(b) Should any defect develop during the guarantee period and the defect be due to faulty handling the produce will be replaced free of charge. This guarantee is in lieu of, and expressly excludes, all liability to compensate for loss or damage, howsoever caused.

(c) The alleged defect must be verified by the Vendor within a day subsequent to the date of receipt of the written notice which shall be given by the Purchaser.

(d) The replacement of the defective produce may be effected by the Vendor from their farms failing which they shall obtain the produce from other suppliers within a period of 14 days reckoned as from the date of receipt of claim by the Vendor.

(e) The replacement of faulty produce may be effected direct by the Vendor or it may at its option compensate the Purchaser for the expenses which the latter may incur.

(f) This warranty is restricted to the replacement of produce which become defective during the period established in paragraph (a) above due to defects of manufacture or the use of unsuitable materials but not due to improper storage.

This warranty will not come into operation unless the Schedule to this document is completed and signed by the Purchaser. No work will be carried out under the terms of this warranty until this document completed and signed as aforesaid is presented in advance to our service reception.

The rights under this document or the warranty above referred to are not transferable without our written consent.

This warranty shall be of no effect if the produce has at any time been used after the date of sale for the purposes other than those specified in pre-contractual negotiations.

Clause six:

If subsequent to the signature of this contract contingencies should arise such as fire, floods, droughts, disasters, rain, wind, hailstorms, earthquakes, war, military operations of any class, blockade or of any other class outside the control of the parties which totally or partially prevent the performance thereof by the parties, the period of time stipulated for performance of the contractual obligations shall be deemed to be extended for a period of time equivalent to the duration of such contingencies. In the event of these contingencies lasting more than six months each of the contracting parties is entitled to terminate the contract notifying the other party in writing. In this event neither of the parties shall be entitled to be compensated for any loss which might exist.

The party prevented from performing its contractual obligations on account of any of the contingencies above mentioned shall immediately notify the other party in writing of the existence and duration of same.

The existence of such contingency and its duration in the country of the Vendor or the Purchaser must be proved by a certificate issued by the Chamber of Commerce of the country of the Vendor or the Purchaser respectively.

Clause seven:

The contracting parties agree to perform this contract in good faith. Any difference which might arise as a result of this contract shall be settled by means of amicable negotiations. If such negotiations should fail and it should not be possible to reach understanding the parties shall submit the matter in dispute to an arbitration tribunal whose decision shall be final. The arbitration tribunal shall be set up in the City of Paris and shall consist of a representative of each of the parties and a presiding arbitrator appointed by both parties by mutual agreement. The award of the arbitration tribunal shall settle the amount of the arbitration expenses and the party which is to pay the same. An award adopted by a majority of votes shall be final and binding on both parties.

Clause eight:

The Vendor contracts as a principal and not as an agent of the growers of the produce and has no authority to make any representation or otherwise act on behalf of the growers of the produce.

The produce is not sold subject to any Warranty or other benefit whatsoever unless expressly agreed in writing between the parties.

PURCHASER'S DECLARATION

I/We agree that I/We have not been induced to make this offer by any representation as to the quality, fitness for any purpose, performance, or otherwise of the Goods and subject to the Vendor's acceptance of this offer. I/We agree to be bound by the terms and conditions hereof in all respects including the conditions of sale printed overleaf. In making this offer I/We have not relied on the skill, judgment or opinion of the Vendor, his servants or his agents in relation to the Goods.

Angie Kellaher............................. Date ....

> *Subject to the proviso that 10% of the payment price will be knocked off for each hour that delivery is delayed!*

Kirsty Hellman
on behalf of Earth2 Earth!

VENDOR'S ACCEPTANCE

I/We accept and confirm this offer subject to its terms and conditions.

Claude de Valera...............................Date............................

(Signature of Director or other authorised person for and on behalf of the Vendor.)

Wacky machine company – Rental agreement for super slicer carrot washer and cutter

IMPORTANT – YOU SHOULD READ THIS CAREFULLY.

Orders placed with the Company will only be accepted on the following terms and conditions. No variation or modification of or substitution for any such terms and conditions shall be binding unless expressly agreed by the Company in writing. No buyer's conditions of order or purchase and no other conditions, particulars, standards, specifications, statements or other matters whether printed, written or verbal shall form part of or be deemed to be incorporated into any contract with the Company unless specifically referred to in the Company's acceptance:

1   TERM OF HIRE

We shall supply the super slicer carrot washer and cutter and you shall rent the Equipment for the minimum period of 10 years and after that until terminated.

2   OUR RESPONSIBILITIES/RIGHTS/LIABILITIES

(a) We shall not be responsible for any direct or indirect or consequential injury, damage or loss to any person or any property arising out of the installation, possession, use or condition of the Equipment. We shall only be responsible for personal injury caused directly by Our negligence.

(b) We shall in no circumstances be responsible for loss of business or profit arising from a breakdown of the Equipment.

(c) We shall not be responsible for any breach of copyright resulting from the use of Equipment rented under this Agreement.

3   YOUR RESPONSIBILITIES/RIGHTS/LIABILITIES

(a) You shall indemnify Us against all liability arising out of the possession or use of the Equipment except liability for personal injury caused directly by Our negligence.

(b) From the date of delivery of the Equipment to You the Equipment shall be at Your risk and You shall insure the same with the Insurers in respect of Equipment Failure on the terms of Group Policy a summary of which is set out in the Insurance Certificate available for perusal at our premises.

4   PROPERTY INSURED

The Insurers insure the Equipment which you have hired under the Agreement, while you maintain it at the Premises.

5   BENEFIT

The Insurers will indemnify you against the cost of Failure. The cover is limited to the lowest of the current market value of the Equipment, or its replacement cost, or £2,000. The Insurance can either meet the cost of repairs which have already been carried out or they can send in repairers at their own expense. Repairs can only be carried out by Authorised Repairers. Such payments will be made to the Rental Company for the benefit of the insured customer.

6 EXCLUSIONS

Failure does not include failures caused by such things as defects in the electrical supply, misuse, neglect, wilful act, theft or accidental damage, or any other extraneous cause, or interference by any third party or use of the Equipment anywhere except at the Premises or for any unauthorised use. The benefit is limited to that described above, and will not cover any other loss (such as consequential loss, damage to other property, or death or bodily injury).

7 HOW TO CLAIM

Claims should be made by telephone to the Service centre shown in your Welcome Pack, or to your local Rental Company shop within a reasonable time of the Failure. Failure to make a claim within a reasonable time will invalidate any claim.

QUESTIONS

(1) Before you learn any more about the law of contract and wealth of cases which you are likely to have to read, we would like you to make a list of what you consider would be a fair solution to the problems faced by the various parties in 'The Sad Tale of Angie and Georgie'. Once you have completed the list, keep it somewhere safe and use it as a resource as you progress through the book in order to gauge the ways in which the law of contract complies with your ideas about common-sense fairness.

(2) Is there any additional information you would like to have about the story before you progress? If so, make a list of the additional information you would like to gather before advising the parties. Give reasons why you think it is important to have this information.

(3) If you could go back in time, how would you alter what the parties do in order to minimise the number of disputes which arise?

(4) How many agreements can you identify?

PART TWO:

BIG IDEAS IN THE LAW OF CONTRACT

CHAPTER 3

THE RISE AND FALL OF FREEDOM OF CONTRACT

INTRODUCTION

The law of contract cannot be fully understood without reference to the history of ideas which underpins it. It will become apparent in the course of this book that the law of contract has undergone several important transformations in the last few decades. Reading cases and statutes from this period will lead to familiarisation with the detail of such changes but it is unlikely to lead to a full appreciation of how it was possible for them to come about and the wider political context which made transformation acceptable to influential stakeholders. In a book of this kind, it is almost impossible to do justice to the rich spectrum of ideas which have been reflected in debates between academics, politicians and the wider community of users of law. Instead, what we aim to do in this chapter and the next is to sketch out some key ideas which have influenced the ways in which we look at contracts. Of particular relevance here is the question of the extent to which the State in the guise of the legislature or the judiciary should interfere with contracts made in order to redress imbalances of power between the parties or impose obligations upon them.

Even the briefest perusal of the newspapers will demonstrate that the issues which lie at the heart of this debate reflect a much wider controversy about the role of the modern State. The issue remains a contentious one which has troubled successive governments and debate has become particularly intense since the setting up of the Welfare State. The political imperatives of the Conservative Party under Thatcher, the 'rolling back of the State', debate about the 'third way' and the regulatory State, and visions of socialism in post-communist States, all hinge on the same critical issue of what constitutes the appropriate boundaries between public and private, autonomy and regulation, collective ideals and individualism. When you come to argue your first case in front of the Court of Appeal, a sound knowledge of the intricacies of former precedents and 'black letter' law will serve you well. But it is unlikely that your arguments will stimulate the judges you stand before unless you can provide justification for why the court should make a departure from what has gone before.

LEGAL AND OTHER VIEWS OF CONTRACT

The early history of contract is extensive, complex and not entirely free from controversy. Medieval law was primarily concerned with crime and land. From an early stage it recognised formal agreements which were written and 'understood' but slowly began to validate claims arising out of informal, oral transactions as well. Of particular significance is the common law's recognition by the 16th century of claims involving four key elements. These were: reliance by the claimant on an undertaking given by the defendant; faulty performance, and later non-performance, of the undertaking by the defendant; loss to the claimant; and compensation in the form of damages.

Later, the language of the courts began to link the idea of undertaking with that of promise. At that time the moral force of, and duty to keep, promises was very strong. In the view of the American contract lawyer, Professor Corbin, writing in the earlier part of the last century:

> That portion of the field of law that is classified and described as the law of contracts attempts the realisation of reasonable expectations that have been induced by the making of a promise. Doubtless, this is not the only purpose by which men have been motivated in creating the law of contracts; but it is believed to be the main underlying purpose, and it is believed that an understanding of many of the existing rules, and a determination of their effectiveness, require a lively consciousness of their underlying purpose.

Nevertheless, in terms of a person's word being 'as good as their bond', the law stopped short of declaring that all promises were binding. Starting from an inquiry into the reasons why a promise was given, the doctrine of consideration came to set limits to promissory liability. It eventually did so by requiring that some form of *exchange* took place. This, as we explained in Chapter 1, allowed contracts to be distinguished from gifts or gratuitous promises made out of kindness rather than as part of a bargain. The types of bargain recognised by the law might be the exchange of money for a service or the exchange of one possession for another. But it was also accepted that promises could be exchanged to form binding contracts as long as there was a connection between them. So if Ethelred offered to pay Edwina three cows for a stable of manure and she accepts, then it can be seen that their promises to give up the cows and transfer manure are related to each other and form a bargain. Edwina's promise would only have been made if Ethelred had made his.

Thus, even before the onset of the industrial and commercial revolutions, contract law had developed considerably. It contained basic, interconnecting concepts such as undertaking, promise, expectations, bargain in the sense of commercial exchange, reliance, loss and compensation. By the 19th century, the concept of contract came to be discussed more broadly by philosophers, political scientists, economists, sociologists and others and became an important element in the political philosophy of the era. Contract came to be seen as the key to wealth and happiness in the emerging market society. The 'utmost liberty in contracting' became a prime ethical, political, economic and legal goal. In the words of the American jurist, Roscoe Pound:

> Justice required that each individual be at liberty to make free use of his natural powers in bargains and exchanges and promises except as he interfered with like action on the part of his fellow men, or with some other of their natural rights.

According to this view of society, the autonomy of individuals took precedence. Not only was this considered a laudable goal in its own right, but it was also seen as the key to the economic success of society. It was argued that the individual was best placed to know what their needs were and should be allowed to make whatever contracts on whatever terms they thought appropriate.

Adam Smith's work proved to be particularly influential in this context. In his *Wealth of Nations*, published in 1776, Smith analysed exchange in terms of people's 'natural propensity' to 'truck, barter and exchange'. In his view it was this inclination which gave rise to contract, trade and the division of labour. His wide-ranging arguments sought to show how the individual's self-interested pursuit of optimum gain and happiness was both regulated and harnessed to the general good by the economist's law of demand and supply. His thesis was that, by trading with others, individuals not only got what they wanted but gave others what they desired. The magical ingredient converting individual acquisitiveness into universal good was the 'invisible hand'. In Smith's view, the individual 'generally neither intends to promote the public interest, nor knows how much he is promoting it ... He intends only his own gain, and he is in this, as in other cases, led by an invisible hand to promote an end which was no part of his intention'. Smith advocated minimal regulation of the economy, and therefore of contracts, by the State. He saw it as a prime function of the law to uphold and enforce contracts and stressed that promises were not binding as a consequence of some inherent quality but rather because of the reliance they created in the market, which was not to be disappointed.

A number of commentators have shown an interest in why the individual came to play such an important role in the philosophical works of this era. Maine attempted to explain the reasons for this shift in his work on the movement of progressive societies from 'status' to contract. In this he distinguished two theoretical 'ideal' types of society. The first was essentially a pre-industrial type of society in which power and relationships were based on those you were unavoidably connected to and the status you 'enjoyed' as a result. These included kinship, marriage, neighbourhood and engendering close, continuing relationships. The second was a society in which the individual becomes the central figure and their associations are predominantly motivated by reason and economic gain. Drawing on these ideas, Tönnies talked of a similar drift from social union to an essential 'separation' of individuals in an industrial society. For him, the latter was merely an 'artificial construction of an aggregate of human beings' in which rationality and calculation were the lynchpins.

The rational, impersonal relationship was also examined by Weber, who also drew a distinction between what he called 'status' and 'purposive' contracts. The first 'more primitive' type involved the creation of continuing 'total' social and legal relationships, such as those between husband and wife or landowner and serf. By way of contrast, the archetypal purposive contract was 'the money contract'. This was specific, quantitatively delimited, abstract, economically conditioned and usually achieved some specific, generally economic, performance or result. In his view, what distinguishes such contractual relationships from status relationships is the fact that the reciprocal rights and obligations are limited to those specified in the contract. The purposive market exchange contract created only a tenuous and temporary association. Because these impersonal associations were incapable of inspiring high trust of the kind seen in status contracts, Weber argued that it was necessary to establish legal machinery, which, while not raising levels of trust, did at least provide a greater required measure of economic certainty. Others have also argued that trade and industry would break down if business agreements could be broken with impunity. So, for instance, Professor Hart, in *The Concept of Law* (1961) argued that 'where altruism is not unlimited, a standing procedure providing for such self-binding operations is required in order to create a minimum form of confidence in the future behaviour of others, and to ensure the predictability necessary for co-operation'.

THE RELATIONSHIP BETWEEN THE COURTS AND THE MARKET

The perceived role of the courts in this scheme of things can be summed up by reference to the words of Sir George Jessel who advised the judiciary that 'you have this paramount public policy to consider in that you are not lightly to interfere with this freedom of contract'. In a similar vein, Henry Sidgwick in his *Elements of Politics* (1879) argued:

> Suppose contracts freely made and effectively sanctioned, and the most elaborate social organisation becomes possible, at least in a society of such human beings as the individualistic theory contemplates – gifted with mature reason and governed by enlightened self-interest.

Viewed in this way the function of contract is to facilitate trade. It is significant that in the early part of the 19th century, the legal focal point for contract focused on the binding nature of reciprocal promises, that is, *executory* contracts. In contrast to the *executed* contract in which exchange is immediate, executory contracts involve the exchange of promises about future conduct. The importance of the courts' recognition of executory contracts was that it allowed the business community to plan ahead. If Sunil knows that he can rely on the courts to enforce Angie's promise to pay him £20,000 for a consignment of outdated mobile phones taking up room in his warehouse, he can enter into negotiations with manufacturers of this year's latest mobile phones to supply him with stock for his showroom, confident that he will have funds to pay for it. Moreover, now that the manufacturer has a firm order, they can enter into discussions with different suppliers about the purchase of parts, and so the contract chain goes on without any material object having yet changed hands. In this example, the parties are able to enjoy the confidence and predictability that Hart talks about. With clear recognition that promises bind future performance, contract showed obvious potential for planning and risk allocation in the marketplace.

Two further developments in contract law, following fuller recognition of the executory contract, must be mentioned. It was accepted by the judiciary that an action for breach of an executory contract can be brought if one of the promisors fails to do what they promised to do. In other words, a party liable on an executory contract is liable not for what they have done but for what they have not done. In Professor Atiyah's view, 'he must be liable because of his intention, his will, his promise. There is nothing else'. At the same time, in the early 19th century, wide acceptance of the idea of liability based on promises allowed a general theory of contract law to emerge which distinguished it from other areas of law. Academics and judges began to use the idea of promise and freely given consent as the basis of the law, and contract was no longer merely regarded as an adjunct of the law of property or a discussion of particular types of transactions. Books came to be written about 'the law of contract in its general and abstract form apart from its specific practical applications'.

The vision of contractual relations which emerged at this time has come to be known as the 'classical' model and we shall use this shorthand throughout the book. The approach was clearly designed to serve a free market economy – to act as a framework within which the free play of competitive forces could operate. Roscoe Pound has summed the approach up by saying that in '*laissez-faire* style the law was conceived negatively as a system of hands off while [people] do things rather than as a system of ordering to prevent friction and waste'. As we proceed to examine substantive elements of contract law in this book, we will time and again be reminded of the legacy of 19th century thinking and its continuing effect on the law today. For this reason, it is of value to review the key features of the 'classical' model as it emerged from around 1800 onwards:

- there was a presumption that contracting parties were possessed of equal bargaining power and were self-motivated and self-assertive;

- a party was bound not so much because they had made a promise as because they had made a bargain;

- agreement was based on consent and free choice. This meant that contractual obligations were viewed as self-imposed. Imbalances, whether measured in terms of consideration or unfairness, were irrelevant;

- pursuit of the parties' intentions carried the courts beyond express statements of intention in the contract itself to presumed intention through the notion of implied terms. Such a shift from a subjective view of contract which focuses on what the parties intended to an objective view of contract which focuses on what they are presumed to have intended is to be seen, for instance, in the use of implied terms to make sense of the parties' agreement;

- this was not, however, true where there was a lack of consent. Absence of this critical element of agreement would, within narrow limits, allow the court to strike down a contract. Among others, fraud, misrepresentation and fundamental mistake were recognised as factors vitiating consent;

- the binding nature of contract was, in the words of Atiyah, 'in principle, a matter of pecuniary calculation. Each party is bound; he must therefore perform, or pay damages for his failure to perform'.

THE CHANGING NATURE OF CONTRACT

Approaches to contracts have changed significantly since the heyday of the classical period. But change has taken the form of adjustments to the 'classical' model rather than a grand scale reformulation of the law. The main thrust of modern critiques of contract law is that a new model which moves more firmly away from the classical paradigm is required. For some, the classical model is unsatisfactory even in its neo-classical guise and often ignored by the business community either as a guide to planning or as a means of dispute-solving. These are themes to which we shall return in the next chapter. In the remainder of this one, we describe how the classical model has adjusted to the changed circumstances of the modern world.

As we have seen, enthusiasm for freedom of contract went hand-in-hand with support for the operation of a free market. But as Hunt and Sherman remind us, assumptions underpinning the free market approach could be seen to be erroneous:

> One's view of the desirability of the market system depends on whether one is more impressed with the efficacy and impersonality of this allocation mechanism or with its lopsided results. Thus one defender of capitalism writes: 'The case for capitalism is at its strongest on the simple thesis that the market knows best how to allocate and use the scarce resource of capital.' A critic of capitalism sees it differently: 'The main reason that freedom of contract has never been as free as advertised – and it is a painfully obvious reason – is that sellers and buyers are not equal in bargaining power. So the terms of sale will simply reflect the power, or lack of it, that each party brings to

the market place. So a market is also a financial slaughterhouse, where the strong chop up the weak.'

Responding to the challenge raised by such arguments, Weber cut straight through the simplistic abstractions of earlier legal and economic thinking on the subject of freedom of contract. In his view, markets for goods and services might be more plentiful and factors of production more mobile, but this did not in itself result in more 'real' freedom. In his view, the exact extent to which the total amount of 'freedom' within a given legal community is actually increased depends entirely on the concrete economic order and especially on the property distribution.

Weber's argument was that new developing markets threw up new economic groups with powerful 'market interests' based on capital and entrepreneurship. As was becoming clear to most people, it was the power relations in society, not economic and legal abstractions, which determined the operation of markets and the degree of real freedom in those markets. In his words: 'The result of contractual freedom, then, is in the first place the opening of the opportunity to use, by the clever utilisation of property ownership in the market, these resources without legal restraints as a means for the achievement of power over others.' As others had done, Weber illustrated his analysis by means of the contract of employment in which the employer was commonly the more powerful party and could offer jobs on a 'take it or leave it' basis. Given the more pressing economic needs of the worker, it was possible in this way for an employer to impose their terms on the employee.

Weber is not only pointing to the difference between formal and real freedom but indicating how formal freedom protects and exacerbates inequality:

> The increasing significance of freedom of contract and particularly of enabling laws which leave everything to 'free' agreement implies a relative reduction of that kind of coercion which results from the threat of mandatory and prohibitory norms. Formally it represents a decrease of coercion. But it is also obvious how advantageous this state of affairs is to those who are economically in the position to make use of the empowerments.

Durkheim was also amongst the first sociologists of law to attack the prevalent individualist, self-interest view of contract and the idea that contract could be regarded as a microcosm of society or a model for human relations. He argued that, within the contractual bond, the element of self-interest inevitably created an inherent contradiction. In his view each contracting party, while in need of the other, seeks to obtain what they need at the lowest price, that is, to acquire the most rights possible in return for the fewest obligations possible.

In contrast to many of his contemporaries, he was concerned with undermining the prevailing vision of contract as an essentially individualistic and utilitarian act rather than a social one. He suggested that unregulated self-interest would in no way enable the mechanism of contract to serve as a model for what he termed 'organic solidarity' in society. Contrary to much thinking at the time, Durkheim would not accept that a society splintered by increasing division of labour could achieve 'solidarity' through the pursuit of economic self-interest within a loose framework of *laissez-faire* control. He opined: 'In the fact of economic exchange, the different agents remain outside one another, and with the termination of the operation each one finds himself alone again ... Indeed, interest is the least constant of all things in the world.

Today it is in my interest to unite with you. Tomorrow the same reason may make me your enemy.'

It was necessary, in Durkheim's opinion, to place contract in a context wider than that of party autonomy and individual will. For him, the true focal point was not individuals but society, which should provide a framework of norms and laws able to promote social justice. Most significantly, in his view, social regulation of contract required clear recognition of the social facts of unequal bargaining power as opposed to the economic and legal myth underlying freedom of contract. Again, he turned to the example of the employee:

> What can the poor worker reduced to his own resources do against a rich and powerful boss, and is there not a palpable and cruel irony in assimilating these two forces which are so manifestly unequal? If they enter into combat, is it not clear that the second will always and without difficulty crush the first? What does such a liberty amount to, and does not the economist who contents himself with it become guilty of taking the word for the thing?

Durkheim insisted that society and the law must no longer passively uphold unjust contracts which are 'anti-social' as the 'agreement of parties cannot render just a clause which in itself is unjust'. He appreciated that not all 'interest' or 'conflict' could be removed from either society or contract, but he advanced the view that there must be awareness of the need for an agreed mechanism to find the 'middle term between the rivalry of interests and their solidarity'. Gurvitch, who re-examined the rivalry of interests in contract, was later to refer to this as 'equilibration'.

POWER IN THE MODERN MARKETPLACE

A series of transformations in British society have served to reinforce the arguments made by scholars such as Weber and Durkheim. These have fuelled a partial transformation of the philosophy of contract and include concentration of power in the marketplace, the growth of the Welfare State and changes in judicial attitudes. In the remainder of this section, we shall consider each in turn.

(a)   The concentration of power in the market

Commentators have observed that competitive capitalism inevitably tended towards monopoly. The legal result of this has been *the mass-produced standard form of contract* presented on 'take-it-or-leave-it' terms by those who are powerful in the market. The allocation of resources in the British economy no longer centres on the free market contracts of 'small enterprisers' but on the operations of massive multinational corporate groups and governmental agencies. A variety of factors have contributed to this movement in Britain. Some, such as cartelisation schemes designed to combat the worst effects of economic depression, the nationalisation of basic industries and the creation of a 'public sector' of the economy, have come about as a direct result of government policies. Others, such as the growth of trade associations, of mergers in the private sector, the development of mass production and the tendency for large companies to take over small ones, have come about more naturally. The result is that, in many areas of trade and industry, tickets, model forms and standard conditions of the kind used in 'The Sad Tale of Angie and Georgie' are now the order of the contractual day. These developments clearly dilute key concepts such as choice and consent in contract and undermine the importance of pre-contractual negotiations.

(b)   The tremendous expansion of the welfare and social service functions of the State

The creation of the Welfare State has led to the proliferation of statutorily imposed terms of contract and an increase in contracts to which government departments and other public authorities are themselves parties. The use of contract as an instrument of governmental social and economic policy through the medium of public control over standard 'implied' terms has led to many contracts becoming institutionalised. This development can be seen in consumer-protection policy, in landlord-and-tenant legislation, and in measures to be found in statutes concerning sexual discrimination and equal pay at work. According to this vision of contract, choice and consent are sacrificed. As Atiyah has said: 'The legislation of the past century has carried to great lengths the circumstances in which the individual's freedom of decision is overridden, either in the direct interests of a majority, or to give effect to values which a majority believe to be of overriding importance.' The greater the government's control over terms, the less likely that contractual rights and duties are agreed as a result of the parties' real agreement.

It should be emphasised that the 20th century also saw a dramatic increase in the State's involvement in contract, not just as a regulator but as a party. This involvement has primarily taken three forms. First, as a *provider* of services such as health-care, social security, education, motorways and defence, the State is required to buy in construction and engineering works, technical services, hardware and vast quantities of other supplies and materials from independent contractors. It is in this area of public sector activity that contract has been the subject of major transformation. It is not merely that where the State is involved as purchaser, we are dealing with the problem of one party having massive bargaining strength and 'dictating' terms, but that rules of contract which draw on the notion of one-off and private exchanges begin to look obsolete.

The second, related development regarding public sector contracting saw the taking into State-controlled public ownership such major utilities as gas, electricity, water supply, the coal industry, rail transport and health-care in the course of nationalisation programmes introduced shortly after the Second World War. Here the State, through public authorities such as Education Authorities or the National Health Service, has become the *supplier* of key services. We will see that in this context contract may play no part at all in the relationships between pupils and teacher or doctor and patient. More recently, the State has also become a regulator of contracts. Subsequent government re-privatisation schemes have meant that national and local public services such as the prison service and refuse collection are now being provided on a 'contracted-out' basis. Key services are no longer carried out directly by public authorities but by private sector organisations under contract to the authority in question overseen by State-funded regulatory bodies. Since privatisation, many of the interests of consumers as regards prices, terms and quality of supply are provided for by statute-based regulatory agencies and not by the law of contract. For example, the Office of Electricity Regulation (OFFER) is an independent body set up by Parliament to protect the interests of electricity consumers. Problems which cannot be resolved satisfactorily with the supplier can be referred to the regional OFFER. If no solution is found, the matter may be considered by the regional consumer committee. Such a committee's decisions are not binding but decisions taken by the head of the regulatory mechanism, the Director General of Electricity Supply, do have the same effect as a county court judgment: see *R v Director General of Electricity Supply ex p Redrow Homes (Northern) Ltd* (1995).

Whether or not these arrangements satisfy the need to balance value for money with the public interest continues to be hotly contested in the political arena. But it is noticeable that in several sectors (eg, gas supply), the number of consumer complaints has risen dramatically since privatisation. As Collins concludes:

> The real substance of the issue of the scope of contracts in this context should turn on whether the statutes regulating public utilities provide adequate alternative means of redress for consumers, so that the exclusion of contractual rights is the price paid for the advantages of the statutory scheme for complaints.

Contract specialists frequently draw attention to the need to regulate business activity where an organisation has become so powerful that it can dictate terms to anyone with whom it contracts. In this context it is sometimes easy to forget the fact that government contracts, made on behalf of us all with public money, also pose a significant threat to those concerned about inequality of bargaining power. It has been argued that one of the main social causes for the transformation of contract in the 20th century has been the tremendous expansion of the welfare and social services function of the State in all common law jurisdictions. One of the legal corollaries of this development was a vast increase of contracts where government departments or other public authorities are on one side, and a private party on the other.

In principle, the general law of contract applies to government 'procurement' contracts. There is no special branch of 'government contract law' in this country, no legislative code as for consumer credit or fair trading, and administrative law is largely irrelevant in this context. In fact, the complaint has been made that *no* adequate law has been evolved on public contracts. Any question of the 'adequacy' of the private law rules of contract is also largely redundant. This is a field dominated by standard-form contractual documents, prepared on behalf of the government authority involved and rarely negotiated. The government contract is an instrument of a power relationship, and only vaguely resembles the consensual agreement extolled by Maine and Adam Smith. In Turpin's view 'the classical law of contract' which was formulated by 19th-century judges was:

> ... a law of the market ... This law in general did not, and does not, make provision for the peculiar circumstances of government procurement, the unique relationship between the government and its principal contractors, or the specific issues of the public interest that arise in government contracting.

Government procurement contracts are, in broad terms, an expression of economic and social policies and the contractor is the instrument whereby services and functions are executed. However, government expenditure of taxpayers' money on goods and services raises questions of public accountability. Although the relationship between the government and its major suppliers used to be described as a partnership with 'fair and reasonable prices' at its base, the current economic climate and concern about the government being ill-served by the private sector have led to changes. In particular, the rules of the European Union have led to more competitive tendering and a more 'free market' approach to procurement. Hard bargaining, best value for money and the attainment of contract targets are now the order of the day.

It is clear, even from this brief survey, that government-procurement contacts are a rather special area, having only vague links with the general principles of contract law. From procurement policy to regulatory remedies, the contracting process is directed from somewhere along the corridors of power. In the absence of litigation or forms of public hearing other than occasional references in *Hansard*, fears of misuse of the system, as highlighted by various corruption trials in the 1970s, may well remain.

(c)   Changes in judicial approaches

It will become clear throughout this book that changes in political ideology, in social and economic conditions, and, bit by bit, in the law itself have moved the judicial focus away from freedom and sanctity of contract, voluntary agreement and fixed rules. This has involved more than a change in judicial approaches; it has involved a change in ideas about the appropriate role of the judiciary. There has been a discernible shift away from strict rules towards less certain notions of 'fairness', 'reasonableness' and 'judicial discretion'. Contract law has always struggled to serve the conflicting aims of certainty and flexibility. Certainty, it is said, makes for predictability and a legal framework in which planned relationships can proceed with confidence. In the alternative, advocates of flexibility argue that certainty leads to rigidity and a failure of the law to reflect the needs of a volatile and increasingly complex business world. However, it must be stressed that no new 'social welfare mixed economy model' has wholly taken its place. The character of contract as a legal instrument of contemporary society is undergoing profound changes, in which elements of the old mingle with the new. If we take it that the 19th century contract law supported the free market system, what policy is revealed in present-day contract? To what extent has the law moved away from the 'classical' model?

Of particular value in understanding these fundamental issues is the analysis of judicial decision-making put forward by Adams and Brownsword in their book *Understanding Contract Law*. They argue that the common law increasingly displays signs of the *tensions* created by two *competing* judicial philosophies. These are a formalist approach which focuses on rules and a *realist*, result-orientated approach. Out of a number of possible stances along the continuum between these two positions, a judge may be seen as a strict adherent to the 'paper rules' (a textural formalist) at the expense of justice or commercial convenience. Alternatively, they may be a 'strong realist', even an iconoclast, like Lord Denning, for whom precedent is no bar to achieving the right result. As you read the chapters which follow, it would be useful for you to keep these different approaches in mind as you will see some excellent examples of both.

Adams and Brownsword (2000) argue that these different approaches to legal method actually reflect the broader political ideologies discussed above. In their words:

> Market individualism has two limbs, a market philosophy and an individualistic philosophy. The market philosophy sees the function of the law of contract as the facilitation of competitive exchange. This demands clear contractual ground rules, transactional security, and the accommodation of commercial practice. The individualistic side of market individualism enshrines the landmark principle of

'freedom of contract' and 'sanctity of contract', the essential thrust of which is to give the parties the maximum licence in setting their own terms, and to hold parties to their freely made bargains ... judges should offer no succour to parties who are simply trying to escape from a bad bargain ... Consumer-welfarism stands for reasonableness and fairness in contracting. More concretely, this is reflected in a policy of consumer protection and a pot-pourri of specific principles. For example, consumer-welfarism holds that contracting parties should not mislead one another, that they should act in good faith, that a strong party should not exploit the weakness of another's bargaining position, that no party should profit from his own wrong or be unjustly enriched, that remedies should be proportionate to the breach, that contracting parties who are at fault should not be able to dodge their responsibilities, and so on. Crucially, consumer-welfarism subscribes to the paternalistic principle that contractors who enter into bad bargains may be relieved from their obligations where justice so requires.

It should be readily apparent that in line with political and economic developments, 'consumer-welfarism' has been the main driving force behind contract decision-making over the last 50 years or so. The trend has been such that some commentators have argued that the protection offered to some categories of contractor, most notably 'consumers', is such that the legislature and judiciary have recreated the status contract.

CONCLUDING REMARKS

When one attempts to put the 20th century's 'transformation' of contract into overall perspective, it is possible to discern two outstanding and related features. First, as regards the institution of contract itself, account must be taken of the new widespread use of the standard, non-negotiable form of contract and the vastly increased involvement of the State as a regulator, supplier and purchaser. Secondly, as regards the changing nature of the law itself, the essential point is that what has occurred is not so much a transformation but a bifurcation of contract law brought about in large part by the competing ideologies identified by Adams and Brownsword as 'market-individualism' and 'consumer-welfarism'. Throughout our examination of the case law we will meet shifts of approach by the courts away from traditional, 'classical' analysis to a range of different approaches to the issue in question. The tension that this creates may be expressed in a variety of ways and is not easily alleviated. For example, should the courts adopt a 'hands-off' approach or adopt a paternalistic, interventionalist role? Is the key objective freedom and facilitation of exchange for the parties or one of fairness? Are the requirements of contract-makers best served by legal certainty or does justice requires flexibility in the law? Perhaps it may be said, as Atiyah argues, that contract theory is in a mess and has in its modern formulation to serve too many different masters.

REFERENCES AND FURTHER READING

Adams, J and Brownsword, R (2000) *Understanding Contract Law*, 3rd edn, London: Sweet & Maxwell.

Atiyah, P (1979) *The Rise and Fall of Freedom of Contract*, Part III, particularly Chapters 14–16, 21 and 22, Oxford: Clarendon.

Campbell, D and Vincent-Jones, P (eds) (1996) *Contract and Economic Organisation*, Aldershot: Dartmouth.

Daintith, T 'Regulation by contract: the new prerogative' (1979) 34 Current Legal Problems 41.

Durkheim, E (1964) *The Division of Labour in Society*, New York: Free Press.

Friedmann, W (1972) *Law in a Changing Society*, 2nd edn, Chapter 4 'The changing function of contract', Penguin.

Gilmore, G (1974) *The Death of Contract*, Columbus, OH: Ohio State University Press.

Harden, I (1992) *The Contracting State*, Milton Keynes: Open University Press.

Kessler, F 'Contracts of adhesion – some thoughts about freedom of contract' (1943) 43 Columbia Law Review 629.

Renner, K (1949) *The Institutions of Private Law and Their Social Functions*, London: Routledge.

Turpin, C 'Government contracts: a study of methods of contracting' (1979) 31 MLR 241.

Turpin, C (1989) *Government Procurement and Contracts*, Harlow: Longman.

QUESTIONS

(1) 'The economic correlate of common law contract is a free enterprise society.' Put forward detailed arguments in support of this proposition.

(2) Discuss the following view of contract:

'During the process of production, the owner assumes a mask, increasingly severe, sinister, and in the end almost despotic. Now, as he leaves the intimidating and gloomy factory with his wares, his features unwrinkle, they become bland, modest and agreeable. The man who stands in the market with his goods, though the same person, now wears a disguise that changes his appearance beyond recognition, that of the "guardian of commodities". Every recollection of that lower sphere of production ... of despotism ... has vanished from the thoughts of the man, and the appearance of the commodity reveals no traces of it. The capitalist has now become ... an equal among equals. He has dealings with his own kind only' (Renner, *The Institutions of Private Law and their Social Functions*).

(3) To what extent does the classical contract model help you to identify what constitutes a legitimate contractual arrangement in 'The Sad Tale of Angie and Georgie'?

(4) What are the benefits of applying an exchange model to distinguish contracts from gifts and promises in that case study?

(5) Do you think that marriage vows should be enforceable as a contract? Give reasons for your response. Would your response change if you were asked the same question in relation to Angie and Georgie's exchange of vows?

CHAPTER 4

FROM FORMALISM TO REALISM: CONTEMPORARY CRITIQUES OF CONTRACT LAW

INTRODUCTION

In the last chapter we visited classical contract theory and considered the various challenges to it posed during the welfarist era. On the whole, the response of members of the judiciary and academia has been to try to adjust the classical model so that it better suits the goals of social policy and the marketplace of today. What has emerged is a mixture of approaches in which market-individualism still competes for attention with the more modern notion of consumer-welfarism. Later chapters in this book such as those on implied terms, consideration and unfair terms will sketch out some of the detail of how some sense of balance has been achieved during the 'neo-classical' period. What this new label makes clear is that the classical model, albeit in a modified form, continues to have much influence over how we approach contracts. In the minds of many contemporary academics in the field, this is an unsatisfactory development. To some, all that has happened is that the classical model has been tinkered with when what is needed is a rethinking of the principles which should underpin doctrine and a reformulation of the techniques used to recognise the nature of the obligations contained in contracts. A growing number of scholars have argued that the very relevance and legitimacy of the assumptions underpinning the classical model are in crisis.

In this chapter we seek to look at some contemporary critiques of contract which encourage us to look at contractual relationships in different ways. The strength of these various theories and the reason why they have so much resonance in a book of this kind is their attention to how contract is used and operates in everyday life. Rather than seeing the function of law as being to declare how contract ought to be, many of the approaches we will examine are based on the premise that law should *reflect* what constitutes ethical and workable commercial practice. The shift which is plotted is that from formalism to realism. The new breed of authors whose work is considered owe much to a socio-legal or realist tradition of scholarship which takes as its starting point the need to understand how the law on statute books and precedents is received in the community it seeks to regulate.

THE LEGAL REALISTS

The intellectual origins of the legal realists can be traced to the emergence of a sociology of law. Drawing on the earlier work of jurists and moral, social and political philosophers, a group of 19th century writers began to focus on law as a social phenomenon. In other words, they did not take at face value the justifications provided by lawyers for particular rules. This sociological movement in law was in large part a reaction against contemporary approaches to studying law which tended to focus on the importance of the rules at the expense of studying their reception. Legal formalism, with its emphasis on how things ought to be, tended to encourage the spurious idea that law is in some way autonomous, an end in itself, rather than a means to social order. Sociologists of law have, by way of contrast, sought to put law firmly in its social, political and economic contexts. They look for relationships between law, legal systems and the wider society, and ask questions about the functions, effects and efficiency of rules. Some lawyers have welcomed the growth of this 'external' view of law. A former Lord Chancellor, Lord Hailsham, said that his:

> ... only abiding concern ... is my fear that the study and practice of law may become too narrowly based and tend to divorce itself from the general culture of which we are all a part, and in which history, language, literature, the physical sciences and philosophy have an equal and distinctive part to play in the framing of our institutions and our system of justice.

Realists in this mould have argued that there should be a connection between law and the standards of everyday life if law is to retain its legitimacy. By way of example, it can be seen that over 90 years ago, the Austrian jurist Eugen Ehrlich argued that there should be more research into brewers' supply of beer than 'on the concept of the juristic person'. Ehrlich's preoccupation was with the rules and practices by which individuals and groups *actually* govern their relations. His conclusion was that these consist only partly of the law to be found in statutes and judicial decisions. He called these other rules and practices 'living law' in support of his argument that 'the centre of gravity of legal development lies not in legislation, nor in juristic science, nor in judicial decision, but in society itself'. 'Living law' and formal law were, for Ehrlich, different though related phenomena. 'Living law' was the prime incentive for human activity in the field of contracts. It was seen as running ahead of the law and often growing apart from it. In his view, this practice was encouraged by lack of access to the courts. Enforcement of contracts in the courts has been an expensive process for at least a century with the result that contract litigation was often considered only as a last resort. Moreover, profits earned from relationships maintained through goodwill and the compromise of differences often outweighed damages awarded against a company that now trades elsewhere. It could be argued then that the business community has, for reasons of perceived convenience, efficiency and cost, been virtually impelled to develop its own customs, practices and techniques designed to avoid or mitigate business or 'legal' risk and loss.

The judiciary has not been insensitive to the need for the law to remain relevant to practice. For example, in the 17th century, in order to remedy weaknesses in the common law of the time, the judges began to incorporate into it what was known as the 'law merchant'. This was a body of relatively sophisticated rules and techniques applicable previously only between merchants, or in particular trades or centres of business. But the question of whether it is the law which should be sensitive to practice or the everyday practice of contracts which should primarily be mindful of formal law remains controversial. It is an issue which poses serious questions about the role of law and the judiciary.

Professor Gower has suggested that 'though contact between law and business has not been lost it seems to be less direct, with a growing aloofness on the part of the businessman and a growing remoteness from commercial realities on the part of the law'. It would seem that business has to a large extent withdrawn from contract law because of its irrelevance to everyday notions of obligation. This is particularly the case as far as dispute resolution is concerned. The business community has come to place much greater reliance on negotiation, commercial mediation and arbitration than adjudication which in turn means that the raw material from which judicial precedents are set is depleted. Some observers have gone further and suggested that the formal contract of the classical model is no longer the essential vehicle for economic exchanges. These arguments suggest that we should go beyond the material contained in textbooks on the subject which focus only on the issue of what the formal law is. Instead, it could be argued that we need to pose a different set of questions, such as what is the relationship between contract practice and the law? Do business people make contracts on the basis of the legal rules? Do they use the courts to enforce contracts? Is law relevant? By asking these questions we move from a position in which law is taken to be synonymous with commerce to a position where the most logical question to pose is of whether commercial exchange needs law.

NON-CONTRACTUAL RELATIONS IN BUSINESS

In the latter half of the last century a number of important empirical studies of the operation of contract law on a day-to-day basis were undertaken which provided fertile ground for reconsideration of the relevance of classical and neo-classical models. These studies are important not only because they help us to answer the questions posed above, but because they have prompted the emergence of new theories about the role of contract which help us to visualise alternatives to the traditional models. The most obvious starting point for a discussion of the real world of contract is the work of Stewart Macaulay who was the first socio-legal researcher to explore in a systematic way the use that the business community made of contracts. He argued that contracts had the *potential* to serve two key functions. The first of these is the rational planning of the transaction with careful provision for as many future contingencies as can be foreseen. The second is the existence, or use of, legal sanctions to induce performance of the exchange or compensate for non-performance. Macaulay saw planning as involving such things as the definition of performances, the effect of defective performances and the legally binding nature, or otherwise, of the agreement. His expectations about the role that contract might play in exchanges would have been familiar to classical scholars who focused considerable attention on planning and dispute resolution. What was to prove innovative about his work was the response of manufacturers to his questions about the actual use to which contract was put.

In his study of the car industry, Macaulay found, somewhat surprisingly, that business people were not very concerned about planning their transactions. Other studies have also shown that business people are not particularly worried about the initial terms of the agreement and that detailed negotiations at the beginning of a relationship can even appear to be a sign of mistrust. It would seem that it is good relations and profit margins rather than legal rights and duties which are uppermost in the minds of commercial contractors when they make deals. In Macaulay's study, most manufacturers discussed what constituted performance and the effect of certain things happening during performance, but less than half negotiated the consequences of non-performance and even less gave thought to the type of legal sanctions which would apply in such situations. However, he did find evidence of two widely accepted norms of business practice which bound the parties and business community in other ways not anticipated by the classical model with its heavy emphasis on individualism and self-interest: first, an adherence to the principle that commitments should be honoured in almost all situations and a strong feeling that one should not welsh on a deal; and secondly, that one ought to produce a good product and stand behind it. Neither of these motivations was as altruistic as might at first appear to be the case. Firmly behind these norms was a sure knowledge of the commercial value of trouble-free, continuing relationships with good customers.

It is clear from the burgeoning empirical literature on the day-to-day use of contract that, contrary to the classical model's assumption about the importance of certainty, flexibility is highly valued within the business community. Performance of contractual obligations often takes a significant amount of time. So, for instance, the supply of aircraft parts to the Royal Air Force might involve a contractual relationship spanning many years. Similarly, an architect might be employed to design a building and supervise its construction over a three year period or longer. During this time the agreement is likely to alter. Changes in market conditions, technology and costs mean that adjustments to contracts are common. So, for instance, the country's entry into war at short notice will mean that more aircraft parts need to be produced or that the price of imported components increases rapidly. Similarly, the design of a civic theatre may have to be reconsidered when the builders find a site of archaeological interest when digging the foundations. Macaulay found a number of instances in which one party sought such an adjustment once an agreement had been made. In law, such unilateral proposals to vary an existing agreement require a new agreement to be negotiated and a new exchange to take place to seal the bargain. Macaulay found that in the business world such adjustments, and even withdrawals, were in many instances allowed by the other party 'without dispute' or renegotiation. Cancellation was not always cause for an action for breach but, like bad debts, a recognised risk that could be budgeted for. As one lawyer commented: 'There is a widespread attitude within the business community that one can back out of any deal within some vague limits.'

Even when such adjustments to the working agreement do not occur, there are limits to what those drafting a formal paper deal can predict will happen and provide for. This means that when a judge or lawyer looks for the plain meaning of the original contract it is often the case that it does not reflect what the parties want to achieve. As a result it has been argued that traditional forms of analysing contracts are inadequate for they fail to understand the importance of the *implicit dimensions* of contracts. That is not to say that traditional doctrines have ignored the need for flexibility. It will be seen from the chapters that follow that even the most traditional of lawyers anticipates the need for such things as variation of contracts and interpretation of agreements in the context of a previous course of dealing or trade custom. But the emphasis of the classical model is on treating contracts as disembedded associations between individuals motivated only by financial gain in the short or medium term. For some, this is an inadequate response to contractual realities in the marketplace. Campbell and Collins (2003) have argued that legal reasoning has developed only a weak capacity to incorporate these dimensions into its analysis of contract. In their words:

> If the law seeks to protect and enforce contractual agreements, the recognition that it has a partial and incomplete understanding of those agreements suggests that it fails in many instances to achieve its goals by enforcing not the agreement of the parties in all its relevant dimensions but a truncated perception of that agreement ... misunderstandings of this practice create the risk that legal regulation will either fail adequately to support the practice when required or misdirect its controls so that they are ineffective.

Macaulay's study also found that the use of litigation in the business community was rare and many participants argued that they would *actively avoid* introducing lawyers into a dispute because they did not understand the give and take of business. In fact, the parties would frequently disregard the contract or legal sanctions available in negotiating a dispute. As Macaulay (2003) has argued more recently:

> Business people do know that there are such things as actions for breach of contract. They also know that their reputation with their trading partner is valuable, and they do not knowingly do things that would damage it without a good reason. Most of the time, I would guess, avoiding breach of contract litigation is not something that business people spend much time thinking about. Insofar as this is true, the style of contract analysis used by judges will not matter much to people who are not law professors.

Macaulay and others have also discovered that it is not just that law is marginalised but that other normative frameworks are used to replace it. These studies suggest that widespread use is made of non-legal sanctions such as complaints, replacement procedures, negotiated settlements, gossip and blacklisting and that the effectiveness of these measures renders recourse to the courts unnecessary. Underpinning these various informal sanctions is an economic need to stay on good terms with those parties with whom business people were likely to want to contract with again. This finding alone provides a stark contrast to the classical model of contract which envisages a 'discrete' one-off exchange between strangers.

However, the failure of so many legal doctrines to reflect how contracts work in an everyday context and the fact that the courts may rarely be used by some sectors of the business community should not necessarily lead us to the conclusion that the law completely lacks legitimacy. It is possible that law plays a more indirect role in the contractual sphere than has been suggested so far. Other authors have argued that while business people honour informal norms and sanctions while a contractual relationship is progressing well, when it breaks up they may well want recourse to the sort of 'end game' rules which appear in formal written agreements. Moreover, although they may not use the courts, that is not to say that formal doctrine, favourable precedents and the threat of legal enforcement of contractual obligations are not used as bargaining tools in the process of negotiating an out-of-court settlement or compliance with a demand. In this way, it may be that formal doctrine continues to have a radiating effect or symbolic power not anticipated by some empirical studies. Even where disputes do not arise, the law may play some part in fostering confidence. If litigation is not thought about on a day-to-day basis, it may nonetheless constitute a vague symbolic threat which serves to encourage reliability. The question which remains is whether we want the law of contract to be more than this?

FEMINIST CRITIQUES OF CONTRACT

The argument that the beliefs which underpin social relations are co-operative rather than constantly antagonistic is one which has been taken up in feminist critiques of the law of contract. The identification of a correlation between the characteristics of masculinity and the ethos and philosophy of classical legal doctrine has been central to feminist engagements with the law. Three broad themes could be said to run through feminist texts on contract law. First, that the exclusion of women from the legal profession has meant that feminist concerns have been marginalised. Secondly, that for much of the history of contract law women, and married women in particular, were severely limited in their ability to make contracts which would be legally enforceable. Finally, and most importantly, that the values with which the classical model of contract are associated are essentially masculine values.

It has been argued that since men have been the visible architects of the courts, civil process and doctrine, it is therefore likely that masculine values have dominated the courtroom. Women were not able to vote for those who made laws until the last century, nor were they admitted to the House of Commons as representatives. They have been physically absent from the courts in any role other than victim, witness or observer for much of the history of the courts and were only able to enter the legal profession as recently as the 1920s. Even today, precedent continues to be largely determined by men of English descent. Only one Lord of Appeal in the Ordinary is a woman, as are just 6% of Lord Justices of Appeal or High Court Judges.

The history of contract law also reveals that women have been largely excluded from the contractual sphere. In some cases the exclusion has been obvious. This was the case, for instance, when married women were not allowed to make contracts except as agents of their husbands or when they had to terminate certain contracts of employment on marriage. The fact that the contractual sphere was one in which women were not expected to participate is reflected in the 6th edition of *Chitty on Contract*. In this influential treatise, married women find themselves referred to in the same chapter as lunatics, felons and outlaws. Other instances of exclusion have been less obvious, as is the case, for instance, with the doctrine of intention to create legal relations. The overt aim of the doctrine was to ensure that only those who intended to enter into a commercial agreement would be bound by it, but indirectly the doctrine served the purposes of rendering unenforceable agreements made in the 'domestic' sphere by married couples or close relatives. As it was women, rather than men, who have tended to dominate the domestic sphere and lack influence in the commercial sphere, such prohibitions have served to disadvantage them in the promotion of their perspective more than was the case with the interests of men.

However, it is not just the physical exclusion of women from the contractual sphere or courtroom which has been of concern to feminists. Commentators have also remarked on the exclusion of feminine values from the philosophy of classical contract law. There is a clear resonance between their concerns and those of the empiricists discussed above. Although the subject remains controversial, feminist writers have suggested that whilst feminine subjects prefer to focus on context, relationships and discretion in resolving disputes, masculine subjects prefer to work with pre-determined and logical rules which, although inflexible, produce certainty. Empirical work in the field suggests that feminine subjects typically see moral dilemmas in the context of long-term goals. Their worlds are worlds of connection and network in which an awareness of the links between people give rise to a recognition of context and responsibility for one another. Most significant for present purposes is the way in which this approach can be seen as opposed to an individualistic justice model of the type favoured by classical theorists.

It is arguable that there is no branch of the law in which the hostile egoism of possessive individualism is more clearly reflected than in classical contract and neo-classical models which take people away from the pre-existing web of community emphasised by writers such as Macaulay. It has been argued that doctrinal writers and judges alike have tended historically to legislate against the emotive and relational dimensions of contracts and that, in its most extreme form, the legal subject of contractual exchange has been viewed as a mere expression of economic relationships or callous cash nexus divorced from intimacy. According to this way of thinking, exchanges are the only way in which individuals come to recognise the needs of others. Applying this reasoning to contracts, the late Mary Jo Frug saw as masculine a position which stressed the plausibility of only one outcome in a model of contract predicated on discrete and abstract relationships. In her view, this led somewhat inevitably to a literal interpretation of the relevant contract texts and an emphasis on the value of certainty. By way of contrast, she characterised as feminine a position that was grounded in a pluralistic, context-sensitive model of contract relationships which offered a multiplicity of objectives and was centred on good faith, forbearance and sharing.

It follows that, for the feminist critic, the classical and neo-classical models have become associated with masculine values such as performance, control, security of transaction and standardisation for their survival. But it is context which has been of particular importance to feminist scholars. They have argued that contractual doctrine removes disputes from their everyday existence by narrowing the issues for discussion into distinctive and limited legal categories which stifle the setting in which the dispute occurs. Not only do classical and formalistic approaches to the subject concentrate on specific events and moments in time, they purport to rely on linear modes of reasoning. In this way, it has been argued that accounts of disputed events which are entirely adequate by the standards of common sense morality prove to be legally inadequate because of judicial assumptions about how a story should be told and how and when blame should be assessed. The emphasis placed by the judiciary on abstract principles and linear accounts also reflects the tendency of the common law to seek universal and guiding principals to frame all decisions. Such generalisations assume universal truths and a neutral or objective way of seeing things which tend to suppress alternative ways of framing accounts or grievances. Viewed in this way, it is clear that the classical model is ill-equipped to create a space in which the sort of context discussed in empirical studies and by feminists can be heard and understood.

RELATIONAL CONTRACT THEORY

It is, however, in the work of relational contract theorists that the most successful attempt has been made to address the concerns raised by empiricists and feminists about context and substantive norms of justice. The work of Ian Macneil has been particularly influential in this respect. His interest in contracts has focused on the ways in which context can be used in interpreting contractual behaviour. The themes which characterise his work are how legal doctrine should respond to long-term relationships, recognise and engender trust and respect the sort of diverse interpretations of legal obligations which empiricists and feminists talk about. Four core propositions inform the relational approach to contract:

- Every transaction is embedded in a complex web of relations. Even the most casual and brief of contracts such as the purchase of a daily newspaper involves a complex network of suppliers of paper, journalists and transport.

- Understanding any transaction requires an appreciation of anything which is significant to the transaction regardless of whether it is something which is relevant to formal legal rules about contracts.

- Effective analysis of any transaction requires a recognition of all relationships and sequences which impinge on performance.

- This contextual analysis produces a more sensitive approach to the contractual relationship than an approach which privileges the formal agreement.

Macneil draws an important distinction between two types of contract. The *discrete* contract is one where the parties come together for one transaction. This happens, for instance, when Angie buys a packet of chewing gum from a petrol station on the way to France, to which she never returns. This type of contract is one in which the goods and money are exchanged immediately and the parties do not necessarily anticipate dealing with each other again. At the opposite end of the spectrum is the *relational* contract which forms part of a long-term relationship between the parties whose business interests become more integrated as a result. In this sort of contract, flexibility, trust, co-operation and harmonious settlements of disputes are likely to be privileged. It is for these reasons that relational contracts have been likened to marriages and discrete exchanges likened to one night stands. But as Wightman (1996) reminds us:

> Although such terms as trust and co-operation are used here, it is important to see that there is no suggestion that relational contracting is just a mush of altruism, where self-interest has disappeared. The issue is not the existence of self-interest, but the form of its expression. Take, for example, the relationship between a main contractor and various subcontractors on a major construction project such as a large bridge. It will be in the self-interest of all the firms for the project to be completed successfully, but this will not happen if every technical breach is pounced on as an excuse for terminating and claiming damages.

Macneil has argued that all contracts, whether discrete or relational, rely on shared understandings about the particular meanings to be attributed to contracts and contractual behaviour. For him the failure of the classical model is its inability and unwillingness to recognise the importance of context, humanitarian factors and implicit understandings in contract. In his view this renders it obsolete in practical terms because of the ways in which it distorts understanding of the marketplace. It would seem then that the importance of relational contract theory lies not only in its revelations about the components of contracts which are vital to an understanding of them but in its revelations that these are the very elements which are marginalised by classical theorists.

This point is beautifully illustrated in *Baird Textile Holdings Ltd v Marks & Spencer plc* decided in 2001. The claimant in this case argued that they had been one of the main suppliers of clothes to Marks & Spencer for 30 years. The parties operated according to a 'supplier partnership' arrangement which allowed Marks & Spencer to play an active role in the design and manufacture of the clothes. Over time, the claimant organised their workforce in a way which allowed them to be flexible and responsive to requests from the retailer. They claimed that the relationship had been terminated by Marks & Spencer without notice contrary to the understanding between them that the relationship would be long-term. The Court of Appeal was asked to determine whether there was a cause of action and it came to the conclusion that the relationship was made up of a long series of discrete contracts for the supply of garments rather than a more holistic and long-term contractual relationship based on established understandings of the kind identified by the claimants. The court's reasoning was based in part on the finding that Marks & Spencer had made it clear that they did not intend to enter into a long-term contract. It would be difficult to find a case where the tensions implicit in the common law's focus on discrete exchanges is more apparent. The court's reluctance to recognise that over time the entirety of the relationship between the parties had become more than the sum of a series of particular exchanges is a considerable blow to those who believe that the law should be more sensitive to the normative frameworks and understandings which arise out of exchanges. These cannot be found in discrete exchanges: they are the spirit of the relationship.

The common law's reluctance to take greater account of relational elements to contracts leads us back to the important questions about the role of contractual doctrine and the judiciary posed earlier in this chapter. We have learnt that relational contracts are likely to be less specific than discrete ones and may, as a result, pose additional problems of interpretation, because they are highly dependent on implicit understandings. If one takes Macneil's arguments to their logical endpoint, it could be argued that it is the context in which the contract takes place which should be looked at before the formal contract. In his view, looking at the express terms of a contract before context skews understanding of what has fuelled and nurtured the formal agreement. This represents a complete reversal of the position of traditionalists who have preferred to begin, and sometimes end, with formal written documents or negotiations which take place at the beginning of the contract.

CONCLUDING REMARKS

There is no doubt at all as to the importance of empirical work on contracts for anyone interested in the relationship between business transactions, contract and contract law. These studies indicate that business policy and practice often operate to marginalise the role of the formal law of contract in everyday business transactions. To the extent that business transactions operate 'outside' contract, this amounts to a rejection by the business community of legal doctrine. Does this matter? According to Macaulay's evidence, it would seem that it does not, unless you are a lawyer who is losing fees. None of the business people that Macaulay interviewed appeared to be losing sleep over their non-contractual relations. However, another view is that it would be dangerous to 'write off' contract as a business device on the strength of the empirical studies conducted. Rather, it could be argued that greater efforts should be made to make the law relevant to the business community. After all, the basic function of contract has long been identified as facilitating business exchanges.

What becomes clear from the analysis contained in this chapter is that the theories underpinning the law of contract are in a state of flux. Criticisms of the classical model focus on its emphasis on procedural justice at the expense of substantive justice, its privileging of rules over understanding and context, and its inability to reflect the day-to-day world of contracts. We saw in the last chapter that welfarist interventions on behalf of consumers have mitigated the more extreme injustices of a model based on the assumption that the parties to a contract exercise free will. Conceptually, though, these interventions remain exemptions to general rules rather than a general platform from which to launch a more general discussion about the importance of looking at inequality or context in all contracts. It becomes clear that the pragmatism of the common law confers status on certain types of contracting parties but fails to address the issue of whether there is such a thing as a general law of contract in English law. In the chapters which follow, we will see these issues being raised again and again. But what remains important for present purposes is whether and how relations contract theory can deliver its promise of a more responsive law of contract which is relevant to all of us.

REFERENCES AND FURTHER READING

Adams, J and Brownsword, R 'The ideologies of contract' (1987) 7 Legal Studies 205.

Beale, H and Dugdale, T 'Contracts between businessmen: planning and the use of contractual remedies' (1975) 2 British Journal of Law and Society 45.

Bernstein, L 'Merchant law in a merchant court: rethinking the code's search for immanent business norms' (1996) 144 University of Pennsylvania Law Review 1765.

Bottomley, A (ed) (1996) Feminist Perspectives on the Foundational Subjects of Law, London: Cavendish Publishing.

Campbell, D and Collins, H (2003) 'Discovering the implicit dimensions of contracts' in Campbell, D, Collins, H and Wightman, J (eds), Implicit Dimensions of Contract: Discrete, Relational and Network Contracts, Oxford: Hart Publishing.

Campbell, D and Harris, D 'Flexibility in long-term contractual relationships' (1993) Journal of Law and Society 166.

Deakin, S, Lane, C and Wilkinson, F '"Trust" or law? Toward an integrated theory of contractual relations between firms' (1994) 21 Journal of Law and Society 329.

Epstein, R 'Confusion about custom: disentangling informal customs from standard contractual provision' (1999) 66 University of Chicago Law Review 821.

Macaulay, S 'Non-contractual relations in business – a preliminary study' (1963) 28 American Sociological Review 55.

Macaulay, S 'Elegant models, empirical pictures, and the complexities of contract' (1977) 11 Law and Society Review 507.

Macaulay, S (2003) 'The real and paper deal: empirical pictures of relationships, complexity and the urge for transparent simple rules' in Campbell, D, Collins, H and Wightman, J (eds), Implicit Dimensions of Contract: Discrete, Relational and Network Contracts, Oxford: Hart Publishing.

Macneil, I 'Contracts: adjustment of long-term economic relations under classical, neoclassical and relational contract law' (1978) 72 Northwestern University Law Review 854.

Macneil, I (1980) The New Social Contract: An Inquiry into Modern Contractual Relations, New Haven, CT: Yale University Press.

Pateman, C (1988) The Sexual Contract, Cambridge: Polity Press.

Vincent-Jones, P 'Contract and business transactions: a socio-legal analysis' (1989) 16 Journal of Law and Society 166.

Wightman, J (1996) Contract – A Critical Commentary, London: Pluto Press.

QUESTIONS

(1) Read over 'The Sad Tale of Angie and Georgie' and note down all the agreements made in the story which you think *ought* to be enforced by the courts, regardless of whether they would be. Look back at your notes. Can you identify common characteristics which each of the agreements you have identified share? What are these?

(2) How important do you think context is to Angie and Georgie in determining whether or not to sue for breach of these agreements? Would you advise them to try and sue? What would they achieve? Give reasons for your response.

(3) Imagine that you have been asked to prepare a 10 minute presentation for a radio programme in which you need to convey the distinction between relational and discrete contracts using examples from 'The Sad Tale of Angie and Georgie'. Sketch out what you would say and then add a section which makes the case for the importance of the distinction.

PART THREE:

MAKING A DEAL

CHAPTER 5

APPROACHES TO FINDING AGREEMENT AND PRE-CONTRACTUAL NEGOTIATIONS

INTRODUCTION

The rules relating to the formation of contracts are designed to establish the moment a contract comes into existence so that the parties are clear about the exact time and place that their obligations to each other begin. This is clearly important if people are to be able to plan in advance or if a contractual relationship breaks down and one of the parties seeks to be compensated. In considering whether a contract has been formed, English law looks for agreement between the parties. The typical contract is conceived of as a two-sided bargain voluntarily and deliberately entered into by two people. This chapter focuses on agreement and is concerned with the following questions. First, how do lawyers analyse the process by which the parties to a contract reach agreement? Secondly, how does business practice relate to the legal analysis of agreement?

Most lawyers would say that the answer to the first question is well-settled by the leading cases which provide a rational and structured account of the negotiation and agreement process. However, others whose views were rehearsed in the last chapter would say that the 'rules' of offer and acceptance, on which the legal concept of agreement rests, are unsatisfactory: first, because they are largely irrelevant to the conduct of business today; and, secondly, because they are often awkward tools which are only rarely used by the courts for the settlement of disputes. Who is right?

DEFINITIONS, FORM AND OBJECTIVITY

In the search for agreement the courts have for some time looked for an 'offer' and an 'acceptance'. *Offers* have traditionally been defined by the courts as expressions of a willingness to enter into a legally binding contract. The expression may manifest itself in words or in conduct. The purchase of a daily newspaper may, for instance, be completed without the buyer or seller saying anything to each other. However, they must do something which expressly or impliedly indicates that the offer is to become binding on the person making it (the offeror) as soon as it has been accepted by the offeree.

An *acceptance* is a final and unqualified expression of assent to the terms of an offer. So, if Sally emails Carl to say 'Would you like to buy a consignment of 20 of the latest skateboards for £2,000? I can deliver next Thursday', and Carl emails back the response 'Great. I promise to send you a cheque for £2,000 and will stay in on Thursday', there is an agreement which would be recognised by English law. It can be seen from this simple example that acceptance turns an offer, so defined, into agreement. Figure 5.1 shows this transaction in pictorial form.

Traditionally, the courts have *not* sought to protect the expectations of parties as they negotiate with each other during the pre-contractual stage. This is logical. It is not until a contract is formed that the law of contract has a role in governing the relationship.

Figure 5.1: Elements of a contract

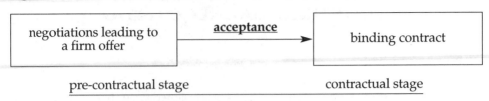

| negotiations leading to a firm offer | acceptance → | binding contract |

pre-contractual stage   contractual stage

It should also have become clear from previous chapters that English law recognises as valid those exchanges which are contemporaneous with the process of the acceptance matching the offer (executed contracts), as well as exchanges of promises about future conduct (executory contracts).

It often comes as a surprise to students to discover that only in certain cases does the law require contracts to be in writing. Carl and Sally's agreement would have been just as valid if they had communicated by telephone or had the conversation face to face over coffee. Although written contracts are common, the fact that transactions are frequently conducted on the basis of printed standard forms of contract is a matter of business expediency and is not a *legal* requirement. A contract may be in writing. It may be signed by the parties, but it could also be concluded verbally, by conduct, or some mixture of all three. What marks out a written contract and makes it attractive is that having something in writing is often the best evidence of the terms agreed by the parties. For this reason the Consumer Credit Act 1974 requires that hire purchase and other credit transactions be in writing and signed by the parties as a consumer protection measure.

When looking for agreement the courts are not concerned with what the parties were thinking or really intended to do. The tests imposed by the courts are *objective*. This means that, for practical reasons, the courts infer intention from what the parties do and say rather than from what they are thinking. If the parties have, to all outward appearances, agreed in the same terms on the same subject matter, generally neither can deny that they intended to agree. So, in the email transaction between Carl and Sally discussed above, the court would not be concerned with Carl's objection that he never really intended to buy Sally's skateboards but was just exploring possibilities. They would focus instead on what the reasonable person would assume to have been his intention on reading the email exchange. The subjective *consensus ad idem* theory, popular in the 19th century, which required that there could be no contract without a genuine 'meeting of the minds' has largely passed from the law, although we shall see that it continues to have some influence in cases where mistakes are made in the pre-contractual negotiations. However, whatever the test in looking for agreement, it commonly involves *construing* the language and behaviour of the parties in order to establish whether the parties have, from an objective viewpoint, reached agreement.

In reality, finding an offer and acceptance may not always be as straightforward as the example involving Carl and Sally suggests. Often this is because negotiations leading to a contract may be prolonged and involve a series of statements made by the parties as they move slowly towards agreement. For instance, before sending the email in which he accepts Sally's offer, Carl may have asked for further information about the colours of the skateboards, their condition or suitability for use on ramps. By the same token, Sally may have specified convenient collection times and methods of payment which were not acceptable to her. But greater levels of complexity are also introduced when one begins to study the *context* in which commercial transactions take place. Consider, for example, the position if Sally had been supplying Carl with a consignment of the most up-to-date skateboards for his shop for over 15 years. Every time she hears of a new business opportunity she lets him know about it and he has come to rely on her to always deliver skateboards she is confident she can obtain. As a result he is prepared to let her use his shop in her advertising. On one occasion she emails him to say that she is excited about a new design of skateboard from Australia which she is bidding for on an internet auction organised by one of her long-time suppliers. On the strength of this, Carl organises a launch of the new range in his shop. He orders posters and balloons and places an advertisement in the local paper as he usually does on the strength of Sally's communications. But on this occasion, she is not able to supply the skateboards as she fell asleep when she should have been placing a bid. Is it appropriate for the courts to recognise contractual obligations in this situation?

WHAT ARE THE COURTS LOOKING FOR?

The exact moments when offers and acceptances occur are not always clear, as the parties often proceed by nudging slowly towards contractual responsibility. As a result, the notions of offer, counter offer, invitation to treat and acceptance can be elusive. As Treitel has remarked, 'When parties carry out lengthy negotiations it may be hard to say exactly when an offer has been made and accepted ... Business people do not, any more than courts, find it easy to say precisely when they have reached agreement', but a court must 'decide whether an apparently unqualified acceptance did in fact conclude the agreement'.

As the arguments in subsequent chapters unravel it will become apparent that inter-business contracts often refuse to fit neatly into the 'doctrinal handcuffs' of rigidly interpreted rules. As the work of Macaulay discussed in the last chapter has shown, business people are much less strict than lawyers as regards contractual certainty. Directors or managers often feel that insistence on adherence to contractual 'detail' is bad for continuing business relations and, in any case, it may amount to poor strategy to tie oneself too tightly at the time of agreement when the future is uncertain. While acceptance must be unconditional, contractors often prefer to punctuate the agreement with a variety of adjustment devices which allow for flexibility as market conditions change and performance proceeds. Renegotiation and price variation clauses are two examples of such devices. In his book, *Government Procurement and Contracts*, Turpin cites a pertinent comment by the chief of defence procurement in 1986: 'We know that in these major contracts everything is fine while the project is running well but when a project goes wrong everybody starts reading the contract. We want to be sure that when we read it, it still means what we hoped it meant at the beginning.'

A close study of doctrine reveals that the frameworks for analysis handed down to generations of students has involved a formal set of rules which prescribe exactly what has to be done before a contract comes into place. You will undoubtedly learn a lot about these 'rules' of offer and acceptance during your course. Exam papers across the country will be full of problem questions in which emails are sent and not delivered, letters lost and answerphone messages unheard. It will become clear to you that the English courts have developed highly distinctive methods for analysing the point at which a contract comes into being which rest on the identification of particular sequential stages in the course of negotiations. In line with this approach the courts have developed a number of objective tests to determine whether agreement had been reached. Pre-contractual negotiations have to go through a number of formal stages before a contract can be found. In time these have become rather formulaic and divorced from the original notion of true agreement. It will be seen from the cases discussed in this chapter that this approach can often produce unsatisfactory results. The most obvious example of this is when the parties clearly intend to do business with each other, have reached an understanding and have begun to perform their part of the bargain without satisfying all the rules. Although the courts have found ways to enforce many of these agreements, they have done so at the expense of coherence. This in turn has led to much debate about the modern day relevance of this formalistic approach.

CRITICS OF THE FORMALIST APPROACH

Critics of this formalist approach assert that the offer-acceptance-consideration model presents an unrealistic, rigid and oversimplified view of business agreements. They argue that undue emphasis is placed on the idea of binding promises, or on the notion of offer and unqualified acceptance. The critics complain that the degree of certainty required by the law offends against the need for a degree of flexibility in business. The American commentator Mooney is scornful of the traditional textbook analysis:

> We learned that there are certain expressions of mutual assent to which the law appends an obligation arising from the express or plainly implied 'promises' of the parties. The legal obligation is strictly limited to the promises. These promises are discovered in *the* unvarying method by which human beings contract with each other, namely by means of 'offers' embodying 'promises' directed by 'offerors' of particular 'offerees' who 'accept' by manifesting assent either by tendering a promise or an act ... Case variations were hung on the construct like ornaments on a Christmas tree, glittering but essentially useless.

In the everyday world of business, promises seldom occur in the manner suggested by the case law. Over-emphasis on promises reflects simplistic 'party autonomy' and 'as you promise so you shall be bound' views of contract, and fails to pay attention to the realities of business negotiations, the safeguard and contingency 'buffers' which the parties themselves build into agreements and the mass of contract terms now emanating from statutory provisions.

However, although the courts' rules relating to agreement are based to a great extent on the relatively simple contractual situations of a century or more ago, it could be argued that they are not as immobile or 'black letter' as some would suggest. From a generally stated 'base line', it has been argued that they shade off towards a more realistic middle ground more in keeping with the complexity and approximate certainty of business life today. Collins, for instance, suggests that many of the leading cases can be much better understood if seen as attempts to determine the exact point at which it is *reasonable* for the parties to rely on what the other has said rather than an analysis of whether they have done particular things at particular points. We shall return to the idea of reasonable reliance as a basis on which to impose obligations in Chapter 7. For present purposes, suffice it to say that this alternative construction may get no closer to determining whether there has been a true agreement but it does produce results which are more flexible and attuned to business culture and practice. In a complicated commercial case a few years ago, *New Zealand Shipping Co Ltd v Satterthwaite & Co Ltd* (1975), Lord Wilberforce argued in a similar vein:

> It is only the precise analysis of this complex of relations into the classical offer and acceptance, with identifiable consideration, that seems to present difficulty, but this same difficulty exists in many situations of daily life, eg sales at auction; supermarket purchases; boarding an omnibus; purchasing a train ticket; tenders for the supply of goods ... these are all examples which show that English law, having committed itself to a rather technical and schematic doctrine, in application takes a practical approach, often at the cost of forcing the facts to fit uneasily into the worked slots of offer, acceptance and consideration.

What was striking about this case was that a majority of their Lordships were willing to engage in an ingenious application of the legal concepts of agreement and consideration in order to achieve 'commercial reality', and that it was the minority that stayed within the bounds of traditional analysis. It is also worth noting that numerous editions of Cheshire and Fifoot's *Law of Contract* have issued this warning regarding offer and acceptance:

> It must again be emphasised that the phrase 'offer and acceptance', though hallowed by a century and a half of judicial usage, is not to be applied as a talisman, revealing, by a species of esoteric art, the presence of a contract. It would be ludicrous to suppose that businessmen couch their communications in the form of a catechism ... The rules which the judges have elaborated from the premise of offer and acceptance are neither the rigid deductions of logic nor the inspiration of natural justice. They are only presumptions, drawn from experience, to be applied in so far as they serve the ultimate object of establishing the phenomena of agreement.

The quotation above warns us against over-dependence on the 'rules' of offer and acceptance as problem-solvers where contract formation is concerned. The 'rules' must be used with extreme care in an area where considerations such as the parties' intentions, trade custom, special circumstances and policy may all play their part. The student's dilemma and a plea for pragmatism have been neatly put by Lewis (1980):

> The formation of contracts by offer and acceptance is an aspect of law that has always aroused considerable academic interest, primarily for the opportunity it offers to pose largely unrealistic problems that permit varied, inconclusive and interminable intellectual analysis. Generations of students are acquainted with the noisy river that drowns the voice of the offeree as he accepts the offeror's offer (latterly a low-flying aircraft may be substituted for the clamorous flood); with the letter of acceptance that never arrives; with the epistolary revocation of offer that arrives after the letter of acceptance has been posted but before it has been delivered.

CASE STUDIES OF ALTERNATIVE STYLES OF REASONING

Before going on to consider the formal rules relating to the formation of contracts, it is useful to reflect on the different *approaches* to contract formation which are discernible from the case law. This can be done quite succinctly by analysing the judgments in two similar cases in which the parties moved slowly towards agreement. In the 1970s, the Conservative City Council in Manchester had a policy of selling council houses to tenants who wished to buy them. They devised a simple procedure to be followed which the tenants could use without the help of a solicitor. Following an election, the Council became Labour-controlled and the new administration discontinued the sales except in cases in which there was already a binding contract to sell in place. Two tenants who were informed that their sales could not proceed decided to sue the Council, as they believed that a contract for sale had been formed which they should be allowed to enforce.

In *Storer v Manchester City Council* (1974), Mr Storer had applied to buy his council house and the town clerk had forwarded to him an 'Agreement for Sale' detailing the purchase price and mortgage arrangements. Mr Storer had signed and returned the Agreement before the Conservative Council's policy had been discontinued by Labour. In their analysis of the case, the Court of Appeal adopted a conventional approach to finding a contract based on a series of authorities dating back to the classical contract period. They looked for a firm offer and a firm acceptance of that offer and decided that the procedure followed by the parties had reached the stage at which a binding contract had been concluded. Lord Denning stated that:

> [Mr Storer] had done everything which he had to do to bind himself to the purchase of the property. The only thing left blank was the date when the tenancy was to cease ... The corporation put forward to the tenant a simple form of agreement. The very object was to dispense with legal formalities. One of the formalities – exchange of contracts – was quite unnecessary. The contract was concluded by offer and acceptance. The offer was contained in the letter of 9 March in which the town clerk said: 'I ... enclose the Agreement for Sale. If you will sign the Agreement and return it to me I will send the Agreement signed on behalf of the Corporation in exchange.'

> The acceptance was made when the tenant did sign it, as he did, and return it, as he did on 20 March. It was then that a contract was concluded. The town clerk was then bound to send back the agreement signed on behalf of the corporation. The agreement was concluded on Mr Storer's acceptance. It was not dependent on the subsequent exchange.

> The final point was this. Counsel for the corporation said that the town clerk did not intend to be bound by the letter of 9 March 1971. He intended that the corporation should not be bound except on exchange. There is nothing in this point. In contracts you do not look into the actual intent in a man's mind. You look at what he said and did. A contract is formed when there is, to all outward appearances, a contract. A man cannot get out of a contract by saying 'I did not intend to contract', if by his words he has done so. His intention is to be found only in the outward expression which his letters convey. If they show a concluded contract that is enough.

In the later case, *Gibson v Manchester City Council* (1979), the facts were slightly more challenging for those disposed to use a traditional approach to finding an offer and acceptance as the purchasing procedure was slightly different and had not advanced as far as in *Storer*. Mr Gibson had applied to the Council for details of the price and mortgage terms applicable to the purchase of his council house. The City Treasurer replied that the Council 'may be prepared to sell the house to you at £2,725 less 20% = £2,180'. The letter gave details of the mortgage likely to be made available and asked Mr Gibson, if he wished to proceed, to make a formal application. He did this and the Council took the house off the list of council-maintained properties and placed it on their house purchase list. Mr Gibson claimed that the City Treasurer's letter amounted to an offer which he had accepted.

The Court of Appeal agreed with this analysis despite the fact that the transaction did not fall neatly into a conventional analysis of offer and acceptance. Bearing in mind the court's decision in *Storer* and prompted by considerations of fairness, Lord Denning supported the decision as follows:

> To my mind it is a mistake to think that all contracts can be analysed into the form of offer and acceptance. I know in some of the textbooks it has been the custom to do so; but as I understand the law, there is no need to look for a strict offer and acceptance. You should look at the correspondence as a whole and at the conduct of the parties and see therefrom whether the parties have come to an agreement on everything that was material. If by their correspondence and their conduct you can see an agreement on all material terms, which was intended thenceforward to be binding, then there is a binding contract in law even though all the formalities have not been gone through. For that proposition I would refer to *Brogden v Metropolitan Railway Co* (1877).

> It seems to me that on the correspondence I have read (and, I may add, on what happened after) the parties had come to an agreement in the matter which they intended to be binding.

What makes his judgment so worthy of note is that Denning is suggesting that there is no need for one component to be identified as an offer and another as acceptance. He argues that we should be looking to the overall transaction rather than becoming bound by formalistic rules which do not capture the *spirit* of the transaction. To use a simple metaphor, Denning is looking for the presence of a cake whereas those adopting a more formalistic analysis have looked for the ingredients of the cake and whether they have been put together in a 'correct' sequence.

Denning's approach in this case was, however, rejected by the House of Lords who adopted the traditional, formalist position. In Lord Diplock's words:

> My Lords, there may be certain types of contract, though I think they are exceptional, which do not fit easily into the normal analysis of a contract as being constituted by offer and acceptance; but a contract alleged to have been made by an exchange of correspondence between the parties in which the successive communications other than the first are in reply to one another is not one of these. I can see no reason in the instance case for departing from the conventional approach of looking at the handful of documents relied on as constituting the contract sued on and seeing whether on their true construction there is to be found in them a contractual offer by the council to sell the house to Mr Gibson and an acceptance of that offer by Mr Gibson. I venture to think that it was by departing from this conventional approach that the majority of the Court of Appeal was led into error.

As a result, it was decided that no offer to sell had been made by the Council. The City Treasurer's letter had stated that the Council *may* be prepared to sell and it invited Gibson to make a formal application to buy. It was argued that no clear intention to be bound could be evinced on a true construction of the words used and the letter amounted to no more than an invitation to negotiate further. It should also be noticed that two of the things that 'happened after' the correspondence were that the council took the house off their maintenance list and Gibson made some alterations to the property. However, it cannot be said that the English courts recognise and protect reliance on *expected* contracts, although protection is afforded to reliance on agreed variations to *existing* contracts as will be seen in the next chapter. We will also see in the next chapter that Lord Denning's approach, whereby he was willing to look at the 'whole transaction' rather than insist on strict offer and acceptance analysis, has been applied in other cases and so it cannot be said that it has been entirely rejected. Moreover, for present purposes it provides us with a challenging and alternative view of contract which helps us to critique the credibility of the formalistic approach.

CONCLUDING REMARKS

In the chapters which follow, we will begin to take a closer look at the rules of offer and acceptance referred to in this chapter and other tests of enforceability which rely on particular types of behaviour. It may well be of use to return to this chapter again when the detail of these rules has become more apparent. The purpose of this chapter has been to encourage you to interrogate traditional ways of analysing agreement and, as you read through the cases, to consider whether the formalist approach is serving the needs of the business community and wider society. The interface between theory and practice, the competing needs of certainty and flexibility and concerns about open-ended standards are all issues which will be revisited again and again.

REFERENCES AND FURTHER READING

Beale, H and Dugdale, T 'Contracts between businessmen: planning and the use of contractual remedies' (1975) 2 British Journal of Law and Society 45.

Collins, H (2003) *The Law of Contract*, London: LexisNexis Butterworths.

Furmston, M (2001) *Cheshire, Fifoot and Furmston's Law of Contract*, 14th edn, London: Butterworths.

Lewis, C 'The formation and repudiation of contracts by international telex' (1980) LMCLQ 43.

Turpin, C (1989) *Government Procurement and Contracts*, Harlow: Longman.

Wheeler, S and Shaw, J (1994) *Contract Law: Cases, Materials and Commentary*, Oxford: Oxford University Press.

QUESTIONS

(1) Read through the decisions in *Gibson v Manchester City Council* (1979) and draw up a list of reasons why the sale of the council house should *not* have gone through. Now rehearse the opposing arguments. Would you apply the same reasoning if the case concerned a deal between the council and a local construction company with its own team of lawyers?

(2) In the example involving Carl and Sally cited on page 58, do you think that Carl should be able to get compensation from Sally for the special launch he has had to cancel? Give reasons for your answer.

(3) Look through the list of agreements in 'The Sad Tale of Angie and Georgie' which you identified at the end of the last chapter. Analyse each of these according to 'formalist' and 'material agreement' methods discussed in this chapter. What are the effects of the different methods on the outcome?

CHAPTER 6

PRE-CONTRACTUAL NEGOTIATIONS: OFFERS, INVITATIONS TO TREAT AND COLLATERAL CONTRACTS

INTRODUCTION

In this chapter, we move on from the broader issues raised in the last chapter to consider specific issues which have been tested before the courts in relation to negotiations leading up to an offer. The chapter which follows on from this moves on to look at problems which have arisen in relation to acceptance. Although they have been separated out in the interest of introducing topics in an accessible and manageable format, these chapters should be read together as there is considerable overlap. Despite the tendency to aspire to clear, if somewhat illogical, rules to govern the law relating to offer and acceptance, in practice it is often difficult to separate the two concepts out.

If the courts are disposed towards a formalistic approach, it is important for students to understand the method of analysing negotiations in this way. An examination of the various things that occur in the pre-contractual stage requires an appreciation of a range of terms such as invitation to treat, tenders, collateral contract and unilateral offers which are used to distinguish the various situations which are akin to an offer but do not quite fulfil the relevant criteria. It is to these various terms that we now turn. In its reasoning, the judiciary turns again and again to consideration of whether statements by the offeror are capable of being converted into a contract or whether further negotiation is necessary. A major issue underpinning many of the judgments we will be considering is the courts' reluctance to bind the parties to a contract at an unexpectedly early stage.

OFFERS, INVITATIONS TO TREAT AND ADVERTISEMENTS

As a general proposition, offers must be distinguished from other statements made at a pre-contractual stage which are known as 'invitations to treat'. This is an old-fashioned expression which describes attempts by one party to encourage the other to enter into negotiations with them or make an offer to them. Most people come across several examples of invitations to treat each day without being aware of the term of art used by lawyers to describe them. Each time you pass a shop which declares that it has the 'lowest prices in town' or an advertising board which declares that a certain airline offers 'lower prices than all its competitors' you are being tempted, or invited, to approach them with a view to buying a product or service from them. But few would expect the claims made to be substantiated. They are part of the 'puff' or sales technique used to encourage customers to enter a shop or access a website. But, as one moves on to look at other inducements and more specific wording, it becomes clear that there are fine lines to be drawn between what should be taken seriously and what should not.

A number of problems have arisen over whether the display of goods in a shop window or on the shelves of a shop with prices attached amounts to an offer. One would think so and presumably shopkeepers who display signs reading 'Special offers – exceptional bargains' and the like think so too. However, as early as the mid-19th century, the courts took a different view, which was endorsed in the supermarket case of *Pharmaceutical Society of Great Britain v Boots Cash Chemists (Southern) Ltd* (1953). A Boots customer selected goods from the shelves and presented them at the cash desk where she paid the prices marked. Some of the goods were required by the Pharmacy and Poisons Act 1933 to be sold only under the supervision of a registered pharmacist and a pharmacist was present at the cash desk for this purpose. Boots were alleged to have infringed the 1933 Act because the contract had been formed before the woman presented the goods at the cash desk. When did the sale take place? The society argued that it was when the customer put the goods into her wire basket, so accepting the offer constituted by the display on the shelves. If this were so, certain medicines and poisons would be 'sold' without supervision contrary to the 1933 Act. However, the Court of Appeal disagreed and ruled that the sale took place at the cash desk. They argued that display of the goods did not mean that they were on offer. Instead, they argued that an offer to buy was made by the customer at the cash desk subject to supervision and possible refusal. In their view, the display of goods was merely an invitation to treat.

This decision really rests on a policy choice which supported commercial innovation and convenience rather than on orthodox analysis of contract formation. The same issue usually arises in the context of criminal statutes where the *Boots* ruling has led to difficulties (see *Pilgram v Rice-Smith* (1977)). In *Fisher v Bell* (1961), a case involving the alleged offence of 'offering for sale' a 'flick knife' contrary to the Restriction of Offensive Weapons Act 1959, the court was asked to analyse the law in relation to priced goods in a shop window. Although the statute was clearly intended to cover such goods, it was held that the display was merely an invitation and that no offence had been committed because an offer had not been made.

It has been argued that the law would be better served to regard displays or advertisements as offers subject to the condition, sometimes found in advertisements, that stocks remain available, as this position would better reflect the expectations of the public and business community. Parties may of course indicate that their statements do not constitute offers. Estate agents often do this by including a form of words on details of properties, such as the statement that: 'These particulars do not form, nor constitute any part of, an offer, or a contract, for sale.' However, the courts are not well-disposed to this approach and have often been driven by pragmatic concerns in the cases before them. Even where an advertisement in the 'For Sale' columns of a newspaper contains specific wording, a court would almost certainly, on the basis of the 'limited stocks' argument, regard the advertisement as an invitation to treat. This was 'business sense' according to Lord Parker in *Partridge v Crittenden* (1968), another statutory offence case in which the defendant inserted in a periodical a notice stating 'Bramblefinch cocks and hens 25s each'. If the advertisement had been construed as an offer and demand had exceeded the defendant's supply, he could have faced any number of breach actions, as well as being guilty of an offence under the Protection of Birds Act 1954.

The issue of identifying whether a statement in an advertisement was *specific enough* to be construed as an offer which was intended to be binding was also addressed in the famous case of *Carlill v Carbolic Smoke Ball Co* (1893). The case concerned a slightly different type of contract from the bilaterally negotiated ones we have discussed thus far. The offer was of a type known as a unilateral offer to the world at large capable of being transformed into an agreement when someone came forward to perform the conditions specified. However, for present purposes, our concern is with the issue of what the case had to say about defining an offer.

The facts of the case were that the defendant company produced a medical preparation called the Carbolic Smoke Ball. They inserted an advertisement in the *Pall Mall Gazette* in which they offered to pay £100 to anyone who caught influenza after having used the Smoke Ball in a specified manner and for a specified period of time. They also stated that they had deposited £1,000 with the Alliance Bank as a sign of their good faith. On the strength of the advertisement, Mrs Carlill bought a smoke ball from a chemist, used it as prescribed, but nevertheless caught influenza. It was held that there was a contract between the parties and that the plaintiff could recover £100.

Much discussion in the case centred on the specificity of the wording of the poster. Bowen LJ stated that the advertisement in question 'was intended to be understood by the public as an offer to be acted upon' and Lindley LJ said: 'Read this how you will ... here is a distinct promise, expressed in language which is perfectly unmistakeable, that £100 will be paid by the Carbolic Smoke Ball Co to any person who contracts influenza after having used the ball three times daily, and so on.' In finding that the company's advertisement was to be construed as an offer, the court rejected the claim that it was 'a mere puff' or a vague and non-actionable invitation to treat. The offer therefore constituted an express promise to pay £100 to any party who fulfilled its terms. When Mrs Carlill used the smoke ball as prescribed, she should be regarded as having accepted the company's offer. The fact that normal communication of acceptance was not required was inferred from the wording of the offer and the nature of the transaction. The offer was seen as a serious one, showing an intention to create legal relations and therefore imposing a legally enforceable obligation on the company. Many commentators view the case as one which challenges the traditional conceptualisation of offer, but it is clear that policy issues also underlay the court's ruling, decided as it was in an age of 'quack' medical preparations produced by rogues who did not deserve to succeed.

More recently, new challenges to these rules about the formation of contract have been posed by the development of the internet and e-commerce. People have been making contracts through the agency of machines for some time. Every time you buy a bar of chocolate from a vending machine or put your car through an automatic car wash, you use a machine to make a contract. But cyberspace poses new challenges and has been identified as the fastest growing marketplace in the world. The web facilitates the making of more specific and customised contracts than is possible with a vending machine. It also allows people to make contracts across jurisdictions and continents with more ease than was previously possible. To date, most commentators have attempted to apply traditional reasoning to electronic contracts by looking for invitations to treat, offers and acceptances in the same way as lawyers have done for decades. Analogies with exchanges in a real marketplace are often facilitated by the design of websites. Many allow you to browse through their products in the same way you might in a shop, provide you with a virtual shopping basket and, once browsing is complete, instruct you to proceed to a virtual checkout. These 'click-wrap' contracts are negotiated by the seller displaying their terms and conditions and the buyer clicking on buttons to evidence their satisfaction with the choices being displayed. Goods displayed on the virtual shelves of a website can by analogy be treated as an invitation to treat in the same way as the goods on the shelves in the *Boots* case. The supplier's programme checks the availability of the item and if it is in stock the purchaser can make their offer by entering their credit card details and clicking on a button to confirm their choices.

But while we tend to think of the web as akin to an instantaneous form of communication such as face-to-face negotiations, in many ways this new technology gives consumers more time to ponder the terms and conditions prescribed by the seller in the comfort of their own home or office. Many websites do not allow a buyer to proceed to the stage where they can order a product or service without first ensuring that they have called up a screen with the company's terms of business on it. Some also allow the buyer to proceed along the 'negotiation' process in a number of clear-cut stages in which they are given several opportunities to reconsider their position and choices. It is important then to recognise the distinctive nature of electronic negotiations and contracts and question whether traditional modes of analysis can be applied to them. Documents on the web may not be perceived to be as trustworthy or permanent as paper documents. Text can be very easily manipulated in an electronic document without leaving a trace of previous versions. Electronic documents can also be linked to other sites and documents in a more random way than print documents, allowing connections and information flows that might be inconceivable in traditional paper deals. Concern that this renders the transaction somewhat different from those cases discussed so far is reflected in the fact that there are a growing number of European regulations which focus specifically on electronic contracts.

PERFORMANCE DURING FORMATION OF THE CONTRACT

A host of empirical studies and a burgeoning number of cases have revealed that in the business sector, people often commence performance before they have completed all the formal stages of contract formation. This provides a real dilemma for the judiciary. On the one hand, they are eager for the law to reflect efficient commercial practices; on the other, a number clearly feel constrained by the expectation that they should look for a particular sequence of events which anticipates that formation of the contract will be complete before performance begins. The fact that business practice so often flies in the face of traditional analysis of formation tempts us back to Lord Denning's more holistic approach to the issue outlined in the *Gibson* case above.

Difficulties over performance prior to completion of negotiations occur in a number of settings but debate around 'letters of intent' provides a good example of a practice which has caused problems for traditional models of analysis. A letter of intent, sometimes called 'an instruction to proceed', states that the sender *intends* to enter into a contract with the addressee. This is a common device in the construction industry where business people regularly rely on such letters. On their true interpretation, letters of intent probably create no obligation on the parties which would be recognised in English law. But where they include an instruction to proceed with performance and *such performance has begun*, the courts have been prepared to allow that when the contract is eventually agreed it will relate back to the performance that has taken place. In other words, the contract is given retrospective power.

This practice was extensively discussed in the case of *Trollope & Colls Ltd v Atomic Power Constructions Ltd* (1962). The facts were that in February 1959, Atomic Power received a tender for civil engineering work in the construction of a nuclear power station from Trollope & Colls. The tender was for a lump sum price and incorporated conditions authorising variations in the form, quality or quantity of work and provided that such variations were to be taken into account in ascertaining the contract price. The tender further incorporated a fluctuation clause relating to labour and material costs. Considerable changes were made after the date of tender, necessitating amendment of drawings, specification and bills of quantities. Trollope & Colls were notified of these changes and in June 1959 they were asked to start work by a 'letter of intent' from Atomic Power which stated: 'We have to inform you that it is our intention to enter into a contract with you for [the works]. As soon as matters outstanding between us are settled we will enter into a contract agreement with you, and in the meantime please accept this letter as an instruction to proceed with the work necessary to permit you to meet the agreed programme.' Work began and, on 11 April 1960, all outstanding matters were agreed but no contract was signed. A dispute arose over the basis on which Trollope & Colls should be paid for the work they undertook before 11 April. They contended that they should be paid on a *quantum meruit* basis for the work carried out before that date. *Quantum meruit* is a quasi-contractual remedy which allows payment to be made for the value of the work done where there is no formal contract. Atomic Power argued that the tender, as adjusted, outlined how payment should be assessed. It was held that the parties having acted in the course of negotiations on the understanding that, if and when a contract were made, it would govern what was being done meanwhile, the contract which came into existence on 11 April 1960 governed the rights of the parties as to *prior* work. This approach was said to be justified on either of two grounds: first, by the implication of a stipulation, necessary for the business efficacy of the contract, that the variations clauses should apply retrospectively; or, secondly, that the tender constituted an offer that contemplated variation of the work and the ultimate acceptance of that offer was an acceptance which embraced the changes requested and agreed in anticipation of the ultimate acceptance. Megaw J concluded that there is 'no principle of English law which provides that a contract cannot in any circumstances have retrospective effect'.

A similar situation arose in the case of *Trentham Ltd v Archital Luxfer Ltd* (1993), but in this case complete performance took place before negotiations on the way to a contract had been finalised. Here, Trentham were engaged to design and build industrial units and entered into negotiations with Archital Luxfer for them to supply and install aluminium windows. This work was completed and paid for but Trentham sued Archital Luxor for alleged defects in the windows, after they were sued by their client for delays and defects. Archital denied the existence of any contract. Whilst no written contract had come into existence, Trentham claimed that a binding contract was nevertheless formed on the basis of written exchanges, oral discussions and the performance of the transaction by both parties.

According to the leading judgment in the Court of Appeal, this was a contract which could not 'be precisely analysed in terms of offer and acceptance'. Was the contract in *Trentham* one of the 'exceptional' types of formalised contracts recognised by Lord Diplock in *Gibson*? Steyn LJ delivered the only full judgment and held that 'in this fully executed transaction a contract came into existence during performance even if it cannot be precisely analysed in terms of offer and acceptance'. He based this decision on the following points. First, he argued that English law adopts an *objective* approach to contract formation in which 'the governing criterion is in the reasonable expectations of [in this case] ... sensible business people'. Relying on *Gibson*, he further argued that although the coincidence of offer and acceptance is the normal mechanism of contract formation, 'it is not necessarily so in the case of a contract alleged to have come into existence during and as a result of performance'. Following the line of reasoning in *Trollope*, he suggested that if a contract only comes into existence during and as a result of performance of the transaction, it will frequently be possible to hold that the contract impliedly and retrospectively covers pre-contractual performance.

When reviewing these cases it is interesting to reflect on the 'contractual' nature of such agreements in the construction industry. They are undoubtedly 'messier' deals than those made by Carl and Sally in Chapter 5. The method of analysis used by judges such as Denning and Steyn is also undoubtedly more challenging. But it could also be claimed that decisions such as these, whilst flying in the face of formalist analysis, bring the law into line with the reality of practice in this field and increase the legitimacy of the law within the communities it aims to serve.

The ability of judges to provide a remedy in such cases has been challenged even further in a set of cases in which performance occurred but negotiations did *not* result in a contract. The fact that a contract has not been formed clearly hampers the court in applying contractual remedies, just as it did in the collateral contract cases discussed above. However, the courts have shown themselves willing to entertain restitutionary or 'quasi-contract' claims based on the notion of unjust enrichment in these situations. The idea is that natural justice and equity require those who have received a benefit must pay for the value of the work on the *quantum meruit* basis discussed above (see *Peter Lind & Co Ltd v Mersey Docks and Harbour Board* (1972)).

This solution to the absence of a contract and contractual remedies arose in *British Steel Corp v Cleveland Bridge & Engineering Co Ltd* (1984). In that case, Cleveland entered into negotiations with British Steel for the supply of a number of steel nodes and issued a letter of intent to British Steel requesting them to start work pending the preparation and issuing of the official form of sub-contract. British Steel declined to contract on Cleveland's terms as they had their own standard forms of contract and were concerned about the question of liability for loss caused by late delivery. Negotiations continued but no agreement was reached. All of the nodes were eventually delivered late but none of them were paid for. British Steel sued for the reasonable value of the nodes on a *quantum meruit*, restitutionary basis because no contract had been concluded. It was held by Robert Goff J that the parties had not reached agreement and no contractual relationship had come into existence. Thus, the letter of intent could not be used to identify terms as to payment and performance. But British Steel recovered £230,000 on its *quantum meruit* claim and Cleveland's counter claim failed, there being no binding terms regarding delivery or payments for late delivery for the claim to be measured against.

The remedy offered in this case straddles the boundary between contract and restitution. It could be seen to cause problems for the integrity of contractual doctrine since it undercuts the purpose of making certain contracts unenforceable. It would seem that responding to business reality can create a dangerous 'no man's land' between practice and the conventional view of contract formation. We will return to these issues in the next chapter.

CONCLUDING REMARKS

In this chapter we have identified some of the problems which emerge when we start to look at the identification of contractual liability. We have also begun to unravel some of the dilemmas which have arisen when law on the books is compared with the everyday realities of commercial practice. What the cases reveal are the tensions which become apparent in judicial reasoning when common sense tells us that an obligation has arisen which the traditional doctrines of the law of contract are not equipped to recognise. In the interests of pragmatism, we have seen from the cases in this chapter that the judiciary has found ways of getting around these limitations. But this has been at the expense of clear principles and there is a danger that the exceptions and reasoning involved begin to make a mockery of the philosophy underpinning the doctrines. This suggestion should be borne in mind as we progress in the next chapter to look at the notion of agreement.

REFERENCES AND FURTHER READING

Adams, J and Brownsword, R 'More in expectation than hope: the Blackpool Airport case' (1991) 54 MLR 281.

Ball, S 'Work carried out in pursuance of letters of intent – contract or restitution' (1983) 99 LQR 572.

Collins, H (2003) *The Law of Contract*, 4th edn, London: LexisNexis Butterworths.

Cumberbatch, J 'In freedom's cause: the contract to negotiate' (1992) 12 Oxford Journal of Legal Studies 586.

Howarth, J 'Contract, reliance and business transactions' (1987) JBL 122.

Jones, D 'Claims arising out of anticipated contracts which do not materialise' (1980) 18 University of West Ontario LR 447.

Lewis, R 'Contracts between businessmen: reform of the law of firm offers and an empirical study of tendering practices in the building industry' (1982) 12 British Journal of Law and Society 153.

Simpson, A 'Quackery and contract law: the case of the Carbolic Smoke Ball' (1985) 14 Journal of Legal Studies 345.

QUESTIONS

(1) Is it appropriate for tendering problems identified in this chapter to be remedied through use of quasi-contract rather than mainstream doctrine?

(2) Imagine that you have just started in a new job as a legal officer in the Department of Trade and Industry. Your line manager tells you that she is under a lot of pressure from the business sector to introduce regulations about tendering practices following the decision in *Trollope*. She asks you to draft some regulations to help her clear up 'this terrible mess'. Do you think regulations would be a good idea? What principles do you think should underpin such regulations?

(3) Do you think that Angie and Georgie's customers should be able to hold them to all the promises made in their Charter of Standards? Give reasons for your answers.

(4) Brian Fairs is an airline company and places the following advertisement in a
    national newspaper: 'Rock bottom prices. Flights from Liverpool to Chicago for
    £1 return plus taxes. Enough for everyone!' On the morning the advertisement
    appears Martha-Marie immediately phones the booking line to be told that there
    are no flights at that price left. Do you think she should be able to take her case to
    court and demand a ticket at the price advertised? What arguments can you
    think of which could be used by Brian Fairs to refute her claim?

CHAPTER 7

THE MOMENT OF RESPONSIBILITY

INTRODUCTION

In the last chapter we looked at the various things that can happen during pre-contractual negotiations. It became clear in the course of analysis that the exact moment an offer is made is not always clear as the parties often proceed slowly towards contractual responsibility. In this chapter we build on this understanding of the negotiation process but focus instead on the issue of how the courts go about deciding when there has been an acceptance of the offer and the birth of a contract. Collins (2003) refers to this marrying of offer and acceptance as the 'moment of responsibility'. The main focus of case law in this area has been on finding a way of determining when it is appropriate to attach legal liability to statements or conduct of the negotiating parties. In some cases it will be clear that a moment arrives when both the parties intend to be bound to each other and understand what they are committing themselves to. In this context, Collins gives the example of two parties signing a written contract in front of each other. But agreement is often much more difficult to pin down. One of the difficulties facing the judiciary is whether it should prescribe what the parties need to do in order for a contract to be enforceable or merely enforce what seems to be standard business practice. The dangers of the first approach are that the law could become irrelevant to the business community and begin to lack legitimacy. The problem with the alternative is that poor practice in the business community might be left unregulated.

COUNTER OFFERS

The law relating to counter offers provides a good example of the formalistic tendencies of much precedent in this field. As we have already made clear, negotiations are expected to take place in a sequence and it is the act or words of the offeree alone which transforms an offer into a contract. Moreover, acceptance is expected to correspond *exactly* to the terms of the offer, like a mirror image. So if, for instance, we return to the contract between Carl and Sally concerning a consignment of skateboards, discussed at the beginning of Chapter 5, agreement would not have been reached if Carl had emailed back to say, 'Great, I would like 19 and will send you a cheque for £1,800'. This is because he is not accepting what is on offer. Negotiators cannot be selective about the parts of an offer they choose to accept. Moreover, once an effective acceptance has come about, the person who made the offer can no longer withdraw it because the acceptance binds them to what they have offered and turns the terms of the offer into the terms of a contract. It follows that acceptance does not take place when the person to whom the offer is made rejects the offer, accepts it subject to certain qualifications or claims to be accepting an offer which is different from the one made.

An offeree's response to an offer which significantly differs from the offeror's terms is labelled a counter offer. Counter offers are viewed as rejections of the original offer and bring them to an end. The point is well-illustrated in the case of *Hyde v*

Wrench (1840) in which Wrench offered to sell his farm to Hyde for £1,000. Hyde said in reply that he would give £950 for it. Wrench turned down this proposal. Later Hyde wrote that he was prepared to pay £1,000 after all. This communication was ignored and Hyde sued to enforce an alleged sale at £1,000. It was held that no contract existed. Hyde had rejected Wrench's original offer by his counter offer of £950 and he was unable to revive it by changing his mind and tendering a purported acceptance which was nothing more than a new offer which Wrench was entitled to refuse.

The rigid application of this rule can cause difficulties where the intention of the offeree is clear but they introduce an additional element to the negotiations which has the effect of nullifying their 'acceptance'. In *Northland Airliners Ltd v Dennis Ferranti Meters Ltd* (1970), the sellers, a company in North Wales, negotiated with the buyers, a Canadian company, for the sale of an amphibian aircraft. The sellers sent the following telegram: 'Confirming sale to you Grummond Mallard aircraft ... Please remit £5,000.' The buyers replied: 'This is to confirm your cable and my purchase Grummond Mallard aircraft terms set out your cable ... £5,000 sterling forwarded your bank to be held in trust for your account pending delivery ... Please confirm delivery to be made thirty days within this date.' The sellers did not reply but sold the aircraft to a third party at a higher price. The Court of Appeal held that there was no contract between the claimant and defendant. The buyers' reply introduced two new terms, one as to payment and the other as to delivery and the sellers were not bound to reply to this counter offer.

However, case law suggests that an inquiry as to *whether* the offeror might modify his terms does not necessarily amount to a counter offer. In *Stevenson, Jacques & Co v McLean* (1880), it was held that Stevenson could still accept McLean's offer of a certain quantity of iron 'at 40s nett *cash* per ton', even though he had telegraphed to McLean requesting details of possible credit terms. Bearing in mind that Stevenson was buying for resale in an unsettled market, his words were 'nothing specific by way of [counter] offer or rejection, but a mere inquiry which should have been answered'. The case makes clear that the dividing line between a request for additional information and a counter offer is a fine one.

THE BATTLE OF THE FORMS

The main significance today of the counter offer rule lies in its use in litigation over the 'battle of the forms'. It is not uncommon to find business buyers and sellers who appear to have agreed but are 'separated' by the express wording of the documents they exchange. This is markedly so where standard forms are prepared by each party setting out the terms and conditions on which they are prepared to do business and these accompany or are referred to in all their communications. If both parties do this there is a battle as to whose terms and conditions take priority. The case of *Butler Machine Tool Co Ltd v Ex-Cell-O Corp Ltd* (1979) is illustrative of one sequence of events which gave rise to the 'battle of the forms', and to which the Court of Appeal rather unconvincingly used the rules relating to counter offer to solve the problem. The facts of the case are presented in Figure 7.1. The correspondence started with Ex-Cell-O making an inquiry of Butler.

In this case, the buyer's terms differed significantly from the seller's. On whose terms, if anyone's, was the contract made? The court held that the seller's quotation (2)

Figure 7.1: The battle of the forms

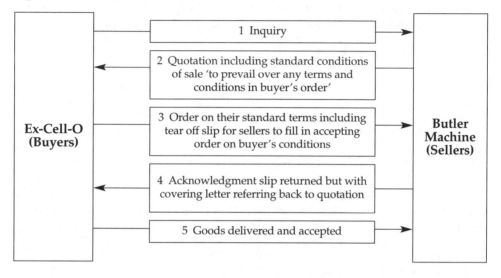

was an offer, the buyer's order (3) a counter offer, and the seller's return of the acknowledgment slip (4) an acceptance of the buyer's counter offer. The contract was therefore made on Ex-Cell-O, the buyer's, terms.

The significance of this finding was that although the price quoted by Butler was £75,500, their terms contained a 'price-escalation' clause under which Ex-Cell-O was required to pay at prices at the date of *delivery*. The buyer's terms contained no such clause. When Butler tried to invoke the clause, claiming a further £3,000, this dispute arose, resulting in Butler's eventual failure in the Court of Appeal. It has been said that ignoring the seller's covering letter (4) was unconvincing, because it seems plain that the sellers did intend to re-import their terms and conditions into the bargain. If this letter had been taken to be another counter offer, it could be said that the buyer's acceptance of delivery (5) was acceptance by conduct of that counter offer, in which case the seller's terms would have prevailed. Or would the buyer's lack of previous response to (4) have meant that there was *no* contract? The possibilities are considerable. But what is clear is that there was no agreement of the kind usually expected by neo-classical doctrine. Possibly there was no agreement at all according to classical doctrine.

The case reveals the limitations of an overly formal understanding to contract formation and reflects the difficulties that such an approach has in coming to terms with everyday business practices which do not fall neatly into the classical or neo-classical paradigm. The parties clearly wanted and intended to enter into *a* contract with each other, but the notion that they were fully attuned to the detail of their commitment is clearly a falsehood. Rather than solving the problem of the battle of the forms, the case could be said to create one by encouraging the parties to keep on sending their forms in the hope that theirs will be the 'last shot'. Whilst the majority of judges in the case were persuaded that the scenario could be analysed according to the rules of offer and acceptance, the judgments provided Lord Denning with another opportunity to argue that traditional analysis of such situations was overly formulaic and out of date. Convinced that the parties had concluded a contract, he argued, in line with his reasoning in *Gibson v Manchester City Council* (1979), for a more holistic approach to contract formation in which the court played a proactive role in determining its contents. Where there are differences in the standard conditions of each party which are irreconcilable, he suggested that the conflicting terms should be scrapped and replaced by a reasonable implication. However, the 'hit or miss' nature of the traditional approach to formation is borne out in subsequent cases. In *British Road Services v Arthur Crutchley Ltd* (1968), BRS delivered a large consignment of whisky to Crutchley's warehouse. The driver handed Crutchley a delivery note which incorporated BRS conditions of carriage. The note was stamped by Crutchley, 'Received under Crutchley's conditions'. The court held that this amounted to a counter offer, which BRS accepted when handing over the whisky. The contract was therefore concluded on Crutchley's terms.

It is clear that some of the reasoning in leading cases is different to reconcile. In *Cie de Commerce et Commission SARL v Parkinson Stove Co Ltd* (1953), Parkinson sent to Cie an order for a quantity of steel sheets on a printed form containing the following provision: 'This order constitutes an offer on the part of Parkinson on the terms and conditions and at the prices stated herein and, to constitute a binding contract on Parkinson, said offer must be accepted by execution of the acknowledgment in the form attached by Cie, it being expressly understood that no other form of acceptance, verbal or written, will be valid or binding on Parkinson.' Cie omitted to sign and return the acknowledgment slip attached to the form, but on receipt of the order replied to Parkinson: 'We acknowledge receipt of … your order No K 4851 dated March 5, which we received today and for which we thank you.' Subsequent correspondence left no doubt that the parties regarded themselves as bound. However, when Parkinson cancelled the order and Cie sued for breach, Parkinson claimed that there was no concluded contract because of Cie's failure to return the acknowledgment slip. In the alternative, they argued that strict compliance with the request for return of the slip was not necessary to create a contract because Cie's letter of acknowledgment could not be construed as a sufficient acceptance of Parkinson's offer. Neither argument found favour at first instance but the Court of Appeal held that there was no concluded contract and, accordingly, that Cie were not entitled to damages. It was felt that Cie's letter of acknowledgment, which did not strictly adhere to the terms of the offer, did not amount to an acceptance of the order. It is difficult to disagree with the case note commentator who wrote: 'It is submitted that the [French claimants] may in the circumstances be forgiven if they are left with a feeling that the requirements of the English law of contract are none too easy to fulfil. It is difficult to envisage how they could have more clearly indicated their acceptance of the order, short of returning the acknowledgment slip itself.' The eventual decision is scarcely an illustration of what Pilcher J, in the court of first instance, referred to as the tendency of the courts 'always [to] lean towards giving legal effect to documents which the parties themselves regard as constituting a binding contract in law'.

COMMUNICATION ISSUES

The general 'rule' is that acceptance does not create a contract until it is communicated to the offeror. Mental acceptance or mere acquiescence, without more, is not sufficient. This is the case even where the offeror waives the need for communication by indicating that acceptance by silence will suffice (see *Felthouse v Bindley* (1862)). The requirement is that the person accepting the offer must say or do something which indicates to the person who made the offer that they accept the terms. It follows that the courts have not been prepared to find acceptance of an offer where there have been faults in the method of communication which mean that a message has not been received. Examples might include instances when acceptance is spoken into a mobile phone as the line goes dead, an acceptance is not heard because of background music in a club or cases where the offeree's fax machine breaks down and fails to deliver a message. In each of these situations the application of the general rule would require the courts to find that no contract had been formed.

There are several explanations for this general rule. First, the requirement reflects the fact that the law expects both parties to be clear about the agreement they are entering into before it imposes legal obligations on them. The courts have also been concerned that the parties should know the exact moment that an offer has been accepted. If acceptance was able to occur without the offeror being told, then only one party would know that a contract had been born and obligations created. Being clear about the exact moment when they are bound to each other also allows each of the parties to enter into further deals with others on the strength of the first. Finally, on an evidential note, it could be extremely difficult to prove acceptance if the offeree was under no obligation to communicate it.

For many years the courts were troubled with relatively simple communication problems involving instantaneous oral negotiations or more time-consuming postal communications. But today, the means by which parties can communicate with each other are much more varied and may include face-to-face contact, the telephone, an answerphone, letter, fax, telemessage, telegram, telex, email or standard forms displayed on websites. As business is becoming more and more impersonal with the growth of large-scale organisations, just what is meant by effective communication of acceptance can be a difficult question. In *Entores Ltd v Miles Far East Corp* (1955), the Court of Appeal was asked to consider the impact of new technologies on the area. In its consideration of new forms of instantaneous communication by electronic telex they followed the general rule that acceptance still took place when it was received rather than when it was sent.

However, the problems of delayed receipt made possible in electronic transactions were also considered by the court in *The Brimnes* (1975), in which a telexed withdrawal of a ship from a charterparty appeared on the charterer's telex machine within office hours but was not read until the following day. It was held that the withdrawal was effective when it appeared on the machine because it was reasonable to assume that someone would look at it then. Moreover, in the case of *Brinkibon Ltd v Stahag Stahl* (1983), the House of Lords gave a qualified endorsement of *Entores*, warning that its 'rule' could not be applied universally in view of the many variants in the use of telex. The court argued that although telex was an instantaneous form of communication, receipt was not always instantaneous. For example, a message could be sent out of office hours with the intention that it would be read at a later time. The court opined that the position should be resolved by reference to the parties' intentions, sound business practice and by a judgment as to where the risk should lie. Remarking on the 'not particularly helpful' lead given by the House of Lords in *Brinkibon*, Stone argued:

> ... in so far as any general principle can be read into it, it would seem ... that the communication should take effect at the time when the acceptor could reasonably

have expected it to be read ... There does not seem to be any reason for treating faxes differently from telex, but electronic mail, sent to an electronic 'post-box' which will only be checked once or twice a day, might well be said only to be communicated once the time for checking has passed. A similar approach might need to be used in relation to messages left on a telephone answering system. That is, the message should only be regarded as communicated once a reasonable time has elapsed to allow it to be heard by the offeror.

If this line is taken, it is clearly to the advantage of the acceptor, in that it allows an acceptance to be treated as effective when the offeror remains unaware of it because of their failure to check incoming messages. The reasoning of the court fits uncomfortably with traditional approaches. But it provides an example of Collins' claim that what the courts are often concerned with and should be concerned with is not the mechanics of offer and acceptance but a consideration of the point at which it is *reasonable* for the parties to assume a contract has come into being.

THE POSTAL 'RULE' AND REVOCATION OF AN OFFER

A more established exception to the general rule that the offeror must receive notification of an acceptance before a contract can come into existence comes in the guise of the 'postal rule'. This allows that where the offeree sends their acceptance by post, the offer is regarded as accepted as soon as the letter of acceptance is posted. The authority for this proposition comes from the judgment in *Adams v Lindsell* (1818) in which the court was more concerned with questions of speed, early reliance by the offeree and convenience than logic. Where the postal rule applies, offerees are protected at the price of hardship to offerors. The offeror is put at risk to the extent that they are bound by a contract before they are aware of the fact of its existence.

In analysing the judgment it is important to stress that it is always open to the offeror to specify how an offer should be accepted. In coming to their judgment the court in *Adams* appears to have decided that an offeror prepared to accept the risks inherent in using the postal system should also bear the risk of an acceptance getting lost or there being a delay. An offeror would be well-advised to *exclude* the postal rule by the terms of their offer and insist that they will only be bound on actual receipt of a posted acceptance. In affirming the rule in *Adams*, Bramwell LJ in the Court of Appeal in *Household Fire Insurance Co v Grant* (1879), advised that the prudent offeror should stipulate that: 'Your answer by post is only to bind if it reaches me.' More recently, in *Holwell Securities Ltd v Hughes* (1974), an offer to sell a house was made in the form of an option stated 'to be exercisable by *notice* in writing to the Intending Vendor'. Such a notice, properly addressed, was posted within the time limit allowed but it never reached the offeror. It was held that there was no contract as the terms of the option, on their true construction, required acceptance to be actually communicated. Indeed, the court went so far as to suppose that there *was no single or universal rule* determining the effect of a posted acceptance and that the postal rule 'probably does not operate if its application would produce manifest inconvenience and absurdity'. It would seem then that the question is one of practical considerations and convenience rather than deductions from a general rule.

E-COMMERCE

There is some debate as to whether the established rules governing instantaneous and postal communications are adequate for modern-day use. In particular, there has been some disagreement between scholars as to whether it is the rule or exceptions to it that cover communications by email. As emails now outnumber paper communications and are the preferred way for many in business to communicate with clients, the point is worth serious consideration. One of the problems posed by emails is whether receipt occurs when the email is downloaded onto a server, when it appears on the computer, or when the email is actually read by the recipient. Another new issue which arises in this context is that an email address may consist of a name or number followed by the name of the service provider but not indicate the physical location of the sender or the recipient. This leaves open the associated difficulty of *where* the acceptance becomes binding, if the acceptance is sent to such an address.

Some have argued that the postal rule should apply to acceptances made by email because they are not transmitted instantaneously and differ from other forms of instantaneous communication in that the information is broken down and sent in 'packets' through different routes. Moreover, emails often go astray. This means that the sender cannot be sure that their message has been transmitted successfully and renders it unreasonable for them to rely on the communication having been received. Even if the sender asks for a delivery receipt, that receipt simply confirms that the message has been delivered to a mailbox, but not the offeror themselves. Seen in this way, an email with a delivery receipt is more like recorded delivery post than an instantaneous communication and should properly be subject to the postal rule.

Others have suggested that the usual receipt rule should apply because the sender is ultimately in a position to know if the email has or has not been sent. It follows from the reasoning in *The Brimnes* that, viewed in this way, the acceptance should become binding when it reaches the offeror's business premises or the place of their internet service provider during normal office hours. Article 11 of the E-Commerce Directive 1999 provides some guidance in respect of non-business to business contracting by requiring that electronic orders and acknowledgments will be taken to be received when the addressee can access them. This would seem to suggest that the downloading of the message from the server would constitute receipt. However, the Directive does not clearly explain the legal position of electronic offer and acceptance, or even define when a contract is concluded. The result is that the law remains uncertain.

Sometimes the process of contracting is completed purely in cyberspace. 'Click-wrap' contracts on the internet allow a contract to be made by providing information and clicking buttons on screen. The process involves the item passing from virtual shelf to virtual shopping basket to virtual checkout where the purchaser orders the item in the basket by clicking another button. The supplier's program checks the availability of the item and whether it is in stock; the purchaser indicates that they intend to be bound by providing payment details and confirming their choice. These communications are more akin to instantaneous telephone conversations as it will be immediately obvious to one of the parties if the other becomes disconnected. Accordingly, the sender of a message in a click-wrap contract is in a position to know whether the message has been transmitted successfully almost as soon as it has been sent. This would seem to make the receipt rule more relevant than the postal rule. The

Consumer Protection (Distance Selling) Regulations 2000 provide some protection for the consumer by requiring that certain information be provided before the contract is concluded. This includes the identity of the supplier, the price, arrangements for the delivery and supply of goods or services and information on cancellation rights. This information must be provided to the consumer in another durable medium which is 'available and accessible' prior to delivery.

AGREEMENT AND CERTAINTY

Even when a valid contract has come about as a result of compliance with the rules discussed above, an agreement may fail to be enforced by the courts as a result of its vagueness or incompleteness. This is a particularly important issue for those interested in studying contract law in perspective because a theme to which we consistently turn in this book is the fact that business people are generally less concerned than lawyers about complete and precise expression of their contractual obligations. What is striking from the decisions discussed in this section is that the judges vary quite considerably in their approach to the tensions between the needs of the law and the needs of the business community.

The issue of vagueness or incompleteness arose in the case of *Hillas & Co Ltd v Arcos Ltd* (1932) in which the court was prepared to temper over-reliance on formality in order to place an agreement into its business context. The facts of the case were that Arcos (sellers) and Hillas (buyers) entered into and performed a contract for the supply of Russian timber for the year 1930. Hillas took up an option for Arcos to supply further timber 'of fair specification' for delivery during 1931, but Arcos was unable to supply this timber because they had sold it to a third party. When sued for breach they argued that the 1931 agreement was void for uncertainty. However, on the basis of the parties' involvement in the Russian timber trade, the concluded 1930 contract and expert evidence on the nature of that trade, the House of Lords felt able to construe the words 'of fair specification' with sufficient precision to establish a binding agreement between the parties for 1931 supplies. In his consideration of the relevant principles to apply to the case, Lord Wright considered how the tension between the need for certainty in the law and flexibility in the business community could be accommodated. He argued that:

> Business men often record the most important agreements in crude and summary fashion; modes of expression sufficient and clear to them in the course of their business may appear to those unfamiliar with the business far from complete or precise. It is accordingly the duty of the court to construe such documents fairly and broadly, without being too astute or subtle in finding defects; but [that] does not mean that the court is to make a contract for the parties, or to go outside the words they have used, except in so far as there are appropriate implications of law, as for instance, the implication of what is just and reasonable to be ascertained by the court as a matter of machinery where the contractual intention is clear, but the contract is silent on some detail. Thus in contracts for future performance over a period, the parties may neither be able nor desire to specify many matters of detail, but leave them to be adjusted in the working out of the contract ... As obvious illustrations I may refer to such matters as prices or times of delivery in contracts for the sale of goods.

Where the dividing line between certainty and uncertainty, enforceability and unenforceability is drawn may well depend therefore on the court's ability and wish to accommodate business practice. A court inclined towards formalism would no doubt reject the argument that they should strive to settle an important matter that the parties had chosen to leave unsettled in their original agreement. Their approach would be to insist that a good contract must be a concluded bargain which settles everything that needs to be settled and leaves nothing to be determined by *further* agreement between the parties. This was the line adopted in *May and Butcher Ltd v The King* (1934). In this case the parties entered into a contract under which the government Disposals Board agreed to sell old tentage to May and Butcher over a certain period of time. The contract required that the price was to be 'agreed from time to time' and disputes submitted to arbitration when a disagreement about the price arose. May and Butcher claimed that a reasonable price should be determined by the court or that a price should be fixed under the arbitration clause. But it was the Disposable Board's contention that there was no contract. Their view was upheld by the House of Lords. Although the Sale of Goods Act 1893 then provided for a reasonable price where the contract was silent on the point, it was held that in this case the contract was not silent because there was a provision for the parties to agree on price. Arbitration was also excluded, there being 'a failure to agree, which is a very different thing from a dispute'.

The Court of Appeal went the other way in *Foley v Classique Coaches Ltd* (1934), a decision which reflects Lord Wright's words in *Hillas*. Here, the contract between the parties provided that Classique Coaches Ltd should buy petrol exclusively from Foley 'at a price to be agreed by the parties from time to time'. There was also an arbitration clause in the contract which the court took to apply to any failure to agree as to price. After three years Classique Coaches Ltd repudiated the agreement on the basis that it was incomplete after coming to the conclusion that they could get cheaper petrol elsewhere. Foley brought an action, claiming a declaration that the agreement was binding, damages for breach, and an injunction restraining Classique from buying petrol other than from them. The court found in Foley's favour, being impressed by the fact that the parties had for three years clearly believed that they had a contract and they had provided machinery for dealing with any failure to agree as to the price. It was held that the petrol should be supplied at a reasonable price.

Similar issues emerged in two cases involving leases. In *King's Motors (Oxford) Ltd v Lax* (1969), it was decided that an option in a lease for a further period of years 'at such rental as may be agreed on between the parties' was, in the absence of an arbitration clause, void for uncertainty. This allowed the landlords to terminate the lease even though the option had been duly exercised. Uncertainties of this kind may prove to be a loophole through which an unwilling party can escape from an agreement. However, in *Sudbrook Trading Estate Ltd v Eggleton* (1983), a lease gave the tenant an option to purchase the premises 'at such price as may be agreed on by two valuers, one to be nominated' by each party. When the landlord refused to appoint a valuer, the House of Lords held that the option in effect provided a formula enabling *a reasonable* price to be fixed. Since the ancillary machinery for determining that price had broken down, the court felt able to substitute its own machinery. It was stressed that with a partly performed agreement 'the court would strain to supply the want of certainty': see also *Didymi Corp v Atlantic Lines and Navigation Co Inc* (1988).

In recent years, a new species of agreements liable to be set aside because of uncertainty have emerged in the form of agreements to negotiate. In *Walford v Miles* (1992), Walford brought an action for breach of an oral 'lock-out' agreement in which

Miles promised not to negotiate with or consider offers from third parties during the pre-contractual stage. In exchange for this undertaking, Walford supplied a letter of creditworthiness from their bank. However, the 'lock-out' agreement contained no time limit and their Lordships considered that Miles had in no legal sense locked himself *into* negotiations with Walford. Arguments claiming that the agreement contained an implied term that Miles would continue to negotiate in good faith with Walford for a reasonable period of time failed to impress the House of Lords which considered the agreement to be too uncertain. In Lord Ackner's view, 'the concept of a duty to carry on negotiations in good faith is inherently repugnant to the adversarial position of the parties when involved in negotiations', a view which is clearly out of line with relational thinking. It may be doubted that Lord Ackner's analysis was entirely appropriate to describe the relationship between these parties which envisaged close co-operation between them. Miles had agreed, for instance, to continue working in the business as Walford lacked expertise in the field.

The decision has not met with unanimous approval. Adams and Brownsword see it as based on 'a formalist concern for certainty of terms in conjunction with a robust market-individualism'. However, the case has subsequently been applied by the Court of Appeal in *Pitt v PHH Asset Management Ltd* (1993) with a different outcome. In this case Pitt was twice 'gazumped' when PHH withdrew from an agreement for the sale of a property 'subject to contract'. In each case PHH received a higher offer from a third party. Nevertheless, PHH later agreed to sell to Pitt and they promised not to consider any further offers in return for Pitt's promise to exchange contracts *within two weeks* of receipt of the draft contract. It was held that this was a binding 'lock-out' agreement which PHH, who had again withdrawn, had broken. The key factor which distinguished this agreement from the one in *Walford* was the specified time limit which provided the requisite degree of certainty. Otherwise, it would appear that certainty will only be found, and reliance protected, where performance has already taken place: as in such cases as *Hillas, Foley* and *Trentham Ltd v Archital Luxfer Ltd* (1993).

TENDERS, REASONABLE RELIANCE AND LEGITIMATE EXPECTATION

An issue which sits outside traditional analysis of offer and acceptance is the position of tenders in the pre-contractual process. Contracts governing important, high-cost business projects such as major construction, engineering works or the supply of military equipment are usually negotiated on a competitive tender basis. This means that interested parties are invited to bid for the contract work. The request for tenders may be communicated by an advertisement or it may be invited from a selected group of favoured companies. According to traditional rules of analysis this would normally be seen as an invitation to treat. A contractor who chooses to submit a tender in the form of a quotation would thereby be making an offer, which might be accepted or not. Unless the initial invitation stated that the contract would be awarded to the lowest bidder, *any* tender may be chosen on the basis of business considerations. For example, in March 1995, the government decided to buy a mixed fleet of 35 helicopters from a British/Italian consortium and a US company at a cost of £1.2 billion rather than accept a £300 million lower bid from the US company alone. This option was taken against financial advice from the Ministry of Defence but was justified on the ground that it safeguarded 5,000 British jobs.

However, if a request for a tender clearly indicates that a certain type of bid such as the highest or lowest will be successful, it is viewed as an offer capable of acceptance by the person who puts in the tender which satisfies the condition. This is because of the extra level of specificity. This issue arose in *Harvela Investments Ltd v Royal Trust Co of Canada Ltd* (1986) in which sellers of shares invited tenders from two parties and bound themselves to accept the higher bid. A bid was accepted by the sellers which, although the higher, was arguably not a firm bid in compliance with the seller's terms. The bid in question mentioned a fixed sum which was slightly lower than the other bid but stated in the alternative that the bidders would offer $100,000 Canadian in excess of any other offer. It was held that the invitation to bid was a unilateral offer, like the one in *Carlill*, to be bound by whichever bid was the higher. This was because it requested the performance of an act (the submission of the higher bid) which, once performed, converted the offer into a bilateral contract of sale to the higher bidder. As the bid which had been 'accepted' did not conform to the seller's own instructions, it was invalid. By accepting that bid, the sellers were breaking their own rules.

The issue of whether the pre-contractual tendering process warranted special protection was considered in *Blackpool and Fylde Aero Club v Blackpool Borough Council* (1990). In that case, the council also invited tenders for a concession to operate pleasure flights from Blackpool airport to be submitted by noon on a given day. The Aero Club, who had operated the flights prior to the licence coming up for renewal, submitted a tender in time but, due to an error on the part of a council employee, it was marked as having been received late and was consequently not considered. The concession was awarded to another bidder. The club's claim that the council was in breach of a contract to *consider* all valid bids was upheld.

What was the contract that the club claimed had been breached? Earlier in this chapter we argued that the period during which negotiations take place is one in which the law of contract has traditionally given no protection to the parties. What is significant about this case is the way in which the court sought to protect the pre-contractual period by using the terminology of contract. It did this by arguing that in addition to the contract which resulted from the council agreeing to accept a bid from the organisation which put forward the most attractive tender, there was a second contract governing the conduct of the tendering process which was laid down by the council itself and which protected all those putting forward a tender. As Bingham LJ observed:

> Where, as here, tenders are solicited from selected parties all of them known to the invitor, and where a local authority's invitation prescribes a clear, orderly and familiar procedure ... the invitee is in my judgment protected at least to this extent: if he submits a conforming tender before the deadline he is entitled, not as a matter of mere expectation but of contractual right, to be sure that his tender will after the deadline be opened and considered in conjunction with all other conforming tenders.

The court did not go as far as to claim that this contract was like the other contracts we will consider in this book. Rather, it suggested that it was a *collateral* contract, that is to say an additional contract which was subordinate to the main contract. There is another reason why this case is relevant to a book which seeks to place contract law in perspective. Bingham LJ argued that to have come to an alternative conclusion would have allowed an unacceptable discrepancy between the law of contract and the confident assumptions of the commercial parties involved that their tenders would be considered as long as they complied with the conditions laid down by the council (see also *Heathcote Ball & Co v Paul Barry* (2000)).

CONCLUDING REMARKS

In the *Gibson* case discussed in Chapter 5, Lord Diplock argued that the law relating to the mechanics of contractual agreement is 'well settled, indeed elementary'. He recognised that there may be certain types of contract which do not fit easily into the normal analysis of a contract as being constituted by offer and acceptance, but he considered these to be exceptional. In the last three chapters we have argued that these well-polished 'rules' are not always capable of satisfactorily meeting the demands made upon them by the business world. There is clearly a danger in regarding them as 'black letter' rules to be rigidly applied. Instead, there is considerable merit in viewing them as presumptions that are flexible and adaptable to new situations if the law is to be seen as relevant to the business community.

However, on another level, if you read the cases discussed in these chapters through the lens of relational contract theory, there is greater cause for concern. The difficulties which arise when the judiciary focuses on contracts as discrete exchanges, rather than part of an ongoing commercial relationship in which certain standards and expectations have arisen over time, have been revealed most recently in *Baird Textile Holdings Ltd v Marks & Spencer* (2001) case. A relational reading of this case goes beyond looking at the context of the relationship. It goes beyond a flexible approach to understanding when the agreement which is being adjudicated came into being. As we learnt in Chapter 4, Macneil's vision of the relational approach is to start with the relationship and then move on to the contract. The change in emphasis may seem to be a subtle one but the implications for the methods used by the judiciary when trying to identify agreement are considerable. When context comes before rule, a very different vision of the role of the judiciary and law of contract is promoted.

REFERENCES AND FURTHER READING

Adams, J 'The battle of the forms' (1983) JBL 297.

Ball, S 'Work carried out in pursuance of letters of intent – contract or restitution' (1983) 99 LQR 572.

Collins, H (2003) *The Law of Contract*, 4th edn, London: LexisNexis Butterworths.

Dickie, J 'When and where are electronic contracts concluded?' (1998) 99(3) Northern Ireland Legal Quarterly, pp 332–34.

Gardner, S 'Trashing with Trollope: a deconstruction of the postal rules' (1992) 12 Oxford Journal of Legal Studies 170.

McKendrick, E 'The battle of the forms and the law of restitution' (1988) 8 Oxford Journal of Legal Studies 197.

Murray, A (2000) 'Entering into contracts electronically: the real W.W.W.' in Edwards, L and Waelde, C (eds), *Law and the Internet: A Framework for Electronic Commerce*, 2nd edn, Oxford: Hart Publishing, pp 17–36.

Rawlings, R 'The battle of the forms' (1979) 42 MLR 715.

QUESTIONS

(1) On 1 April 1995, Monumental Marble Masons Limited wrote to Decor and Fittings Limited the following letter:

Dear Sirs,

We have the following remainders in Italian Marbles which we are pleased to offer to you as one of our regular customers, in whole lots, delivery to be taken at our Tomb Street Yard, at the prices marked below, which we are sure you will agree are well below current market rates for these excellent quality marbles. This special offer is open for acceptance up to the end of the month. Do not miss this splendid opportunity to lay in a stock which cannot fail to improve in value, even if you have no immediate use in mind.

Offer in whole lots – Delivery to be taken at our yard

Lot No 1 Piastraccia – 45 No slabs ¾" thick by 3'6" x 1'9" at £75

Lot No 2 Rosso Levanto – 58 No slabs ¾" thick by 4'6" x 1'6" at £35

Lot No 3 Botticino – 37 No slabs ¾" thick by 4'0" x 1'9" at £75

Lot No 4, etc, etc …

Yours faithfully …

Decor and Fittings Limited received the letter by post on 3 April and replied on 4 April as follows:

Dear Sirs,

Thank you for your offer of marble remainders in yours of the 1st instant. We will be pleased to take delivery of Lot No 3, 37 Botticino slabs 4'0" x 1'9" x ¾", and we enclose herewith our cheque for £75. Please advise the soonest that we can collect from your yard.

Yours faithfully …

The letter was posted on the evening of 4 April but due to a misdirection by the Post Office it did not arrive at Monumental Marble Masons' office until Monday 14 April. In the meantime, on Friday 11 April, Shop and Salon Services Ltd, who had received a similar letter from MMM, called at the Tomb Street Yard, paid £100 cash and collected both Lot 2 and Lot 3. MMM immediately dispatched a telemessage to Decor and Fittings Limited and the three other firms to whom they had sent their offer, saying: 'Our letter of 1 April Lots 2 and 3 withdrawn from offer.' Decor and Fittings Limited did not man their offices on Saturday, so that the telemessage was not delivered until Monday 14 April. When MMM received Decor and Fittings' letter and cheque on 14 April, they immediately returned the cheque by post and confirmed details of their telemessage. Advise Decor and Fittings of their rights, if any.

(2) In 'The Sad Tale of Angie and Georgie' there are a number of agreements. Can you identify a specific point when agreement between Angie and Georgie and the following come into being:

(a) Mister C;

(b) Chelsea;

(c) Orange Peril plc;

(d) Wacky Machine Company and Ned;

(e) Dipti;

(f) Marcus;

(g) Monkish Soup Company;

(h) Claude;

(i) Kirsteen;

(j) St Ives Bank;

(k) the multi-storey car park?

What are the terms of the various agreements? Can you give any examples from the case study where the timing of an agreement was critical to the identification of terms included in it?

(3) 'In stressing objective certainty and completeness the requirements of traditional contract have perpetuated the idea of a contract as a rationally complete and discrete transaction' but 'most contracts are part of a wider relationship composed of previous dealings, other contracts or shared business standards, which are ignored by this objective, individualised approach': Ball (see 'References and further reading'). Critically appraise this statement.

(4) If you could change one aspect of the law relating to acceptance, what would it be? Give reasons for your response.

CHAPTER 8

CONSIDERATION, ESTOPPEL AND INTENTION

INTRODUCTION

In the final chapter in this section which focuses on how deals are made, we look at the second key component which has been required in the law of contract if an agreement is to be enforced – consideration. The doctrine is fundamental to the classical model and is the mechanism through which the judiciary have sought to distinguish between gifts and commercial exchanges. It is important to understand from the start that evidence of consideration may be needed more than once in the life of a contractual relationship. Whenever the parties need to vary the terms of the original agreement they will need to provide fresh consideration as, in the eyes of traditionalists, this is a fresh deal. It will be seen that it is this condition which has caused the most tension between the requirements of doctrine and the needs and practices of the business community. We learnt when looking at the work of Macaulay and others in Chapter 4 that business people are not as concerned with formalities as lawyers. The commercial pressures or tight deadlines which they work with on a daily basis mean that they are often prepared to accept changes to contractual arrangements suggested by the other party to the deal without even considering what new thing they need to offer in exchange in order to make the variation legally binding.

Attempts have been made to circumvent the rigour of the doctrine by the development of the equitable doctrine of estoppel. One of the most significant characteristics of the doctrine is the fact that it shifts the conceptual focus away from exchange to reliance. The focus is on whether a party has acted reasonably when relying on an undertaking relating to variation of the contractual terms. The notion of reliance has been much discussed in academic circles and is widely acknowledged to be an alternative to understanding contractual obligations as exchanges. Estoppel is one of the areas in which this thinking has found its way into doctrine. As a result, the comparison of these two models is a major focus of this chapter and a theme which we carry over to the next, when we look at the problems of misrepresentation in pre-contractual negotiations.

CONTRACT AS BARGAIN AND EXCHANGE

We shall start with an exploration of the fact that since the classical period, the common law concept of contract has been founded on the concept of exchange and bargain. In 1915 in *Dunlop Pneumatic Tyre Co Ltd v Selfridge & Co Ltd*, Lord Dunedin said he was content to adopt from a work of Sir Frederick Pollock the following definition of consideration: 'An act or forbearance of one party, or the promise thereof, is the price for which the promise of the other is bought, and the promise thus given for value is enforceable.' What does this mean? It should be obvious that, in the simplest terms, the vast majority of contracts involve the parties swapping something. Every time you buy a newspaper you give money in exchange for it. We get paid a monthly salary in exchange for the services we provide as teachers, researchers and administrators. Those of you who have taken out student loans have been given money in exchange for a promise to pay it back. It is clear that each party to the contract is expected to give something to the other and also to lose something if they are to satisfy the requirement that both offer and acceptance must be supported by consideration.

What the parties exchange reflects the bargain they have reached. It is for this reason that informal, gratuitous promises lack the required reciprocity needed to make them enforceable – nothing is given for the gift. Lord Dunedin's definition also makes it clear that forbearance from doing something can also constitute consideration. So, if a bank agreed to refrain from pursuing legal action to recover a loan if the person who took out the loan agreed to sell some assets and pay back half of what they owed, the bank's forbearance also constitutes consideration. We can also see from these examples that a promise to do something in the future can amount to consideration. The ability to enforce a contract which concerns something which has yet to happen is an important feature of the classical model of contract and allows for forward planning in the commercial sector. In a bilateral contract, consideration commonly consists of mutual promises. At this stage the contract is said to be *executory*. Actual performance of the act (or the forbearance) embodied in such a promise amounts to *executed* consideration: the promise is performed. In the case of a unilateral contract a promise is always exchanged for an act.

Contract law textbooks reveal almost three centuries (from 1602 to 1884) of 'leading' cases on consideration, cases concerning a variety of legal propositions and exceptions regarding the nature of this contractual requirement as 'the sign and symbol of bargain'. However, for an introductory study of the law as it operates *today*, it is doubtful if full attention need be given to the extensive and complicated accumulation of 'old' case law on consideration. Points from such cases do still arise but, more often than not, modern cases tend to demonstrate moves in judicial thinking *away from* strict bargain theories based on exchange or bargain. Support for a 'playing-down' of consideration can be found in recent extra-judicial statements. Sir Frederick Lawton has said that:

> Students always seem to spend a lot of time on the formation of contract, consideration and mistake but little on the discharge of contract and remedies, with which the practitioner is usually concerned. Occasionally problems arise as to whether there has been a contract and whether the parties were thinking of the same subject matter; but in all my time in the law I have never met a problem about consideration.

In a similar vein, Lord Denning expressed the view that the effect of the doctrine of promissory estoppel since 1947 'has been to do away with the doctrine of consideration in all but a handful of cases. During the 16 years while I have been Master of the Rolls I do not recall any case in which it has arisen or been discussed'. Taking these statements as our cue, we will confine ourselves to an examination of consideration's main features and then proceed to a closer look at promissory estoppel and other moves away from traditional requirements.

The consideration supplied by the parties must be 'something of value in the eyes of the law' to make it binding. Generally speaking, 'value in the eyes of the law' has been taken to mean *economic* value. The economic value of goods received, services rendered or cash paid is usually obvious. Although, as was stated in one case, 'natural love and affection' do not amount to consideration, the courts are willing to acknowledge merely nominal economic consideration such as peppercorn rent. This is because the notion of freedom of contract which dominates the classical model of contract requires that there be a bargain, but not necessarily a *good* bargain in business terms. It has long been argued that the parties should be free to set their own price or promise in accordance with the value they personally attach to the exchange. It is for this reason that the agreement between Angie, Georgie and Chelsea to pay her more than the market rate in wages would be enforceable in the courts. As Lord Blackburn said in 1973: 'The adequacy of the consideration is for the parties to consider at the time of making the agreement, not for the court when it is sought to be enforced.'

Whilst this general approach to bargains continues to frame the case law, nowadays, when courts are more sensitive to imbalances of bargaining strength and the use of excessive commercial pressure or undue influence, a grossly inadequate consideration may militate against a court's sense of 'fairness in exchange'. For example, in *Lloyds Bank Ltd v Bundy* (1975), although Lord Denning stated that 'no bargain will be upset which is the result of the ordinary interplay of forces', the court struck down a contract of guarantee by which the defendant, an elderly farmer not well-versed in business affairs, mortgaged his house as security for the debts of his son's business. This was done at a time when the company was already in dire financial straits, and not long before its eventual collapse. It was felt that in the circumstances, 'the consideration moving from the bank was grossly inadequate' and, at the late stage at which the guarantee was given, 'all that the company gained was a short respite from impending doom'. The legislature has also played an increasingly active role in the regulation of exchange in certain contexts, such as carriage of goods by sea, rents and interest rates. The concept of free bargaining still plays an important part in judicial thinking, but judges and legislators have increased their level of control over consideration in a variety of ways.

PAST CONSIDERATION ✗

The classical view of contract, rooted in the idea of reciprocity, expects consideration to be exchanged as part of a bargaining process. Thus, it is said that something wholly performed *before* exchange is agreed cannot amount to consideration: instead, it is known as *past* consideration. The idea rests on the assumption that if something has been voluntarily done before exchange has occurred then this should be treated as a voluntary gift or service. Once given or performed, the same thing cannot be used as consideration in a subsequent exchange. For example, if I give you some legal advice in connection with problems you are having with your landlord and afterwards you agree to pay me for it, I could not claim that we had made a contract. My contribution to the pact occurred before the subject of money was discussed and its 'bargaining value' has thus been used up or spent. However, in a business context it may be argued that if you originally requested the service it must have been understood by the parties that payment would be forthcoming and the later express promise to pay merely confirms and quantifies an earlier implied promise on your part: see *Re Casey's Patents* (1892). This alternative reading of such situations has proved controversial and undermines the whole notion of contemporaneous bargain on which traditional reasoning is based.

The sort of problems which might arise in connection with this rule in the commercial sector are illustrated in *Pao On v Lau Yiu Long* (1980). In this case, the defendants sold shares to the plaintiff who promised not to put them on the market for at least 12 months. The defendants, who retained a large block of shares, had required this, as they did not wish to see the value of their holding depressed by a sudden sale of the plaintiff's shares. The defendants later promised to indemnify the plaintiff against any loss he might incur if the shares fell in value during the year. The Privy Council was willing to marry together the plaintiff's promise not to sell, albeit given as part of the original contract of sale, and the defendants' subsequent promise to indemnify. It has been said that the plaintiff was 'only getting what he was really, morally and commercially, entitled to'. The case also supports the growing idea that in appropriate circumstances, the court should have regard to a *continuing commercial relationship* between parties rather than concentrating on 'discrete' transactions or arrangements within that relationship, a proposition which sits comfortably with the arguments of relational contract theorists.

CONSIDERATION AND EXISTING CONTRACTUAL DUTIES

The courts have shown themselves willing to 'find' consideration in a number of cases in which it did not at first sight appear to be present. The case of *Carlill v Carbolic Smoke Ball Co* (1893) is a good example. Moreover, in *Gore v Van der Lann* (1967), a senior citizen's 'free' bus pass was held to form the basis of a contract. But it is a much more recent development for the courts to recognise as consideration for a new contract something that someone is already under a contractual duty to do. It follows from what has been said about past consideration that a party can not offer up as consideration something that they have a pre-existing duty to do. If a duty already exists then this 'consideration', like past consideration, has already been used and spent. The position can be outlined by using an example from the case study in Chapter 2. Chelsea agreed to carry out certain obligations as a shop assistant for Angie and Georgie at a fixed price. Angie and Georgie later agreed to pay Chelsea a different wage if she promised to perform her existing obligations. Is this 'deal' binding? The traditional view must be that Angie and Georgie's promise is not binding because it is not supported by fresh consideration from Chelsea. The consideration is spent because it has already been used to support another agreement and, as we have already made clear, each new contract or variation of an existing one requires 'fresh' consideration. It might be useful to think of the issue in two stages. There is an original contractual agreement followed by a variation of it. The variation, it would seem, can only stand if Chelsea in return for Angie and Georgie's later promise agrees to do *more* for Angie and Georgie. This would be a new agreement with additional consideration for the second contract. But Angie and Georgie provide no additional consideration. However, a further issue remains in relation to motivation: whilst there is no new consideration in a traditional sense, the agreement is beneficial to each party. Should the courts take account of this?

A strict line on this issue has been taken in much of the case law. In *Stilk v Myrick* (1809), a crew had been engaged to sail a vessel from London to the Baltic and back at the rate of £5 a month. Following the desertion of two of the 11 crew members, the captain promised to share the deserters' wages among the remaining crew if they would work the ship back to London, but the owners refused to honour the captain's promise when the ship returned. It was held that the seamen's claim failed for lack of consideration. The crew were already bound by their contract to meet the normal emergencies of the voyage and were doing no more than their duty in sailing the ship back. But in *Hartley v Ponsonby* (1857), a case which is often compared with *Stilk v*

Myrick, 17 out of 36 crew deserted and the voyage became very hazardous. It was held that the remaining crew had in consequence been discharged from their original contract and were therefore free to enter into a new one at higher wages. One report of *Stilk v Myrick* stresses the danger that a shift in bargaining power, as was afforded the crew in the case, could lead to instances of extortion. While this policy argument is not taken to be the main reason for the decision, it provides a context in which the differences in the judgments can more easily be understood. It is also of interest in view of later developments.

In the 1950s, in two cases where a party merely promised to perform an existing legal duty in return for a promise, Lord Denning felt able to find that such a promise was good consideration. In *Ward v Byham* (1956), a case involving a statutory duty, he argued: 'I have always thought that a promise to perform an existing duty, or the performance of it, should be regarded as good consideration, because it is a benefit to the person to whom it is given.' And in *Williams v Williams* (1957) he opined:

> Now I agree that, in promising to maintain herself while she was in desertion, the wife was only promising to do that which she was already bound to do. Nevertheless, a promise to perform an existing duty is, I think, sufficient consideration to support a promise, so long as there is nothing in the transaction which is contrary to the public interest.

The cases shift the focus from strict formulae of bargain and exchange to *practical benefit* to the person to whom the promise is given (*Ward*), and to the possibility of public policy reasons for not enforcing the promise (*Williams*). These points re-emerge in the more recent case of *Williams v Roffey Bros and Nicholls (Contractors) Ltd* (1991) which, like *Stilk v Myrick*, concerns an existing contractual duty. In that case, Roffey, as main contractors, entered into a contract with a housing association for the refurbishment of a block of flats. Roffey sub-contracted the carpentry work to Williams for £20,000. Part way through the work, Williams was in financial difficulties because he had tendered too low and had failed to supervise his workmen properly. There was a distinct possibility that Williams could not complete on time or would stop work altogether. Facing a penalty clause in the main contract for late completion, Roffey agreed to pay Williams a further £10,300 at a rate of £575 per flat completed. The carpentry work on eight more flats was finished but, with only a further £1,500 having been paid by Roffey, Williams stopped work and sued for damages in respect of the eight completions. In line with the judgment in *Stilk v Myrick*, Roffey argued that Williams had provided no consideration to support their promise of additional payment and Williams was merely doing what he was already obliged to do.

The Court of Appeal held that Roffey were bound by their promise. In the view of Glidewell LJ, the present state of the law on the subject could be expressed in six propositions:

(i) if A has entered into a contract with B to do work for, or to supply goods or services to, B in return for payment by B, and

(ii) at some stage before A has completely performed his obligation under the contract B has reason to doubt whether A will, or will be able to, complete his side of the bargain, and

(iii) B thereupon promises A an additional payment in return for A's promise to perform his contractual obligations on time, and

(iv) as a result of giving his promise B obtains in practice a benefit, or obviates a disbenefit, and

(v) B's promise is not given as a result of economic duress or fraud on the part of A, then

(vi) the benefit to B is capable of being consideration for B's promise, so that the promise is legally binding.

In his view, the benefits obtained or detriment avoided by the main contractors were agreed for three reasons. First, in order to seek to ensure that the plaintiff continued work and did not stop in breach of the sub-contract; secondly, to avoid the penalty for delay in the main contract; and, finally, to avoid the trouble and expense of engaging other people to complete the carpentry work. The application of the six conditions outlined by Glidewell allows for the possibility that *Stilk v Myrick* can be distinguished. It would seem that the legacy of the case is that emphasis should be on whether the promisor gains some tangible benefit from the rearrangement and that no wrongful pressure or fraud is exerted to give rise to that promise, but the case certainly stretches the limits of consideration.

Stepping back from the detail, it could be said that this decision can be explained in terms of good business sense. Both parties are business contractors. The main contractor, when giving his promise of additional payment, is making the best of a bad job. In his estimation, it is less disadvantageous to pay the sub-contractor more than to run the very real risk of having to pay his client even more under the terms of the penalty clause in the main contract. On this basis, the court leaves the parties to their rearrangement. The case also takes account of the long-term commercial advantages of the renegotiation of terms during the performance of the contract. Treating each variation of terms as a new contract requiring fresh consideration may be a logical approach to contracts where an ongoing relationship of dependence does not exist. But, as *Williams v Roffey* shows, an overly formalistic approach to the issue in all contracts can create an absurd situation in which the law undermines perfectly fair and logical alterations which benefit both parties.

This view of the case can be seen, in more technical language, in the words of Russell LJ: 'Consideration there must be but in my judgment the courts nowadays should be more ready to find its existence so as to reflect the intention of the parties to the contract where the bargaining powers are not unequal.' This view is far from being a new critique of the law in this area. Over 60 years ago, the American realist lawyer Karl Llewellyn insisted that a true understanding of business law's purpose assumes an understanding of the facts of business life. He summed up the position as follows and in so doing leads us to the next issue:

> Law and logic go astray whenever such dealings are regarded as truly comparable to new agreements. They are not. No business man regards them so. They are going-transaction adjustments, as different from agreement-formation as are corporate organisation and corporate management; and the line of legal dealing with them which runs over waiver and estoppel is based on sound intuition.

PROMISSORY ESTOPPEL: EXCHANGE OR REASONABLE RELIANCE?

Our discussion of consideration has centred on the idea of bargain or exchange as a reasonable basis for an historical explanation of the doctrine. We have seen that the legal approach to bargain excludes from the province of contract formation promises which have not been 'paid for'. In *Williams v Roffey*, the formalistic concepts of consideration were stretched to their limits but it was clear that modification of the contract enabled Roffey to obtain benefits. Although Williams merely promised to continue his original obligations, the practical benefit to Roffey was sufficient to make his promise binding. In this section, we consider the position where the variation of the contract involves one party *giving up* some of their rights in a situation in which the other party provides no further consideration to support the promise.

This position was discussed in *Pinnel's Case* (1602) in which it was stated that payment of a lesser sum in satisfaction of a greater one did not satisfy the law of contract. The rule in *Pinnel's Case* was affirmed by the House of Lords in *Foakes v Beer* (1884). In that case, Foakes owed £2,000 to Beer who sued and obtained judgment. Foakes needed time to pay and it was eventually agreed that Beer would take no further proceedings in return for an immediate payment of £500 plus specified instalments until the whole judgment was satisfied. After the £2,000 was paid, Beer claimed £360 interest on the judgment debt. The court upheld her claim. Foakes's payment of the lesser (capital) sum did not discharge the greater (capital plus interest) debt. The court determined that Beer could recover the full amount, even if she had promised to forego interest, as Foakes had provided no consideration for that promise. The 'remorseless logic' of this common law approach can be applied to the new deal between Angie, Georgie and Chelsea:

(1) a contractual relationship exists between Angie, Georgie and Chelsea;

(2) a new agreement is made in which Chelsea promises or assures Angie that she will accept *less than* is due to her under the contract;

(3) therefore, Chelsea's promise is *not* supported by fresh consideration from Angie;

(4) there is no new agreement supported by consideration which discharges the original contract;

(5) Chelsea can therefore retract her promise, insist on her strict legal rights and sue for the full, original debt.

Despite its logic, the common law rule has never been free from criticism, not least because it does not always make sense in a commercial context. Financial compromise, involving the waiving of part of a debt, may be good business sense especially in times of cash-flow problems. In *Foakes v Beer* itself, Lord Blackburn, reluctantly acquiescing in the majority view, stated that:

> I think it is not the fact that to accept prompt payment of a part only of a liquidated demand can never be more beneficial than to insist on payment of the whole. And if it be not the fact, it cannot be apparent to the judges ... What principally weighs with me ... is my conviction that all men of business, whether merchants or tradesmen, do every day recognise and act on the ground that prompt payment of part of their demand may be more beneficial to them than it would be to insist on their rights and enforce payment of the whole. Even where the debtor is perfectly solvent, and sure to

pay at last, this often is so. Where the credit of the debtor is doubtful it must be more so.

However, the cases do not always focus on allowing a creditor to renege on his promise: the villain of the piece may be a debtor whose reluctance, or worse, drives the creditor into accepting less than is due. In such cases, it was argued in *D & C Builders Ltd v Rees* (1966) that the unscrupulous debtor should be bound to pay in full either by use of the common law rule or by applying ideas of unfair pressure or duress (see Chapter 12).

In any event, the rule in *Pinnel's Case* is now so hemmed in by exceptions that there must be few cases today in which the principle is in fact applicable. At common law the original agreement can be avoided so as to exclude the rule by making sure there is some *variation* in the debtor's performance. This may include a variation in the method, time or place of payment by the debtor to support the creditor's promise to waive part of the debt so that, for instance, the debtor may make payment of a smaller sum in a different currency. Provision by the debtor of something different in kind, such as stocks and shares instead of £2,000, also falls under this heading. Although case law suggests that the variation must perhaps originate with the creditor and be to their advantage, it is clear that, as in *Williams v Roffey*, the common law has shown itself prepared to respect variations of contract where nominal fresh consideration is provided as long as it benefits the creditor.

In 1994, the Court of Appeal decided a case which not only revived disquiet regarding the mismatch between the rule in *Pinnel's Case* and regular business practice, but also presented an opportunity to bring the prevailing argument in *Williams v Roffey* to bear upon that early 17th century decision. In *Re Selectmove Ltd* (1995), the company owed large sums in unpaid tax and national insurance contributions (NIC) to the Inland Revenue, which presented a petition to wind up the company. The company alleged a later agreement by which the Inland Revenue would not take such action on the debt if the company paid future tax and NIC as they fell due and paid off arrears at £1,000 per month. In return for these forbearances, the company were in effect only doing what they were already obliged to do. In the event they made late payments of both new demands and arrears instalments and the Inland Revenue sued to enforce the original agreement. The court was sympathetic to the *Williams v Roffey* argument that a promise to perform an existing obligation may amount to good consideration if there are practical benefits to the promisee. As in that case, the rearrangement with the Inland Revenue made good business sense in the circumstances. The company had been kept out of liquidation by paying off its debts over a period and this was apparently the outcome the Inland Revenue preferred. However, it was held that the second agreement was unenforceable for lack of consideration. It was analytically possible for the Court of Appeal to find that a benefit to the creditor was sufficient consideration, but the court decided that it was bound by the House of Lords' decision in *Foakes v Beer*. Thus, the rule remained that in common law part payment of a debt is no consideration, subject only to the exceptions considered above.

The upshot is that *Williams v Roffey* does not apply where the pre-existing obligation is an obligation to pay, as opposed to an obligation to supply goods or services, otherwise *Foakes v Beer* would have no application. It must be the case that further developments are required to eliminate the 'rough edges' that presently exist in this area of the common law. Taking a cue from *D & C Builders*, it may be that the answer is to abolish the requirement of consideration for contract renegotiations in all cases where the agreement does not come about as a result of illegitimate pressure.

EQUITABLE INTERVENTION IN THE FIELD

However, the rule in *Pinnel's Case* has been all but eroded by an equitable doctrine which allows the common law position to be subverted. In 1947, in *Central London Property Trust Ltd v High Trees House Ltd*, it was established that a promise by one of the parties not to enforce their full contractual rights has a *degree* of binding effect in equity even though this renegotiation and variation of the contract is not supported by consideration. In the *High Trees* case, the facts were that in 1937 CLPT let a block of flats in London to their subsidiary company HTH for 99 years at a ground rent of £2,500 pa. In 1940, as a result of bombing raids, many of the flats were empty and CLPT agreed to reduce the rent to £1,250 pa because the original rent could not be paid by HTH out of the profits they received from the flats. HTH provided no consideration to support CLPT's promise to forgo half the ground rent. By 1945 the flats were again fully let, and the receiver of CLPT wrote to HTH claiming future payment of rent at the full rate and 'arrears' of almost £8,000. Friendly proceedings were later instituted. Denning J accepted the claim for full rent from mid-1945. He reasoned that the 1940 agreement had been a *temporary* expedient and the conditions giving rise to it had disappeared. The judge, however, added that CLPT could not sue for the full rent in the period from 1940 to 1945 because of the equitable doctrine of estoppel espoused in *Hughes v Metropolitan Railway Co* (1877). It was held that if a claim for arrears had actually been made, HTH would have been able to use CLPT's promise as a *defence* to the action. The effect of the doctrine of promissory estoppel is to hold promisors to their word and prevent them from going back on their promise where it would be unjust or inequitable. This doctrine of promissory estoppel operates in the following way:

(a) There must be a *pre-existing legal relationship* giving rise to rights and duties between the parties such as the rental agreement between Angie, Georgie and Mister C or Chelsea's contract of employment.

(b) One party must later make a clear *promise* or assertion that they will *not fully enforce their existing rights* against the promise, such as when Mister C and Chelsea do not insist on full rent or payment of wages. They may do this for a variety of reasons including sound business practice in changing circumstances.

(c) The *effect* of promissory estoppel is to *stop* the promisor from denying this promise, from retracting it and insisting on his strict legal rights under the existing contract. Unlike the common law rules relating to variation of contract, no consideration moves from the promise. There is no bargain; the equity lies in the promisee's reliance on the other's word.

The doctrine can be used even though the promisee provides *no fresh consideration* for the new promise and satisfaction. However, it must be intended that the promise be *relied upon* and the promisee must in fact rely upon it. According to Lord Denning, in *Alan & Co Ltd v El Nasr Co* (1972), this does not necessarily mean detrimental reliance. Instead the person relying on the estoppel must have been led to alter his position. This only means that they must have been led to an act differently from what they would otherwise have done, such as paying the agreed lower rent. The effect is to make it *inequitable* for the promisor to go back on the promise they have given. Where there is no bargain involved, it is the mere action in reliance on the promise which usually makes it just to enforce the promise.

However, it is generally considered equitable to allow the promisor, on giving *reasonable notice*, to insist on a *resumption* of their strict rights. But this will not be possible and the promise will become final and irrevocable if the promisee cannot resume their position before the promise was given. It follows that where their rights are only suspended, the promisor can sue to enforce their original rights as to *the future*, but cannot recover any balances 'owed' while their forbearance took effect. Moreover, the promisee can use the *promise as a defence* to such an action but cannot sue on the promise to waive their full rights as they provided no consideration for it. In other words, the doctrine can be used as a 'shield and not a sword'. Technically then, it does not create new rights so as to abolish the doctrine of consideration by the 'back door' (see *Combe v Combe* (1951)).

As it is an equitable doctrine, one of the requirements for the application of promissory estoppel is that it must be unjust for the promisor to go back on the promise they have given. As a result of this use of the principle is in the court's discretion. It was on this ground that Lord Denning based his judgment in *D & C Builders Ltd v Rees* (1966). In that case, D & C, a small firm of builders, did work for Rees at a cost of £482. Having pressed for payment for several months, they eventually and reluctantly agreed with Rees's wife, who knew they were in financial difficulties, to accept £300 'in completion of the account'. Mrs Rees told them that if they refused to take the lesser sum, they would get nothing. D & C later sued for the balance of the original debt. The court decided that their promise to accept £300 not supported by consideration from Rees was of a type to raise the estoppel principle, but agreed it was necessary to take account of 'the dealings which have thus taken place between the parties'. They found that Mrs Rees had held the plaintiffs to ransom and, as such, her conduct amounted to unfair pressure. The judges concluded that as a result it was inequitable to permit D & C to go back on their promise and recover the whole debt.

The *High Trees* decision has found basic acceptance with the House of Lords, subject to some uncertainty about its limits. Academic lawyers, however, have continued to question not only the limits but the basis of this erosion of *Foakes v Beer* and the rule in *Pinnel's Case*. Some writers seem satisfied if its effect is a mere suspension of the rights of the creditor and if, on giving notice, they can withdraw their promise to waive their strict rights. Certainly, in *High Trees*, notice was given but the £1,250 pa agreement was in any case stated to be only 'for the duration' of the war (see also *Tool Metal Manufacturing Co Ltd v Tungsten Electric Co Ltd* (1955)). But there have been judicial differences between Lord Denning, who sought to extend the doctrine as forcibly as possible, and the House of Lords, which has given warnings about the need for 'coherent exposition'. Lord Denning did not accept that the doctrine is limited to the mere suspension of rights and has argued that the principle may be applied so as to preclude the subsequent enforcement of them.

Further argument relates to the promisee's actions following the promise. Must they act to *their detriment* for the doctrine to apply? It is perhaps true to say that this is the wrong approach. The key to the doctrine is more logically seen as *reliance*. All that is necessary is that the promisee places reliance on the promise and acts upon it. So, in *High Trees*, HTH paid. Similarly, in *Charles Rickards Ltd v Oppenheim* (1950), the seller, who had been promised further time in which to make delivery beyond the agreed date, continued to make efforts to perform the contract. Another development comes with the suggestion that promissory estoppel can be a sword as well as a shield and *can* provide the basis of a cause of action. According to this vision, the doctrine is not merely a defence available for the party to whom the promise was made if and when sued by the promisor.

The practical result of the establishment and development of promissory estoppel in the post-war years and the decision in *Williams v Roffey* is an increasing number of cases where agreements are being enforced which traditionally would not have been enforced because of a lack of consideration. The cases reveal a serious tension between law and practice. On one side is the orthodox analysis in which each renegotiation of a contract is seen as a separate and distinct deal required to satisfy all the formalities of the classical model. On the other side is the reality of the business environment in which sensitivity to changing market conditions and flexibility in dealings is crucial to the efficient operation of the market. Whilst the 'rules' of contract formation may make philosophical sense, they do not always make sense in a commercial context. Business deals often involve a complex array of dealings over time with a vast web of contractors, sub-contractors and financiers. The pragmatism of the English judiciary is such that they have tried to respond to the needs of commerce, but this has tended to result in a tinkering with key doctrinal concepts which has led to a lack of clarity about their application. But perhaps more significantly, the attraction of a reliance model of contract as better reflecting the needs of the parties and fairness has led to an increasing interest in this alternative vision of contractual relations and the foundations of contractual doctrine. It is in the field of consideration that supporters of the bargain-exchange model have most to defend.

INTENTION TO CREATE LEGAL RELATIONS

We have learnt so far that an *agreement* may be supported by valid *consideration* but it is not a binding contract unless it is also accompanied by an *intention to create legal relations*. This is a feature of the law which was imported from continental legal thought in the 19th century and gradually accepted by the courts. No doubt the idea of 'a concurrence of intention' in the parties was attractive at a time when the law concentrated on party autonomy and two wills becoming one in true *consensus*. Nevertheless, attribution of such an intention *to the parties* is, in the vast majority of cases, unrealistic and the approach has become rather unfashionable as a result. In part, this is because it is doubtful whether negotiating parties ever turn their minds to this question. A feature of the research done by Macaulay and others is the finding that the business community's prime concern is with good, continuing *business* relations, and that in most cases an intention to create a binding relationship is assumed. As Lord Cross stated in *Albert v Motor Insurers' Bureau* (1972):

> It is not necessary in order that a legally binding contract should arise that the parties should direct their minds to the question and decide in favour of a legally binding relationship. If I get into a taxi and ask the driver to take me to Victoria Station it is extremely unlikely that either of us directs his mind to the question whether we are entering into a contract.

As a result, while the common law still pays attention to the need for an intention to create a binding relationship, the test is now an objective rather than a subjective one.

The 'intention of the parties' does not mean the real intention of these particular parties. It means that intention which reasonable parties would have had in those circumstances. To put it another way, it is not actual but 'constructive' intention that settles the matter if the question is in issue. The courts decide to do this by working from *presumptions* as to the presence or absence of such an intention. Where business transactions are concerned, there is a presumption that legal relations are intended – and that such agreements are therefore binding. It is possible, though rarely found, for business parties to *exclude* the intention to be bound by an express statement to that effect in the agreement itself (see *Rose and Frank Co v Crompton & Bros Ltd* (1923)). These are known as binding in honour clauses. However, they must do this in the clearest possible terms before the court will allow that the basic presumption has been overturned: see *Edwards v Skyways Ltd* (1964).

For social and domestic arrangements there is presumed to be no intention to create legal relations. The practical effect of the doctrine is that it serves to protect certain types of agreement from being enforced by the courts. These include social and domestic arrangement such as agreements to meet for dinner, go for a walk, share information in study groups or give lifts in a car to friends. Each of these agreements might satisfy the requirements of offer, acceptance and exchange but they are unlikely to be enforced because the parties are not expected to use the courts to enforce their compact, nor indeed would they want to. In this way the doctrine enables the court to hive off and exclude from the jurisdiction of the law of contract 'unwanted' agreements. Thus, as regards most purely domestic or marital agreements, it is, in Atiyah's view, 'probably true that in these cases the result depends not so much on the lack of intention to create legal relations, as on the courts' view that it would be unseemly and distressing to allow husbands and wives, while still living together, to use the court as an arbiter for their matrimonial differences'.

The distinction which the courts have made between the worlds of business and home are well illustrated in *Balfour v Balfour* (1919). In this case, the defendant husband, while on leave with his wife from his work in Ceylon, agreed to pay her £30 a month maintenance while she remained in England for medical treatment. Later the husband suggested that his wife stayed in England, and eventually she obtained a divorce. This action concerned the husband's failure to pay monthly sums prior to the divorce. The Court of Appeal held that the agreement, made by a husband and wife 'in amity', was not a binding contract but a merely domestic arrangement which, in the absence of indications to the contrary, the parties did not intend to give rise to legal relations. Atkin LJ was of the opinion that 'the small courts of this country would have to be multiplied one hundredfold if these arrangements were held to result in legal obligations'!

It follows that an agreement between a couple who are no longer 'in amity' may well be held to be binding. So, for example, the court may uphold an agreement between a separated couple which relates to the future arrangement of their financial affairs (see *Merritt v Merritt* (1970)). However, there is only a narrow dividing line between the domestic and the business nature of some agreements and there are circumstances in which a binding *business* agreement may clearly be made between couples. For instance, a wife may employ her husband or sell property to him.

It is worthy of note when examining the husband and wife relationship that we are back with Weber's prime illustration of the 'status' contract – the 'total' relationship which differs from the 'purposive' contract with its limited commercial aims. One can hear echoes of this distinction in Atkin LJ's judgment: 'Agreements such as these are outside the realm of contracts altogether ... The consideration that really obtains for them is that natural love and affection which counts for so little in these cold courts ... and the principles of the common law ... find no place in the domestic code.' Not surprisingly, the distinction between the private world of the home and the public world of business has been criticised by feminists. In their view, the division has facilitated an indirect form of discrimination against women. Because women have traditionally spent more of their working lives in the home and take greater responsibility for child care and management of the domestic sphere, the failure of the courts to recognise agreements between couples is much more likely to affect them adversely. Consider the situation, for example, where a couple have a baby and the woman offers to take primary responsibility for the child while the man studies in return for an undertaking that once he has graduated they reverse roles. Common sense tells us that there is agreement, an exchange and an intention to enter into a binding agreement. The fact that it is unlikely that the courts would enforce the agreement possibly suggests more about the assumptions made by the judiciary about the appropriate jurisdiction of the law of contract than it does about logic or fairness.

COMFORT LETTERS

It is generally true to say that little account is taken of the doctrine of intention to create legal relations in modern day publications, but it remains important in two particular contexts in which the business community has an interest. The first is comfort letters and the second is collective bargaining. In this section and the next we shall consider these in turn. A comfort letter is a representation by one party which reassures the other about their commitment to the contract or ability to carry it out. Their purpose is to increase confidence in pre-contractual negotiations but the question has arisen of whether they carry sufficient intention to be bound to form part of the contract. The cases involving 'comfort letters' suggest that the doctrine may be becoming overly subtle in this area. So, for instance, in *Kleinwort Benson Ltd v Malaysia Mining Corp* (1989), Malaysia Mining set up a wholly owned subsidiary, Metals Ltd, to trade in tin on the London Metals Exchange. Malaysia Mining also sought a loan of £5 million from Kleinwort Benson, a merchant bank, to supplement Metals' existing capital. Before making the loan, Kleinwort Benson asked Malaysia Mining for a guarantee of their subsidiary's indebtedness to them. A guarantee is a binding promise to pay another's debts if he fails to pay. Malaysia Mining declined to do this but said that the loan would be covered by their 'comfort letter'. Kleinwort Benson replied that this would be 'no problem' but that the rate of interest charged would be slightly higher. Malaysia Mining's comfort letter stated that: 'It is our policy to ensure that the business of Metals Ltd is at all times in a position to meet its liabilities to you.' Malaysia Mining also said they would not reduce their current financial interest in Metals Ltd until the loan had been repaid. In 1985 the world tin market collapsed and Metals Ltd went into liquidation with the loan (now £10 million) unpaid. Kleinwort Benson sued Malaysia Mining for the full amount on the basis of the comfort letter, which they maintained had contractual effect.

The Court of Appeal held that the correct test to determine the status of a comfort letter was to ask whether a promise was being made, rather than the test applied at first instance of whether there was an intention to create legal relations. The court held that the letter amounted to a policy statement only and did not form the basis of a contract. Ralph Gibson LJ considered that a 'true' construction of the relevant parts of the comfort letter made clear that Malaysia Mining were accepting 'a moral responsibility only' to pay its subsidiary's debts. His reasoning implies that appropriate wording could establish a promissory obligation which would appear to make the comfort letter a guarantee or the equivalent. The facts of this case do not fit easily into the concept of a clear rebuttal of the presumption that business agreements are binding and raises difficult questions about risk and reliance.

Other jurisdictions have not been so cautious. In *Banque Brussels Lambert v Australian National Industries Ltd* (1989), the wording of the comfort letter was such as to enable the Australian court to find a promissory obligation and a breach of contract. The New South Wales court considered comfort letters to be little different from letters of guarantee. But this does not address the issue of why Malaysia Mining would provide one but not the other. If the Court of Appeal had 'found' a promise to pay, as the court of first instance did, it would at least have avoided criticism to the effect that its decision was commercially unrealistic. As Brown (1990) has commented:

> There should be no room in the proper flow of commerce for some purgatory where statements made by business people, after hard bargaining and made to induce another business person to enter into a business transaction would, without any express statement to that effect, reside in a twilight zone of merely honourable engagement. The whole thrust of the law today is to attempt to give proper effect to commercial transactions. It is for this reason that uncertainty, a concept so much loved by lawyers, has fallen into disfavour as a tool for striking down commercial bargains.

COLLECTIVE BARGAINING

There are other business agreements which the courts have refused to enforce on the ground of an absence of constructive intention. The most important example is the industrial collective bargaining agreement which has developed in significance and complexity since the formative days of contract's 'classical' period. It is therefore not surprising that contractual concepts which might have been appropriate to the private bargains of the 19th century have failed to transplant into this new and specialised area of group bargaining.

Collective bargaining agreements are negotiated by trade unions and employers over such matters as pay and conditions of work. Contract law has to a large extent been supplanted in the employment area in modern times by a growing mass of 'special' statutory measures and voluntary codes of practice making up, at least in part, the field of labour law. On the assumption that litigation is not the best way of promoting industrial relations, legislation keeps the courts away from such an agreement. The point was clearly made by the Royal Commission on Trade Unions in 1968:

> This lack of intention to make legally binding collective agreements, or better perhaps, this intention and policy that collective bargaining and collective agreements should remain outside the law, is one of the characteristic features of our system of industrial relations which distinguishes it from other comparable systems.

In line with this approach, modern legislation requires that agreements are 'conclusively presumed not to have been intended by the parties to be a legally enforceable contract' unless they are in writing and expressly provide to the contrary. In other words, it reverses the usual presumption about intention in commercial settings. Few, if any, collective agreements contain such express provision, although the terms of such unenforceable collective agreements can become binding when incorporated into individual contracts of employment: see *National Coal Board v Galley* (1958).

This policy suggests that although the question of intention to create legal relations is not taken by commentators to be a very important aspect of contract law, it is, like several others, a controversial issue if one penetrates below the surface. Some commentators argue that it could be abolished and the cases to which it has been applied could or should have been decided on a different basis. But there is no doubt that the doctrine remains an important tool where the judiciary and legislature want to exclude certain groups or practices from consideration by the courts. Feminists and left-wing scholars have argued that such exclusions are based on a particular ideological or political reading of the role of contract which needs to be exposed to greater interrogation. Seen in this way, the doctrine of intention to create legal relations is far from being a device to separate out the casual from the formal arrangement.

CONCLUDING REMARKS

In this chapter we have visited the doctrines which, in addition to the law relating to offer, acceptance and agreement, determine how the making of an enforceable contract is evidenced. It is clear from the doctrines and cases analysed that there are a number of tensions which have arisen and that different visions of contract have emerged. We have looked at the notion of exchange and bargain but made clear that these notions, founded on the classical model, have been challenged by the idea of reliance. These competing ideas about what needs to be evidenced before the courts are prepared to recognise and enforce a contract have considerable repercussions for the subject as a whole. Significantly, the challenge has come from the equitable doctrine of promissory estoppel, but the courts in *Williams v Roffey* have shown an ongoing commitment to fitting agreements which make sense in the business community into a traditional framework of analysis. We shall leave you to draw your own conclusions about whether this is an acceptable state of affairs until you have read the cases. But, in the chapter which follows, we shall turn once more to the notion of reliance and its close and developing relationship with the concept of contract.

REFERENCES AND FURTHER READING

Contractual intention

Brown, I 'The letter of comfort – placebo or promise?' (1990) JBL 281.

Goodrich, P (1996) 'Gender and contracts' in Bottomley, A (ed), *Feminist Perspectives on Foundational Subjects in Law*, London: Cavendish Publishing.

Tettenborn, I 'Commercial certainty: a step in the right direction' (1988) CLJ 346.

Unger, J 'Intent to create legal relations, mutuality and consideration' (1956) 19 MLR 96.

Wheeler, S and Shaw, J (1994) *Contract Law: Cases, Materials and Commentary*, Oxford: Oxford University Press.

Consideration and promissory estoppel

Adams, J and Brownsword, R 'Contract, consideration and the critical path' (1990) 53 MLR 536 (*Williams v Roffey*).

Denning, Lord (1979) 'High Trees' in *The Discipline of Law*, Part Five, London: Butterworths.

Dugdale, A and Yates, D 'Variation, waiver and estoppel – a re-appraisal' (1976) 40 MLR 680.

Gordon, D 'Creditors' promises to forgo rights – a study of the *High Trees* and *Tool Metal* cases' (1963) CLJ 222.

Peel, E 'Part payment of a debt is no consideration' (1994) 110 LQR 353 (*Re Selectmove*).

Phang, A 'Consideration at the crossroads' (1991) 107 LQR 21.

QUESTIONS

(1) 'Consideration is a perfectly adequate test of liability in contract, the so-called doctrine of intention to create legal relations is superfluous.' Discuss this statement in the light of decided cases.

(2) Can you apply what you know about the doctrine of consideration to the problems facing Angie and Georgie? For instance, are the following variations of contract supported by fresh consideration? Would they be upheld by the courts?:

   (a) Kirsteen's claims that Angie and Georgie are obliged to pay her £500 commission for the help she gave them in finding a carrot supplier.

   (b) The reduction of Chelsea's wage.

   (c) Mister C's demand that they should pay him the 25% of the rent he didn't collect while he was living with Missy J.

   (d) Marcus's demand for additional payment.

   Please cite the relevant case law when giving your response. Do you think the variations should be upheld?

(3) Are there reasons why Georgie's medical insurance contract should be enforceable but the agreement between Angie and Georgie recorded in their tapestry should not?

(4) Explain the doctrine of promissory estoppel in terms of its being:

   (a) a moral principle;

   (b) the bending of a rule of higher generality;

   (c) good business sense.

PART FOUR:

BARGAINING NAUGHTINESS AND FORMATION PROBLEMS

CHAPTER 9

MISREPRESENTATION

INTRODUCTION

So far in this book we have looked at the big ideas which underpin the modern law of contract and the doctrines, rules and ideas which govern the way we look at formation. Determining when the parties became legally obliged to each other and the detail of how they are bound is crucial and a point we shall return to again and again. We cannot determine whether there has been a breach unless we understand what the parties have agreed. If one of the parties claims there has been a mistake, we cannot determine the validity of their claim unless we determine what it is that each of the parties assumed about performance as they entered into the agreement.

In this section of the book we look at a number of problems which relate to formation which may allow one of the parties to have the contract set aside or to claim an extra-contractual remedy. Some of this behaviour is termed bargaining naughtiness and you will discover that many of the cases we turn to involve fraudsters. But in other instances agreement is defective because misunderstandings have arisen or because one of the parties has been reckless in what they said. The main doctrines with which we are concerned here are those relating to misrepresentation, mistake, duress and unconscionability. These are all doctrines which operate in the 'twilight zone' of the law of contract.

MISREPRESENTATION AND PRE-CONTRACTUAL NEGOTIATIONS

During the course of pre-contractual negotiations people tend to make a variety of representations to each other. These might include comments about the condition of the thing being negotiated about, the standard of a service, special characteristics of an item and the price and method of payment. This is particularly the case in the business community where negotiations may be protracted. Many of these representations are sufficiently important that they will eventually become terms of the contract concluded between the parties. But it is also the case that negotiations break down or the parties do not expect all their statements to become contractual promises. This chapter focuses on whether negotiating parties can be found liable for the representations made before a contract is formed which do not become part of the contract.

In the previous chapter it was made clear that the judiciary in this country is reluctant to impose unexpected obligations on the parties prior to them reaching agreement. This is in contrast to other jurisdictions where a pre-contractual duty of good faith is proving increasingly popular. It has been argued that the traditional English approach increases market efficiency and benefits the business community. It protects the parties' freedom to negotiate at length, explore possibilities and exchange the sort of information on which efficient dealings are based prior to the moment of responsibility. The rationale for this position is that when the parties are inhibited by legal regulations during the negotiation process they may not feel so free to exchange information relating to the deal they plan to make. Traditionally then, the boundaries of contractual obligations have been set from the moment at which agreement is reached.

Judicial attitudes have changed and no longer accord with this approach. Atiyah has argued that the law relating to misrepresentation was one of the first areas of law to show signs of retreat from the high water mark of Victorian individualism. In *The Rise and Fall of Freedom of Contract*, he sketched out the background to developments in this area:

> The older notion that a man could say what he liked to a prospective contracting party, so long only as he refrained from positively dishonest assertions of fact, seems to have come up against a new morality in the late nineteenth century. The courts began to insist on the duty of a party not to mislead the other party by extravagant or unjustified assertions ... in their determination to stamp out the laxer business morality.

But even the modern cases reflect the hold which individualism and adversarialism continue to have on the English law of contract. The approach adopted to these problems is not to impose a positive duty on negotiating parties to behave well but rather to declare certain types of behaviour unacceptable. The distinction may appear subtle but it has considerable connotations. The approach of contract can be compared with that of tort which has not been so shy of intervening in the regulation of pre-contractual negotiations. Here, interference has been justified on the basis that dishonesty in the pre-contractual period can distort the market which relies on the exchange of *accurate* information for its optimal efficiency. Viewed in this way, it has been argued that deliberate and dishonest inducements to enter into a contract which incurs expenditure for one of the parties abuses the notion of freedom to contract and standards of morality. However, the law remains a somewhat confusing mixture of tort and contract, common law and equity. Underpinning this confusion is ambiguity about the proper ambit of contract and contractual principles and concern that they should be stretched to cover a pre-contractual period. Elsewhere in this book it will be argued that the courts and legislature have been prepared to step in to regulate the negotiation process where consumers are concerned but have continued to make certain assumptions about contracting parties who trade as businesses.

IS IT A TERM?

Since most contracts are made orally or are a mixture of oral and written terms, it can be difficult to decide which pre-contractual representations become terms of the contract and which are excluded from the contract and become what lawyers refer to as 'mere' representations. Although the latter affect the contract, they do not become an integral part of it and, if untrue, do not give rise to a breach of contract. In practical terms the distinction is less important than it was before the Misrepresentation Act 1967, since the remedies available to those who are the victims of pre-contractual misrepresentations are now akin to, but not the same as, the remedies for breach of contract. However, there continue to be reasons why it is important for a lawyer to argue that a representation has become a term of the contract. These include the fact that breach brings with it an automatic right to damages whereas this is discretionary in the case of mere representations. Moreover, there are different rules relating to the amount of damages that should be made available in the two cases which may affect the litigation strategy adopted.

The relevant case law must be seen in its historical context. The claim that a pre-contractual statement has become part of the contract has traditionally been made to secure a contractual remedy where no tortious remedies existed at the time, to secure damages as of right or to provide a defence to a claim for breach from the other party. Today, the test of whether a representation has become a term of the contract depends on an *objective* appraisal of whether the representor intended to be bound to the truth of the statement so as to render themselves liable to an action for breach. The courts have laid down certain guidelines when seeking an answer to this question, but the essential criterion adopted by the courts would seem to be that of fairness in the particular circumstances presented to them.

So, for instance, in *Oscar Chess Ltd v Williams* (1957), Williams sold a car for £280 to a car dealer. He innocently described it as a 1948 model but unbeknown to him the logbook had been forged. In fact it had been registered in 1939 and was worth £175. The statement was held to be a misrepresentation but not a term of the contract. This was because the dealer might have bought the car anyway and the buyer was in a good position to discern the age of the car. Lord Denning LJ laid down a number of criteria to distinguish terms from mere representations. He argued that:

(a) the more important a statement made during negotiations, the more likely that it is a term;

(b) the longer the time between the making of the statement and the agreement being concluded, the more likely that it is not a term;

(c) if an oral statement is not recorded in a written contract, it is evidence against a term being intended;

(d) the statement is more likely to be a term if made by a person possessing special skill or knowledge regarding its truth.

These criteria suggest that there are no hard and fast rules when trying to determine whether a representation is a term or not. The main theme running throughout the case law is a consideration of whether it was reasonable in the circumstances to rely on the representations made. Thus, in *Bentley v Harold Smith (Motors) Ltd* (1965), where the positions were reversed, a pre-contractual statement made by a dealer to a private purchaser was held to be a term of the contract. The dealer stated that a car had done 20,000 miles when it had in fact done almost 100,000. The statement by the dealer, who was in a much better position to check its truth, was held to be a term and contractual damages were awarded.

MISREPRESENTATION: THE GENERAL RULES

As attitudes towards pre-contractual negotiations have changed, the law has provided some relief through the doctrines of fraud and misrepresentation for those who have been misled in pre-contractual negotiations. Misleading statements about the price of goods and services, quantity, composition, strength and fitness for purpose have also been singled out for regulation by legislation such as the Trade Descriptions Act 1968 and the Consumer Protection Act 1987. As a general rule a party must not make any false and misleading statements to the other party which induce them to enter into a contract. If they do they may result in successful claim of misrepresentation. The courts have defined misrepresentation as an untrue statement of existing fact made by one party to the other which, while not forming part of the contract, is nevertheless one of the reasons that induces them to enter into it. Figure 9.1 below shows what needs to be proved in pictorial form. As with promissory estoppel, the essence of the doctrine is reliance. Although there is no general duty to *disclose* material facts, a single word, a nod, a shake of the head or a smile may amount to a misrepresentation of fact and allow the misled party to avoid the obligations posed by the subsequent contract if the statement subsequently turns out to be untrue. In these circumstances, consent to enter the contract is said to be vitiated and the agreement false.

Figure 9.1: The elements of misrepresentation

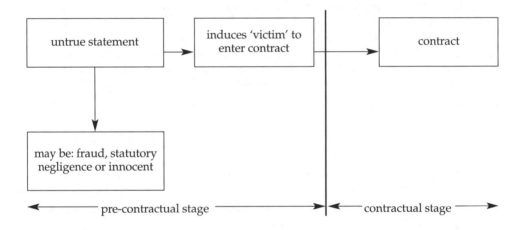

Although silence does not amount to misrepresentation, a partial non-disclosure may do so. For example, a statement may omit facts which render what is actually said false or misleading. Also, a statement may be made which is true at the time, but which subsequently ceases to be true to the representor's knowledge before the contract is entered into. Here, a failure to inform the representee of the change in circumstances will amount to misrepresentation. So, for example, in *With v O'Flanagan* (1936), a medical practice was stated to be worth £2,000 during negotiations for its sale. By the time the contract was entered into some months later, the practice had become worthless owing to the illness of the vendor. The contract was set aside as the changed circumstances had not been revealed.

STATEMENTS OF FACT, OPINIONS AND PROMISES

Much of the case law on misrepresentation is concerned with determining the sort of statements which it is reasonable for people to rely upon. In this context, statements of fact, which are actionable, have been distinguished from other sorts of statement which cannot form the basis of an action. These include extravagant and unverifiable sales talk, statements of opinion, statements of intention and statements of law. The rationale behind the distinction remains sensible. It seems reasonable, for instance, to expect people to read contracts or get legal advice rather than rely on a statement of law made by a layman. Similarly, statements of opinion and sales talk are commonly understood as 'puff' which should be believed with caution. For example, in *Bisset v Wilkinson* (1927), the vendor of land which, to the knowledge of both parties, had not previously been used for sheep farming stated that it would support 2,000 sheep. It was held that this was merely a statement of opinion which, when it proved to be unfounded, was not actionable. However, the courts have shown themselves less willing to apply the 'rule' relating to opinions where one party is in a position to know more than the other about the matter being discussed. So, in *Esso Petroleum Co Ltd v Mardon* (1976), an expert's inaccurate estimation of the future petrol sales of a filling station based on negligently prepared data was found to be a 'considered judgment' which was actionable.

A formulaic approach to distinguishing the sorts of statements which are actionable or not is dangerous as in some situations the distinction has become a rather subtle one. Indeed, it has been argued that the distinctions between facts, opinions, intentions and other statements as to the future that can be found in the cases over many years have now reached a state of over-subtle complexity. For example, it is a misrepresentation of fact for a person to say that he holds an opinion which he does not hold. Moreover, it might appear that a pre-contractual statement as to future conduct made by one party to the other which is later not borne out by the facts cannot be a misrepresentation. However, in *Quickmaid Rental Services Ltd v Reece* (1970), the company's representative, shortly before concluding a written rental agreement for a coffee machine with Reece, told him that they would not be installing another machine on the same road. Later, another machine was installed and the representative's statement was held to be a promise in a contract partly written and partly oral. See also *Evans & Son (Portsmouth) Ltd v Merzario Ltd* (1976).

An alternative to placing too heavy a reliance on distinctions of this type would be to ask whether, in all the circumstances, it was reasonable for the representee to rely on the statement rather than on his own judgment. As Collins (2003) has argued:

> These attempts to reduce to the form of rules the situations and contexts when it will be reasonable to rely upon pre-contractual statements looked doomed to failure for two reasons. In the first place, the reasonableness of reliance must depend upon numerous features of the particular case, such as the relative expertise and knowledge of the parties, and the context in which a statement is made. For example, a statement about the legal effects of a document such as a Will might be reasonably relied upon if made by a qualified lawyer to a client, but not if made by someone without legal expertise ... We should also be aware that the issue of whether it was reasonable to rely on a statement is not simply a question of fact. It involves a normative judgement about which kinds of statements negotiating parties ought to be able to rely on.

INDUCEMENT AND RELIANCE

In order to lodge a successful claim for misrepresentation the representee must also be able to show that they relied on the statement and that it induced the contract, though it need not be the sole inducement. Thus, once it is established that the misrepresentation was calculated to induce entry into the contract, and that the representee has in fact entered, it is a fair inference that they were influenced by it. It used to be the case that it was defence to a claim of misrepresentation that the representee might have discovered its untruth by the exercise of reasonable care. But, since the coming into force of the Misrepresentation Act 1967, the judiciary have distinguished between those cases in which it was reasonable for the representee to make use of an opportunity to discover the truth and those in which it is not. Again, the courts have shown themselves willing to look at relative equality of bargaining power in these situations.

For instance, in *Smith v Eric S Bush* (1989), the plaintiffs relied on a negligent valuation of a house they were buying which was undertaken by a surveyor under contract to the building society they were using. Their claim against the surveyor succeeded even though they might have established the truth if they had employed their own surveyor. The House of Lords decided that it was not reasonable for them to take this step as the house was of modest value but that their decision might have been different had the house had a high value or had it been a situation involving commercial premises.

THE DIFFERENT TYPES OF MISREPRESENTATION

Three types of misrepresentation are currently recognised and can be classified according to the state of mind of the representor (see Figure 9.2). These are fraudulent misrepresentation (a dishonest assertion); negligent misrepresentation (not dishonest but careless); and wholly innocent misrepresentation (not dishonest, not careless but nevertheless incorrect). All are capable of causing loss and are actionable, but the remedies of the injured party are generally broadest in the case of fraud and much narrower for negligent and innocent misrepresentations. A party who proves that a misrepresentation induced them to enter into a contract is entitled to rescind the contract or in certain circumstances claim damages. Rescission involves setting the contract aside and treating it as though it never happened. This means that both the parties must be able to return what they have exchanged.

Figure 9.2: The types of misrepresentation

type of misrepresentation	test	damages available?	rescission available?
fraudulent	deceit	special tortious	subject to usual bars
common law negligent	special knowledge	normal tortious	not applicable
statutory negligent	careless	special tortious	subject to usual bars
innocent	honest and on reasonable grounds	on discretionary basis	subject to usual bars

Lord Herschell in *Derry v Peek* (1889) stated that 'fraud is proved when it is shown that a false representation has been made (1) knowingly, or (2) without belief in its truth, or (3) recklessly, careless whether it be true or false'. However, a person who honestly believes his statement to be true cannot be liable for fraud, however careless he might be. The claimant who alleges fraud must prove the absence of an honest belief, and although this burden is the same as in other civil proceedings, that is, proof on the balance of probabilities, it is not easily discharged in practice. By way of contrast, innocent misrepresentation occurs in situations in which the defendant is able to establish that they had reasonable grounds to believe in the truth of their statement.

A misrepresentation is negligent if it is made carelessly and in breach of a duty, owed by the representor to the representee, to take reasonable care that the representation is accurate. It used to be argued that such a duty only arose in cases where there was an existing contract between the parties or a fiduciary relationship of some kind existed. But it became clear from the House of Lords' landmark decision in *Hedley Byrne & Co Ltd v Heller and Partners Ltd* (1964) that where a 'special' professional or business relationship, short of contract, existed, a duty of care was recognised in the law of tort as regards statements made and relied upon which caused financial loss. Significantly, in the case of such negligent misstatements, it is not necessary for the parties to enter into a contract following their negotiations.

These developments led up to the decision in *Esso Petroleum Co Ltd v Mardon* (1976), mentioned above, where it was held that the relationship between the negotiating parties could be regarded as 'special' in the sense referred to in *Hedley Byrne*. Although the estimated throughput of 200,000 gallons a year was only a forecast, it was based on the superior knowledge of a senior sales representative who held himself out to be experienced in the field. Thus, it would seem that if a person who has, or professes to have, a special knowledge or skill makes a representation in the form of advice, information or opinion with the intention of inducing the other party to enter a contract, they are under a duty to use reasonable care to ensure that what they have said is reliable.

The development of a common law doctrine of negligent misrepresentation was rendered largely irrelevant with the introduction of the Misrepresentation Act in 1967. Under s 2(1) of the 1967 Act, a statutory liability for negligent misrepresentation was created which does not rely on any 'special relationship' (see Figure 9.3).

Figure 9.3: Section 2(1) of the Misrepresentation Act 1967

Where a person has entered into a contract after a misrepresentation has been made to him by another party thereto and as a result thereof he has suffered loss, then, if the person making the misrepresentation would be liable in damages thereof had the misrepresentation been made fraudulently, that person shall be so liable notwithstanding that the misrepresentation was not made fraudulently, unless he proves that he had reasonable ground to believe and did believe up to the time the contract was made that the facts represented were true.

The fact that it is the representor who has to prove their case is one of the most significant characteristics of the statute as it reverses the normal burden of proof in civil proceedings in which it is for the person making the claim to prove their case. It is also the factor which makes an action under the statute much more attractive than an action under the common law doctrine of negligent misstatement. However, the *Hedley Byrne* principle will still be of use in situations in which no contract results from the parties' dealings or the party making the statement is not a party to the final contract.

THE REMEDY OF DAMAGES

Two remedies need to be discussed in the context of actions for misrepresentation. These are damages and rescission. Debate about the availability of damages in misrepresentation is difficult to understand without an appreciation of the different ways in which the law of tort and contract approaches the subject of what the injured party should be compensated for. Liability for misrepresentation may arise in tort where the representation is made fraudulently or negligently, but it will only arise in contract where the representation has also become a term. Where damages are assessed on tortious principles the object is to put the misrepresentee into the pre-contractual financial position they would have been in had the tort not been committed. By way of contrast, where damages are assessed on contractual principles the object is to put the party who has suffered as a result of breach in the position they would have been in had the contract been performed and their *expectations* fulfilled. Figure 9.4 compares these two positions in diagrammatic form but the fact is that in practice the distinction can be a difficult one to draw.

Figure 9.4: Damages

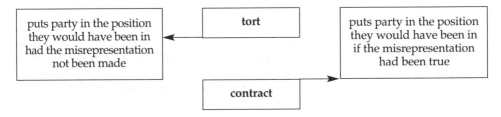

The fact that damages in cases of misrepresentation are based on the principles relevant to an award of damages in tort means that the claimant cannot claim compensation for the profits they might have expected from entry into the contract. The usual rule in calculating tortious damages is that the claimant is entitled to any loss which is foreseeable. However, a special rule has been applied by the courts in considering cases involving fraudulent behaviour. In these instances the courts have been more generous to the claimant and have allowed them to recover for any damages which flow from the tort whether or not they are foreseeable (see *Doyle v Olby (Ironmongers) Ltd* (1969)).

In *East v Maurer* (1991), the court reconsidered whether 'all the actual damages flowing directly from the fraudulent inducement' covered loss of profits. This could be classified as an 'expectation' loss of a type usually found only in breach of contract. The facts of the case were that East bought one of Maurer's two hair salons in Bournemouth for £20,000 in 1979. Maurer fraudulently claimed in the course of negotiations that he did not intend to work in the other salon except in emergencies. In fact he continued to work full-time in that salon. The effect was that the plaintiffs' business was never profitable. East sold it in 1989 for £5,000 and sued Maurer for fraudulent misrepresentation. At first instance, damages were awarded to cover the difference in value of the business between the purchase price and its true market value. They also included an award of £15,000 for loss of profits more in keeping with the award of contractual damages. On appeal, it was held that 'all the actual damage' did include loss of profits in this case, on the basis that where deceit is concerned the law should compensate the plaintiff for all the loss suffered, so far as money can.

The distinction made with contractual damages was that the court claimed to be assessing the profit the plaintiff might have expected to make in another salon bought for a similar sum, and not on the contractual basis of the profits that the salon might have made if Maurer had *promised* that he would not work in the other salon. Nevertheless, the loss of profits award was, somewhat surprisingly, reduced to £10,000.

The judgment suggests there is a very fine line between the contractual test and the tortious test. It will be appreciated that in this case Maurer did not contractually bind himself not to work in the other salon. The statement he made was a pre-contractual statement of intention which was held to be a misrepresentation of *fact* because it was proved that he did not have this intention when he made the statement. Significantly, however, the outcome was virtually the same as if he had bound himself.

Some of the same issues have arisen in the context of statutory misrepresentation. Section 2(1) of the 1967 Act, reproduced above (see Figure 9.3), gives a statutory right to damages but considerable confusion has also revolved around the section. Whilst it makes clear that assessment is to be calculated on a tortious basis, opinion has been somewhat divided over whether it should be calculated according to the more generous level of damages under the tort of deceit or the less generous level used more generally in the tort of negligence. Until recently the weight of academic opinion was in line with Treitel's analysis in 1987:

> Where the action is brought under s 2(1) of the Misrepresentation Act, one possible view is that the deceit rule will be applied by virtue of the fiction of fraud. But the preferable view is that the severity of the deceit rule can only be justified in cases of actual fraud and that remoteness under s 2(1) should depend, as in actions based on negligence, on the test of foreseeability.

It will be recalled that the 'deceit rule' means that a representee can recover all loss flowing directly from the fraud even if the loss was not foreseeable. The 'fiction of fraud' referred to by Treitel is an allusion to the wording of s 2(1) itself where it states that the liability for damages should arise *as if* the statement had been made fraudulently. In the case of *Royscot Trust Ltd v Rogerson* (1991), the Court of Appeal held that s 2(1) liability gave rise to liability under the 'deceit rule'. The facts of the case were that a car dealer negligently misrepresented to the plaintiff finance company both the price of a car and the amount of deposit paid by a customer who wished to take the vehicle on hire purchase terms. The company financed the deal but the customer (first defendant) sold the car in breach of the HP agreement and defaulted on his payments. The finance company brought proceedings against both customer and dealer for loss suffered. It was held that the measure of damages under s 2(1) of the 1967 Act is tortious, not contractual, and that the dealer's liability was such that, in the judgment of Balcombe LJ, 'the finance company is entitled to recover from the dealer all the losses which it suffered as a result of entering into the agreements with the dealer and the customer, even if those losses were unforeseeable'. The finance company was awarded £3,625 plus interest. The literal interpretation of s 2(1) in this case means that as regards the measure of damages a negligent misrepresentor is in the same position as the fraudulent one and that the more generous award applies in either case. However, it is difficult to appreciate why the traditional distinction in tort between intentional and negligent conduct should be disregarded in this way, so making the negligent misrepresentor liable beyond the bounds of forseeability (but see also *Naughton v O'Callaghan* (1990)).

There is no *right* to damages for a wholly innocent misrepresentation under s 2(2) of the 1967 Act, but the court is given a *discretionary* power to declare the contract subsisting and to award damages in lieu of rescission if it would be equitable to do so. The court must bear in mind the nature of the misrepresentation and the loss caused to the representee if the contract were upheld and the loss caused to the representor if the contract were set aside. This discretionary power extends to negligent misrepresentation so making available the remedies of rescission *and* damages under s 2(1) or, if appropriate, rescission or damages under s 2(2) in cases of this kind. However, the court's power to award damages in lieu of rescission where this remedy is not barred (see below) is more likely to be used where the representor is not at fault and compensation is an adequate remedy. The assessment of damages under s 2(2) is the normal tortious measure which excludes consequential loss.

THE REMEDY OF RESCISSION

Rescission is an equitable remedy which is available in *all* cases of misrepresentation. If the representee chooses to rescind the contract, and the court so orders, it is and treated as if it never existed. It can be gleaned from this that the remedy is a drastic one and it is for this reason that the courts are sometimes reluctant to use it, as it involves both the parties giving back what they have exchanged. Alternatively, the representee may rely on the misrepresentation as a defence and as the basis for a counter claim in an action brought on the contract by the representor. A party who wishes to rescind should, if possible, do so by taking active steps against the representor such as seeking a cancellation of the contract. But legal proceedings will be necessary if, say, money paid by the victim (representee) is claimed and the representor refuses to pay it back.

However, there are four bars or limitations to rescission. First, if the representee continues with the contract in the knowledge of the other party's misrepresentation as happened in *Doyle*, then the contract is treated as affirmed and will be allowed to continue. Secondly, it may be impossible to put the parties back into their original positions before the contract was made. This may be because the representee has made changes to the subject matter causing its value to decline or it may be a wasting asset such as a cargo of fruit or a mine. However, a representee who can make substantial, though not precise, restitution can still rescind the contract if he returns the subject matter and makes allowance for its deterioration. Thirdly, the right to rescind will be lost through the intervention of third party rights. Thus, for example, a person who has been induced by fraud to sell goods on credit cannot rescind the contract after the goods have been bought by an innocent third party (see *Lewis v Averay* (1972) in Chapter 10). Finally, in cases of *non*-fraudulent misrepresentation a lapse of time may bar rescission. This point was illustrated in *Leaf v International Galleries* (1950) in which a five year delay in a case of innocent misrepresentation was held to bar the plaintiff's claim. In cases of fraud, lapse of time is merely evidence of affirmation, time running from the discovery of the truth.

EXCLUSION OF LIABILITY FOR MISREPRESENTATION

A clause in a contract excluding or restricting liability for misrepresentation is subject to the rules to be discussed in Chapter 15 regarding incorporation and construction. It is also subject to s 3 of the Misrepresentation Act 1967, as amended by the Unfair Contract Terms Act 1977, which applies the requirement of reasonableness to the clause. This use of this test was looked at in *South Western General Property Co Ltd v Marton* (1982). In this case, Marton, an experienced builder, bought land at auction. It was described in the particulars of sale as building land for which planning permission had previously been refused because the proposed house was out of character. The sale was subject to an exclusion clause which stated that 'any intending purchaser must satisfy himself by inspection or otherwise as to the correctness of each statement contained in the particulars'. Marton, who had bought the land as a site for his own residence, later discovered that planning permission had been refused in terms that made any further application futile. The court held that the description in the particulars was misleading because it implied that the land could be used for building if the house was in character and this was untrue. The defendant had relied on the description, which 'failed to tell more than a part of the facts which were material to the whole contract of sale'. Moreover, the attempt to exclude liability was held to be unreasonable in the circumstances. Context is extremely important in such cases. In cases involving experienced dealers and an individual, an exclusion may be found to be unreasonable, whereas the same clause might be regarded as reasonable if found in a contract with a property speculator.

CONCLUDING REMARKS

The issues raised in the chapter are important as they encourage us to think about the role of private laws in encouraging responsible rather than selfish behaviour. What is clear from the chapter is that a range of standards apply, depending on the intentions and behaviour of those disclosing the information and the characteristics of the contracting parties. The approach of the judiciary has, quite logically, been to impose the harshest penalties on those who are deceitful in pre-contractual negotiations. It is also increasingly evident that different standards apply depending on the relative bargaining strengths of the parties. The last few decades have witnessed an increasing use of legal devices to protect consumers with little power in the market place or experience of commerce. But the case law in the field of misrepresentation also displays a sensitivity towards inequality of bargaining power in intra-business relationships. The influence of tortious principles is clear as the courts have had to turn their attention to notions of superior knowledge. It is within this context that the notion of reliance rather than bargain, discussed in the last chapter, begins to make sense.

Many of the debates touched upon in this chapter will continue to have resonance as discussion of the effect of information asymmetry continues to trouble economists in their attempts to improve market efficiency. The judiciary and academics are also under much greater pressure than ever before to take the concept of good faith seriously in their discussions of pre-contractual negotiations. In this book, we return to discuss the matter in later chapters. For present purposes, it is perhaps sufficient to reflect on what Macneil and others have said about the importance of trust and co-operation in the business sector. If, as relational contract theorists argue, these standards have a commercial as well as an altruistic value, it may be that the cases we see before the courts where trust has broken down because of misrepresentation are atypical of the vast majority of business relationships.

REFERENCES AND FURTHER READING

Atiyah, P (1979) *The Rise and Fall of Freedom of Contract*, Oxford: Clarendon.

Atiyah, P and Treitel, G 'Misrepresentation Act 1967' (1967) 30 MLR 369.

Bishop, W 'Negligent misrepresentation through economists' eyes' (1980) 96 LQR 360.

Brownsword, R 'Case note on *Howard Marine* decision' (1978) 41 MLR 735.

Cartwright, J (1991) *Unequal Bargaining*, Oxford: Oxford University Press.

Collins, H (2003) *The Law of Contract*, London: LexisNexis Butterworths.

Fairest, P 'Misrepresentation and the Act of 1967' (1967) CLJ 239.

Hooley, R 'Damages and Misrepresentation Act 1967' (1991) 107 LQR 547.

Taylor, R 'Expectation, reliance and misrepresentation' (1982) 45 MLR 138.

Treitel, G (1987) *The Law of Contract*, London: Sweet & Maxwell.

QUESTIONS

(1) In 'The Sad Tale of Angie and Georgie', could it be argued that any of the following are guilty of misrepresentation:

   (a) Ned and Monkish;

   (b) Claude;

   (c) Angie and Georgie?

   What would the parties to any action have to prove before their actions was successful?

(2) Over a year ago, Greene bought Powell's dental practice in the village of Hotwell. At the beginning of negotiations in October 1993, Powell assured Greene that there was no other practice within a 40 mile radius of the village and told him that the practice grossed about £30,000 per annum. He said Greene could examine the accounts for the last six years if he wished but Greene declined. Whilst he was thinking about the purchase, he met his brother-in-law, a dentist in Moorside (a town about 50 miles from Hotwell) and made casual enquiries as to whether he thought the practice would be a good buy.

   In fact, the practice had never grossed over £25,000 per annum. Furthermore, two months after the negotiations started (but before the sale was completed in mid-1994) a new practice opened up two miles away, taking many of Powell's patients. Powell did not tell Greene about this.

Greene raised a loan of £40,000 on which interest of £250 per month was payable, in order to finance the transaction (along with capital of his own which he had available).

Later in 1994, Greene found out that the rival practice had been set up and that Powell's practice could never have grossed £30,000. Nevertheless, he continued with the practice in the hope that he would be able to build it up. He has failed to do so despite considerable further injections of capital to buy new equipment. He wishes to take action against Powell. Advise Greene.

(3) In *Howard Marine & Dredging Co Ltd v Ogden & Sons (Excavations) Ltd* (1978), it was claimed that a statement (i) amounted to a collateral warranty, (ii) gave rise to a claim for damages under the Misrepresentation Act, and similarly (iii) for damages in negligence. There was little unanimity between the members of the Court of Appeal on these three claims. Where do you stand on these points?

(4) In what manner, if at all, does the measure of damages differ in cases of (a) fraudulent misrepresentation, (b) negligent misrepresentation, and (c) breach of contract?

(5) In an action in tort for negligent advice, it is not necessary to show that the statement complained of was a representation in the sense in which this term is understood in contract law. Discuss.

CHAPTER 10

MISTAKE

INTRODUCTION

We have already discovered that if two people appear, according to an objective test, to have reached an agreement supported by consideration, they are bound by it. But in certain limited circumstances the courts have been prepared to set contracts aside on the basis that there is no true agreement in reality because one or both of the parties were mistaken about something which strikes at the root of the contract. But the mistake doctrines discussed here remain narrow, despite the attempts of some members of the judiciary to expand them. In part this is because the judiciary has expressed discomfort with an expansive doctrine aimed at setting contracts aside. They have preferred instead to see themselves primarily as upholders of agreements and expectations.

The limited rationale for allowing certain contracts to be set aside came into the English common law from continental jurisprudence in the second part of the 19th century. Like the notion of intention to create legal relations, it grew out of strict 'consensus' or 'will' theory which insisted that obligations must be voluntary. If there were any factors present which vitiated consent, then this was considered fatal to the binding nature of the parties' agreement. In other words, contrary to the objective test which places emphasis on what the parties actually say and do rather than what they intended, there was a need for 'real', subjective concurrence of minds or intention. An early leading case of relevance is the House of Lords' decision in *Cundy v Lindsay* (1878). Simpson urges us to see this decision as an example of a case decided under the influence of a then 'full blown' consensus theory of contract. In that case it was argued, for instance, that: 'If contract requires *consensus ad idem*, there must be a real subjective concurrence of minds ... whatever the outward appearance if the parties were not in fact in agreement there is no contract.' This subjective approach to agreement has now been almost entirely superseded by the objective view of agreement but the vestiges of the theory remain in cases relating to mistake more than in any other contractual doctrine. In *Bell v Lever Bros Ltd* (1932), Lord Atkin said that 'If mistake operates at all, it operates to negative or nullify consent'.

The subject is one which is rife with decisions that are difficult to reconcile and in addition there is a wealth of 'explanatory' academic theory and counter theory on the issue. A disproportionate amount of time can be spent on mistake which will be of little commercial use. One can imagine a number of commercial situations in which mistakes might arise. So, for example, an offer on a cereal packet relating to trips to a theme park may be open to more than one interpretation with the result that the cereal company gets requests to supply cut price tickets from consumers it had not anticipated would qualify. The possibility of mistake being pleaded in such circumstances might be discussed by lawyers instructed by the cereal company, but it is unlikely to be favoured as a line of defence. This is because the threshold for proving mistake is extremely high. This explains why there is little modern case law. It is, then, a confused area of little business significance and only a few general introductory points will be made.

CATEGORIES OF MISTAKE

Two main types of mistake are discernible from the case law but in this chapter we are only concerned with the first type, which can be labelled 'agreement mistake'. The second type of mistake known as 'common' mistake or 'possibility mistake' is conceptually different. For that reason we discuss it in the chapter on impossibility where it is discussed alongside the connected doctrine of frustration. Agreement mistake, with which we are concerned here, occurs where the parties are at cross-purposes or one party is deceived by the other. So, for instance, in a cross-purposes case, Slapper Trains might offer to sell its fleet of excess trains to Europa Snail, a new rail operator. But it may be that Slapper are referring to old rolling stock whereas Europa Snail think they are negotiating about the latest models which Slapper will no longer need when a branch line is shut down (see Figure 10.1).

Figure 10.1: Agreement mistake: cross purposes

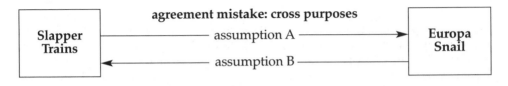

Alternatively, the agreement may be faulty because one party makes a mistake which the other is aware of but does not correct. This commonly happens in cases involving rogues and fraudsters where their intention is to defraud the other party. This type of mistake is often referred to as unilateral agreement mistake because only one party is mistaken and bears a close relation to the claims for fraudulent misrepresentation discussed in the last chapter. It might happen, for instance, where a fraudster pretends to be the Chief Executive of Slapper trains and Europa Snail enters into a contract with her as a result.

Figure 10.2: Agreement mistake: unilateral

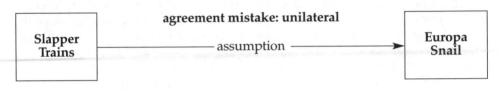

THE PARTICULAR PROBLEM OF MISTAKEN IDENTITY

Many of the cases about mistake involve situations in which a unilateral mistake comes about as a result of a fraudulent deception about the identity of one of the parties. As Lord Millett made clear in the House of Lords in *Shogun Finance Ltd v Hudson* (2003), the mistaken identity problem is far from being an esoteric one for academics. In the modern age of e-shopping and 'identity theft', impersonations and fraudulent purchases are on the increase. Case law suggests that a number of decisions in this category involve a fraudster obtaining valuable goods on credit by representing themselves as someone else, often against a worthless cheque. The fraudster then disposes of the goods to an innocent third party, for cash. A mistaken identity case might arise, for instance, where one party represents themselves as a well-known tennis player to a sports clothes designer in order to obtain their sports clothes at a significantly reduced price. The name of an actual player is assumed in order to inspire confidence in their fraudulent claim.

What can the deceived party do? It would be possible to bring an action for fraudulent misrepresentation against the rogue and claim damages or rescission. Unilateral agreement mistakes involving fraudsters bear many similarities to fraudulent misrepresentation discussed in Chapter 9 and the two heads are often pleaded in the alternative. In the cases in Chapter 9, the misrepresentation related to the attributes of the contractual subject matter such as a filling station's annual turnover of petrol. By way of contrast, mistake cases tend to focus on the notion of who a party is. The differences can be difficult to discern in practice and it has been argued that the distinction is meaningless, that a person cannot be distinguished from their qualities or attributes.

Either way, the remedies available for fraudulent misrepresentation are often not of much use because the fraudster will have disappeared without leaving a forwarding address! Instead, the action is usually brought by the person deceived against an innocent third party to whom the goods have been sold on. The action is not based directly on contract as there is no contractual relationship between the deceived and the third party. Instead, it is an action in the tort of conversion for recovery of the goods or their value based on the claim that the innocent third party cannot own them. It is argued that because the contract between the fraudster and the deceived was based on a fundamental mistake, then ownership did not pass to the fraudster. It follows that, as a result, they cannot have transferred ownership to the innocent third party. The dilemma faced by the courts is clear. Which of the two innocent parties should suffer for the dishonesty of the fraudster?

Understanding of the issues at stake also relies on an appreciation of the difference between contracts rendered void and those which are merely voidable. If the deceived can prove mistaken identity, their contract with the fraudster is void; it is treated as never having existed. As a result, neither the fraudster nor the innocent third party can obtain ownership of the goods. If the action rests on fraudulent misrepresentation, then the deceived's contract with the fraudster can, at best, be declared voidable. This means that the court can decide whether to treat it as though it never existed or allow it to live. But the involvement of an innocent third party also stops the deceived from avoiding the contract because an unchallenged contract between the deceived and the fraudster was in existence when the fraudster passed on ownership to the innocent third party. In this situation the court protects the interests of the innocent third party and will not upset the arrangement. As a result, it is the innocent third party who is able to retain the goods.

These points are illustrated in the leading case of *Cundy v Lindsay* (1878). The plaintiffs, Lindsay, received an order for goods from a fraudulent person, Blenkarn, who gave his address as 37 Wood Street, Cheapside. He signed his letter in such a way as to make it appear that the offer came from Blenkiron & Co, a firm known by reputation to the plaintiffs whose address was 123 Wood Street. The goods were despatched to Blenkiron & Co, 37 Wood Street. Blenkarn took possession of them but, without paying the plaintiffs, sold them to the defendants, who were sued by the plaintiffs for conversion. It was held that there was no contract between the plaintiffs and Blenkarn, and therefore no title to the goods passed to Blenkarn or consequently to the defendants, who were accordingly liable.

The court inferred that the plaintiffs intended to sell to Blenkiron & Co and not to the person who traded at 37 Wood Street. In other words, they thought they were accepting Blenkiron & Co's 'offer', as Blenkarn knew full well. As a result, there was no 'concurrence of minds', consent was negatived and no agreement arose between the plaintiffs and Blenkarn. Lord Cairns stated that 'The principal parties concerned ... never came into contact personally' and later, 'how is it possible to imagine that ... any contract could have arisen between the respondent Lindsay and Blenkarn, the dishonest man? Of him they knew nothing, and of him they never thought. With him they never intended to deal. Their minds never, even for an instant of time, rested upon him, and as between him and them there was no consensus of mind which could lead to any agreement'.

If, alternatively, the court had inferred that the plaintiffs, though misled by Blenkarn's fraud, had intended or at least were content to deal with the person at 37 Wood Street from which address the offer had come and to which the goods were sent, then there would have been a contract between the plaintiffs and Blenkarn. It would have been voidable for fraud but the defendants' title to the goods would have been secure since they would have acquired a good but voidable title from Blenkarn before the plaintiffs had avoided their contract with Blenkarn and so defeated any transfer of title. The reasoning in the case has not received universal support. Commentators have been concerned that a finding of mistaken identity unnecessarily prejudices third parties who later deal in good faith with the fraudulent person.

By highlighting the 'subjective concurrence of minds' basis of the decision in *Cundy*, it is not suggested that the 'no contract' ruling was wrong. For the case to remain relevant today we must ask from an objective viewpoint whether the plaintiffs had clearly shown that their intention was only to deal with Blenkiron & Co who were known to them. Thus, in line with what is now the basic test for establishing agreement, we must answer the following questions. Did Lindsay so conduct themselves that a reasonable person would think that they were accepting an offer from Blenkiron & Co? Moreover, did Blenkarn the rogue know, or ought he reasonably to have realised, that Lindsay were prepared only to contract with Blenkiron & Co? Put in this alternative way, in order to agree with the decision in the case, both questions must be answered in the affirmative.

It is clear from the decision in *Cundy* that the main stumbling block in the claimant's case is their need to overcome the legal presumption that, despite a mistake, the parties entered into a binding contract. In order to rebut the presumption, the claimant must prove that the person whose identity is assumed is a definite and identifiable person. In other words, the claimant must show that they intended to deal with a specific person other than the fraudster with whom they apparently made a contract. If there is no confusion between two distinct entities, there is no fundamental mistake. In addition, the claimant must prove that the other party was aware of their intention to deal with some person other than himself. This requirement is easily met where it is a fraudster who has induced the alleged mistake. The issue arose in the case of *King's Norton Metal Co Ltd v Edridge, Merrett & Co Ltd* (1897). Here a fraudster obtained goods from the plaintiff by business letter using the alias 'Hallam & Co'. Since the fraudster and 'Hallam & Co' were the same person, the plaintiff could not be said to have made a mistake of identity. The plaintiff did mistakenly believe that 'Hallam & Co' existed as a separate entity but was unable to show that they meant to contract with 'Hallam & Co' and not with the fraudster. They had taken a risk as to the credit-worthiness of the letter writer, with whom they had made a voidable contract on the basis of fraud but the contract was not void for mistake.

More recently, there has been a trend against finding an operative mistake in similar cases in favour of finding that there is a contract between the claimant and the rogue which is only voidable for fraud. There are a number of reasons for this. First, the courts are now primarily concerned with the objective 'outward and visible signs' of agreement and not with the presence of an 'inward and mental assent'. Moreover, in the significant 'mistake' cases since *Cundy*, the plaintiff and the rogue have dealt with each other face-to-face rather than through the medium of writing. In line with the objective view of agreement, a strong presumption has been developed to the effect that, when dealing face-to-face, the claimant intended to contract with the person physically present before them and identified by sight and hearing. So, for instance, in *Citibank NA v Brown Shipley & Co Ltd* (1991), Waller J stated that: 'The no contract situation, as opposed to a voidable contract, only arises if it is fundamental to the contract that one party to the contract should be who he says that he is. That is easier to establish where contracts are made entirely by documents and is less easy to establish in an *inter praesentes* position.'

Moreover, a Law Reform Committee Report of 1966 recommended 'that contracts which are at present void because the owner of the goods was deceived or mistaken as to the identity of the person with whom he dealt should in future be treated as voidable so far as third parties are concerned'. This recommendation has, however, never taken legislative effect. Whether these arguments render *Cundy* irrelevant or distinguishable from 'face-to-face' cases is debatable. What is clear is that the courts are more likely to place the claimant's behaviour under closer scrutiny. Situations in which the claimant has been careless in his dealings with the rogue are more likely to prompt the courts to decide in favour of third party rights. So, for instance, it has been argued that one should get a cheque cleared before parting with property worth several hundred pounds (see *Lewis v Averay* (1972) and *Gallie v Lee* (1971)). Further, it is established that the claimant must also prove that during negotiations and before entering into the contract, they regarded the 'identity' of the other contracting party as being of vital importance and indicated as such. They must also demonstrate that they took all reasonable steps to verify that 'identity'.

The outcome of judicial analysis is that a mistake of identity occurs where the victim confuses the attributes of two particular persons. But the expectation is that to be successful the claimant must be independently aware of some of the attributes of the person the rogue is pretending to be. In other words, they must be aware of the existence of a famous tennis player with the name being used by the rogue or that a reputable company called Blenkiron exists. Moreover, the attributes being claimed or inferred must be important in the context of the deal. So, for instance, if the tennis wear designer referred to above was giving substantial discounts to anyone who approached them then they could not rely on the doctrine of mistake to help them set aside the contract. What the cases seem to show is that the claimant's mistake as regards the attribute of credit-worthiness is not one which can be relied upon to negate consent. The credit-worthiness of a party can be checked. But what has tended to happen is that the claimant relies on their own personal and mistaken judgment to assess credit-worthiness and so takes a deliberate business risk. The result is that the courts have decided that they, and not an innocent third party, must bear the loss.

When we come to the actual decisions and the reasoning of the various courts in the mistaken identity cases, there are problems of reconciling one decision with another and of establishing the principles upon which the courts are proceeding. It is useful to start with a key case, *Lewis v Averay*, decided by the Court of Appeal in 1972. In that case, Lewis advertised his car for sale and was approached by a fraudster who falsely claimed to be Richard Greene, a film and television actor. When the fraudster wrote a cheque for £450, Lewis, on asking for proof that he was Greene, was shown a film studio pass with the name 'Richard A Green' and the fraudster's photograph. Lewis took the cheque signed 'RA Green' and the fraudster took the car. The fraudster then sold the car to Averay who bought it in good faith. The cheque was subsequently dishonoured and Lewis sought to recover the car from Averay. It was held that the contract was not void for mistake and that title in the car had passed to Averay.

The reason for this outcome was that the presumption was that the plaintiff intended to contract with the person physically before them. However, the contract was considered to be voidable for fraud. In his judgment, Lord Denning took into account the rights and needs of innocent third parties. He contrasted the position of the innocent third party, who knew nothing of what had passed between Lewis and the fraudster, and the position of Lewis 'who let the rogue have the goods and thus enabled him to commit the fraud'. Lewis's mistake was as to credit-worthiness and it is clear that he did less than was reasonable to establish that the fraudster was Greene. Even if he was, that was no guarantee that the cheque would be honoured. In order to reinforce his approach, Denning also expressed agreement with the Law Reform Committee's recommendation of 1966 to the effect that contracts entered into in these circumstances should be voidable so far as the acquisition of title by innocent third parties was concerned.

Similar issues have arisen in other cases. In *Phillips v Brooks Ltd* (1919), a rogue entered the plaintiff's shop and selected pearls worth £2,550 and a ring worth £450. He wrote a cheque for £3,000, stating that he was Sir George Bullough of St James' Square, a wealthy man known by name to the plaintiff. Phillips checked the address in a directory and, at the rogue's request, allowed him to take away the ring. The rogue pawned the ring with Brooks Ltd and the cheque he gave to Phillips was subsequently dishonoured. Horridge J held that Phillips had 'contracted to sell and deliver [the ring] to the person who came into his shop ... who obtained the sale and delivery by means of the false pretence that he was Sir George Bullough'. In his analysis the judge started by considering the *prima facie* legal presumption about face-to-face dealing. He argued that the plaintiff's intention was 'to sell to the person present and identified by sight and hearing'. Moreover, the jeweller had failed to prove that he intended to contract with Bullough and with nobody else. His looking up the address was scarcely sufficient to verify the rogue's claim. In summary, the plaintiff took a risk as regards credit-worthiness and his case failed. The contract was voidable for fraud rather than void for mistake and had not, in this case, been avoided in time to defeat the defendant's title (see also *Shogun Finance Ltd v Hudson* (2003) on this point).

The importance of placing emphasis on distinguishing between the type of action proven and whether this rendered the contract void or voidable has been criticised elsewhere. Adopting a different stress in *Ingram v Little* (1961), Devlin LJ expressed the view in his dissenting judgment that:

> ... the relevant question in this sort of case is not whether the contract was void or voidable, but which of two innocent parties shall suffer for the fraud of a third. The plain answer is that the loss should be divided between them in such proportion as is just in all the circumstances ... if the fault or imprudence of either party has caused or contributed to the loss, it should be borne by that party in the whole or in the greater part.

This suggestion, with its relevance to apportionment, was found to be 'plainly attractive at first sight' by the Law Reform Committee in 1966. Nonetheless, it was rejected by them as leading in some cases to 'uncertainty' consequent upon 'a wide and virtually unrestrained judicial discretion'. Problems were seen in particular where the goods passed from the rogue to an innocent purchaser and then on to subsequent innocent parties.

CONCLUDING REMARKS

It is clear from this chapter that the law of mistake is a complex and intricate subject. Given the paucity of cases on the subject it is questionable as to whether it is essential to study the topic in any depth in an introductory text of this kind. For that reason, treatment of the subject has not been comprehensive. Instead, we have tried to introduce some key themes which will encourage students to think about the subjective and objective tests of agreement, the extent to which third party rights should affect the remedies of the main parties to the contract, the ways in which issues relating to formation of contracts overlap and the issue of how risk should be allocated between the parties when something goes wrong. In the chapter which follows we shall go on to develop some of these themes in the context of fairness in the bargaining process.

REFERENCES AND FURTHER READING

Greig, D 'The passing of property and the misidentified buyer' (1972) 35 MLR 306.

Jackson, B (1988) *Law, Fact and Narrative Coherence* Liverpool: Deborah Charles.

Sutton, P 'Reform of the law of mistake in contract' (1976) New Zealand Universities Law Review 40.

Williams, G 'Mistake as to party in the law of contract' (1945) Canadian Bar Review 271, 380.

Wheeler, S and Shaw, J (1994) *Contract Law: Cases, Materials and Commentary*, Oxford: Oxford University Press.

QUESTIONS

(1) Could any of the contracts in 'The Sad Tale of Angie and Georgie' be set aside on the grounds of mistake? What would the disadvantages of bringing such an action be?

(2) Appraise critically the argument put forward by Adams and Brownsword that mistake is not to be used as an excuse for bad bargains and nor is it to be allowed to jeopardise the security of market transactions.

CHAPTER 11

THE IMPOSSIBILITY DOCTRINES

INTRODUCTION

The vast majority of business agreements proceed to satisfactory completion without disputes arising or claims that there has been a breach, but some commercial ventures may be thwarted because of something happening which is beyond the contracting parties' control. So, for instance, the goods contracted for may have perished, making performance impossible. Alternatively, war may unexpectedly break out in a country in which components are being made for a UK-based computer company. This may make it difficult for the manufacturer to make or deliver the components. Moreover, if the war is with the UK, what constituted a legal and legitimate contract for the supply of the components on Monday suddenly becomes trading with the enemy on Tuesday and is rendered unlawful. Events of this kind may render performance of the contract impossible, difficult or illegal. How do the courts respond to such unexpected circumstances? Are the parties absolved from responsibility to perform their contract or do the courts hold them to their contract? What happens where the parties have already begun performance or been involved in a significant financial outlay in anticipation of performance?

COMMON OR POSSIBILITY MISTAKE

In Chapter 10 we looked at the problems surrounding agreement mistakes and indicated that a second category of mistake existed which involved a situation where both parties share a common misapprehension. This would be the case, for instance, where oranges have, unbeknown to either party, perished while their sale was being negotiated or if Slapper Trains' whole fleet is destroyed by fire as the talks about their sale take place. For this reason, this type of mistake is often referred to as common or possibility mistake, although the use of nomenclature differs considerably between commentators.

Figure 11.1: Possibility mistake

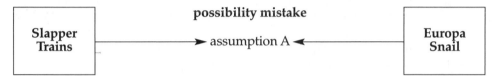

The problem which arises in such instances is that it is impossible to perform the contract. What distinguishes this type of impossibility from the doctrine of frustration discussed in later sections is timing. Possibility mistake occurs because the contract has been negotiated on a mistaken assumption about the existence or quality of the consideration. In cases of frustration the contract is capable of being performed at the time it is made, but a subsequent event renders it impossible or futile. However, the main problem with possibility mistake, as in cases of frustration, lies in deciding when an incorrect assumption is sufficiently fundamental for the courts to justify setting the contract aside. As regards mistake, the weight of opinion is that a contract will only be void in such circumstances where there is in fact nothing to contract about and the agreement is devoid of all content.

For some years there has been disagreement between commentators and members of the judiciary as to whether there is a second doctrine of common mistake founded in equity which allows the courts to intervene in circumstances where the contract would not be rendered void by the common law. The decision in *Bell v Lever Bros Ltd* (1932) suggests that this is not the case, but Lord Denning argued in *Solle v Butcher* (1950) that the court did have this power and that common mistake could also render a contract *voidable*. In contrast to void contracts, those rendered voidable can be set aside at the discretion of the courts. The more recent decision of the Court of Appeal in *Great Peace Shipping Ltd v Tsavliris Salvage (International) Ltd* (2002) makes clear that this is not an appropriate statement of law. Applying *Bell v Lever*, the judges argued that there was no equitable jurisdiction in cases of common mistake and that the judgment in *Solle* had been an attempt to usurp the common law. The equitable doctrine envisaged by Denning was seen as bearing no difference to the common law doctrine and could not be used to revive a contract which the common law considered never to have existed. However, they argued *per curiam* that there was scope for the legislature to intervene to mitigate the harshness of the common law. We wait to see whether the legislature will take up the challenge.

In the *Great Peace* case, the defendants offered salvage services to a vessel in distress. The offer was accepted and the defendants approached a merchant vessel which they both believed to be 35 miles from the ship in distress. They entered into negotiations and concluded a contract but then discovered that the merchant ship was actually 410 miles away. However, the defendants did not cancel the contract until they had found an alternative ship to undertake the work. When challenged they pleaded fundamental mistake of fact and that the contract was either void or voidable at law. The court found in favour of the merchant vessel.

The judgment makes clear that the test for common mistake is extremely narrow. In a lengthy judgment, the judges rejected the contention that the doctrine was based on the notion of an implied term that the contract would be rendered void in the circumstances which had occurred, as had been argued. It was argued that the circumstances were far removed from the contemplation of the parties that it was something of a falsity to imply agreement about such a term. In finding for the merchant shipowners they were influenced by the fact that the ship could still have played a part in the rescue operation even though it was so far away, whereas the test for common mistake was that the circumstances had to render performance impossible rather than something which was just substantially different.

THE DOCTRINE OF FRUSTRATION

It has been argued that the security of contract is increasingly affected by the spread of such political, economic and social upheavals as war, strikes, revolution or rampant inflation. Globalisation of markets has contributed to this as more and more businesses form links with contractors in other States. The courts have responded to such problems by developing the doctrine of frustration, known elsewhere as the impossibility doctrine. Like the doctrine of mistake which deals with a pre-existing impossibility problem, the doctrine of frustration is a narrow one. This is because the courts have been reluctant to allow the parties to escape their obligations to each other in anything but the most extreme circumstances. A claim that a contract has been frustrated will not be successful, for instance, when one party merely finds performance difficult or unprofitable, although it is often pleaded in such circumstances in an attempt to avoid contractual obligations. The courts have preferred to see the doctrine as one of last resort which should be used rarely and with reluctance.

There are few modern authorities that deal with the doctrine and trainee lawyers will not hear frustration being discussed with clients on a regular basis. Neither are there any empirical studies of the doctrine which allow us to place the formal law in its social, political or economic context. However, the doctrine of frustration remains important because it provides an example of the importance of planning contractual performance in advance. The allocation of commercial risk is something that all contractors are interested in and often bears a close relation to the price to be paid. Careful drafting and allocation of risk prior to performance means that the parties can often avoid the need for costly litigation should something unpredictable happen to disrupt the contract.

THE BASIC TENETS OF THE DOCTRINE

Taylor v Caldwell (1863) is generally acknowledged to be the first case which heralded the introduction of a general principle of frustration and provides a good example of the use of the doctrine as a defence to a claim of breach of contract. In this case Caldwell agreed on 27 May to let Taylor have the use of the Surrey Music Hall at £100 per day for four concerts. The first of the concerts was to be held on 17 June but on 11 June the Hall was accidentally burnt down and it became clear that the parties had made no provision in the contract for such a contingency. Taylor claimed damages in respect of wasted advertising expenses but it was held that the contract was discharged by frustration and that Caldwell was not liable. Blackburn outlined the reasons for the decision:

> Where, from the nature of the contract, it appears that the parties must from the beginning have known that it could not be fulfilled unless ... some particular specified thing continued to exist, so that, when entering into the contract, they must have contemplated such continuing existence as the foundation of what was to be done; there ... the parties shall be excused in case, before breach, performance becomes impossible from the perishing of the thing without the fault of the contractor.

Subsequent leading judgements were keen to make the point that the doctrine is a restrictive one. In *Davis Contractors Ltd v Fareham UDC* (1956), Davis in effect agreed to build Fareham UDC 78 houses in eight months for £92,000. Serious shortages of labour and materials resulted in the contract taking 22 months to complete and costing Davis £18,000 more than estimated. Davis claimed that the contract had been frustrated by economic conditions and that as a consequence he was not bound by the agreed price. Instead he claimed a larger sum for services rendered on a *quantum meruit* basis. The

House of Lords held that the delay caused did not mean that the basis of the contract was displaced. Lord Radcliffe famously explained the basic tenets underpinning the doctrine when he said that:

> ... frustration occurs whenever the law recognises that without default of either party a contractual obligation has become incapable of being performed because the circumstances in which performance is called would render it a thing radically different from that which was undertaken by the contract ... The court must act upon a general impression of what its rule requires ... But, even so, it is not hardship or inconvenience or material loss itself which calls the principle of frustration into play. There must be as well such a change in the significance of the obligation that the thing undertaken would, if performed, be a different thing from that contracted for.

In this case the thing contracted for was 78 houses. These had been built so, in the circumstances, the court considered it appropriate that the risk fell upon the builder.

In 1981, in *National Carriers Ltd v Panalpina (Northern) Ltd*, the House of Lords upheld Lord Radcliffe's 'radical change in the obligation' test, which was restated by Lord Simon as follows:

> Frustration of a contract takes place when there supervenes an event (without default of either party and for which the contract makes no sufficient provision) which so significantly changes the nature (not merely the expense or onerousness) of the outstanding contractual rights and/or obligations from what the parties could reasonably have contemplated at the time of its execution that it would be unjust to hold them to the literal sense of its stipulations in the new circumstances; in such a case the law declares both parties to be discharged from further performance.

In the same case, Lord Hailsham identified a number of different ways of justifying the setting aside of the contract in such circumstances. These included the inclusion of an implied term in the contract to the effect that if the parties had known what was going to happen they would have assumed that the contract should have been terminated. Alternatively, he said it could be argued that the contract should be set aside because of a total failure of consideration. He noted that broader concepts employed by the judiciary to rationalise interference included a requirement that justice be done in these exceptional cases or the assumption of an obligation to search for the real 'meaning' of the contract.

Unfortunately, the vast majority of frustration cases are not clear-cut. They frequently concern pleas of commercial futility brought about by a wide variety of political, economic or other disabling factors rather than the more obvious physical impossibility of the type in *Taylor v Caldwell*. So, for instance, in *Krell v Henry* (1903), Henry hired rooms in Pall Mall at a high price for the purpose of viewing the coronation procession of Edward VII. The procession was cancelled owing to the King's illness but Krell sued for the hire charge and the doctrine of frustration was pleaded in defence. The court held that Krell's claim failed. The contract had been frustrated and was therefore void. In their opinion it was the coronation procession and the relative position of the rooms which was the basis of the contract rather than the value of having a hired room (see also *Amalgamated Investment & Property Co Ltd v John Walker & Sons Ltd* (1977)).

However, in another 'coronation case', *Herne Bay Steam Boat Co v Hutton* (1903), Herne Bay Steam Boat Company hired a boat in order to offer cruises on coronation day. The aim of the trip was to see the royal naval review which had been organised to celebrate the coronation together with a day's travelling around the fleet at Spithead.

In contrast to *Krell v Henry*, which involved the same frustrating event, the contract was held not to be frustrated when the royal review was cancelled because of the King's indisposition. The reason given by the court was that in this case the royal review was not the sole basis of the contract. As Sir Frederick Pollock said: 'In point of fact the fleet was still there and it was very well worth seeing without the review.'

At first glance the cases seem difficult to reconcile but it has been argued that they can be distinguished by reference to the relative economic positions of the parties. In *Krell v Henry* it was a consumer who would have suffered had the contract not been frustrated. In the latter case it was a businessman taking advantage of a commercial opportunity and charging a high price for the cruise who would have had to bear the risk. Moreover, Brownsword has argued that the real problem Hutton was trying to avoid was the fact that insufficient people were willing to pay high prices for the trip. The cases demonstrate the point that the doctrine of frustration will not be invoked to allow a party to escape from a contract, the basic obligation of which has not been displaced but which has merely become a bad bargain for him.

A number of frustration cases also arose as a result of the closure of the Suez Canal in 1956. In these cases a fine distinction was made between the main purpose of the contract and *the way* in which the seller was to carry out this basic obligation. So, for instance, in *Tsakiroglou & Co Ltd v Noblee Thorl GmbH* (1962), Tsakiroglou agreed to ship groundnuts to Noblee Thorl in Hamburg from Port Sudan. The agreement was made in line with international standard form contracts known as 'cif' contracts. It was agreed that shipment was to be made during November and December 1956 but no specific delivery date was named. Following the closure of the Suez Canal in early November, Tsakiroglou made no effort to ship the goods and, when sued for damages, pleaded frustration. It was held that the closure of the canal did not fundamentally alter the contractual obligation into one of a different character. The thing undertaken was still the same. The carrier could still ship goods from Port Sudan to Hamburg, albeit under the changed circumstances, by a lengthier and more expensive voyage round the Cape of Good Hope. As a result, the court held that Tsakiroglou was liable to pay £5,600 damages to Noblee Thorl for breach of contract. It has been said that it would require circumstances such as a contract to carry perishable goods from Port Sudan to Alexandria to bring about frustration in such a case.

Delay is frequently a factor in frustration cases. It may be, for example, that goods cannot be shipped on time because flooding prevents them reaching the port of loading, a strike holds up their movement, or the government requisitions the delivery vessels. But again, delay only frustrates a contract when it defeats the commercial venture. As Lord Roskill made clear in *The Nema* (1981): 'Whether or not the delay is such as to bring about frustration must be a question to be determined by an informed judgment based upon all the evidence of what has occurred and what is likely thereafter to occur.' This exercise involves the court trying to determine how long the delay is likely to occur and whether one of the parties can reasonably be asked to wait for a delayed performance. The task is an extremely difficult one as judges, like the contracting parties themselves, cannot see into the future. This point is illustrated in *Tamplin SS Co Ltd v Anglo-Mexican Petroleum Co Ltd* (1916), where a five year delivery by sea agreement signed in December 1912 was disrupted when the government requisitioned the vessel for war service in February 1915. The majority of the court felt that it was likely *at the time the case was decided* that the vessel would be released in time to render further substantial services under the contract. On that basis the contract was not held to have been frustrated even though the contract was in fact delayed for longer.

In an effort to clarify the position, distinctions have been made between indefinite delays and temporary interruptions. In *Metropolitan Water Board v Dick, Kerr & Co Ltd* (1918), Dick, Kerr agreed in 1914 to build a reservoir at Staines for the Metropolitan Water Board. The work was to be completed in six years but in 1916 the Ministry of Munitions ordered the work to stop and Dick, Kerr to sell all disposable plant. It was held that the interruption created by the statutory order was of such a character and probable duration as to make the contract, if resumed, a different contract from that entered into. It would seem then that where indefinite delay, as opposed to temporary interruption, is all that can be envisaged for the parties from the time of the intervening act then the contract is discharged by frustration. It is not the case that the contract is definitely impossible to perform some time in the future, such as when peace is restored, but that, in the circumstances, it is not reasonable to hold the parties to their obligations in the new circumstances.

The discharge of a contract through supervening *illegality* is justified on different grounds. Where, for instance, war breaks out between the two States in which the contracting parties are based or a statutory ban is placed on trading certain produce, such as red meat, then the use of the doctrine is explained by reference to public policy and not by physical impossibility or even a radical change from the original obligation. Instead, it is reasoned that there cannot be default in not doing what the law forbids to be done. So, for instance, in *Fibrosa Spolka Akcyjna v Fairbairn Lawson Combe Barbour Ltd* (1943), the export of textile machinery to Lithuania via the port of Gdynia was held to be frustrated by the occupation of that port by German troops in September 1939.

LIMITATIONS ON THE DOCTRINE

We have already seen that the doctrine does not apply in situations where the alleged frustrating event does not displace the basic obligation of the contract but merely makes its performance more onerous or expensive for one party. But other limitations also apply. The doctrine does not operate where the alleged frustrating event is the result of a party's own voluntary act or negligence. So, for example, in *The Eugenia* (1964), it was stated that a charterer who ordered a vessel into a war zone, with the result that she was detained, could not rely on the detention as the basis for frustration of a contract of hire. This was because the detention was due to the charterer's action, which was interpreted as a breach of contract in the circumstances and an instance of 'self-induced frustration'.

The leading case on the notion of 'self-induced frustration' is *Maritime National Fish Ltd v Ocean Trawlers Ltd* (1935). In this case, Ocean Trawlers operated five trawlers for fishing with otter trawls. Three of the trawlers were owned by Ocean Trawlers and of the other two, one was called the *St Cuthbert* and was chartered from Maritime National Fish. In order to use the otter trawls a licence was required from the Canadian government and as a result of a change in government policy, Ocean Trawlers was granted only three licences. They allocated two to their own vessels and one to the chartered vessel *not* owned by Maritime National Fish. When challenged, Ocean Trawlers argued that the charter of Maritime National Fish's vessel was frustrated. This claim was rejected by the Privy Council because the frustration was taken to be 'self-induced'. In the court's view it was this act and election of Ocean Trawlers which prevented the *St Cuthbert* from being licensed for fishing with an otter trawl rather than the action of the government. In other words, Ocean Trawlers could have allocated one of the three licences to the *St Cuthbert* rather than to one of their own vessels. The supervening event was not beyond their control and so did not frustrate the contract.

The rather harsh rule has been applied elsewhere. In *The Super Servant Two (Lauritzen AS v Wijsmuller BV)* (1990), a shipowner lost one of his two vessels capable of transporting oil drilling rigs. This meant that a contract for the transportation of the plaintiffs' rig from Japan to Rotterdam could not be performed because the defendants' other vessel was being used to perform other contracts. The defendants claimed that the contract was frustrated but the plaintiffs argued that the impossibility sprang from the defendants' own decision regarding their 'election' to use their remaining vessel on other work. The Court of Appeal held that although the defendants were neither negligent nor in breach of contract as regards their allocation of duties, the problems were not sufficient to render the contract frustrated. Such interpretations of events are not without their critics. It has been argued that where a party has entered into a number of contracts, supervening events may deprive them of the power of performing them all, without depriving them of the power of performing some of them. It could be submitted that frustration should not be excluded by a party's 'election' where their only choice was which of two contracts to frustrate. See also *Constantine (Joseph) SS Line Ltd v Imperial Smelting Corp Ltd* (1942).

The courts have also refused to apply the doctrine where the parties have clearly foreseen the precise risk but have nevertheless gambled on its non-occurrence, although this restriction has been applied narrowly. For example, the fact that the parties foresee and provide for a possible delay does not prevent frustration if the delay which actually occurs is of a totally different order of magnitude which was not foreseen. Also, where the contract is rendered illegal as a matter of public policy, foreseeability does not prevent frustration if to allow continuance of the contract would, as seen in the *Fibrosa Spolka* case, involve giving assistance to an enemy economy. Finally, the doctrine does not generally apply where the parties have made express provision for the event which occurs. Here it is the contract which will govern the position. Since this involves contractual planning this is an issue to which we turn in the final sections of this chapter after considering the impact of statutory intervention in the field.

THE LAW REFORM (FRUSTRATED CONTRACTS) ACT 1943

Even where the contract is brought to an end by the operation of the doctrine of frustration, the aim of the law is to allocate or distribute the loss brought about by the supervening event. The Law Reform (Frustrated Contracts) Act 1943 improved on earlier common law rules and now governs such circumstances. According to the Act, the court's decision that a frustrating event took place means that the contract is automatically brought to an end *from the time of frustration*. What was a binding contract becomes void and the parties are excused from further performance by operation of law. The Act also deals with liabilities arising in the period during which the contract subsisted, between agreement and the time of the frustrating event.

During this time, work may have been undertaken, expenses incurred, and advance payments made. In these circumstances the Act seeks to achieve a just settlement between the parties. The effect of the Act is that:

(a) money *paid* before the frustrating event is recoverable whether performance is total or partial;

(b) money *payable* before the frustrating event, but not in fact paid, ceases to be payable;

(c) a party who has incurred *expenses* in performance of the contract prior to its discharge may, at the court's discretion, be awarded those expenses. However, they can only be awarded up to a maximum of *sums paid or payable* under the contract before the frustrating event occurred. In exercising this discretion, the court or arbitrator can split the loss in such proportions as they think just. They will be influenced by the extent to which the expenses have been rendered useless following frustration. So, for instance, very little will be awarded if the expenses have been incurred in manufacturing machinery for one party can readily be sold to another;

(d) a party who has gained a *valuable benefit* other than money under the contract before the frustrating event may be required to pay a just sum for it. In *BP Exploration Co (Libya) Ltd v Hunt (No 2)* (1979), Robert Goff J explained 'the fundamental principle underlying the Act itself is prevention of the unjust enrichment of either party to the contract at the other's expense'.

However, the Act does not apply to all contracts. Excluded from its remit are voyage charterparties and other contracts for the carriage of goods by sea, contracts of insurance and certain contracts for the sale of goods where the goods have perished. This has been justified on the basis that common law rules which were well-known and respected in these areas needed to be preserved. Most importantly for present purposes, s 2(3) of the Act provides that where the parties have included a clause in the contract which determines what should happen if an event renders performance impossible or difficult, then this clause will take precedence over the Act. As Lord Denning made clear in *The Eugenia* (1964), 'To see if the doctrine [of frustration] applies, you have first to construe the contract and see whether the parties have themselves provided for the situation that has arisen. If they have provided for it, the contract must govern. There is no frustration'. However, there are exceptions to this provision. The first is where frustration renders a contract illegal. The second, as Lord Denning implies, is where the clause is incomplete or narrowly construed and cannot, on the reading of the contract, be said to cover the situation which has arisen (see, for instance, the *Metropolitan Water Board* case).

CONTRACTUAL PLANNING AND THE ALLOCATION OF RISK

Risk is a familiar concept in the business community. Business people deal with it on a day-to-day basis and the allocation of risk is a crucial part of the bargaining process. It can never be eliminated. A person who makes a contract can never can be absolutely certain that they will be able to perform it when the time comes. Instead the very essence of it is that a contractor takes the risk as part of the deal struck.

However, business people have shown themselves reluctant to run the risk of a contract being set aside by the court through no fault of their own. While a frustrating event or circumstance may be beyond their control, it is nonetheless possible for them to use the contract to plan what arrangements may govern the aftermath. It may be difficult to predict the unusual but it is possible to organise obligations in the contract in a way which makes it clear who shall bear the burden of contractual performance becoming difficult or impossible. It is also logical to suppose that in most deals the party who takes more risks can expect to negotiate a lower price. Indeed, one of the incentives for determining what will happen in the event that something unlikely or unpredictable occurs is that it will normally affect the price of the contract, so someone who is risk averse will prefer to pay more under the contract and be sure that their interests are protected whatever happens. Moreover, businesses are constantly sensitive to new risks. So, for example, after the 1956 closure of the Suez Canal, sellers began to stipulate for a 'Cape Surcharge' to be paid by the buyer if the Canal was closed again, as it was in 1967 (see *Henry Ltd v Clasen* (1973)). Similarly, Davis Contractors were in a position to, and had tried to, protect themselves by a letter stating that their tender was subject to adequate supplies of labour and materials being available, or by the use of price fluctuation and extension of time clauses.

It would seem, then, that this is an area of contract in which careful wording of contractual terms is of the essence. So, for example, a seller who needs an export licence in order to ship goods assumes a greater risk if they agree to 'deliver as soon as licence granted', which would be interpreted as an absolute undertaking, than if they agreed to a conditional obligation to 'deliver subject to licence'. In the first instance, if the seller fails to get a licence they will be liable in damages for the buyer's lost expectations; in the second, if they fail after reasonable efforts to obtain a licence, they will not be liable. Where the parties expressly allocate risk and loss in the contract, or apportion it between them, their agreed terms will govern the situation if the contingency arises. For this reason, the doctrine of frustration is properly limited to contingencies not specifically provided for in the contract. If the change in circumstances could lead to a successful plea of frustration, but the parties have nevertheless properly provided for the supervening event which has arisen, then their contractual terms will govern the situation (see s 2(3) of the Law Reform (Frustrated Contracts) Act 1943). As Lord Wilberforce has argued when outlining the policy behind the Unfair Contract Terms Act, 'in commercial matters generally, where the parties are not of unequal bargaining power, and where risks are normally borne by insurance, not only is the case for judicial intervention undemonstrated, but there is everything to be said ... for leaving the parties free to apportion the risks as they think fit and for respecting their decision'.

The application of the doctrine of frustration to an event which has occurred and which is now the subject matter of litigation rests, of course, in the hands of the courts and it is often a difficult question as to whether the doctrine does or does not apply. Therefore, the prudent business person may well consider it wiser to introduce into their contract a clause defining *in advance* the rights and duties of the parties if certain events beyond their control occur. This is the case *whether or not* such events would result, in legal terms, in frustration of the contract. A clause should also provide an agreed basis for assessing the allocation of risk and expense following delay or cancellation. Alternatively, the question of risk and additional expense or loss may be covered by an appropriate clause relating to insurance coverage. Such a clause is generally known as a *force majeure* clause and it is the prime example of what Macaulay describes as planning for contingencies. The practice of including such clauses in contracts has gained official recognition in the UNIDROIT Principles of International Commercial Contracts which sets out best practice in modern international contracts. According to Art 6, non-performance is excused if one party can prove that it was caused by an unpredictable impediment.

By way of contrast a 'hardship' clause serves a different purpose from a *force majeure* clause and operates in the context of long-term contracts such as those involving the construction of works, or crude oil or natural gas supply. In the face of unforeseen and fundamental changes in circumstances the parties may not want to bring the contract to an end either by invoking a *force majeure* clause or by litigation involving a plea of frustration. The problem is that English courts have no power to adapt the terms of long-term contracts in such situations. However, by including a hardship clause the parties can make allowance to re-negotiate their contract so as to minimise losses and avoid undue hardship. As Trakman (1983) has explained:

> Businessmen often prefer to modify rather than to terminate their arrangements in the face of disruptions of trade. They choose to increase or decrease their contract price ... or alter the quality of their performance because part-performance is usually better than non-performance. They modify their promises because salvaging segments of a contract is preferable to salvaging no segments at all.

FORCE MAJEURE CLAUSES

The expression *force majeure* has been judicially defined to cover all circumstances beyond the will of contractors, which it is not in their power to control, and such *force majeure* is sufficient to justify the non-execution of a contract. Although the wording of these clauses varies according to the nature of the contract, as regards contracts for the international sale of goods they usually contain a list of possible *force majeure* events capable of impeding or preventing performance, together with a 'sweeping up' phrase designed to ensure that there are no gaps in the formula. For example, a clause of this kind might read:

> Strikes, lockouts, labour disturbances, anomalous working conditions, accident to machinery, delays en route, policies or restrictions of governments, including restrictions of export and other licences, *or any other contingency whatsoever beyond seller's control*, including war, are sufficient excuse for any delay or non-fulfilment traceable to any of these causes.

The purpose of these clauses is not to have the contract set aside immediately. Instead, it is typical for *force majeure* clauses to suspend performance for an agreed period of time whilst requiring that each party is under a duty to keep each other notified as regards their respective positions. Once this agreed period of time has elapsed, one party will then have a right to exercise an option to cancel the contract. This can be invoked on the occurrence of a contingency which might or might not call for frustration in the legal sense. The risk, or loss contingent upon invoking the clause, may again be allocated by the parties under the terms of the clause, whether the contract is cancelled or not. *Force majeure* clauses provide for the parties to suspend or cancel the contract depending on the circumstances.

However, careful planning does not necessarily keep you out of court. In *Czarnikow Ltd v Rolimpex* (1978), Rolimpex, a Polish foreign trading organisation, agreed to sell 200,000 tons of sugar to Czarnikow as part of the annual export quota. In Polish law Rolimpex had a separate legal entity, distinct from the government, although it was subject to ministerial directions. The rules of the Refined Sugar Association were incorporated into the contract and rule 18(a) provided that if delivery was prevented by 'government intervention beyond the seller's control', the contract would be void without penalty. The seller was made responsible for obtaining the requisite export licence under rule 21. The contract stipulated that failure to obtain such a licence was not 'sufficient grounds for a claim of *force majeure* if the regulations in force ... when the contract was made, called for such licences to be obtained'. The 1974 crop was poor and was needed for domestic consumption. A ministerial resolution imposed an immediate ban on all sugar exports. On the same date a formal decree was issued giving legal effect to the ban, though it did not revoke the export licences already ordered in compliance with rule 21. In reliance on the *force majeure* clause, Rolimpex informed Czarnikow that the contract could not be fulfilled and the dispute was referred to arbitrators in London, who, relying on rule 18(a), found in Rolimpex's favour.

On appeal it was held that, first, the arbitrators had established that Rolimpex was not an organ of the Polish government but an independent State organisation. The contract was therefore frustrated by 'government intervention' within rule 18(a) and was *not* self-induced, as it would have been if they had been part of the government. Rolimpex was accordingly relieved of liability under the contract. Secondly, the obligation under rule 21 to 'obtain' the requisite export licence implied no obligation to maintain it in force; Rolimpex was not thereby precluded from relying on rule 18(a).

In *Toepfer v Cremer* (1975), the seller sold the buyer 5,000 tons of soya bean meal. The contract was on the Grain and Feed Trade Association Ltd Form No 100, which contained a *force majeure* clause entitling the seller to an extension of time for shipment and a clause which stated that, in the event of default by the seller, the damages were to be based upon the actual or estimated value of the goods 'on date of default'. The goods were to be shipped by 30 April 1973 but the worst floods on the Mississippi for over 20 years caused great delays to shipping. On 16 May the seller invoked the *force majeure* clause, and by an extension notice informed the buyer that he intended to ship the goods from 'Mississippi port(s)'. The date of shipment was thereby extended to 31 May, with a further extension, at the buyer's option, to 30 June, which was the latest date for shipment. If goods of the contract description had been shipped by 30 June, the seller could have fulfilled their contract, provided the buyer had been so notified by 10 July. The seller did not ship the goods. The buyer claimed damages for non-delivery and, the market price having risen, contended that the date of default was 10 July. The seller maintained that the date of default was another, earlier time and that their extension notice was bad because it did not state any definite port. The Court of Appeal held that damages would be assessed on the basis that the date of default was 10 July, for that was the last day for the performance of the contract. The extension notice was valid, for it was perfectly possible for the seller to intend to ship at one of the ports on the Mississippi. Further, since the seller had themselves invoked the *force majeure* clause and had given the extension notice, they could not be permitted to say that the notice was bad.

CONCLUDING REMARKS

In this chapter we have looked at two doctrines which practitioners will have little cause to use. Not only are the disastrous array of events detailed in the case law unlikely to happen on a regular basis but the doctrines are designed to deter excessive use of the power of the court to set a contract aside. Regular attempts have been made to expand the doctrines in an attempt to help parties who through no fault of their own find themselves to have suffered loss, but these attempts, though understandable, have met with mixed success. However, the most important aspect of the discussion in this chapter has been the focus on risk and planning which are central to an understanding of the interface between law and economics. The fact that contracts, however carefully planned, cannot anticipate everything that will happen is an important reminder of the need for flexibility in contractual relations discussed in earlier chapters.

REFERENCES AND FURTHER READING

Brownsword, R 'Rules and principles at the warehouse' (1977) 40 MLR 467, case note on *Amalgamated Investment v John Walker* (1977).

Brownsword, R 'Henry's lost spectacle and Hutton's lost speculation: a classic riddle solved?' (1985) 129 Solicitors' Journal 860.

Cartoon, B 'Drafting an acceptable *force majeure* clause' (1978) JBL 230.

Colinvaux, R 'Suez survey' (1964) JBL 176 (and see also the detailed analysis of the *Suez Canal* cases by Mocatta J: [1970] 2 Lloyd's Rep 21).

Cornwell-Kelly, H 'The Community concept of *force majeure*' (1979) NLJ, 8 March at 245.

Frug, M (1992) 'Rescuing impossibility doctrine: a postmodern feminist analysis of contract law' in *Postmodern Feminist Jurisprudence*, New York: Routledge.

Hedley, S 'Carriage by sea: frustration and *force majeure*' (1990) CLJ 209, case note on *The Super Servant Two*.

Lasok, K 'Government intervention and State trading' (1981) 44 MLR 249.

McKendrick, E (ed) (1995) *Force Majeure and Frustration of Contract*, 2nd edn, London: Lloyds of London Press.

Schmitthoff, C (1990) *Schmitthoff's Export Trade. The Law and Practice of International Trade*, 9th edn, London: Stevens, Chapters 12 and 34 on hardship clauses.

Schmitthoff, C 'Hardship and intervener clauses' (1980) JBL 82.

Stannard, J 'Frustrating delays' (1983) 46 MLR 738.

Trakman, L 'Frustrated contracts and legal fictions' (1983) 46 MLR 39.

Treitel, G (1994) *Frustration and Force Majeure*, London: Sweet & Maxwell.

QUESTIONS

(1) Do you agree with Collins when he argues that the doctrine of possibility mistake is not only inconsistent with the objective test of consent and based upon little authority, but that the problems in such cases are better handled through construction of the express and implied terms of the contract? Give reasons for your response.

(2) Could any of the parties in 'The Sad Tale of Angie and Georgie' rely on the doctrine of frustration? What would the barriers to pleading their case be?

(3) Ali agreed to allow Lin and her family the use of Ali's holiday villa for a week for £1,000. Lin paid a deposit of £400, with the balance payable the day before the holiday was to commence. Two days before the holiday was due, Lin's children were taken ill with measles and she sent a doctor's certificate to this effect to Ali, saying that the holiday would have to be cancelled. Ali expressed regret, but demanded the balance of the agreed sum. Advise Lin.

What difference would it make if:

(a) the villa was washed away the day before the holiday was to start?;

(b) the previous occupiers of the villa had left the place filthy and Lin refused to stay and booked hotel accommodation which cost £500 for the week?;

(c) Ali was paying for the chalet by means of a hire purchase agreement and because of non-payment of the instalments the owner of the chalet had retake possession and refused admittance to Lin when she arrived?;

(d) the children had contracted smallpox instead of measles?

(4) 'The subject of frustration of contract has been associated, or confused, with various subjects, such as mistake, impossibility of performance, breach of contract, failure of consideration, illegality, failure of what is referred to as the common venture, and general considerations said to depend on reason and justice': Latham CJ in the Australian case of *Scanlan's New Neon Ltd v Toohey's Ltd* (1943). Discuss.

CHAPTER 12

UNFAIRNESS AND COERCION

INTRODUCTION

The standard of fairness is central to much of what is discussed in this book. In one sense we have learnt that the common law does not investigate whether an exchange is fair as that is for the parties to determine, but considerations of what is fair cannot be avoided by the judiciary. When the courts come to determine what is reasonable in the circumstances or deterimine the fate of a fraudster, it is inevitable that notions of fairness will come into play. Ideas of what constitutes a fair deal or negotiation process differ considerably but there is no doubt that the matter is important to contract lawyers. While discussion of the issue is pervasive, debate about the concept has also continued in a number of specific contexts. In the last section we looked at misrepresentation and in subsequent chapters we will be concerned with the idea of unfair and unreasonable contract terms. In this chapter, we will look at a number of particular doctrines which the courts have tentatively developed in order to mitigate the most extreme types of unfairness in contract and the illegitimate use of power. We will be examining ideas around inequality of bargaining power, unconsionablility and duress. The chapter raises a number of important questions. Is there a universal notion of unfairness? Does an agreed notion of unfairness make any sense at all? Should we look to what the parties think is fair or is there a general standard that can be applied? Can any one agreement between the parties be analysed alone or should we look to the backdrop of circumstances such as age, intelligence and market position? Does our concern amount to anything more than value for money? When is intervention justified?

Many different approaches to the mitigation of gross unfairness are revealed by the doctrines discussed in this chapter. In some cases the approach is to look at the victim and to ask whether their consent to the contractual terms can be considered genuine when unacceptable levels of pressure have been put on them. Another standpoint is to look at the position of the oppressor and to impose particular duties on them because of their specialist knowledge or economic power. A third approach, less discernible in the English doctrines discussed, is to look at the terms of the contract in the search for oppression and unfairness. In each of these cases the most pressing issue is how we separate the acceptable from the unacceptable.

We have already considered the ways in which 19th century rules of contract were developed in the context of *laissez-faire* and a free-market economy. The parties' capacity to bargain freely and equality of bargaining power were assumed. Fierce competition and commercial pressure were taken for granted and the courts generally declined to recognise a requirement for a general legal standard of reasonableness in transactions. The concepts of freedom and sanctity of contract inevitably led the courts to assume a primary role as upholders and enforcers of contracts rather than agents of their destruction. The contractual engines of private enterprise were paramount and the judges were not prepared for the courts to be used to relieve parties from the normal incidents of business risk-taking.

However, even the most conservative judicial statements regarding freedom and sanctity of contract were qualified. The courts, then as now, would set aside contracts and grant relief to parties where, as in cases of fraudulent misrepresentation, agreement was clearly not genuine. Similarly, some parties, such as infants and persons of unsound mind, were afforded protection against those who would take advantage of their lack of business acumen. The fundamental idea that agreement or consent to a contract must be free and voluntary also let in a number of narrow rules regarding forms of pressure exerted by one party on the other which the law regarded as improper. Such pressures ranged from actual physical violence to the improper use of a position of trust, such as that existing between solicitor and client.

GENERAL STANDARDS

A key question to be resolved in this area is whether relief should be granted to parties in such cases because the voluntary nature of the undertaking was called into question or because there is a general standard of fairness which pervades *all* contractual doctrines. The first of these possibilities was not necessarily offensive to proponents of the classical or neo-classical contract model because of the emphasis on the inadequacy or lack of agreement, but the second suggests a more interventionist approach to the policing of bargains than traditionalists would find acceptable. Case law in the area suggests that extreme caution has been exercised in reaction to the suggestion that a general standard would be the most fruitful approach to concerns about improper pressure or unscrupulous conduct. This has been characterised by the conservative development of specific doctrines relating to particular types of behaviour. English courts have not committed themselves to one overriding principle such as that of 'good faith' and the development of the law has been piecemeal. This lead has been followed by the legislature which has tended to concentrate on the needs of particular classes of people it assumes to be in a relatively weak bargaining position. The protection of consumers in sale of goods legislation is an excellent example of this.

That is not to say that attempts have not been made to develop more generic standards of fairness. So, for instance, Waddams, writing in 1976, argued that:

> Despite lip service to the notion of absolute freedom of contract, relief is every day given against agreements that are unfair, inequitable, unreasonable or oppressive. Unconscionability, as a word to describe such control, might not be the lexicographer's first choice, but I think it is the most acceptable general word.

Unfairness, protection against improper pressure and inequality of bargaining power were also linked together by Lord Denning in the case of *Lloyds Bank Ltd v Bundy* (1975), where he argued that English law should give relief to people who, without independent advice, enter into contracts on terms which are very unfair or transfer property for a consideration which is grossly inadequate when their bargaining power is seriously impaired. He anticipated that this might come about as a result of needs, desires, ignorance or infirmity, coupled with undue influences or pressures brought to bear by or for the benefit of another. In his words:

> There are cases on our books in which the courts will set aside a contract ... when the parties have not met on equal terms, when the one is so strong in bargaining power and the other so weak that, as a matter of common fairness it is not right that the strong should be allowed to push the weak to the wall. Hitherto these special

categories have been treated as a special category in itself. But I think the time has come when we should seek to find a principle to unite them.

In his analysis, Denning considered the various doctrines considered in this chapter as all being examples of one species of doctrine rather than separate ones.

The development indicated by Denning appeared at the time to promise the emergence of a new judicial doctrine operating to provide relief against harsh bargains where there existed a patent inequality of bargaining power between the parties. It was assumed by many commentators that later case law would allow the courts to define more clearly the scope of the emergent principle, whether expressed in terms of unconscionability or inequality of bargaining power. Indeed, there was some support for Denning's approach in *Schroeder Music Publishing Co Ltd v Macaulay* (1974). However, for some, the difficulty with the judgment was that the notion of inequality of bargaining power outlined could be seen to be enunciating the rule that any exercise of abnormal market power is *prima facie* reviewable by the courts in a civil action. But further clarification was not forthcoming beyond statements that the principle would not operate where the bargain was 'the result of the ordinary interplay of market forces'. Moreover, in *National Westminster Bank v Morgan* (1985), Lord Scarman argued that discrete doctrines dealing with unfair contract had not been sufficiently developed to need the support of a general principle of inequality of bargaining power (see also *Barclays Bank plc v O'Brien* (1993) and *TSB Bank v Camfield* (1995)).

It is important to emphasise that this narrow approach to unfairness is not evident in all common law jurisdictions. The inclusion of a clause relating to 'unconscionability' in the United States Uniform Commercial Code is perhaps the most widely cited example of an attempt to develop a general doctrine. Under the Code the courts are required to examine the commercial setting of the contract, and it has been said there that the doctrine is 'one of the prevention of oppression and unfair surprise'. The concept of good faith which sits alongside the notion of unconscionability as a macro doctrine designed to capture a variety of different types of unfairness has also become more commonplace elsewhere. For instance, the French and German civil codes require that agreements are to be performed in good faith as does the American Uniform Commercial Code. They impose a positive duty on contracting parties to 'play fair' and engage in open dealing. In a practical sense this would mean, for instance, that terms are expressed fully, clearly and legibly and that notice should be given of particularly onerous terms. Acting in good faith might also include not taking advantage of someone's lack of experience or weak bargaining position. The idea is not totally alien to the English legal system. The idea of a general standard of good faith has attracted some support amongst the judiciary (see, for instance, Bingham LJ in *Interfoto Picture Library Ltd v Stiletto Visual Programmes Ltd* (1989)) and amongst academic writers. Moreover, certain types of specialist contracts such as those used in the insurance industry make use of the notion of good faith. Moreover, the Unfair Terms in Consumer Contract Regulations 1999 use a test of whether a term is contrary to good faith and there are many modern developments, such as negligent misrepresentation, which encourage good behaviour in the pre-contractual period.

However, despite these innovations English lawyers have remained suspicious of a general doctrine of good faith and the judiciary's preference for pragmatic rather than principled decision-making has mitigated against the progression of the idea. Concerns that the introduction of this standard would introduce uncertainty into the law and call for difficult inquiries into contractual terms and negotiations have been widely expressed. Others have argued that the piecemeal solutions to specific instances of unfairness offer as adequate a solution as a general requirement.

Adams and Brownsword (2000) outline the dilemmas posed by the suggestion that the concept of good faith be adopted:

> For, what precisely does 'good faith' mean? Does it simply mean that a party must act with a clear conscience or are there some external standards of good faith dealing? If the latter, are these external standards set by a particular commercial community, or is there a critical moral benchmark for good faith? Moreover, where are the boundaries of a good faith requirement to be drawn?

A conservative judicial approach was much evident in the case of *Walford v Miles* (1992). In that case, the plaintiffs were in negotiations with the defendant over the purchase of a business and during the course of their discussions it was agreed that the sellers would not negotiate with another party. When the sellers broke off the discussions the buyer claimed that there had been a collateral contract to negotiate in good faith, but the House of Lords rejected the argument that the sellers were bound to negotiate this standard. Indeed, Lord Ackner went so far as to say that the concept of a duty to carry on negotiations in good faith is inherently repugnant to the adversarial position of the parties in pre-contractual negotiations. The toleration of such opportunism clearly makes it difficult to introduce general standards of acceptable behaviour.

Commentators have suggested that the adoption of a general principle would allow the English judiciary to avoid the excessive contortion of specific doctrines to achieve fairness which has characterised much of the piecemeal development in the field. More fundamentally, it has been suggested that discrete common law doctrines are particularly ill-suited to regulate contracts and that a new approach is essential. Moreover, it is evident that resistance to the concept of good faith is likely to be challenged as model contracts for international trade which contain good faith clauses are adopted and European legislation requires the adoption of such standards. Moreover, it is clear from the empirical studies visited in Chapter 4 that good faith is already an accepted norm within the business community where co-operative behaviour is much more common than Lord Ackner would have us believe, especially where a contract is likely to be long-term. Collins has argued that rather than imposing uniformity, 'open textured' standards, such as good faith, allow the judiciary to explore such conventions within the business community with a view to bridging the gap between formal law and practice.

PROCEDURAL AND SUBSTANTIVE FAIRNESS

Before going on to discuss the specific doctrines which have emerged to deal with particular types of unfairness, it is important to say a little about how instances of unfairness, unconscionability or inequality of bargaining power may be classified. In their treatment of the notion of unfairness, commentators have tended to make distinctions between two different types of unfairness which might manifest themselves in the field of contract. The first of these is *procedural unfairness*. This deals with unfairness during the making of the contract: what some academics have called bargaining naughtiness. Concerns about this type of unfairness, for instance, are reflected in the doctrines of misrepresentation which allow relief to parties who have been deliberately or recklessly misled about the quality of the thing they are trying to obtain.

The second type of unfairness is substantive. Here, commentators have been concerned with the fairness of the deal which has come about as a result of the bargaining. We have already seen that on the whole the courts are not concerned with whether adequate consideration has been given. Treitel (2002) has explained why this is so:

> The reason for this is not that the courts cannot value the promise of each party: they have to do this when assessing damages. It is rather that they should not interfere with the bargain actually made by the parties ... Such problems are however, more appropriately dealt with by special legislation or by administrative measures than by the ordinary process of civil litigation. The courts are not well equipped to develop a system of price control, and their refusal, as a general rule, to concern themselves with the adequacy of consideration is a reflection of this fact.

This position places emphasis on the sort of respect for individual autonomy so valued in the classical model. As Atiyah explains:

> It is assumed that the parties know their own minds, that they are the best judges of their own needs and circumstance, that they will calculate the risks and future contingencies that are relevant, and that all these enter into the bargain. It follows that unfairness of the bargain – gross inadequacy or excess of price – is irrelevant, and that once made, the contract is binding.

Viewed in this way, what the parties achieve is their own affair and their failures are likewise their own responsibility. Treating individual contractors as economic actors means that superiority in bargaining power is left for the market to regulate. Another justification for the emphasis on procedural rather than substantive fairness is that it is assumed that fair process tends to lead to outcomes considered fair by the parties. But some commentators have offered a more sophisticated analysis of the possibilities. Leff, for example, outlines the various scenarios which are possible. These are summarised in Figure 12.1.

Figure 12.1: The dynamics of procedural and substantive unfairness

fair process	⟶	fair result
fair process	⟶	unfair result
unfair process	⟶	fair result
unfair process	⟶	unfair result

According to this conceptualisation of the interface between process and substance, a fair process might lead to an unfair result where, for instance, an open and honest bargaining process leads to the payment of consideration which would generally be considered to be an inadequate price for what has been acquired. Conversely, a bargaining process in which misrepresentations and posturing are rife may nonetheless lead to a deal in which the parties both get what they want. In practice then it would seem that the notions of procedural and substantive unfairness are often intertwined when cases come before the courts. Moreover, although classical contract theorists are reluctant to look at the fairness of the deal entered into, the judiciary frequently uses unfair terms as evidence of a procedural impropriety. Closer scrutiny reveals that the cases in which the courts have been prepared to recognise procedural unfairness are invariably those where a bad deal has also been made. This is a theme to which we shall return as we review the discrete doctrines concerned with fairness.

SPECIFIC DOCTRINES

Duress

The notion of inequality of bargaining power espoused by Denning has been shadowed in English law by a related but narrower concept, that of duress. Duress involves coercion or compulsion as in the case of a contract entered into under a threat of physical violence. The essence of duress is a threat. The idea in the doctrine of duress is that the party's will is overborne during the bargaining process. Far from working against traditional contract principles, this concept complements them. The idea, like that of mistake, is that if consent to a contract is not given freely, then it cannot constitute true consent or meeting of the minds. This might happen, for instance, if someone was induced to sign a contract because they had a gun held against their head or other physical violence was threatened. A successful plea of duress can have significant implications. When duress is proven the contract can be avoided by the victim of the duress if they so elect.

Over the last three decades the courts have extended the idea of duress to cover situations where excessive *economic* pressure is brought to bear on one of the parties. Economic duress arises where a contract is formed or a contract is varied following a threat not to the party themselves or their property but to their economic well-being or financial standing. The courts have established the concept of economic duress based on the idea of *wrongful* commercial pressure involving coercion. The modern beginnings of this development are perhaps to be found in another judgment of Lord Denning's in *D & C Builders Ltd v Rees* (1966). Here, Rees, knowing that D & C were in desperate financial straits, put pressure on them to accept £300 in full settlement of a bill for nearly £500. In Lord Denning's view: 'No person can insist on a settlement procured by intimidation.' Pressure and even threats are commonplace in the modern business world but the new concept demonstrates, however indistinctly, that there is now a legal limit which must not be exceeded. The task for the courts is to distinguish acceptable levels of pressure such as those in *Williams v Roffey Bros and Nicholls (Contractors) Ltd* (1991) from unacceptable levels. How then is economic duress, which is actionable and grounds for setting a contract aside, to be distinguished from normal, if fierce, commercial 'cut and thrust', which is not actionable?

Threats and reluctant acquiescence to demands were examined in *The Atlantic Baron (North Ocean Shipping Co Ltd v Hyundai Construction Co Ltd)* (1979). In that case, Hyundai agreed to build a supertanker for North Ocean Shipping for $30 million. The dollar was devalued during construction and Hyundai, without any legal justification, demanded a 10% increase in the remaining instalments of the price and stipulated that otherwise they would terminate the contract. Being anxious to fulfil a very lucrative charter for the new vessel, North Ocean Shipping agreed to this demand but under protest. It was held that the shipbuilder's threat amounted to economic duress but, as the buyers had not taken the matter further, had paid the extra instalments and taken delivery of the ship, they had by implication affirmed the variation in price. As a result, it was held that they could not recover the extra payments. The shipbuilder's problems in this case began as a result of a failure in negotiating a fixed price dollar contract, thereby accepting the risk of adverse currency fluctuations during the construction period. Their transfer of this risk to the shipping company was seen by the court as illegitimate, coercive opportunism founded on a strong bargaining position and it was only North Ocean Shipping's inaction which allowed Hyundai to retain the extra payments.

The idea of a doctrine of economic duress was approved by the Judicial Committee of the Privy Council in *Pao On v Lau Yiu Long* (1980), although it was not proven on the facts. In that case, Lord Scarman was of the opinion that 'there is nothing contrary in principle in recognising economic duress as a factor which may render a contract voidable, provided always that the basis of such recognition is that it must always amount to a coercion of will, which vitiates consent'. In other words, the effect of the coercion is to 'cancel out' the consent given. According to the judges in that case, drawing the line between mere commercial pressure and actionable duress is a question of fact in each case, but Lord Scarman identified four questions to assist the courts in future cases:

(1) Did the person alleged to have been coerced protest at the time?

(2) Did that person have an alternative course open to them, such as an adequate legal remedy?

(3) Was that person independently advised?

(4) Did they take steps to avoid the contract as varied?

The matter was further considered in *The Universe Sentinel* (*Universe Tankships Inc of Monrovia v International Transport Workers' Federation* (1983)). In that case, Universe Tankships' vessel, which flew the Liberian flag, was prevented from leaving Milford Haven harbour by the ITWF who were engaged in a campaign of blacking 'flag of convenience' vessels in efforts to combat exploitation of their crews. The union had threatened Universe Tankships that they would induce tug operators not to assist the ship until various union demands were met. The ship was in fact delayed, at great expense to the owners, for 11 days. Tugs were not made available in breach of the operators' contracts until the demands were acceded to. Shortly afterwards, Universe Tankships themselves demanded the return of payments made to the ITWF as money paid under duress. The union did not dispute that their demands amounted to economic duress. In Lord Diplock's words, 'it is conceded that the financial consequences to the shipowners of the Universe Sentinel continuing to be off hire … while the blacking continued, were so catastrophic as to amount to a coercion of this shipowner's will'. However, the ITWF argued that their threat had been made in contemplation or furtherance of a trade dispute and that they were therefore protected by the immunity against actions in tort conferred by the Trade Union and Labour Relations Act 1974.

A majority of the House of Lords held that there was no trade dispute (within the meaning of the 1974 Act) and the pressure exerted by the union was illegitimate. The agreement regarding the payments in question was voidable and Universe Tankships could recover the payments made.

Following criticism from academic circles, Lord Scarman conceded that duress should not be seen as negating the existence of consent on the part of the person coerced. He argued that the victim's decision is better seen as intentional and voluntary, but as a conscious choice between the lesser of two evils. In his words, the victim has 'no practical choice but to submit to the duress'. A factor that may influence the court in coming to a conclusion that the victim had no other practical course but to submit to the duress is the extent of the loss they would have suffered if they had not submitted. In the court's view, the coercive effect of the pressure must be 'sufficiently great' in the circumstances to render it illegitimate.

Neither this nor subsequent cases have really made clear the meaning of 'illegitimate' in this context. Treitel states that 'the threat must be illegitimate either because what is threatened is a legal wrong ... or because the threat itself is wrongful'. In *The Universe Sentinel* there would appear to have been intimidation by threats to induce, breaches of contract by third parties upon whom the victim heavily relied. Cartwright (1991) has explained the position as follows:

> So we have only limited guidance on the circumstances in which economic pressure will be illegitimate for the purposes of duress. If the thing threatened, or the circumstances in which the pressure is exerted, amount to a crime or a tort, it appears from *The Universe Sentinel* that the coercion will be illegitimate; if the pressure was overwhelming, so as to give the coerced party no choice but to submit, then economic duress is likely to be held to have been established. Moreover, the threat of a breach of contract may be 'illegitimate', and so the question will be whether the threat was sufficiently overwhelming to constitute duress.

Where one party to the contract exerts pressure on the other by threatening breach of the contract, it has been suggested that such a threat is only illegitimate if accompanied by bad faith or malice or the deliberate exploitation of difficulties of the other party. Again, it has been said that the party threatening must be exploiting a 'situational monopoly', which gives the victim no realistic alternative but to comply. This point was considered in *Atlas Express Ltd v Kafco (Importers and Distributors) Ltd* (1989). The facts were that Atlas discovered that they had badly underpriced a contract to transport Kafco's goods to retailers throughout the country, particularly to Woolworths, with whom Kafco had a valuable, long-term contract. Shortly before Christmas, Atlas demanded an increase in the carriage charges. They said that unless a new agreement, drawn up by them, was signed by Kafco, no deliveries would be made. Fearing being in breach of their contract with Woolworths and with no alternative transport available, Kafco signed but only under protest. When Atlas sued to recover the increased charges, Kafco pleaded economic duress. It was held that Kafco were not obliged to pay the additional charges.

An application of Lord Scarman's four questions in *Pao On v Lau Yiu Long* readily substantiates the decision in *Atlas Express*. The possibility of losing the Woolworths contract presented Kafco with the gravest financial consequences and an action against Atlas for breach of the original contract would not have compensated them for the loss of their lucrative business relationship with Woolworths (see also *CTN Cash and Carry v Gallaher* (1994)). Despite these deliberations, the ambit of this common law doctrine has not yet been fully determined and it could be argued that there is a need to make its conceptual basis more clear.

Undue influence

The more expansive equitable doctrine of undue influence has developed alongside duress to prevent bargaining unfairness not captured by the common law doctrine which originally only recognised physical threats and not economic pressure as grounds for avoiding a contract. Undue influence covers situations which fall short of duress but which are nonetheless inequitable. There are two types of undue influence which have been recognised by the courts. The first group of cases fall under the heading of *actual* undue influence. This arises where one of the parties to a contract can prove that they entered the transaction as a direct result of undue influence from the other party. So, for example, in *Bank of Credit v Aboody* (1992), a husband exerted undue pressure over his wife. He bullied her into signing some documents and she signed them just because she wanted some peace. The emphasis in the cases has tended to be on procedural fairness (see *CIBC Mortgages v Pitt* (1994)), but the case law is not settled and in *National Westminster Bank v Morgan* (1985) Lord Scarman argued that substantive unfairness or 'manifest disadvantage' is also a threshold requirement.

The second category of cases falls under the heading of *presumed* undue influence. This arises when the parties have a certain type of pre-existing relationship in which one party places their trust in the other. The type of relationships envisaged are those where one party displays a particular vulnerability or the other can be expected to display altruism in a relationship of care. Relationships covered are often professional and are seen as transcending the commercial world with its focus on pure economic exchanges. In *National Westminster Bank v Morgan*, the House of Lords argued that it must be obvious to any independent and reasonable person that the relationship has special elements and the transaction is explicable only on the basis that the stronger party dominated the weaker. But again the law is far from clear as, in *CIBC*, Browne Wilkinson argued that this formula might have to be reworked (see also *Barclays Bank plc v Coleman and Another* (2000)).

The significance of being able to argue under this heading is that once a presumption is raised it is for the stronger party to prove that they have not taken advantage of the weaker party. Claimants attempting to raise a presumption have to prove that the contract between them 'calls for explanation' (see *Royal Bank of Scotland plc v Etridge (No 2)* (2001)). This significantly reduces the evidential burden placed on a claimant as, once this presumption is raised, the stronger party has to prove that they have not taken advantage of the weaker party. The defendant can, however, rebut the presumption of undue influence by showing that there was procedural fairness and that as a result the claimant entered into the contract freely. This is usually done by establishing that independent advice was taken but the gaining of independent advice does not necessarily save the transaction nor is its absence fatal (see *Royal Bank of Scotland plc v Etridge (No 2)* (1998) *per* Stuart Smith LJ).

The relationships of trust with which the courts are concerned in cases of presumed influence are called fiduciary relationships and may arise in one of two ways. First, there are some relationships in which it is automatically presumed to arise. These include contracts involving parent and child, religious adviser and disciple, guardian and ward, solicitor and client, trustee and beneficiary or doctor and patient, which raise an irrebuttable presumption. Alternatively, where the relationship does not automatically fall into one of these headings, the presumption can be established and rebutted on the facts. In principle then, any type of relationship could theoretically fall within the remit of this type of undue influence; it all depends on the circumstances of the case. It is because of this feature that cases which fall under this heading have tended to be contentious.

One of the most widely cited examples of cases in which a fiduciary relationship arose on the facts is *Lloyds Bank v Bundy* (1974). In that case, the plaintiff and his son both used the same bank. The son ran into business difficulties and his father was asked to secure his son's overdraft and to put his farm up as security. He did this but when the son was unable to pay the bank they tried to repossess the farm. The father claimed undue influence. He argued that he had banked with Lloyds for a long time and placed considerable trust in them. It was his contention that they had abused the confidence he placed in them by not making an effort to warn him fully that it was not in his financial interests to put up the farm as guarantee. The Court of Appeal agreed that the presumption of undue influence should be raised in this case as there was a relationship of trust on the facts and the transaction was obviously disadvantageous. Moreover, the bank was unable to rebut the presumption.

Looking to both process and substance, Lord Denning outlined the specific factors which needed to be proved. He reasoned that: (a) the relationship between the bank and the father was one of trust and confidence; (b) the relationship between the father and son was one in which the father's natural love and affection had much influence on him; and (c) that, on the facts, the consideration moving from the bank was grossly inadequate. The court also found that since the bank would derive an interest from the transaction, there was a conflict of interest. In their view, Lloyds were under a duty to advise the farmer to seek independent advice and that, as they had failed to do that, they had breached that duty.

The types of relationship capable of coming under this category are constantly expanding and being reviewed. In the past 20 years, for instance, the House of Lords has laid down no fewer than three sets of rules to determine in which circumstances a mortgagee will be bound by a transaction obtained through undue influence. *National Westminster Bank v Morgan* (1985) was the first case to recognise the undue influence of a husband on a wife in respect of their shared matrimonial home and this point was further discussed in *Barclays Bank plc v O'Brien* (1993). One of the most interesting aspects of the latter was that Browne Wilkinson accepted that a relationship of trust and confidence may arise on the facts where there is an emotional relationship between cohabiting parties who are not married. His deliberations were taken further in *Etridge (No 2)* (1998) which has now extended the rule to encompass *all* non-commercial relationships (see also *Massey v Midland* (1995), *Banco Exterior* (1997) and *Credit Lyonnais v Burch* (1997)).

Unconscionability

The idea of unconscionability has already been discussed in the introduction to this chapter where it was suggested that it has the potential to be used as an overarching term to describe the various doctrines being considered in this chapter. This is certainly the case in other jurisdictions where it has become synonymous with general doctrines of good faith and unfairness. But in the UK the notion has been used instead to describe a very narrow and longstanding equitable doctrine. Many of the early cases concerned with the doctrine involved 'expectant heirs' who borrowed money at extortionate rates and secured the loan on their future inheritance. These claimants were generally taken to be weak because of their youthful ignorance and desire to obtain money. Another group of cases in which the concept has been used involves emergency salvage operations in which the ability of someone to give meaningful consent has been questioned because of the urgency involved. In *The Port Caledonia and the Anna* (1903), a captain whose ship was in trouble agreed to pay £1,000 for a tug to rescue it. Bukhill J said:

> I have to ask myself whether the bargain that was made was so inequitable, so unjust and so unreasonable that the court cannot allow it to stand ... I hope that those who perform such grand services in tugs from time to time, in worse weather than this, and in peril of their own lives, save property around the coast, will note that this Court will keep a firm hand over them if they attempt to do what has been done in this case.

More recently, the decision of *Cresswell v Potter* in 1978 suggests that the doctrine is alive and well and capable of being applied to modern-day transactions. In that case, a wife left her husband and conveyed her half-share in the matrimonial home to him so that she would not be liable for mortgage payments. She later sought to recover her half-share when the husband sold the property. In the words of Megarry J:

> What has to be considered is first whether the plaintiff is poor and ignorant; second whether the advice was at a considerable undervalue and third, whether the vendor had independent advice ... the euphemisms of the 20th century mean that the word poor has to be replaced by 'lower income group' and the like and the word ignorant by 'less highly educated'.

But there are also clear indications that, by the mid-19th century, the judiciary began to be concerned that the doctrine was too broad and that certain judgments brought with them the danger of too many transactions being set aside (see, for instance, *Earl of Aylesford v Morris* (1873)). The result is that there have been very few modern cases on the topic. The task of limiting the doctrine has been made easier by the fact that the legislature has shown itself willing to legislate for unfairness. For example, consumer credit legislation permits extortionate credit bargains to be reopened by the courts and affords a right to consumers who sign certain types of credit agreements at home to cancel then within a 'cooling off' period. As we shall see in subsequent chapters, the Unfair Contract terms Act 1977 concentrates its efforts on consumers and European Directives also allow for the setting aside of certain types of terms in contracts.

CONCLUDING REMARKS

The doctrines considered in this chapter go to the heart of the issues raised in this book. In particular, they focus on debates surrounding the extent to which we desire a level playing field or general standards of positive behaviour in contracts. The doctrines considered in this chapter challenge the classical notion that rough equality between contracting parties can be assumed and that individuals are the best judges of what is in their best interests. But whilst it is clear that courts in the UK are prepared to intervene in cases of unfairness in the worse types of exploitation, they have tended to do so in a piecemeal fashion. The challenge to contractual fairness has been muted by the fact that the emphasis has tended to be on bargaining naughtiness rather than substantive fairness, although the latter continues to influence decisions. Collins (2002) has suggested that this reflects an ongoing commitment to the market philosophies underpinning the classical notion of freedom of contract:

A reluctance to acknowledge the significance of substantive unfairness in contracts as a ground for intervention still characterizes judicial decisions in the common law. A court will stress any elements of procedural impropriety that it can discover rather than address directly the unfairness of the bargain. The substantive unfairness may provide the motive for intervention, but the formal legal reason given for upsetting the contract will be couched in terms of a procedural defect such as deception, manipulation or unfair surprise.

Legislative attempts to tackle unfair contracts have been bolder as they have attempted to create mechanisms for evaluating whether a bargain is fair, such as rent controls, the minimum wage and price setting for utilities. These initiatives suggest that it is viable to regulate the fairness of substance and process but the extent to which the regulation of unfairness in contracts could be said to be based on coherent policy is uncertain. The area is fraught with competing philosophies about the market and the practical difficulties in determining whether there is such a thing as a general standard of fairness. The empirical studies of contract highlighted in earlier chapters reveal that looking at the context in which a deal takes place is crucial, as formal agreements rarely reflect the implicit dimensions of a deal. But what makes the topic so stimulating is an increasing willingness for these issues to be discussed.

REFERENCES AND FURTHER READING

Adams, J and Brownsword, R (2000) *Understanding Contract Law*, 3rd edn, London: Sweet & Maxwell.

Auchmuty, R 'The rhetoric of equality and the problem of heterosexuality' (2005) in Mulcahy, L and Wheeler, S (eds), *Feminist Perspectives on Contract Law*, London: Cavendish Publishing.

Birks, P 'The travails of duress' (1990) LMCLQ 342.

Brownsword, R 'Good faith in contracts revisited' (1996) 49 Current Legal Problems 111.

Brownsword, R, Hird, N and Howells, G (eds) (1999) *Good Faith in Contract: Concept and Context*, Aldershot: Ashgate.

Cartwright, J (1991) *Unequal Bargaining*, Oxford: Clarendon.

Carty, H and Evans, A 'Economic duress' (1983) JBL 218.

Collins, H (2002) *Regulating Contracts*, Oxford: OUP.

Coote, B 'Duress by threatened breach of contract' (1980) CLJ 40.

Dalton, C 'An essay in the deconstruction of contract doctrine' (1985) 94 Yale Law Journal 997.

Dixon, M 'The special tenderness of equity: undue influence and the family home' (1994) 53 CLJ 21.

Halson, R 'Opportunism, economic duress and contractual modifications' (1991) 107 LQR 649.

Lawson, A '*O'Brien* and its legacy: principle, equity and certainty?' (1995) 54 CLJ 280.

Macdonald, E 'Duress by threatened breach of contract' (1989) JBL 640.

Millett, P 'Equity's place in the law of commerce' (1998) 114 LQR 214.

Phang, A 'Whither economic duress?' (1990) 53 MLR 115.

Trebilcock, M (1980) 'An economic approach to unconscionability' in Reiter, B and Swan, J (eds), *Studies in Contract Law*, Toronto: Butterworths.

Treitel, G (2002) *The Law of Contract*, London: Sweet & Maxwell.

QUESTIONS

(1) In 'The Sad Tale of Angie and Georgie' identify aspects of behaviour which you find unacceptable. In how many instances do you think that the law of contract should get involved in mitigating such unfairness? Could existing doctrine be used to help Angie circumvent the agreement she made with St Ives Bank?

(2) Can you identify the advantages of limiting the concepts of economic duress and undue influence?

(3) 'The task of regulating the fairness of contracts is one which the judiciary is singularly ill-equipped to perform.' Critically appraise this statement.

(4) In *Lloyds Bank Ltd v Bundy* (1975), a farmer guaranteed the bank account of his son's company and charged his farm to the bank as security. The Court of Appeal set aside the guarantee and dismissed the bank's claim against the farm. Why?

(5) 'In sum, for both market-individualists and consumer-welfarists, the doctrine of economic duress rightly shields contractors against unacceptable pressure for renegotiation, but ... it is unclear how adherents of either approach will apply this central idea in individual cases': Adams and Brownsword, *Understanding Contract Law*. Discuss.

PART FIVE:

THE CONTRACT

CHAPTER 13

CONTRACTUAL TERMS

INTRODUCTION

So far in this book we have looked at the theories underpinning the law of contract and what happens in the course of pre-contractual negotiations. In this fifth section, we will focus on the contents of contracts. The ingredients or terms of a contract are not always easy to discover. You will already be aware from the earlier discussion of misrepresentation that certain representations made in the course of pre-contractual negotiations will become terms of the contract whilst others will be excluded from it. Even where a contract is written down and signed by both parties, you will discover that other terms may be added by the courts. In some instances, this will be done because the added terms represent what the parties intended but, in other cases, the judiciary and the legislature have shown themselves willing to rewrite parts of the contract made by two autonomous and consenting individuals. The extent to which this offends the classical notion of freedom of contract has been the subject of much discussion. Judicial and legislative activity in this area reflects the way in which notions of contractual responsibility have changed and moved away from the political ideals of individualism and *laissez-faire*.

WHERE CAN TERMS BE FOUND?

Contract law is not usually concerned with the form into which the parties put their agreement. Many business agreements, such as export sales, building contracts and hire purchase agreements, are based on standard printed documents. A contract may be entirely in written form or it may be partly written with the remainder orally expressed. Many agreements are wholly oral and, indeed, certain contractual obligations may simply be implied from the parties' conduct. So, for instance, if you take a newspaper from an unattended pile outside a shop and place 60 pence into a tin left there for the purpose, a contract has been formed without a word having been spoken or a form signed. A variety of factors such as economy, convenience, certainty, security or speed dictate how contracts are expressed and, as one aspect of freedom of contract, the law itself rarely demands a particular form.

The multiplicity of forms that a contract may take is well-illustrated by the case of *Evans & Son (Portsmouth) Ltd v Merzario Ltd* (1976). The facts of the case were that for several years Merzario made the transport arrangements for the importation of machinery by Evans from Italy. The course of dealing between the parties was based on the printed standard conditions of the freight forwarding trade, clause 4 of which read: 'Subject to express instructions in writing given by the customer, the Company reserves to itself complete freedom in respect of means, route and procedure to be followed in the handling and transportation of goods.' It was not disputed that the terms of the standard form had, by the course of dealings, become part of each individual contract made by the parties. After eight years it was proposed that the machinery should be carried in containers, and Merzario's manager, in the course of discussions in Portsmouth with Evans's manager, assured him: 'If we do use containers, they will not be carried on deck where the machinery might go rusty.' Containers were used and invoices, referring as usual to the standard conditions and containing new charges, were sent. Nothing was put in writing about the containers being carried below deck. A container carried on deck fell into the sea and was lost. The court held that Evans was entitled to damages for breach of contract on two grounds, one of which being that the oral assurance amounted to an express term of the contract, which was partly in writing, partly implied by conduct and partly oral. The new oral term and clause 4 of the printed conditions being inconsistent, the court held that the individual assurance overrode the standard form.

This case was mainly concerned with express terms: what was written or said by the parties and what was written in the printed form which they adopted. Other contractual issues centre on the question of implied terms, which are just as binding as express terms and are implied and incorporated into contracts from a variety of sources. Although government policy, through the medium of statute law, is the most important source of implied terms, say as regards consumer protection, the courts themselves possess the power to imply terms into a contract. We have already seen, in the context of certainty, how a court will imply a reasonable contract price in certain circumstances. Similarly, terms may be implied from business practice and other sources.

IMPLIED TERMS

The courts have long argued that they will not make a contract for the parties. So when and on what basis will they 'find' a term which has not been expressed? Judges and academics have gone to great lengths to identify certain categories or groups of implied terms. Opinions vary as to how many categories there are, probably because, as Lord Wilberforce has said, they are not so much distinctive categories but shades on a continuous spectrum. Moreover, you will see that certain terms added to a contract by the courts or legislature are not 'implied' at all by the parties but are *imposed* in the interests of social justice. Despite these provisions, commentators have suggested that implied terms can be divided into three categories: terms implied in *fact*, terms implied in *law* and terms implied by *custom or usage*. We have used this classification scheme to organise the material in this chapter.

Terms implied in fact

These terms are implied on the basis of what the parties *must* have intended. Therefore, such terms can only be implied if *both* parties, had they applied their mind to the matter now in issue, would have considered them to be necessary. As MacKinnon LJ in *Shirlaw v Southern Foundries (1926) Ltd* (1939) stated:

> *Prima facie* that which in any contract is left to be implied and need not be expressed is something so obvious that it goes without saying; so that if while the parties were making their bargain, an officious bystander were to suggest some express provision for it in the agreement, they would testily suppress him with a common 'Oh, of course!'.

For example, in a contract involving the hire of a ship (charterparty), it would be implied that the vessel on hire was seaworthy. In *Banco de Portugal v Waterlow & Sons*

Ltd (1932), a term was implied into a contract for the printing of bank notes for the Portuguese central bank that the London printers should not allow use of the plates to get into unauthorised hands. As Lord Diplock argued in *Hong Kong Fir Shipping Co Ltd v Kawasaki Kisen Kaisha Ltd* (1962): 'No doubt there are many simple contractual undertakings, sometimes express, but more often because of their simplicity ("It goes without saying") to be implied. "It goes without saying" because the term is an established usage within the particular business context.'

The 'officious bystander' test has on occasion been merged with another, 'business efficacy' test. So, for instance, Scrutton LJ in *Reigate v Union Manufacturing Co* (1918) opined:

> A term can only be implied if it is necessary in the business sense to give efficacy to the contract; that is if it is such a term that it can confidently be said that if at the time the contract was being negotiated some one had said to the parties, 'What will happen in such a case?', they would both have replied, 'Of course, so and so will happen; we did not trouble to say that; it is too clear'.

It is important to stress that the test rests on necessity and not merely reasonableness. It must be necessary common sense to imply the term because the parties themselves would have agreed to it. In other words, the test is, rather unusually, a subjective one.

Terms implied in law

By way of contrast, terms implied in law do not depend on the common intention of the parties. Instead, they should be seen as duties arising out of certain types of contracts. Terms are implied by law as a matter of policy and in many instances the implication of the term amounts to the imposition of a legal duty. So, for instance, in *Liverpool City Council v Irwin* (1977), a 15 storey tower block of council flats had rapidly and drastically deteriorated and tenants claimed it should be replaced by the council. The council's obligations under their 'conditions of tenancy' were absent from the document. The contract being incomplete, the court implied terms 'such as the nature of the contract itself implicitly required'. These included the council's duty to take reasonable care as regards repair and usability of common parts. However, the tenants also had their responsibilities as reasonable tenants.

Drawing on the judgment in that case, Lord Denning said in *Shell (UK) Ltd v Lostock Garage Ltd* (1977) that terms implied in law are to be found in:

> ... those relationships which are of common occurrence ... seller and buyer, owner and hirer, master and servant, landlord and tenant, carrier by land or sea, contractor for building works, and so on. In all those relationships the courts have imposed obligations on one party or the other, saying they are implied terms ... The House in *Liverpool City Council v Irwin* ... examined the existing law of landlord and tenant ... to see if it contained the solution to the problem; and, having found that it did not, they imposed an obligation on the landlord to use reasonable care.

What is notable about the implication of terms in law is that the court may be seen to be regulating the contract in terms of distributive justice so that one party does not take advantage of the other. In Lord Denning's opinion, one must look to see what would be reasonable in the circumstances in the general run of such cases '... and then say what the obligation shall be'. In various sectors of business and commerce, terms implied judicially as legal duties have come to acquire the status of general rules. So, for instance, in building contracts it is required that the contractor will supply good and proper materials; in contracts for the carriage of goods by sea it is required that the carrier will provide a seaworthy vessel; and in contracts for the sale of goods it is required that the goods sold must be reasonably fit for their purpose. As we will soon see, some of these 'standardised' implied terms have also been put into statutory form.

Terms implied by trade usage

The courts have also shown themselves prepared to imply terms to reflect common *business practice*. This is a clear illustration of the point that it may be unwise to regard a contract's express terms in isolation. The better course, in appropriate circumstances, is to set them firmly within an overall framework or context of business conduct and relationships. This point is illustrated in *British Crane Hire Corp Ltd v Ipswich Plant Hire Ltd* (1975). The facts of the case were that British Crane supplied a dragline crane to Ipswich Plant. It being a matter of urgency, the agreement was made by telephone and nothing was said about the conditions of hire. Later, British Crane sent their printed conditions to Ipswich Plant but before they were signed the crane sank in marshy ground. The conditions were similar to those used by all firms in the plant hire business and they laid down that the hirer was liable to indemnify the owner of equipment against all expense in connection with its use. When sued for the cost of recovering the crane, Ipswich Plant claimed they were not liable under British Crane's conditions because they had not been incorporated into the oral contract. The court held that as Ipswich Plant knew that such conditions were in common use in the business, British Crane were entitled to conclude that Ipswich Plant were accepting the crane on their conditions, which had therefore been incorporated into the contract, on the basis of the common understanding of the parties.

In this case, a term was implied or incorporated into a contract because it was reasonable and in common use in a trade to which both parties belonged. Similarly, terms may be incorporated into contracts between parties who have established a regular, previous course of dealing, whether or not they are in the same line of business. This has already been seen in the *Merzario* case as regards the printed standard conditions of the freight forwarding trade. Similarly, in *Kendall & Sons v Lillico & Sons Ltd* (1969), poultry feeding stuffs were sold orally on the Bury St Edmunds Corn Exchange by Hardwick Game Farm to the Poultry Producers Association. The next day Hardwick Game Farm sent a confirmation note to the Poultry Producers Association on the back of which were Hardwick Game Farm's conditions of sale, including one that the buyer took responsibility for latent defects. It was established that the parties had regularly contracted in this way over a period of years, and so it was held that the note's written terms could properly be incorporated into the oral contract.

Similarly, it will be recalled that in *Hillas & Co Ltd v Arcos Ltd* (1932), details from a previous contract between two parties engaged in the timber trade were available to 'fill out' and provide sufficient certainty for a subsequent agreement to be declared binding.

STATUTORY INTERVENTION

We have already noted in Chapter 4 the tremendous expansion of the mixed economy and welfare functions of the State since the classical period of contract. Since the end of the Second World War in particular, this has led to vastly increased judicial and governmental involvement in business and social affairs and a multitude of terms substituted for, or added to, the terms agreed between the parties. It is this erosion of freedom of contract by the courts and statute which is mainly responsible for the transformation of contract from a private to a public act and, in a sense, contract is now as 'mixed' as the economy itself. For a variety of social welfare reasons, statutes may now compel us to make certain contracts, such as those for motor insurance coverage. Even more commonly, statutes now regulate the terms of many contracts, such as hire purchase agreements, rent controlled tenancies, contracts of employment and package holidays.

Intervention often stems from the need for Parliament to restore some semblance of balance to the contractual relationship in question. Where the ideal of freedom of contract has degenerated into the freedom of one party to oppress the other owing to an imbalance of economic power between them, the courts and then the legislature have tended to move in on behalf of the weaker party by way of implied contractual terms. An excellent illustration of this process concerns contracts for the carriage of goods and the description given by Gutteridge as far back as 1935 deserves to be quoted at length:

> No part of English commercial law has undergone greater or more fundamental changes than that which concerns the rules governing the carriage of goods. The primary cause of this has been the development of means of communication and transit due to modern inventions, but another influence which has been at work is the desire to secure world-wide uniformity in the rules of carriage by sea and by air which are necessarily international in character. The growth of the law is also marked throughout by the struggle which has taken place between the carriers in an attempt to escape liability for negligence, and the goods owners who have been at a disadvantage when faced with the uncertainty and expense of litigation in which their opponents have been great and wealthy corporations in whose hands the business of carriage has become concentrated during the last 50 years.

> The judges, for their part, have striven to restrain the attempts of the carriers to obtain contractual exemption from responsibility by refusing to recognize such exemption when accompanied by negligence, deviation or unseaworthiness, and this has resulted in a considerable volume of case law which, in its turn, has been followed by further attempts by the carriers to escape liability. The intervention of the legislature became necessary and resulted in such important measures as the Carriage of Goods by Sea Act 1924, the Railways Act of 1921 and the Carriage by Air Act 1932. On the other hand, it has become evident that the interests of the community call for a balancing of the interests of the goods owners and those of the carriers in order to avoid excessive charges for carriage, and the Acts of Parliament which have just been mentioned ... have been framed so as to relieve the carrier, to the utmost extent which is commercially possible, from the more hazardous features of his responsibility.

> It is probably correct to say that no other part of our commercial law reflects, in a similar degree, the interplay of purely economic considerations and those of legal theory.

Interference has also been justified on the basis that there is a need to redress the imperfections of a free market in which traders lack incentives to supply quality products, and meaningful appraisal of the quality of goods by consumers is not possible.

The twin goals of regulating the market and balancing interests through the imposition of obligations on a party possessing stronger bargaining power has a long history in the sale of goods field. The traditional importance of the ideals of free market in this field are clear from the part that the notion *caveat emptor* has played in the development of law in this field. The maxim which can be translated as 'let the buyer beware' has its English origins in the system of trading common to the markets and fairs of the Middle Ages. In these marketplaces the goods were on open display and could be examined, tested and bought on the spot. It was reasonable in these circumstances for the buyer to rely on their own judgment.

At the time of predominantly face-to-face contractual situations, a buyer might obtain a remedy if, on receiving defective or worthless goods, they could prove breach of an express promise made by the seller or fraud. However, goods later came to be purchased mainly by way of description, so a contract could be formed with a buyer who lived a hundred or a thousand miles away, or, in the case of packaged or canned goods, merely sold over a shop counter. As a result of these changes, the law of seller's obligation as to quality did gradually change. By the early 19th century, the court was willing to infer or imply promises as to quality into the sale which related to merchantability and fitness for the buyer's purpose.

The Sale of Goods Act 1893, which codified the law as it existed at that time, represented something of a halfway house between the opposing ideas of *caveat emptor* and consumer protection. The decision in *Jones v Bright* established the rule that if goods are sold for a particular purpose it is impliedly understood that they will be fit for that purpose and this provision later appeared in s 14(1) of the 1893 Act (see Figure 13.1). However, it did so only as an exception to the underlying principle of *caveat emptor*. As a result, the right which it afforded the buyer was hedged round with qualifications, although subsequent case law reveals that the courts interpreted the requirements of the section in a manner favourable to the buyer.

However, the greatest stumbling block to the fulfilment of real consumer protection was to be found in s 55 of the 1893 Act which provided that: 'Where any right, duty or liability would arise under a contract of sale by implication of law, it may be negatived or varied by express agreement.' Seen together, these clauses reflect a certain ambivalence about regulation of contracts which remains today. But reactions to the statute also suggest that by clinging to the notion of freedom of contract, the legislature set its statutory seal of approval on the freedom to exploit. By means of tightly worded, small-print exclusion clauses in their contracts, sellers of goods, backed by economic power, were able to negate whatever protection was afforded the buyer by means of s 14(1) and similar provisions in the 1893 Act and so deprive buyers of their legal remedies.

A shift in legislative approach has been signalled by subsequent statutes which have tended to favour greater consumer protection. It is now clear that exclusion clauses in contracts for the sale of goods which seek to negate or vary the seller's implied obligations as to such things as fitness for purpose will be of no effect in consumer transactions and in other cases will be subject to a test of reasonableness. The complex question of exclusion clauses will be fully examined in Chapters 14 and

---

Figure 13.1: Section 14(1) of the Sale of Goods Act 1893

14 ... there is no implied warranty or condition as to the quality or fitness for any particular purpose of goods supplied under a contract of sale, except as follows ... (1) Where the buyer, expressly or by implication, makes known to the seller the particular purpose for which the goods are required, so as to show that the buyer relies on the seller's skill or judgment, and the goods are of a description which it is in the course of the seller's business to supply (whether he be the manufacturer or not), there is an implied condition that the goods shall be reasonably fit for such purpose, provided that in the case of a contract for the sale of a specified article under its patent or other trade name, there is no implied condition as to its fitness for any particular purpose.

15, but it is worth noting here that the increasing prevalence and severity of such clauses, particularly in the related field of hire purchase, meant that eventually Parliament was prevailed upon to introduce legislation on this specific topic. This was a major advance in the protection of buyers' rights and the implied term is no longer, for parties contracting as consumers, in the shadow of the exclusion clause: see now the Unfair Contract Terms Act 1977.

The Sale of Goods Act 1893 together with its subsequent amendments has now been consolidated in the Sale of Goods Act 1979 (as further amended in 1994). Similar implied terms regarding quality in such contracts as those for work and materials, exchange and hire are to be found in the Supply of Goods and Services Act 1982. This Act also provides that there is an implied term that the supplier of services will carry out the service with reasonable care and skill: see *Wilson v Best Travel Ltd* (1993) concerning package holidays.

CONCLUDING REMARKS

In this chapter we have introduced you to some of the key themes of this section of the book. Our consideration of express and implied terms demonstrates that this is an area in which the courts have looked at relational elements of contracts through the notion of previous course of dealing and industrywide understandings of common practice. Whilst the judiciary has expressed reservations about writing the contract for the parties, the courts have steered away from literal interpretations of words to try and give meaning to agreements made in a business context. They have been cautious of stepping over the threshold to become writers rather than interpreters. But, as Collins (2003) reminds us, invoking the implicit dimensions of contracts is of fundamental concern to those who wish to promote the efficiency of the market as well as those concerned about social justice. He argues that greater efficiency can be achieved through the observance of conventions that augment mutual trust and confidence. In this way, the legal system can make a profound contribution to the creation of trust in inter-firm relations which may help to reduce transaction costs, avoid disputes and reinforce the legitimacy of the law. An understanding of the implicit dimensions of contracts can be used by the courts to understand how successful economic organisations are established and evolve.

REFERENCES AND FURTHER READING

Collins, H 'The research agenda of implicit dimensions of contract', in Campbell, D, Collins, H and Wightman, J (2003) *Implicit Dimensions of Contract: Discrete, Relational and Network Contracts*, Oxford: Hart Publishing.

Gutteridge, H (1935) 'Contract and commercial law 1885–1935' (1935) 51 LQR 91.

Macdonald, E 'Express and implied terms and exemptions' (1991) 107 LQR 555.

Phang, A 'Implied terms revisited' (1990) JBL 394.

Phang, A 'Implied terms in English law: some recent developments' (1993) JBL 242.

QUESTIONS

(1) In 'The Sad Tale of Angie and Georgie', what terms, if any, would be implied into the contract between Chelsea and the company she booked a ferry ticket with?

(2) In Chapter 7 you were asked to identify the points at which agreements between the parties in 'The Sad Tale of Angie and Georgie' had come into place. Building on that analysis, can you now identify all the terms of such agreements? In addition to express terms, can you think of any terms which might be implied into the agreements?

(3) 'To place an emphasis on negotiated agreement in contract may well be a mistaken emphasis nowadays' (Friedmann). Discuss this statement and consider why Friedmann thinks things are so different today.

(4) Collins has argued that any legal system that enforces contracts must develop techniques for determining the legal significance of the context and conventions surrounding the social practice of entering into contracts. Can you think of any arguments which undermine this point of view?

CHAPTER 14

STANDARD FORM CONTRACTS

INTRODUCTION

The classical contract model developed at a time when most negotiations were conducted face-to-face by two parties. Doctrines associated with this model and its neo-classical offshoot continue to dominate the modern development of the law of contract despite the fact that a considerable number of legal agreements are now standard form contracts containing written express terms prepared in advance of negotiations and exchange by parties other than those contracting. Standard form contracts probably account for the vast majority of all the contracts now made. Most people have difficulty remembering the last time they contracted other than by standard form and except for casual oral arrangements, they probably never have. Most of us contract by standard form several times a day. Car park and cinema tickets, department store charge slips and petrol station credit card purchase slips are all standard form contracts.

Similarly, in the parliamentary debate prior to the passing of the Unfair Contract Terms Act in 1977 in the UK, the point was made that: 'It is probably the case that most contracts are based on standard conditions to some extent irrespective of the relative bargaining strength of the parties.' Standard forms of contract can be found in operation in inter-business agreements and business-consumer contracts.

Although the Unfair Contract Terms Act recognises the existence of 'written standard forms of business', there is no statutory definition of a standard form contract in this country. Instead, the legislature preferred to leave exact definitions to the judiciary. But in Israel the legislature has defined it as 'a contract ... all or any of whose terms have been fixed in advance by, or on behalf of, the person supplying the commodity or service ... with the object of constituting conditions of many contracts between him and persons undefined as to their number or identity'. A wider definition, which is adopted in this book, recognises that both suppliers and purchasers can draw up such contracts, and this is especially true of the business sector; otherwise there would have been no 'battle of the forms' in *Butler Machine Tool Co Ltd v Ex-Cell-O Corp Ltd* (1979).

The English judiciary has shown itself able and willing to fill in the definitional gaps left by the legislature. A Scottish case, *McCrone v Boots Farm Sales Ltd* (1981), involving a consumer-business agreement, raised the issue of what constituted a 'standard form contract'. Without attempting a comprehensive definition, Lord Dunpark was of the opinion that the phrase was 'wide enough to include any contract, whether wholly written or partly oral, which includes a set of fixed terms or conditions which the proponer [offeror] applies, without material variation, to contracts of the kind in question'. In *Schroeder Music Publishing Co Ltd v Macaulay* (1974), Lord Diplock gave his views on the nature of standard form contracts at greater length:

> Standard forms of contracts are of two kinds. The first, of very ancient origin, are those which set out the terms on which mercantile transactions of common occurrence are to be carried out. Examples are bills of lading, charter-parties, policies of insurance,

contracts of sale in the commodity markets. The standard clauses in these contracts have been settled over the years by negotiation by representatives of the commercial interests involved and have been widely adopted because experience has shown that they facilitate the conduct of trade. Contracts of these kinds affect not only the actual parties to them but also others who may have a commercial interest in the transactions to which they relate, as buyers or sellers, charterers or shipowners, insurers or bankers. If fairness or reasonableness were relevant to their enforceability, the fact that they are widely used by parties whose bargaining power is fairly matched would raise a strong presumption that their terms are fair and reasonable.

The same presumption, however, does not apply to the other kind of standard form of contract. This is of comparatively modern origin. It is the result of the concentration of particular kinds of business in relatively few hands. The ticket cases in the nineteenth century provide what are probably the first examples. The terms of this kind of standard form of contract have not been the subject of negotiation between the parties to it, or approved by any organisation representing the interests of the weaker party. They have been dictated by that party whose bargaining power, either exercised alone or in conjunction with others providing similar goods or services, enables him to say: 'If you want these goods or services at all, these are the only terms on which they are available. Take it or leave it.'

This account of standard form contracts enables us to consider some important points about their uses and the extent to which they can be considered abusive.

USES, ABUSES AND BARGAINING POWER

The basic reason underlying the widespread use in present-day business of the standard form of contract is the need to facilitate the conduct of trade. Often, this will be because the parties regularly enter into complex technical and legal relations. This is the case, for instance, in the fields of international trade, civil and mechanical engineering and building. In other cases, it is because the dealings in question involve a multiplicity of transactions relating to standardised and mass-produced products, services or marketing techniques. The latter is a particularly common feature of modern business.

Many of the reasons for the development of standard written contracts are positive. In the inter-business field, they may be well-established as models, negotiated by, or on behalf of, parties of approximately equal bargaining power over a lengthy period of time. The cif international contract of sale and the JCT form of building contract, discussed below, are good examples of this. With these types of contracts, the general position is that they are presumed by the courts to be fair and reasonable because of the roughly equal bargaining position. Despite this, it is not uncommon for a powerful business organisation to impose its 'written standard terms of business' upon one possessing less bargaining strength and it will be seen in Chapter 15 that s 3 of the Unfair Contract Terms Act recognises this. Moreover, the 'battle of the forms' is one example of parties either ignoring or being unaware of terms designed to regulate their relationship. It is clear that business parties often proceed without reading the details embodied in their contract: it has been said that the standard form of building contract works very well in practice so long as it is not read or subjected to legal analysis by the courts!

Consumers do not prepare standard form contracts, but the use of standard form contracts does achieve clear economies in transaction costs which can benefit consumers. This is the case where, for example, a firm sells a large number of mass-produced products or standard services on a regular basis to a variety of people. A multiplicity of transactions all on a similar footing calls for a standard document, not for individually negotiated agreements. To the extent that savings are passed on to the consumer, this must count as an advantage. However, weighing against this benefit are problems regarding communication of information, relating to the crucial rights and duties of the parties. All too often, this is contained in the 'small print' of standard form documents.

However, consumer contracts are often prepared by, or on behalf of, suppliers of goods or services on a 'take-it-or-leave-it' basis. The inequality of bargaining strength normally found to exist between businesses and consumers may be the result of a business concentration of market power, be it monopolistic or oligopolistic, or because the interests of smaller firms are regulated by a trade association. Where the use of standard form contracts is accompanied by inequality of bargaining power, there is a greater likelihood of their being used as instruments of economic oppression because their terms can be weighted in favour of the interests of the stronger parties who prepare them. Here there is no presumption that such contracts are fair and reasonable and, as a result, they are more likely to be subjected to legal regulation. In these circumstances, the courts may consider that there is an absence of genuine agreement and choice which justifies their intervention. In doing this, the courts recognise consumer interest in a choice of goods and services of reasonable quality obtainable at reasonable prices and on fair terms.

It must be clearly understood that standard form contracts often run to a great many pages and individual clauses to more than a page. Moreover, there are thousands of such contracts in use at the present time. Superior bargaining strength is often possessed, and oppressively brought to bear, by suppliers of goods and services. The consumer often has no freedom of choice, except between one standard form, or another which is similarly weighted against him; a 'maze of small print' usually means that onerous clauses are either not read or not understood. These contracts are not agreed to in any real sense. It is well-known that the consumer may have no time to read standard form clauses as they may merely be referred to in the contractual document and be contained in another document elsewhere. Contracts with railway or bus companies are an excellent example of this, although practice is changing with greater use being made of the internet for buying and selling services. Many sites do not allow 'click-wrap' contracts to be concluded until the purchaser confirms they have read the standard forms which can be called up at the click of a mouse.

However, it remains the case that even if consumers did have time to read standard contracts, they would probably not understand them, and even if they did understand them, they would probably have little choice but to accept the terms. When was the last time that you renegotiated the terms of a standard form contract with a major airline carrier or web-based bookseller? Assuming that there is someone in the organisation providing the consumer with such a contract who is aware of its wording and legal significance, we have here an example of what economists call 'information asymmetries' in which one party knows more about the contract than the other.

One approach to this problem would be to reject the assumptions about relative bargaining strength made by classical or neo-classical theorists by encouraging judicial and statutory rewriting of these contracts. Another would be to try and create the negotiating autonomy anticipated by traditionalists and to work towards increased consumer awareness and added legal safeguards relating to such matters as the form and layout of consumer contracts, simplified wording, and rules concerning reasonable notice of terms. Examples of both these approaches are evident in modern legislation and case law. Moreover, legislation passed in recent years has removed some of the more obvious causes of social concern, such as high and hidden interest rates in credit transactions, by outlawing them. Changes have also been imposed relating to the form, layout and language of consumer documents in order to make them more accessible and comprehensible. The Unfair Contract Terms Act 1977 and European legislation have also played an important part in the legal struggle against unfair exclusion and liability in standard form contracts. These developments will be considered more fully in the chapter which follows.

CASE STUDIES

In an introductory book such as this it is neither possible nor appropriate to attempt even a general survey of the law and practice of standard form contracts. However, it is important that students become familiar with some of the contexts within which they operate. In the remainder of this chapter, our object is to examine some particular aspects of building and engineering contracts as they come before the courts in order to elaborate on some of the issues and principles touched on in the last chapter. The prevalence of standard form contracts is such that the task of construing the most common is merely part and parcel of a general judicial function. A case may require the court to establish the true meaning of an individual clause, the relationship between two printed clauses, or a printed clause and a written addition. It may involve a question of whether or not a term may be implied into the contract, or the breadth of an exclusion or limitation of liability clause. In such cases, the substantive rules of contract law may at times play little part or operate only on a secondary level.

In broad terms, building and engineering standard forms display many similarities. Both reflect a high degree of planning of complicated technical operations in the absence of the comprehensive statutory control that it is to be found with most commercial contracts. This planning attempts to establish the detailed nature and scope of the rights and duties of the principal parties and third parties connected with it, such as the architect or consulting engineers and sub-contractors.

The importance of sub-contractors in the performance of the main contract has already been amply demonstrated in the case of *Williams v Roffey Bros and Nicholls (Contractors)* (1991). In both building and engineering contracts it is rare for the contractor to be in a position to undertake all the work required, so that a number of sub-contracts have to be tied in to the main contract. The result is the birth of a network of contracts which are intricately connected with each other. The discrete model of contract is a totally inadequate concept through which to understand such relationships as a whole range of contractors rely on strangers to be able successfully to complete their part of a large project.

The two most difficult problems relating to sub-contracts are delay and the weighing of a sub-contractor's possible liability against his contribution to the total venture. So, for instance, the component supplied by a sub-contractor engaged in the building of an aircraft may be of little financial significance but if defective it may be the cause of a major disaster. It is relevant to mention that another third party, such as the consulting engineer or architect, is given extensive duties to supervise work under the contracts. These professionals commonly issue instructions to the contractor and act as arbitrators in disputes between contractor and purchaser.

One of the most important features of these contracts is the amount of effort made to allow for delays and other disruptions which inevitably arise at some point in a complex chain involving expensive machinery, a range of workers with a large number of different skills and a network of contractors, sub-contractors and agents whose efforts are all inextricably linked to the performance of the overall project. The delay and cost of litigation not only disrupts completion but is likely to lead to financial difficulties for all the parties involved. As a result, there is a considerable incentive to plan for contingencies in advance whilst building in a level of flexibility. It is often possible to settle a dispute arising out of the execution of the works on an *ad hoc* basis without reference to the courts. Alternatively, a party with supervisory functions in the contract, such as an architect, may on a relatively informal basis seek to come to an agreed interpretation of the standard form. If no agreed interpretation can be found, resort may be had to the contract's mediation or arbitration clause. The success of those who draft such contracts in avoiding this danger is such that it has been argued that long-established and universally accepted norms have greatly simplified contracting procedure and they have entirely abolished litigation and arbitration throughout the industry. In the sections which follow, we will take a closer look at how this has been achieved.

BUILDING STANDARD FORMS

Standard form contracts have been in use in the construction industry for over a hundred years. Lord Denning argued that the standard form of contract issued under the authority of the Royal Institute of British Architects (RIBA) and the National Federation of Building Trades Employers is so widely used that it has come to resemble a 'legislative code'. This remark throws further light not only on the nature of standard form contracts but also on judicial functions in relation to them. Most building contracts rest not on private negotiations, but on the adoption of a settled formula or model known as the Joint Contracts Tribunal or JCT contract. This has been devised and revised over a period of time by representatives of all interested parties in the building trade, such as builders, architects, surveyors, sub-contractors and local authorities, representatives of whom form the Joint Contracts Tribunal. As a result, it is a form agreed on by the *whole industry* and does not create a situation where the party is contracting on the *other's* 'written standard terms of business' as we saw in *Butler Machine Tool*. The JCT standard form contract rapidly assumed the status of an authoritative agreement as regards the building operations that it covers although it has always been accepted that terms may be implied. Although managers and site operators are assumed to be familiar with the contract and work proceeds more or less in adherence to its terms, it is often the case that the task of resolving disputes arising out of the execution of the works brings out difficult questions of interpretation of the standard clauses.

It is a key theme throughout this book that legal insistence on clarity and precision in a contractual document may well not wholly accord with the looser, more flexible approach to the implementation of the aims of such a document favoured by those in business and this is clearly the case as regards builders, architects and others on site. Indeed, the flexibility of the RIBA form of contract is such that it has been described as a 'farrago of obscurities'. Clearly, too much standardisation can cause problems when broad terms designed to fit all situations render the contract almost meaningless in places. For this reason the JCT standard form has now been published in six varying editions to suit the requirements of different sorts of parties and endeavours. Even so, the benefits of standardisation are often lost in practice. Even the different editions of the JCT form are rarely used exactly as they are printed. Amendments are made, unwanted clauses are deleted and new ones are added.

The importance of flexibility in these contracts and the provisions designed to facilitate this is well illustrated in the case of *Amalgamated Building Contractors Ltd v Waltham Holy Cross UDC* (1952). Where, under an agreed clause, a contractor asks for an extension of time to complete the works because of, for example, events beyond his control, such as the weather or a shortage of materials, it is generally the architect who has to certify the length of extension allowed. Delay in completion beyond that time usually involves the contractor in paying an agreed sum (liquidated damages) to the employer or building owner unless a further extension is granted. In this case, Waltham UDC, the building owners, employed Amalgamated Building, the contractors, to build 202 houses at a price of £230,000. The contractors were given possession of the site on 7 November 1946, but the formal contract was not entered into until 15 June 1948. Under it the contractors agreed to complete the work by 7 February 1949 and there was a provision for liquidated damages in the event of delay at the rate of £50 a week. On 19 January 1949, Amalgamated Building applied for a 12 month extension because of labour and materials difficulties. The architect did no more than acknowledge this request. The work was not completed until 28 August 1950.

On 20 December 1950, the architect wrote letters, in one of which he stated that he had extended the time for completion from 7 February 1949 to 23 May 1949, and in the other he certified that the whole of the contract should have been completed by 23 May 1949. Waltham UDC claimed liquidated damages at £50 a week for the period from 23 May 1949 to 28 August 1950. Amalgamated Building resisted this claim, stating that they were not liable to pay liquidated damages at all. On the face of it, this appears an extraordinary assertion but is explained in the course of the judgment. Lord Denning came to the following conclusions:

> The validity of the claim for liquidated damages depends on the wording of the contract of 15 June 1948. Clauses 16, 17 and 18 provide that the contractors '(16) ... shall thereupon begin the works forthwith and regularly and diligently proceed with the same and shall complete the same on or before the date for completion stated in the said appendix subject nevertheless to the provisions for extension of time contained in Clause 18 of these conditions. (17) If the contractor fails to complete the works by the date stated in the appendix to these conditions and the architect certifies in writing that in his opinion that same ought reasonably so to have been completed, the contractor shall pay or allow to the employer a sum calculated at the rate stated in the said appendix as liquidated and ascertained damages ... (18) If in the opinion of

the architect the works be delayed (i) by *force majeure,* or (ii) by reason of any exceptionally inclement weather ... or (ix) by reason of labour and material not being available as required ... then in any such case the architect shall make a fair and reasonable extension of time for completion of the works ...'

The work was completed on 28 August 1950. Four months later the architect wrote the two important letters of 20 December 1950. In one of them the architect wrote to the contractors: 'I have now been able to give consideration to the question of extending the time of the above contract. The present expiry date is 7 February 1949, and I have decided that an addition of 15 weeks, bringing the completion date to 23 May 1949, would be a fair and reasonable extension. After careful consideration I cannot see any reason why your whole contract should not have been completed by this date.'

That letter is said to be an extension of time. On the same day the architect wrote another letter, this time to the building owners: 'In accordance with Clause 17 of the RIBA form of contract, I certify that in my opinion the whole of the contract should have been completed by 23 May 1949.'

Those are the two letters which are relied on, the one under Clause 18 and the other under Clause 17, making, as the building owners say, liquidated damages payable for the period from the time when the works ought reasonably to have been completed, 23 May 1949, to the date of completion, 28 August 1950.

The contractors say that the extension of time was invalid. It seems strange that contractors should say that the extension (which was in their favour) was invalid, but they do so because, if the extension time was invalid, they will be able to avoid paying the liquidated damages altogether. The building owners are not able to rely on the original contract time, 7 February 1949, because they have not a certificate under Clause 17 that the works ought reasonably to have been completed by that date. In order to make good their claim to liquidated damages, they must show that the time was validly extended under Clause 18 to 23 May 1949.

The point in the case is therefore: Was the extension, given on 20 December 1950, extending the time to 23 May 1949, valid or not? The contractors say that the words in Clause 18 – 'The architect shall make a fair and reasonable extension of time for completion of the works' – mean that the architect must give the contractors a date at which they can aim in the future, and that he cannot give a date which has passed. I do not agree with this contention. It is only necessary to take a few practical illustrations to see that the architect, as a matter of business, must be able to give an extension even though it is retrospective. Take a simple case where the contractors, near the end of the work, have overrun the contract time for six months without legitimate excuse. They cannot get an extension for that period. Now suppose that the works are still uncompleted and a strike occurs and lasts a month. The contractors can get an extension of time for that month. The architect can clearly issue a certificate which will operate retrospectively. He extends the time by one month from the original completion date, and the extended time will obviously be a date which is already past. Or take a case of delay, such as we have in this case, due to labour and materials not being available. That may cause a continuous delay operating partially, but not wholly, every day, until the works are completed. The works do not stop. They go on, but they go on more slowly right to the end of the works. In such a case, seeing that the cause of delay operates until the last moment, when the works are completed, it must follow that the architect can give a certificate after they are completed. These practical illustrations show that the parties must have intended that the architect should be able to give a certificate which is retrospective, even after the works are completed.

The other members of the Court of Appeal being in agreement, it was held that the extension of time was valid and the contractors were therefore liable to pay liquidated damages of £50 a week for the period 23 May 1949 to 28 August 1950.

ENGINEERING STANDARD FORMS

Over the last 90 years, the Institution of Mechanical Engineers has sponsored and recommended to the industry certain standard form conditions of contract which are from time to time revised in the light of practice. These include models for home contracts, export contracts and the sale of electrical and mechanical goods other than electrical cables. The majority of engineering projects are of an individual nature. The basic object of these contracts, where the engineer erects or installs the plant, is to enable the purchaser at an agreed date to take over and operate the plant which has been completed and tested in accordance with the contract. In practice, engineering contracts are frequently of a complex technical nature and the time required for completion may be lengthy. As a result, there is a greater need for them to be governed by specially agreed 'tailor-made' contracts modelled on the general conditions. In contrast to arrangements in the construction industry, it is common for large-scale operators in the industry to produce their own 'in-house' models which follow the appropriate recommended model. These contracts become 'tailor-made' only by a careful process of incorporation, variation and addition of terms to suit the parties' project.

This means that the functions of contract lawyers in the engineering sector are almost exclusively those of planning, non-litigious interpretation and periodic revision of the model forms so that the rights and duties of the principal parties, and third parties, may be clearly established. Some idea of the high degree of planning that is exhibited in engineering contracts may be gained by listing common clauses contained in such contracts which are lengthy. They include clauses about the things found on site; plant list and operating manuals; patent and other protected rights; assignment and sub-contracting; site conditions; variation orders; unforeseen site conditions; access to manufacturers' premises for inspection of plant; ownership of plant; temporary works and contractors' equipment; liquidated damages; currency of payment; dispute resolution; and secrecy.

The complex nature of these contracts is such that it is essential for the parties to be very clear about who is responsible for the various risks inherent in such enterprises. The mechanism of contract is useful for establishing the obligations of the parties who enter into it, but large-scale engineering operations involve a network of parties who are connected other than by contract. As a result, extensive use is made of 'indemnity' clauses in planning for claims which may arise from third parties to a particular contract who are involved in the larger project. The general purpose of such a clause is to enable one party to recover from the other any loss incurred as a result of claims against him by third parties who suffer loss, damage, injury or death arising out of the performance of the contract. Clause 26 of the now privatised British Steel Corporation's contract provides an excellent example of such a clause:

> 26.1 The contractor shall indemnify the Purchaser against all losses, liabilities, claims, costs and expenses that may result from loss of or damage to any property ... or injury or death to any person (who shall be deemed to include any employee of the

Purchaser) that may arise out of or in connection with the execution of the Contract other than loss, damage, injury or death resulting directly from the act or omission of the Purchaser.

...

26.3 The Contractor shall insure in his own name against all those risks the subject of the Contractor's indemnity in Clause 26.1 with insurers, and on terms approved by the Purchaser ...

One might initially think that a principal party to the contract is in no real position to incur liability for loss or injury to third parties in the context of such a clause. However, although the contractor, or their sub-contractor undertaking the work, is the party who is in all probability directly responsible, a purchaser is by no means immune from third party claims of this kind. The purchaser will probably be the owner or occupier of the site on which the work is being carried out and as such owes duties to others under such statutes as the Health and Safety at Work Act 1974 and the Occupiers' Liability Act 1957. They may have their own employees working 'in connection with' the contract for whom they are vicariously liable and they may even be vicariously liable for the acts or omissions of the contractor themselves, even though the contractor is not an employee.

An example of how these clauses operate in practice is provided by the case of *Murfin v United Steel Companies Ltd* (1957), in which a claim was made against a purchaser-factory occupier alone, who then recovered from the contractor. The facts were that United Steel engaged Power Gas on work at their factory. The latter were bound to indemnify the former 'against every claim against United Steel under any statute or common law for ... (b) death ... arising out of or in connection with the carrying out of Power Gas's work and from any cause other than the negligence of United Steel or their employees'. A sub-contractor's employee was electrocuted in the factory owing to the absence of insulating screens. It was held that United Steel were liable in damages for breach of the Electricity (Factories Act) Special Regulations but were entitled to be indemnified by the contractor because United Steel's 'negligence' as excepted from the indemnity did not include breach of statutory duty.

Significantly, wherever liability eventually rests, this will or should mean that the insurance company of the party responsible will bear the loss. For example, if a third party recovers £10,000 damages against a site owner, the contractor must indemnify the site owner in full. This means that the contractor's insurance company must indemnify the site owner's insurance company who have already met the site owner's liability for the damages awarded. A real life example of how such actions may be framed is provided by *Walters v Whessoe Ltd & Shell Refining Co Ltd* (1960). Whessoe were constructing a tank for Shell at their refinery. Shell's employees left an oil drum containing dangerous vapour on the site whilst Whessoe's men were away at the weekend. One of those men, Walters, was later killed because an earthing fault on his welding machine caused escaping vapour to explode.

In an action brought by Walters' widow against the two companies who were responsible for the acts of their employees, Shell was held 80% and Whessoe 20% responsible. Shell sought to recover their share from Whessoe under an indemnity clause in the contract.

Figure 14.1: *Walters v Whessoe Ltd & Shell Refining Co Ltd* **(1960)**

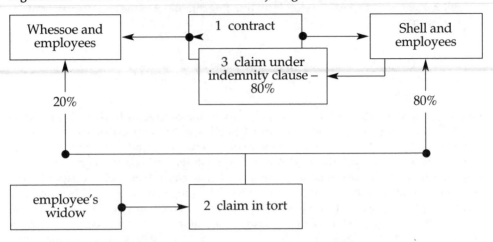

CONCLUDING REMARKS

The importance of standard form contracts in the world of consumers and businesses cannot be overstated. More than any other factor it is the growth of standard forms which has prompted the development of legislative and judicial forms of protection for those who suffer from inequality of bargaining power in the marketplace. Moreover, it is in this field that we have witnessed some of the worst abuses of economic power. Alongside this vision of standard contracts as abusive lies another in which standard form contracts can be seen as facilitating the more efficient working of markets by saving time when the contracting parties are of roughly equal bargaining strength. Seen in this way, they can be conceptualised as a private form of ordering in which industries are able to formalise shared understandings about what constitutes fair practice and sound economic sense. The use of standard contracts to plan future relations and allow for the flexibility needed in a field can be seen in a positive light.

In the chapters which follow we shall look at how the judiciary and legislature have attempted to tread the thin line between efficiency and abuse. In the next two chapters we shall be focusing on the use of clauses which attempt to exclude certain liabilities from contracts. Exclusion clauses can be found in negotiated and standard form contracts, but it is their use in the latter which has most often troubled the judiciary and legislature. The UK government has legislated for regulation of certain types of exclusion clause for nearly three decades, but European intervention in the field has returned the spotlight to standard form contracts and works from a presumption that they have the potential to distort contractual relationships.

REFERENCES AND FURTHER READING

Kessler, F 'Contracts of adhesion: some thoughts about freedom of contract' (1942) 43 Columbia Law Review 629.

McKendrick, E (2003) *Contract Law*, 5th edn, Basingstoke: Palgrave Macmillan.

Rakoff, T 'Contracts of adhesion: an essay in reconstruction' (1983) 96 Harvard Law Review 1173.

Slawson, W 'Standard form contracts and democratic control of law-making power' (1971) 84 Harvard Law Review 529.

Trebilcock, M (1980) 'An economic approach to unconscionability', in Reiter, B and Swan, J (eds), *Studies in Contract Law*, Toronto: Butterworths.

QUESTIONS

(1) How would you distinguish between contracts of adhesion where market power is being abused and standard form contracts which benefit both parties?

(2) In your view, in 'The Sad Tale of Angie and Georgie', does Chelsea need consumer protection when booking the ferry ticket on the web? Can you find out what recent regulations say about these types of contract?

CHAPTER 15

BUSINESSES, CONSUMERS AND UNFAIR TERMS

INTRODUCTION

So far in this section of the book we have concentrated on the terms of a contract and how these reflect the obligations the parties owe to each other. This chapter shifts the focus to look at how the judiciary has dealt with unfair terms in contracts. As in other chapters, it is important to start by making it clear that different approaches to unfair bargains are apparent from case law and these reflect different conceptions of the role of contract law and notions of what is fair and reasonable. Whilst the classical model of contract recognises that unfairness occurs, the focus is on procedural rather than substantive unfairness. This means that traditionalists have been unwilling to intervene to upset a contract which has been negotiated in a fair way. But even with the introduction of legislation and the development of doctrines to protect the parties against manifestly unfair contracts, it remains the case that contractual terms are not set aside lightly. The courts and legislature will only intervene to mitigate the effects of extreme behaviour. As Atiyah (1979) has explained:

> According to this theory, the role of the courts in handling contract cases is very limited, and the same is true for the role allotted to ideas of fairness and justice. Classical theory distinguishes fundamentally between fairness in the process of negotiating and concluding a bargain, on the one hand, and fairness in the result or outcome of the bargain, on the other. Making a contract is thus rather like participating in a contest or game. There are rules designed to regulate the way in which the context is conducted, to outlaw fouls, and so on ... But if the game is played according to the rules, there is really very limited scope for any concept of a 'fair outcome'. Both participants should benefit from taking part in the game, and the best contestant should 'win'.

The view that the best contestant should be allowed to get a better outcome has become more contentious since the time when the classical model first came to dominate the law of contract. In truth, the courts have always found it hard to separate questions of unfair negotiations from unfair terms. The growth of welfarism within the law of contract has encouraged the courts and legislature to intervene to limit the autonomy of contracting parties where significant inequalities of bargaining power are reflected in contractual terms. This approach to the subject has been particularly evident in the field of consumer contracts where there has been recognition that the growth of large-scale businesses and standard form contracts means that consumers have no power to either negotiate the terms of the contract or suggest alterations. The courts and legislature have been particularly diligent in their approach to the regulation of exclusion clauses which tend to limit and exclude liability rather than define positive obligations.

JUDICIAL APPROACHES TO EXCLUSION CLAUSES

The judicial role in the regulation of unfair exclusion clauses has been somewhat overshadowed by the creation of legislation in the field, but there are a number of reasons why it remains very important. First, even with the advent of legislation, the judiciary has a significant role to play in interpreting the meaning of exclusion clauses, legislative tests and the context in which the exclusion clause is being used. Moreover, many contracts in the field of insurance, land, intellectual property and securities do not fall within the ambit of statutes such as the Unfair Contract Terms Act 1977. Finally, the judiciary has taken the lead in limiting the scope of exclusion clauses and legislative intervention cannot be understood fully without reference to the case law. In the remainder of this section we outline the various common law rules which they have developed in their attempts to police terms.

In previous chapters when we have looked at pre-contractual representations, express terms, implied terms and standard form contracts, the focus has been on determining how we know which obligations have been included in the contractual arrangements. By way of contrast, the aim of exemption clauses is to make sure that certain liabilities are excluded from the contract.

Figure 15.1: Elements of the contract

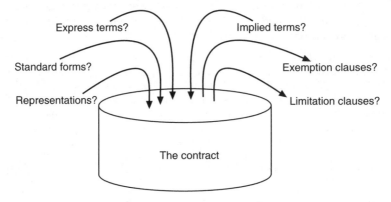

It can be seen from the figure above that there are two types of exclusion clauses: exemption and limitation. Exemption clauses seek to exclude a particular type of liability, whereas limitation clauses merely seek to limit liability. The clear purpose of an exclusion clause in a consumer transaction is to enable the business person to eliminate the risk of having to pay damages to the other party for breach and exclusion clauses are common in business-consumer contracts. In commercial transactions where bargaining strength is more likely to be equal, exclusion clauses are less common, although limitation of liability clauses are often found. These apportion the risk of loss between the parties who can insure accordingly. In fact, in standard form dealings between business organisations, there is a general tendency towards a more sophisticated and wide-ranging concern with risk and its apportionment than is to be found in consumer transactions. The parties, through the use of settled, agreed devices, often display a willingness to combine to avoid or minimise common 'enemies' including the risks of litigation. To this extent, contrary to the classical approach, their contracts emphasise common interests rather than 'separation' and conflict.

As we have already suggested, approaches to attempts by the parties to exempt liability have changed considerably. Seventy years ago a Miss L'Estrange bought a cigarette machine under a sales agreement which contained a clause which stated that 'any express or implied condition, statement or warranty, statutory or otherwise not stated herein, is hereby excluded'. Although the machine soon jammed and became unworkable, she lost her action for breach. This year, one of the authors purchased a car under a sales agreement which stated that: 'Nothing in these conditions is intended to remove, alter or restrict any rights or obligations of either party arising under the Sale of Goods legislation.' On the face of it, all or most of Miss L'Estrange's contractual rights or remedies were removed by the exclusion clause. In the second transaction, the protection afforded by virtue of implied statutory obligations was apparently unimpaired. Why the change? How has the common law approached the issue of unfair clauses in contracts? How have they balanced the needs of autonomous individuals to make whatever deals they see fit with a desire to introduce more substantive notions of unfairness?

Whenever faced with an exclusion clause, it is standard practice to divide an analysis of it into five main questions. First, is the clause which seeks to exclude or limit a party's liability incorporated into the contract? Secondly, if so, as a matter of judicial construction, does the wording of the clause satisfactorily cover the loss or damage at issue? Thirdly, if it does, is it a clause which is rendered ineffective under the 1977 Act? Fourthly, if it passes this test, does the clause satisfy the requirement of reasonableness? Finally, if the term is contained in a standard form contract, is it subject to the test of fairness in European regulations?

The first two questions are addressed in this chapter and, in the next chapter, we go on to consider the remaining issues. But before moving on it is useful to summarise the various questions which you will need to ask when determining whether an exclusion clause is effective and the limitations which might be placed on it. There is no doubt that the law surrounding exclusion clauses is complex as it involves a web of different types of regulatory controls.

The key questions which you should be asking are summarised in Figure 15.2 which you might like to help guide you through the sections which follow.

Is the clause incorporated into the contract?

The issue of how terms become incorporated into contracts has already been touched upon in the section of this book concerned with pre-contractual negotiations and misrepresentation. But the courts' dislike of attempts to exempt liability in contracts involving those in a relatively weak bargaining position has led to a number of rules about these particular clauses being developed in addition to the general rules. Moreover, despite the intervention of the legislature, the pre-statutory case law remains to provide the guidelines in this area. It will soon become clear that the common law cases are almost exclusively concerned with situations in which one party seeks to rely on written terms contained in documents displayed at a place of business or on documents exchanged between the parties in the course of negotiations. In these cases, the courts have imposed the requirements that if such written terms are to form part of the contract, then they must have been brought to the attention of the party whose rights are being restricted. The case law reveals an increasingly restrictive

Figure 15.2: Is an (exclusion) clause effective?

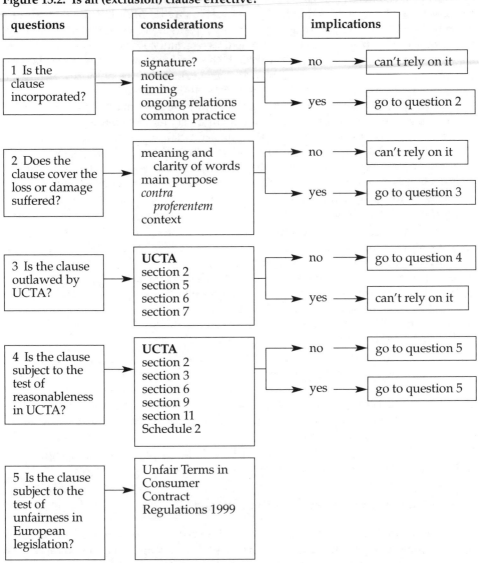

approach to those able to impose their standard conditions on others because of their market power or knowledge.

(a)   Signed documents

The 'rule' in *L'Estrange and Graucob* (1934) reflects the formalistic tendencies of English contract law and an early unsympathetic approach to the plight of those who contract with a stronger party on their standard terms and conditions. The rationale behind the decision is that the best way to prove that written terms on which you are seeking to rely have been brought to the notice of the other party is to ask them to sign the document in which they are contained. This is clearly something of a fiction. In modern-day society, we probably all sign contractual documents without reading the document fully. This does not necessarily reflect our stupidity or lack of business acumen. Rather, it is a reflection of the fact that even if one did object to a particular clause, there is often no practical alternative and the agents with whom we contract are rarely in a position to renegotiate terms. When was the last time that you heard of anyone renegotiating a ticket price or exclusion clauses with a major airline or 'white goods' dealer? Nonetheless, the case of *L'Estrange* is authority for the proposition that a person who signs a contractual document is bound by its terms even though they have not read them. In this case, the plaintiff was bound by her signature even though the exclusion clause was, in the view of the court, in 'regrettably small print'. Putting her signature to the document meant that she could not argue that she had no notice of the clause. This is a case which would now be decided on the basis of the 'reasonableness' of the clause under s 6(3) of the 1977 Act, but its relevance for present purposes is that it reminds us of the fact that the court implies that notice has been given in certain circumstances even if the signatory has not read the clause and has no working knowledge of it. If, however, the true purpose of the signed document has been misrepresented to the party signing, the absolute effect of their signature will not be enforced. So, in *Curtis v Chemical Cleaning & Dyeing Co Ltd* (1951), the restricted scope of an exclusion clause was taken to be as orally represented at the time the contract was being negotiated and not as written (see also *Couchman v Hill* (1947) and *Evans & Son (Portsmouth) Ltd v Merzario Ltd* (1976)).

(b)   Reasonably sufficient notice

In cases which do not involve signatures, it is necessary to prove that the party alleging breach was aware, or ought to have been aware, of the written conditions that the other party was trying to incorporate into the contract to exclude their liability. The courts have required that reasonable notice must be given of a clause set out, or referred to, in such a document, or displayed at the place where the contract is entered into. One way in which they have approached this issue is to ask whether the document containing the conditions is a 'contractual' document. If not, the clause set out or referred to has no force. In *Chapelton v Barry UDC* (1940), for instance, a ticket containing conditions on the reverse handed to a customer after they had paid for hire of a deckchair was held to be merely a 'voucher or receipt'. However, in general, whether a document is one which could reasonably be expected to contain contractual terms is a question of fact which may vary with business practice. This means that a 'receipt' may have contractual force in other business contexts.

Other cases have focused on what constitutes reasonable notice of a restrictive term when documents containing it are not to hand. In 1930 in *Thompson v London, Midland and Scottish Railway Co Ltd*, the court was satisfied that reasonable notice had been given to a passenger of an exclusion clause found on p 552 of the company's sixpenny timetable. The trail to the clause started with the words 'see back' on her ticket. Although a similar point would probably be decided differently today, incorporation by reference to a further document or by the use of a clearly exhibited printed notice may, in many situations, be the only feasible means of communication for the party relying on a clause. Interestingly, the increasing use of the internet to make contracts has improved the position as regards notice as consumers using this medium are often given ample opportunity to read easily accessible written terms. Indeed, in many cases, a contract cannot be concluded until the terms have been called up on screen and the purchaser indicates they have read them.

Despite the general provisions relating to notice, the courts have been prepared to take a more interventionist stance where the exemption clauses concerned are especially onerous. In *Thornton v Shoe Lane Parking Ltd* (1971), Lord Denning insisted on the need for *special steps* to be taken by a party wishing to incorporate unusual or unexpected protective terms into a contract. In that case, Thornton parked his car for the first time at Shoe Lane Parking's car park. A notice outside the entrance stated that: 'All cars parked at owner's risk.' At the entrance, Thornton received a ticket from a machine and an automatic barrier was raised. In small print on the ticket it was stated that: 'This ticket is issued subject to the conditions of issue displayed on the premises.' Inside the building was another notice which purported to exempt Shoe Lane Parking from any liability resulting from damage to the car or personal injury. When collecting his car, there was an accident and Thornton was injured, partly as a result of Shoe Lane Parking's negligence. The court held that, although bound by the exterior notice, the clause relating to personal injury had not been incorporated into the contract. They reasoned that Shoe Lane Parking had not taken sufficient steps to draw Thornton's attention to the 'less typical' personal injury disclaimer at the time the contract was made at the entrance.

The same approach to unfair terms was adopted in a more general commercial context in *Interfoto Picture Library Ltd v Stiletto Visual Programmes Ltd* (1989), which demonstrates the close relationship between substantive and procedural unfairness in practice. The term in question was not an exclusion clause but referred to holding charges for late return of photographs loaned to the defendants for promotional purposes. A two week delay in returning them incurred a charge of £3,783, which was well above comparable rates elsewhere in the trade. The term was described as 'unreasonable and extortionate'. The court decided that because the plaintiffs had failed to take exceptional steps to bring the defendant's attention to their charges, the term did not become part of the contract for lack of reasonable notice and was disallowed as a result.

The courts have also been interested in the timing of the notice, particularly whether notice of the clause had been brought to the attention of the other party before or at the time of making the contract. This was one of the issues discussed in the *Thornton* judgment but was also considered in *Olley v Marlborough Court* (1949). In this case, a contract for the hire of a hotel room was made at the hotel reception desk. However, a clause relating to the safe custody of guests' valuables was to be found in a notice on their bedroom wall. The court in that case barred the hotel from relying on the exclusion clause as the contract had already been 'closed'.

The courts' recognition of relational elements to contracts is reflected in the expectation that a clause may be incorporated into a particular transaction from a regular previous course of dealing. In these circumstances it is argued that it can be assumed that the parties have already been made aware of the existence of a term and had an opportunity to examine it. So, for instance, if the Olleys had regularly visited the Marlborough Court Hotel before and seen or had the opportunity to see the exclusion clause, the clause might have become part of the contract. See also *Kendall &*

Sons v Lillico & Sons Ltd (1969) and *British Crane Hire Corp Ltd v Ipswich Plant Hire Ltd* (1975).

THE JUDICIAL CONSTRUCTION OF EXCLUSION CLAUSES

Those attempting to rely on an exclusion clause will have passed the first important hurdle facing them if they are able to prove to the court's satisfaction that the clause has been incorporated into the contract. But even where the clause *is* incorporated as a term of the contract, the judiciary may interpret the wording used restrictively so as to limit its scope. Long before the advent of legislation the common law has required that exclusion clauses be expressed clearly and without ambiguity if they are to be effective. In particular, the judiciary has required that a clause must clearly cover the liability which it seeks to exclude. The tendency has been to adopt a literal approach to wording. Moreover, if there is ambiguity as to the scope or meaning of an exclusion or limitation clause, the doubt will be resolved by construing it *against* the party who seeks to rely on the clause. This is known as the *contra proferentem* rule. So, for instance, in an inter-business contract for the sale of cotton thread it was stipulated that 'The goods *delivered* shall be deemed to be in all respects in accordance with the contract' unless the buyer complained within 14 days of their receipt. It was held that this clause was no defence to a claim for damages for delivery of less than was anticipated. This was because the damages were being claimed on the basis of goods which were not delivered and the clause expressly mentioned only goods actually delivered. The courts have even been known to 'discover' ambiguity in order to allow them to interpret a clause in the interests of justice and the weaker party.

However, the judiciary have also been shown to favour moderation in some circumstances. In the case of *Ailsa Craig Fishing Co Ltd v Malvern Fishing Co Ltd* (1983), the opinion was expressed that the rules of construction would not normally operate as strictly in the case of limitation of liability clauses. This was because those using limitation clauses were not attempting to absolve themselves of all responsibility but merely to contain it. Moreover, many limitation clauses are considered acceptable in contracts where the point of the deal is to allocate risks between the parties. For instance, clauses which place a financial limit on compensation are generally found in inter-business transactions and are common risk-allocation devices backed by insurance.

Generally, it is true to say that the more extensive the attempt to exclude liability, the clearer the words used must be. So, in applying the *contra proferentem* rule to attempts to exclude liability for negligence, the courts have required that extremely clear words must be required. Perhaps the best guide was established by the House of Lords in the indemnity case of *Smith v South Wales Switchgear Ltd* (1978), in which a business party seeking to exclude liability for negligence was advised to expressly use the word 'negligence' or a synonymous expression such as 'any act or omission' in his clause rather than a general phrase such as 'any liability, loss, claim or proceedings whatsoever' (but see *Scottish Special Housing Association v Wimpey Construction Ltd* (1986)). Moreover, it has also been argued that if there is any doubt as to whether the words used cover negligent liability, it will be assumed that they do not unless there is no other liability to be excluded (see *Alderslade v Hendon Laundry Ltd* (1945)).

In addition to the *contra proferentem* rule, the courts have developed the 'main purpose' rule. This requires that where exclusion clauses are inconsistent with the main purpose of the contract, then they can be rejected because they are in danger of rendering the purpose of the contract nonsensical. So, for instance, an exclusion clause which sought to exclude liability for the roadworthiness of a new deluxe model car would seem to defeat the object of entering into a contract to purchase one. The rule was endorsed by the House of Lords in *Suisse Atlantique Société d'Armement Maritime SA v NV Rotterdamsche Kolen Centrale* (1967) and was subsequently given statutory effect by s 3 of the Unfair Contract Terms Act 1977.

At one point it was argued by some members of the judiciary that if a party committed a 'fundamental' breach of a contract, they were not able to rely on any exemption clause in a contract. The rule had the effect of depriving a party in default of the benefit of their clause. This position was questioned by the House of Lords in *Suisse Atlantique*, where it was suggested that there is no rule of law that an exemption clause can never apply in these circumstances. In *Photo Production Ltd v Securicor Transport Ltd* (1980), the House of Lords re-affirmed that the efficacy or otherwise of an exclusion clause depends upon its construction, and whether or not the contract has terminated. It was argued that although a breach may have occasioned dire consequences, this in itself did not bring into play *even harsher* construction of an exclusion clause than was usual. In any event, their Lordships tended to steer clear of the notion of fundamental breach in this decision. Instead, the court emphasised that business parties, assumed to be of equal bargaining strength, should be left free, through their use of exclusionary and other devices backed by insurance cover, to apportion risks of loss as they thought fit without judicial intervention. This position was reinforced by s 9 of the 1977 Unfair Contract Terms Act 1977.

CONCLUDING REMARKS

It is clear from the various doctrines discussed in this chapter that the judiciary has had a major role to play in the regulation of unfair clauses in contracts. This is nothing new. Many commentators have argued that the common law has always placed considerable emphasis on fairness and that this heritage is particularly obvious in the pre-classical period. But it is also clear that the growth in the use of standard form contracts has encouraged the judiciary in its interventionist tendencies. Whilst a focus on pre-contractual negotiations and procedural fairness is discernible from the case law, consideration of what was fair during the negotiation process is in practice hard to disentangle from an examination of substantive terms, as we saw in the *Interfoto* case. But the discomfort of the judiciary in overtly interrogating the actual terms of the contract rather than the making of it also marks out the boundaries of judicial regulation of contracts. The setting aside of contractual terms agreed between the parties has remained sufficiently contentious for it to require judicial intervention to outlaw particular types of abuse. It is to this issue that we turn in the next chapter, which continues the story of regulation of contractual terms.

REFERENCES AND FURTHER READING

Atiyah, P (1979) *The Rise and Fall of Freedom of Contract*, Oxford: Clarendon.

Nichols, A and Rawlings, R 'Note on *Photo-Production v Securicor*' (1980) 43 MLR 567; also Guest, A (1980) 96 LQR 324.

Whittaker, S 'Judicial interventionism in consumer contracts' (2001) 117 LQR 215.

QUESTIONS

(1) On what basis did the House of Lords in *Photo Production Ltd v Securicor Transport Ltd* (1980) overrule the Court of Appeal decision in *Harbutt's 'Plasticine' Ltd v Wayne Tank and Pump Co Ltd* (1970)? In preparing your answer, summarise the arguments made by Nichols and Rawlings (1980) and respond to them.

(2) How many exclusion clauses can you identify in 'The Sad Tale of Angie and Georgie'? How in your view would their presence alter the liability of the parties?

(3) Yoav goes to Brightpool for a week's holiday. While there he decides to visit the swimming pool. A notice at the turnstile says: 'The Management accept no responsibility for loss or damage to valuables unless left at the office.' Yoav ignores this notice. In his cubicle there is another notice which reads: 'No liability for personal injury.' Yoav ignores this notice and places his mobile phone on the ledge above it. As he runs to dive into the water, he trips over a brush negligently left on the floor by the attendant and breaks his arm. He later finds that his phone was stolen while he was at the hospital having his arm set. Discuss whether Yoav has any claim against the management in respect of his phone or his injury.

(4) Sam leaves his portable computer valued at £2,000 with Sick Electronics to remove a virus. He signed an order form which stated that: 'All machines are expressly accepted at the owner's risk.' Three weeks later, having not heard from Sick Electronics, Sam telephoned and discovered that the computer had been irreparably damaged by a fault in the diagnostic program. Advise Sam.

Explain the position if Sick Electronics had told Sam that they did not do the work themselves and Sam had authorised them to send the computer to Z Ltd, a reputable firm of specialist programmers. The computer had been stolen by an employee of Z Ltd. There is no exclusion clause in the contract between Sam and Sick Electronics but there is a wide and well-worded clause in the contract between Sick Electronics and Z Ltd.

CHAPTER 16

LEGISLATIVE REGULATION OF UNFAIR TERMS

INTRODUCTION

In the last chapter, we looked at how terms are incorporated into contracts and the various devices employed by the judiciary to limit the scope of certain types of exclusion clauses. In time, however, judicial control of such clauses was considered too limited. Social concern regarding the exclusion or restriction of contractual liability for breach of contract by those in business to supply goods and services goes back well into the 19th century. Apart from isolated statutory measures, the legal struggle against such 'unfair terms' was carried on until the 1970s by the judges, who devised a variety of weapons to render such clauses inoperative, particularly where they operated against the interests of consumers in contracts for the sale of goods or supply of services. However, successes by the courts merely drove the drafters of exclusion clauses to renewed efforts to produce 'judge-proof' forms of words such as that which defeated the court in *L'Estrange v Graucob Ltd* (1934). The main problem was that the judges felt that they had no general power to strike down unreasonable exclusion clauses as being, for example, against public policy and therefore void. They felt that the concept of freedom of contract overrode such an approach.

There are now hundreds of statutory provisions dealing with such issues as tenancies, consumer credit, hire purchase and package holidays. Following the lead of the common law, each of these interferes with the freedom to contract by regulating the terms of certain contracts and determining what sorts of liability can be excluded from them. It is not the purpose of this chapter to examine the whole body of civil and criminal law, the regulatory mechanisms and voluntary codes of practice which now exist to protect the consumer from unsafe products, qualitatively deficient goods and services, fraudulent trading practices and the other matters which make up the study of modern consumer protection law and practice. Our main aim is to concentrate on the legal response to unfair and oppressive terms in contracts made with consumers and others, which culminated in the passing of the Unfair Contract Terms Act 1977 (UCTA) and the coming into effect of the European Community Directive on Unfair Terms in Consumer Contracts Regulations of 1994 and 1999. One of the reasons for this emphasis is that this was the first legislative attempt to introduce standards about exclusion clauses into the general law of contract.

The common law approach to exclusion clauses is reflected in many of the provisions of the legislation which has been used in recent decades to complement or reinforce judicial precedent. But UCTA 1977 and the Unfair Terms in Consumer Contracts Regulations 1999 also go beyond the common law and have introduced additional hurdles for those attempting to rely on exclusion clauses. These two pieces of legislation overlap substantially with the result that some types of term are regulated by both and others by just one. Consequently it is now open to consumers to challenge certain contract terms on the basis that they are void or 'unreasonable' under UCTA or 'unfair' under the regulations. In many cases the result will be the same but the fact that the concepts of reasonableness and fairness are different means that there is considerable scope for confusion. For this reason, the Law Commission is currently reviewing both pieces of legislation with the aim of replacing them with a single Act written in plain, accessible language. A final report and draft legislation is due to be published in 2004. It would seem then that, contrary to the classical approach, very serious attempts have been made to tackle inequality of bargaining power and to define what the courts and legislature consider to be unfair or unreasonable terms. In the sections which follow we attempt to introduce you to some of the key concepts which have emerged from these two pieces of legislation without getting overly caught up in complicated detail.

THE UNFAIR CONTRACT TERMS ACT 1977

Despite its title, UCTA does not deal with all contracts or unfair terms but focuses instead on exclusion clauses in an effort to protect consumers and others from particularly unfair limitations of liability. The general thrust of the Act is to regulate those terms which enable one party to offer a performance which is substantially different from that expected. In this way, legislative interventions have provided a hierarchy of protection depending on the type of liability which a party is attempting to exclude, the status of the person seeking to avoid the clause and the characteristics of the person seeking to rely on it. In order to understand fully the provisions of the Act it is necessary to appreciate that it is based on the premise that there are two types of contracting party: those who are dealing as consumers and those dealing as businesses. Potentially, this allows for three different types of contract to be concluded and this point is illustrated in Figure 16.1.

Figure 16.1: The three different types of contract

	contracting with	
business party	+	business party
business party	+	non-business (consumer)
non-business	+	non-business

The Act is limited in its application in that it only subjects contracts made between two business parties or one business party and a consumer to scrutiny. According to s 11, 'business liability' can only occur under the Act if one of the parties is acting in the course of a business or the occupation of business premises. On the other hand, s 12 makes clear that a person deals as a consumer if they do *not* make, or hold themselves out as making, the contract in the course of a business and the other party does make the contract in the course of a business. In other words, you cannot be a consumer under the Act unless you are dealing with someone who is acting in the course of a business. This means that when one party deals with another outside a business environment, neither is treated by the Act as a consumer. Thus, the conferment of the status of consumer depends on the circumstances rather than the person. This approach reflects the fact that the Act is primarily concerned with protecting the interests of consumers when dealing with businesses.

Outlawed clauses

One of the most interesting features of the Act is that it declares void certain types of clauses whatever the circumstances in which they were negotiated. The Act renders six main types of exclusion clauses inoperative on the basis that they attempt to deny specific rights to contracting parties that social policy requires they should have. The ban is total, pays no heed to the intentions of the parties so valued by the classical model and gives the judiciary no discretion to amend the contract in any way where these clauses are present. The relevant clauses are summarised in the Figure 16.2.

Figure 16.2: Unfair Contract Terms Act 1977 outlawed exclusion clauses

outlawed exclusion clauses	section
negligence – any liability for *negligently* causing death or personal injury cannot be excluded by businesses	2(1)
Manufacturers' guarantees – liability for negligence in the manufacture or distribution of goods usually supplied for private use cannot be excluded when the goods are used by a consumer	5
implied terms – statutory implied undertakings as to ownership to title in sale of goods and hire purchase contracts	6(1)
implied terms – statutory implied undertaking relating to conformity with description or sample in sale of goods and hire purchase contracts cannot be used against a person dealing as a consumer	6(2)
implied term – statutory implied undertakings relating to quality or fitness for purpose in contracts for sale of goods or hire purchase cannot be used against a person dealing as a consumer	6(2)
other undertakings – relating to description, fitness, sample or quality cannot be used against a person dealing as a consumer	7(2)

Not all of the outlawed clauses detailed above relate to contractual liability. Section 2 relates to clauses or notices which purport to exclude business liability for negligence. Under s 1(1), negligence means breach of a contractual duty to take reasonable care or exercise reasonable skill as, for instance, in a contract for services, and also breach of a tortious duty. This might arise, for example, in respect of a notice at a sporting event that spectators attend free of charge and for which there is no contract. Section 5 also extends beyond the scope of contract law. It prevents the use in manufacturers' 'guarantees' or 'warranties' for consumer goods of clauses which restrict or exclude liability for loss or damage that arises from defects in the goods while in 'consumer use' and results from negligence in the manufacture or distribution of the goods. The section is therefore concerned with the manufacturer–consumer relationship where there is no contract between the parties rather than the supplier–consumer relationship where there is a contract.

One of the most important provisions for the general law of contract is s 6(2). This establishes that in *consumer* transactions, a business supplier's liability for breach of the statutorily implied obligations relating to the satisfactory quality and fitness for purpose of his goods cannot be excluded or restricted by any contract term. This section follows the lead taken by successive Sale of Goods Acts 1979 and Supply of Goods and Services Act 1982 and Supply of Goods (Implied Terms) Act 1973 in requiring that certain terms are written into consumer contracts by the legislature. Since legislation requires that they be written in, it is natural that the person dealing with a consumer should not be able to exclude them. It would be on this basis that the exclusion clause in the *Karsales (Harrow) Ltd v Wallis* (1956) hire purchase case could now be struck down by reference to the Act rather than the notion of fundamental breach.

The tests of reasonableness

The exclusion clauses which do not fall into one of the six categories rendered automatically void by the Act may nonetheless be subjected to a second type of control introduced by it whereby certain other clauses are subjected to the test of reasonableness. Significantly, the burden of proof regarding reasonableness lies with the party seeking to rely on the clause, a factor which facilitates the undermining of such clause by consumers. Wherever the Act provides that a contract term or notice must meet the requirement of reasonableness, the *time* for assessing its reasonableness is the time when the contract was made. This means that an assessment is made against the background of the circumstances which were, or ought reasonably to have been, known to the parties at that time. If a clause is considered to have been reasonable at the time the contract was made, then its effectiveness will not be impaired by subsequent events or conduct such as the effect of breach. It has been argued that to provide otherwise would amount to 'changing the rules in the middle of the game'.

Figure 16.3 outlines the sort of terms which are subjected to this additional test.

Figure 16.3: Unfair Contract Terms Act 1977 test of reasonableness

key exclusion clauses subject to test of reasonableness	section	can apply to
negligence – terms which attempt to exclude negligent liability for loss or damage other than personal injury or death	2	business and business business and consumer
standard form contract – terms which attempt to exclude or restrict liability for breach when party attempting to rely on clauses is in breach	3(2)(a)	business and business business and consumer
standard form contracts – terms which attempt to allow for a contractual performance which is substantially different from what was expected	3(2)(b)(i)	business and business business and consumer
standard form contracts – terms which attempt to allow for no contractual performance at all to be rendered	3(2)(b)(ii)	business and business business and consumer
implied terms – terms which attempt to exclude or restrict liability for breach of the statutorily implied terms in sale of goods or hire purchase contracts	6	business and business
breach – exclusion clauses in contracts where the contract is justifiably terminated	9	business and business business and consumer

Whilst the provisions relating to outlawed clauses impose an evaluation of what is considered to be unacceptable on contracting parties, the thrust of the reasonableness is to look at the fairness of the term in the context in which it was negotiated (s 11). So, for example, the Act recognises that contracts often reflect agreements as to risk allocation and the price paid. But it also requires that where a term or notice, required to be reasonable, places a maximum *financial limit* on the amount that may be recovered, the court must take account of the resources available to the party seeking the benefit of the clause to meet the liability if it arises (s 1(4)). It is also the case that the Act expects the judiciary to inquire into whether the parties were in a position to cover themselves by insurance.

We have already discovered that attempts to exclude certain implied terms in contracts between a business and consumer are outlawed. But the Act also has something to say about attempts to exclude liability where the contract is between two business parties. Here, the approach has been to attempt to ascertain the extent to which the parties were in a position to make a rational choice about the limitation or exclusion of liability. In these cases, additional guidance is given about the application of the reasonableness test where the clause concerned is in a non-consumer contract for sale or supply of goods. This is contained in Sched 2 to the Act and suggests that the following factors, among others, may be taken as relevant by the court:

- the relative strength of the bargaining positions of the parties;

- whether the claimant received an inducement, such as a lower price, to agree to the exemption;

- whether the claimant knew or ought reasonably to have known of the existence and extent of the term, having regard to, among other things, any custom of the trade or any previous course of dealing between the parties;

- whether any condition for the enforcement of liability such as the need to bring a claim within seven days of performance could practicably be complied with by the claimant;

- whether the claimant had the opportunity to enter into a similar contract with other persons but without having to accept a similar term; and

- whether the goods were specially made to the order of the claimant.

These guidelines apply only to sale and supply of goods cases but they remain significant in other cases. Not only are they one of the first legislative attempts to specify the factors which should be taken into account when accessing what is reasonable in the general law of contract, but they have also been found to have influenced the courts in other cases which are outside the ambit of the section (see *Smith v Eric S Bush* (1989) below).

Negligence liability – 'other loss or damage'

We have already considered the fact that the Act outlaws any attempt to exclude any liability for *negligently* causing death or personal injury by businesses. In addition to this, s 2(2) requires that a business party cannot in the case of loss or damage *other than death or personal injury* exclude or restrict their liability for negligence, except in so far as the term or notice satisfies the requirement of reasonableness. The clause covers inter-business agreements as well as those between consumers and businesses. The application of the test can be demonstrated in *Wight v British Railways Board* (1983). In this case, British Railways Board lost Wight's suitcase but sought to rely on a clause limiting their liability to £1,500 per ton. The drafters of the limitation clearly had commercial consignments in mind rather than those of individuals. Wight's suitcase contained valuable jewellery but, according to terms on display and in the consignment note, the case was carried 'at owner's risk'. The clause having been satisfactorily incorporated into the contract, the judge moved to enquire whether the clause was fair and reasonable in the circumstances. It was held that it was easier for the claimant to insure than the carriers because in the circumstances there were no real means whereby British Railways Board might ascertain the value of the goods consigned. As a result, the clause was considered reasonable (see also *Waldron-Kelly v British Railways Board* (1981)).

The fact that the question of reasonableness depends on the facts of each individual case was brought home in the *Phillips Products Ltd v Hyland* (1987) decision where the Court of Appeal stated that appellate courts should not readily overturn decisions at first instance on this issue. Moreover, in *Smith v Eric S Bush* (1989), a case involving a surveyor instructed by a house purchaser, Lord Griffiths stated that, whatever else, the following matters should always be considered:

(1) Were the parties of equal bargaining power? In this case it was decided that 'the purchaser ... has no effective power to object'.

(2) In the case of advice, would it have been reasonably practicable to obtain the advice from an alternative source, taking into account considerations of costs and time? Here, the house was 'at the bottom end of the market' of a type typically bought by young, first-time buyers who were financially not well-placed to pay for a second opinion.

(3) How difficult is the task being undertaken for which liability is being excluded? The court found that in this case, the work was 'at the lower end of the surveyor's field of professional expertise'.

In their deliberations, the judges in this case considered the practical consequences of the decision on the question of reasonableness. More specifically, they asked whether the risk was one against which the defendant could easily have insured and whether it would have serious consequences for a claimant who was required to bear the loss. It was held that the clause relied upon by the surveyor in this case was not reasonable, but Lord Griffiths also stressed that the decision would have been different if the purchase had concerned 'industrial property, large blocks of flats or very expensive houses'.

Other case law reiterates the importance of determining who is in a position to insure against risks in any commercial relationship. *Photo Production Ltd v Securicor Transport Ltd* (1980) concerned an inter-business agreement which was not decided under the 1977 Act but in conformity with it. Securicor were employed to guard a building but in fact an employee burnt down Photo Production's factory. However, the House of Lords found in Securicor's favour because Photo Production was in a better position to insure its factory against such a contingency than the security firm but had failed to do so. *Phillips* also involved business parties and damage to property. In this case, Phillips Products hired a JCB extractor and its driver. The contract was based on the Contractors' Plant Association model conditions for plant hire. Condition 8 of these conditions stated that the *hirer* was responsible for claims arising from the negligent operation of the plant by the driver. The driver negligently drove the JCB into Phillips

Products' premises and damaged them. It was argued that Condition 8 merely transferred liability to the hirer's insurers rather than acting as an exclusion clause. As a result, it was contended that s 2(2) of the 1977 Act did not apply. The argument was rejected. It was stated that the owner of the excavator 'does most certainly purport to exclude its liability for negligence by reference to Condition 8'. On the facts, it was found that the hirers did not regularly hire plant and drivers, had no control over the driver and no opportunity to arrange insurance (see also *Thompson v T Lohan (Plant Hire) Ltd* (1987)).

Non-consumer sale of goods and hire purchase

Under s 6(3), an inter-business sale of goods or hire purchase contract in which an attempt is made to exclude or restrict liability for breach of the statutorily implied terms is also subject to the requirement of reasonableness. Two cases are instructive here. Although neither was decided on the basis of the 1977 Act and the guidelines in Sched 2, the legislation on which the cases are based had a similar effect to s 13 of the 1977 Act. *RW Green Ltd v Cade Bros Farms* (1978) concerned the reasonableness of a clause in a contract for the sale of 20 tons of seed potatoes which limited claims for compensation to a refund of the price. The potatoes were infected by a virus in breach of s 14 of the Sale of Goods Act 1979, but the limitation clause was found to be reasonable. First, the contract was concluded on standard terms, based on trade practice and agreed over many years by both merchants and farmers. Secondly, certified virus-free potatoes could be bought at a higher price. Finally, the parties were representative of the two sides of the trade and had regularly done business together. However, a further clause requiring complaints to be made within three days of delivery was declared unreasonable as the defect was not discoverable on inspection within the time allowed.

Reasonableness in the context of a contract for a sale of goods was also considered by the House of Lords in *George Mitchell (Chesterhall) Ltd v Finney Lock Seeds Ltd* (1983). In that case, Finlay Lock Seeds supplied cabbage seed to George Mitchell at a price of £192. The seed was planted but the crop failed with a loss to the farmers of an estimated £63,000. The contract was on the supplier's standard terms and the parties had dealt with each other for some years. It contained a clause limiting liability for defective seeds to the contract price. On the facts of this particular case, the Court of Appeal and the House of Lords both adopted an interventionist approach to this inter-business transaction. It was held that the clause was unreasonable. In the Court of Appeal, Kerr LJ stated that:

> The balance of fairness and reasonableness appears to me to be overwhelmingly on the side of the [claimants] ... Farmers do not, and cannot be expected to, insure against this kind of disaster; but suppliers of seeds can ... I am not persuaded that liability for rare events of this kind cannot be adequately insured against. Nor am I persuaded that the cost of such cover would add significantly to the cost of seed. Further, although the present exemption clause has been in existence for many decades, the evidence shows that it was never negotiated. In effect, it was simply imposed by the suppliers, and no seed can in practice be bought otherwise than subject to its terms. To limit the supplier's liability to the price of the seed in all cases, as against the magnitude of the losses which farmers can incur in rare disasters of this kind, appears to me to be a grossly disproportionate and unreasonable allocation of the respective risks.

Standard forms and further consumer protection

Section 3 of the Act extends control of exclusion clauses to cases where one party deals as consumer or on the other's written standard terms of business. The section aims at both unequal bargaining situations and non-negotiated contract situations which may or may not involve a consumer. Where a consumer or a party dealing on another's standard terms is involved, the other party cannot by reference to any contract term:

(a) when himself in breach, exclude or restrict his liability in respect of the breach; or

(b) claim to be entitled: (i) to render a contractual performance substantially different from that which was reasonably to be expected of him; or (ii) in respect of the whole or any part of his contractual obligation, to render no performance at all, except in so far as the contract term satisfies the requirement of reasonableness: see s 3(2).

Section 3(2)(a) came into play in a non-consumer context in *St Albans City and District Council v International Computers Ltd* (1994). In this case, International Computers supplied the Council with a database for its community charge register. The contract was on International Computer's standard terms and limited its liability for loss to £100,000. An error in the software resulted in an overstatement of the city and district population of almost 3,000. The community charge was in consequence set too low with a loss to the Council of £1,314,846. Section 3 applied because the contract was made on International Computer's 'written standard terms of business'. The court held that in this case the determining factors were that the parties were of unequal bargaining power, as International Computers were dealing on their terms and conditions. They also felt that the figure of £100,000 had not been justified in relation to potential risk and actual loss and that International Computers were insured to the extent of £50 million worldwide. In short, they determined that in practical terms it was better that the loss should fall on International Computers and its insurance company than on the local authority and local population by way of increased charges or reduced services. Although here the court adopted an interventionary role, it may be argued that, on the basis of the fourth determining factor, this was at bottom a business–consumer issue.

Effect of breach

Section 9 of the Act confirms an injured party's right, in the face of a serious breach, to *elect* to terminate or to affirm the contract. The Act thus denies, together with the House of Lords' decisions in *Suisse Atlantique Société d'Armement Maritime SA v NV Rotterdamsche Kolen Centrale* (1967) and *Photo Production Ltd v Securicor Transport Ltd* (1980), that fundamental breach could operate to *automatically* terminate a contract and so expunge any exclusionary term in it. Section 9(1) makes it clear that if, by election, the contract is terminated, an exclusion clause survives such termination and it *may*, if not rendered ineffective by the Act, protect the party in breach if it satisfies first the rigours of judicial construction and, second, the requirement of reasonableness.

As discussed earlier, whether fundamental breach has any role to play as a rule of construction in future cases is doubted but not settled. Very serious breaches may or may not be described as 'fundamental'. Statements in *Photo Production* indicate that in any event where business parties of equal bargaining power are involved, the courts should not strain to defeat clearly expressed exclusionary terms. In Lord Diplock's words:

> In commercial contracts negotiated between business people capable of looking after their own interests and of deciding how risks inherent in the performance of various kinds of contract can most economically be borne (generally by insurance), it is, in my view, wrong to place a strained construction upon words in an exclusion clause which are clear and fairly susceptible to one meaning only.

Section 9(2) has the effect of allowing that in the less likely event of a party affirming a contract that they are entitled to terminate following its breach, their affirmation does not eliminate the need for a clause to satisfy judicial construction and the reasonableness test.

THE EUROPEAN COMMUNITY DIRECTIVE ON UNFAIR TERMS IN CONSUMER CONTRACTS (COUNCIL DIRECTIVE 93/13)

In addition to UCTA, UK contracts have more recently been regulated by European legislation. This generally acts in parallel with UCTA, although there are also some overlaps. The European approach to the regulation of contracts appears to offer a regime which is conceptually distinct from that of the common law although many of the same concerns underpin the two pieces of legislation. In the sections which follow, we shall review the European approach to unfair contracts and compare it to that adopted by UCTA.

Visions of economic efficiency underpin the European approach. According to Recital 5 of the Directive, the removal of unfair terms from consumer contracts will facilitate the development of the European single market by giving consumers the confidence to contract outside their own States, thus increasing choice and facilitating competition. The Directive and subsequent regulations provide for a *minimum* level of protection throughout the European Union and make clear that Member States are free to provide additional protection on the basis of their own national law. This has already happened in the UK with UCTA 1977. In contrast to the Act, the regulations of 1999 focus on all contractual terms in contracts between 'consumers' and 'sellers or suppliers' which have not been 'individually negotiated' by the parties. A term in such contracts which is adjudged unfair is not binding on the consumer. The concept of unfairness in the regulations is wider than in the 1977 Act, because it is not confined to exclusion and limitation of liability clauses. In another sense it is narrower, as the regulations do not apply to inter-business transactions. The regulations have met with a considerable amount of criticism and speculation, mainly as regards difficulties of interpretation and the complexity created by having the regulations stand alongside the 1977 Act. As we have already mentioned, it is hoped that these issues will be resolved with the publication of a Law Commission paper on the subject.

Key characteristics of the regulations

Like UCTA, the regulations identify two key players with whom regulation should be concerned. These are 'consumers' and 'sellers or suppliers'. Regulation 3 defines a 'consumer' as 'a natural person who … is acting for purposes which are outside his business, trade or profession'. According to this definition, consumers may be individuals of considerable means (see, for instance, *Standard Bank of London Ltd v Abelowolakis* (2000)). By way of contrast, the seller or supplier is defined as 'a person who sells goods and who ... is acting for purposes relating to his trade, business or profession'. It is noticeable that the expression 'relating to' is wide and that the scope of the term 'business' is similar to that in the 1977 Act. Just as it is impossible under the Act for a business to 'deal as consumer', so there is EC case law to the effect that a business cannot be regarded as a consumer. The effect of the regulations is that a term which is found by the court to be *unfair* will not be binding on the consumer. However, the remainder of the contract will continue to bind the parties if it is capable of continuing in existence without the term in dispute.

The regulations apply to terms which have 'not been individually negotiated'. In essence then it concentrates on standard form, non-negotiable contracts rather than the broader range of contracts which come under the ambit of the UCTA. Regulation 5(2) states that 'a term shall always be regarded as not having been individually negotiated where it has been drafted in advance and the consumer has not been able to influence the substance of the term'. However, the regulations also adopt a technique unknown to the Act. Under Regulation 6(2), certain 'core' terms are *insulated* from regulation. They are not subject to the test of fairness as long as they are in 'plain, intelligible language'. The terms which come within this provision are those which define the main subject matter of the contract, or concern the adequacy of the price or remuneration (see, for instance, *Director General of Fair Trading v First National Bank plc* (2002)). Collins (1994) has argued that the objective of this provision is to preclude claims by consumers that they have paid too much and judicial review of terms that the consumer was fully aware of and appreciated.

Before turning to some of the specific concepts employed in the regulations, it is useful to summarise the ways in which they can be seen to be wider and narrower than domestic legislation. Figure 16.4 attempts to do this in succinct form and should be used to guide you through the provisions discussed.

Figure 16.4: The scope of European regulations when compared to UCTA

	wider provision	narrower provision
European Regulations	1 Concerns go beyond exclusion clauses to all unfair terms in standard form contracts	1 Only relates to terms in *contracts*
	2 Introduces broader concept of good faith?	2 Only relates to contracts which have not been individually negotiated
	3 Allows for the insulation of certain terms	3 Limited to dealings between consumers and sellers/producers

Unfair terms

Regulation 5(1) states that '"unfair term" means any term which, contrary to *the requirement of good faith,* causes a *significant imbalance* in the parties' rights and obligations under the contract *to the detriment of the consumer'*. In common with the Act, the test of fairness is to be made against the background of all the circumstances at the time the contract was entered into. Since no general principle of good faith is explicitly recognised in English contract law, this is a new concept with which the English judiciary has had to grapple. The requirement was described as 'one of fair and open dealing' by the House of Lords in *Director General of Fair Trading v First National Bank plc* (2002). However, some indications of what may constitute good faith are also included in the regulations. Schedule 2 contains a list of matters to which *particular* regard is to be had in determining whether a term meets the requirement. These make clear that, in making an assessment of good faith, regard shall be had in particular to:

(a) the strength of the bargaining positions of the parties;

(b) whether the consumer had an inducement to agree to the term;

(c) whether the goods or services were sold or supplied to the special order of the consumer; and

(d) the extent to which the seller or supplier has dealt fairly and equitably with the consumer.

A non-exhaustive list of terms which *may* be regarded as unfair is to be found in Sched 2 to the regulations. The question of finding 'a significant imbalance … to the detriment of the consumer' is left to the courts, proceeding on a case-by-case basis. The list of 17 different types of potentially unfair terms are not automatically presumed to be unfair. One example is a term which provides for the price of goods to be determined at the time of delivery without giving the consumer the right to cancel the contract if the final price is too high. Other examples deal with provisions relating to negligent liability and death or personal injury; the exclusion or limitation of the consumer's rights in the event of total or partial non-performance; and inadequate performance by the seller or supplier of any of the contractual obligations.

Plain, intelligible language

As regards the drafting of terms, Regulation 7 states that 'A seller or supplier shall ensure that any written term of a contract is expressed in plain, intelligible language', and that 'if there is any doubt about the meaning of a written term, the interpretation most favourable to the consumer shall prevail'. 'Plain and intelligible' will presumably be tested objectively from the point of view of the reasonable consumer and the outcome in cases of doubt is to be determined on the basis of the *contra proferentem* rule of construction. Obscure drafting may be indicative of an absence of fair and equitable dealing and therefore of good faith. In one sense, this provision does little more than was expected in the common law. But the important difference is that this should now become a core standard for the *drafting* of consumer contracts.

Regulation 8: general use of unfair terms – Member States' duties

In contrast to domestic legislation, the European approach has been to take the position that standard form contracts are presumed to be undesirable. Under Article 7(1) of the Directive, Member States are to provide 'effective means to prevent the continued use of unfair terms'. Moreover, the collective interest in achieving this goal is reflected in Article 7(2), which states that such 'means' should include 'provisions whereby persons or organisations having a legitimate interest under national law in protecting consumers may take action ... before the courts ... for a decision as to whether contractual terms drawn up for general use are unfair'. Under clause 10(1) of the Regulations, the Director General of Fair Trading must consider any complaint made to him that a term drawn up for 'general use' is unfair. He cannot act on his own initiative but there is no doubt that he will receive numerous complaints from the Consumers' Association and others.

The Director General has a discretion as to whether to seek an injunction 'against any person appearing to [him] ... to be using, or recommending use' of unfair terms. The Director General will presumably decide not to seek an injunction if he is satisfied with voluntary undertakings he receives regarding discontinuance of unfair terms in general use. Any injunction sought may relate not only to the particular term but also 'to any similar term, or a term having like effect', so as to forestall evasion by re-drafting. According to Regulation 12(3), the court may grant an injunction on such terms as it thinks fit.

CONCLUDING REMARKS

The discussion in this chapter reveals that significant inroads have been made into the regulation of contracts in the last three decades. This is especially true of consumer contracts leading some to argue that we have, in part, returned to the notion of a 'status' contract which relies for its enforceability on the characteristics of the parties rather than the circumstances of the actual deal which has been negotiated. Contrary to the individualistic tendencies of the classical model, modern legislation imposes blanket regulation on certain types of clauses regardless of whether there has been bargaining naughtiness. It is not surprising that this job has been left to the legislature rather than the judiciary as it requires the imposition of a standard of fairness without taking the needs and desires of the parties into account, a task which the judiciary has shown itself nervous of undertaking in a forthright way.

The area is one which also provides a useful case study in legal method. Since the introduction of the European Directive in 1993, the English judiciary has had to grapple with much more open-textured concepts of fairness than they have been used to dealing with. This has caused considerable concern and confusion as they move slowly towards continental ways of determining standards. But this new way of looking at standards also raises more fundamental questions for contract lawyers. In particular, debate has ensued as to whether such open-textured standards achieve anything more than the test of reasonableness with which common law lawyers are so familiar. As Brownsword and Howells (1995) have argued:

> Generally speaking ... the underlying pattern of the protective regime ushered in by the Directive will closely resemble that under the reasonableness test of UCTA. In both regimes, certain sorts of contractual terms are singled out as potentially unfair. Under UCTA it is terms that exclude or restrict liability (and their cognates); under the Regulations, it is terms that involve a significant imbalance (as elaborated by the indicative examples given in Schedule 3). Under UCTA, once a term is subject to the reasonableness test, attention largely focuses on whether it is plausible to assume that there has been free agreement to the provision; under the Regulations, once a term is seen as involving a significant imbalance, attention turns to whether the dealer has acted contrary to the requirement of good faith – which, we have suggested, is largely

a matter (as under UCTA) of satisfying oneself that there has been free agreement to the term.

Whether the 1977 Act and the regulations will at some future date be welded together to form a more 'user friendly' system of protection for consumers or herald the introduction of innovative approaches to unfair terms remains to be seen.

REFERENCES AND FURTHER READING

Adams, J and Brownsword, R 'The Unfair Contract Terms Act: a decade of discretion' (1988) 104 LQR 94.

Adams, J and Brownsword, R 'Double indemnity – contractual indemnity clauses revisited' (1988) JBL 146.

Beale, H 'Unfair Contract Terms Act 1977' (1978) 5 British Journal of Law and Society 114.

Brownsword, R and Howells, G 'The implementation of the EC Directive on unfair terms in consumer contracts – some unresolved questions' (1995) JBL 243.

Collins, H 'Good faith in European contract law' (1994) 14 OJLS 229.

Dean, M 'Unfair contract terms: the European approach' (1993) 56 MLR 581.

EC Council of Ministers, *Council Directive on Unfair Terms in Consumer Contracts: 93/13/EEC* (1993) Official Journal L95/29, 21 April.

Law Commission, *Unfair Terms in Contracts* (2002) Consultation Paper No 166, London.

Macdonald, E 'Mapping the Unfair Contract Terms Act 1977 and the Directive on Unfair Terms in Consumer Contracts' (1994) JBL 441.

Peel, E 'Making more use of the Unfair Contract Terms Act 1977: *Stewart Gill Ltd v Horatio Myer and Co Ltd*' (1993) 56 MLR 98.

QUESTIONS

(1) If you were the law commissioner responsible for consolidating the Act and regulations, what would you do to simplify provisions in this field?

(2) What is meant by an 'unfair term' in the Unfair Terms in Consumer Contract Regulations 1999? Look through the terms of the contracts made by Angie and Georgie. Do you think any of them would fall foul of the regulations? If so, why?

(3) Comment on the validity or otherwise of the following exclusion clauses or notices in 'The Sad Tale of Angie and Georgie':

   (a) A notice on the signpost which narrowly misses Georgie reads: 'The owners of this car park accept no responsibility for damages to property or personal injury which occurs in this car park. The car park is used at the car owner's risk.'

   (b) The effect of the exclusion clause on Earth2Earth!'s Charter of Standards on the potential liability to Dipti.

   (c) Clause 2 of Angie and Georgie's agreement with the Wacky Machine Company.

   (d) Clause 6 of Angie and Georgie's agreement with Claude.

CHAPTER 17

CONTRACT AND COMPETITION

INTRODUCTION

In the last three chapters, we have looked at the sort of terms which are included in a contract and those which are excluded. It will have become clear that this is an area in which the legislature has become increasingly involved and the judiciary progressively more interventionist in stance. As notions of equality of bargaining power and fairness have captured the imaginations of social reformers, lawyers have had to become involved in much more sophisticated analyses of contractual terms than might have been anticipated during the classical period. No longer content to accept that *laissez-faire* philosophies promote the interests of all in society, they have had to engage in debate about what constitutes acceptable behaviour in a contract. The restriction of exclusion clauses is one way in which such concerns have manifested themselves in legislative and judicial policies. The area is one in which concerns about individual terms in particular contracts have been considered alongside debate about the wider impact of such clauses on the fair and efficient operation of the market more generally. In this chapter, we look at these same issues from a different angle, set of doctrines and legislation. What marks this chapter out from the last is the additional focus on behaviour within the business community and across business communities in Europe.

RESTRAINT OF TRADE

By the mid-19th century, contract law was firmly established as the legal corollary of a free-market economy. A significant reason for acceptance of the doctrine of freedom of contract was its links with the principle of free trade. However, it by no means follows that freedom of contract necessarily promotes freedom of trade and competitive markets. In fact, it can be shown that in this respect there is an internal contradiction in the freedom of contract concept. For example, if Megamix, a distributor of compact discs, agrees to take 50% of their requirements of goods from supplier Wicked Ways, they restrict their freedom to contract with a second supplier, Koolite. If Megamix agrees to take all its requirements from Wicked Ways and no one else, they preclude themselves from trading with Koolite. If Megan 'ties' all national distributors in this way, foreign exporters will be prevented from gaining access to the market unless they can secure new outlets for their goods.

Contracts of this type are said to fall within the area of restraint of trade. This is because they restrict or prevent trade and competition. It was clear to business entrepreneurs long before the end of the 19th century that economic advantages might be gained by entering into restrictive agreements among themselves so as to create the economic power necessary to influence and perhaps control markets. But when it comes to regulation of such contracts, tensions are apparent. Somewhat paradoxically, when the courts show a tendency to stand by an agreement made by contracting parties in the interests of freedom of contract, it is possible that they are upholding contracts containing a significant element of restraint. This was recognised by Lord

Atkinson in *Herbert Morris Ltd v Saxelby* in 1916 when he said that: 'Two principles or views of public policy come into conflict in such cases as these, namely, freedom of trade and freedom of contract. While the community is vitally interested in trade being free, it is also vitally interested in people being free to contract and being held to their contracts.' As Macneil (1968) has reiterated:

> It is plain that contracts in restraint of trade may be used in attempts to destroy the market mechanism itself, to destroy its diversity and multiplicity of decision making, and to centralise it in the hands of those who enter the contracts in restraint of trade. This fact is but one facet of potential or actual monopoly control of an economy. The extent to which there is or is not monopolistic control of a given market economy, the extent to which monopoly is not an inevitable accompaniment and outgrowth of a capitalist system, and related problems, are subjects of great dispute among economists and political theorists. For the contract student it is enough to note that contracts in restraint of trade are intimately connected with those political and economic problems, as are the attempts of legislatures and courts to control such contracts.

Assuming that competition and freedom of trade are 'good' things, what efforts did the courts make to control such contracts during the classical period? As regards cartel agreements between formerly competing suppliers of goods and services, they invariably came down on the side of freedom of contract at the expense of freedom of trade. The failure of the courts to look beyond the interests of the parties was a major reason for their inability to stem the rise of restrictive business agreements and monopoly positions. The restraint of trade doctrine remained under the shadow of the *laissez-faire* school of economics and the judges followed the government's lead in adopting a basically non-interventionist role in such business matters when entrepreneurs were concerned. However, the partiality of their approach was illustrated by the fact that at the same time they were doing much to prevent workers forming trade unions.

Somewhat ironically, in 1875, the Master of the Rolls was declaring that businessmen and others must have 'the utmost liberty of contracting' whilst restrictive trading agreements of all kinds were beginning to permeate business. These included market-sharing, price-fixing and resale price maintenance. So, by upholding these agreements, the courts of the time assisted in the destruction of freedom of trade by their pursuit of freedom of contract. The onus of showing that any contract was calculated to produce a monopoly or enhance prices to an unreasonable extent lay on the party alleging it, and once the court was satisfied that the restraint was reasonable as between the parties, this onus was no light one. Naturally, the parties to a successful agreement to 'enhance prices' would themselves consider it more than reasonable and would be extremely unlikely to bring an action on it. Moreover, in 1913 the Judicial Committee of the Privy Council was 'not aware of any case in which a restraint though reasonable in the interests of the parties has been held to be unenforceable because it involved some injury to the public'.

If an agreement was reasonable in the interests of the parties, it was presumed to be in the interests of the public in the absence of proof to the contrary and, since the public was not represented in any litigation, there was no one to argue the case from the public interest point of view or bring 'competition versus monopoly' arguments into the courts. The case of *Mogul SS Co Ltd v McGregor, Gow & Co Ltd and Others* (1892) is a prime illustration of the attitude of the courts during this period. In this case, the defendants were shipowners who formed an association to monopolise the tea-carrying trade from the Far East. On the basis of the agreement, it was possible to regulate the ships that were to call at each port, divide the cargoes between them and fix the freight to be charged for shipment to England. The members allowed a rebate of 5% to cargo-owners who had shipped exclusively on members' vessels during the previous six months, and shipping agents were warned that they would not be given business if they dealt with non-members.

When Mogul, who was not a member, sent vessels to pick up a cargo of tea, the members, acting on the basis of the agreement, arranged that their vessels were in port first. These vessels offered to carry tea so cheaply that the Mogul ships could find alternative cargoes only at unprofitable rates. In an action brought by Mogul, claiming an injunction to prevent agreement in restraint of trade, the House of Lords upheld the agreement and the plaintiff's case failed. Although the agreement regulating routes to be used, rates to be charged and ports to be served was probably an unreasonable restraint of trade, it was argued that the members could not be sued upon it by a company that was not a party to it. The agreement was clearly in the interests of the parties, but was it against public policy and void? It was held that there was no evidence on this wider issue but Lord Bramwell was 'by no means sure that the [agreement] did not prevent a waste and was not good for the public'.

Further light on judicial attitudes towards such restrictive trading agreements is to be found in Bowen LJ's judgment in the Court of Appeal in the same case:

> I myself should deem it to be misfortune if we were to attempt to prescribe to the business world how honest and peaceable trade was to be carried on in a case where no such illegal elements as I have mentioned exist, or were to adopt some standard of judicial 'reasonableness', or of 'normal' prices, or 'fair freights', to which commercial adventures, otherwise innocent, were bound to conform.

The *Mogul* case concerned a *horizontal* restrictive agreement, that is, one between suppliers only. *Dunlop Pneumatic Tyre Co Ltd v Selfridge & Co Ltd* (1915) offers an early illustration of the attempted enforcement by a supplier of *vertical* restrictions imposed on others, such as retailers, further up the chain of distribution. Resale price maintenance is, or was, a common form of restriction of price competition and is designed to ensure that, whatever the channels of distribution through which goods pass, they shall be sold to the retail customer at a price which has been fixed, usually by the manufacturer. In the *Dunlop* case, an attempt by the manufacturer to enforce his resale price maintenance conditions against a price-cutting retailer also fell foul of the privity of contract doctrine which allows only those who are party to the agreement and supplied consideration to support it.

Other arrangements demonstrate both horizontal and vertical restrictive elements, so, for instance, in *Ware and De Freville v Motor Trade Association* (1921), the defendant association of car manufacturers had rules for maintaining fixed prices for their goods. Dealers who departed from these prices had their names put on a 'stop list' and no member of the association was to supply them. An offender could, however, plead his case before a domestic tribunal and be allowed to pay a fine instead. The plaintiffs who had been placed on the 'stop list' complained that all they wanted was to exercise their lawful freedom to deal in cars as they wished, but the Court of Appeal held that the MTA arrangements were not unlawful.

Decisions such as this one reflect a view that was widely held at the time in government and business circles. This was that business people, bent on eliminating or minimising competition throughout British industry, knew their own interests best and should be free to pursue them. Significantly, the courts, which earlier had failed to see the implications of supporting freedom of contract in such cases, began *actively to support* the suppression of competition on 'principled' grounds. They encouraged the fixing of prices at artificially high levels by continuing adherence to the outworn legal concept of *laissez-faire*. Atiyah has argued that: 'A principle which had originally been justified by the political economists was pursued by the courts to an extent which had no economic justification.'

Lord Diplock has written of the same period that:

> By the end of the 19th century the common law had finally given its blessing to the cartel provided that its members were actuated by self-interest, and such legislation as was passed between the first and second World Wars was directed to encouraging the amalgamation of undertakings and the enforcement of restrictive trade practices in the depressed industries of agriculture and coal-mining. The economic theories upon which this legislation was based were reflected in the voluntary adoption of similar restrictions in a whole variety of other trades and industries ... by the beginning of World War II there were few domestic markets in goods and services in which free competition survived.

However, in time, the detrimental effect of such policies became more transparent as politicians became aware that such approaches to the market allowed for economic power to become concentrated in the hands of a few businesses or organisations. An unregulated market came to be seen as one which could be detrimental to the interests of society as a whole because freedom of contract could be said to fetter free trade and competition. The change of economic theory in favour of restricted competition which followed upon World War II was not something to which effect could have been given by the development of the common law. Judges are not economists and the judicial process is not suited to determining where the balance of economic advantage lies. This was a field in which if changes were to be brought about, the only method was by legislation.

And so, the regulation of monopolies, mergers and horizontal and vertical restrictive trade practices became an important part of government policy for the private sector of the economy, with the privatisation programmes of the 1980s and 1990s providing the most recent examples of attempts by government to balance the advantages of free trade and regulation. So important is this legislative trend that in Britain and other countries, the courts have to a large extent been removed from the front line as law-makers and law-enforcers in this field. The common law doctrine of restraint of trade has largely given way to a statutory competition policy, the enforcement of which is the function of administrative bodies and a specially created Restrictive Practices Court. Competition policy and consumer protection are now related areas in modern economic thinking. But perhaps most significantly, competition and consumer law take up ground previously occupied by contract law but have also grown away from it as successive statutory measures seek to serve *the public interest*.

The statutory basis of competition policy was laid down in 1948 and 1956 and at the present time the Office of Fair Trading possesses wide regulatory powers under such restrictive trade practices and competition legislation. Examination of these statutes is beyond our scope, but it is important to note that under the Restrictive Trade Practices Act 1976, a variety of restrictive trading agreements, such as price-fixing, are deemed to be *against the public interest* unless the parties can show that benefits flowing from the agreement, such as price stability, quality, employment and public health, outweigh the detriment to consumers. In addition, it is worthy of note that, while the common law has given limited protection to third parties in challenging restrictive agreements, legislation has focused on the effect of such agreements on those outside of the contract and society as a whole.

Many of the relevant rules are now contained in the Competition Act 1998 which in turn has been guided by Article 81 (formerly 85) of the EC Treaty. These two pieces of legislation prohibit a number of anti-competitive practices although their approach and scope do differ. Under the Act, prohibited agreements are void unless exemption is granted by the Office of Fair Trading or EC authorities. An example of a prohibited agreement is one which directly or indirectly fixed purchase or selling prices. The Act allows for financial compensation to be paid to those who have suffered loss as a result of a prohibited agreement and, where the claimants are consumers, such claims can be brought on their behalf by bodies nominated by the Secretary of State. The focus of legislation is on the effect of such agreements on the economy whereas the common law rules discussed in this chapter are concerned with the effect of restrictions on the parties to the contract. As a result, the common law rules continue to operate alongside and supplement European and domestic legislation. So, it is possible for an agreement to pass the statutory tests of acceptability whilst falling within the scope of common law prohibitions. In the next section we will move to a brief study of a particular form of restrictive business practice: exclusive dealing agreements. This will allow us to take note of their position in the UK, both under statute and in relation to a development in the common law restraint of trade doctrine, and under the competition law of the European Union.

DISTRIBUTION SYSTEMS

Although manufacturers or suppliers of goods employ a variety of methods for distributing their products, we are here concerned with a common method of distribution whereby a supplier sells his goods to intermediary distributors on the basis of a distribution agreement under which restrictions upon their trading activities are accepted by one or both parties. The exclusive distribution agreement is, in practical business terms, probably the most effective way for a supplier to get his goods on to a large market. Under a typical *exclusive* distribution agreement, a supplier agrees to sell their products, for a fixed period and in relation to a defined area, to the just one distributor. The distributor accepts that they will not sell any competing products and will not sell the contract goods outside their territory. In particular, this means that they will not sell in the territory of another of the supplier's 'exclusive' distributors. The key characteristics of such agreements are that they are of a vertical nature and restrictive not only as regards the trading activities of the parties but also of other distributors who are third parties to the contract. So, for instance, in the car distribution industry, a manufacturer or importer of cars will contract with a series of showroom owners to sell their cars within a clearly defined region.

In the UK, such an exclusive dealing agreement is generally exempted from the provisions of the Restrictive Trade Practices Act 1976, so long as it is merely of a vertical bilateral nature. In other words, it should not be based on a horizontal, collective arrangement between the suppliers in question. This was not a decision which met with universal approval when originally taken in 1956. Moreover, it has not always found favour in the European Union where the authorities are seeking to secure a single, *common* market for goods and services. As a result, exclusive distribution agreements which operate to partition that market along national frontiers are not allowed under EC law. This means that exclusive national distributors in the EC cannot secure absolute territorial protection from competition by means of an agreement with their supplier. Article 81 (formerly 85) of the EC Treaty, which is directly effective law in the UK, 'prohibits as incompatible with the common market all agreements between undertakings ... which may affect trade between member states and which have as their object or effect the ... distortion of competition'. Exemptions are allowed where the effect on competition is insignificant and where there are offsetting economic and other advantages.

In *Consten and Grundig v Commission* (1966), the supplier had established a network of distribution agreements. Grundig, a German manufacturer of TV sets and tape recorders, established an exclusive dealing network for the distribution of its products throughout the Common Market. In 1957, Grundig appointed Consten as exclusive distributor in France. Grundig agreed not to sell directly or indirectly to anyone else in France. Moreover, Grundig's other national distributors were bound not to sell outside their allotted territories and Consten agreed not to deal in competing products or to sell outside France. UNEF and other French firms managed to import Grundig's products through a 'back-door' into France and undercut Consten's prices. Consten sued these 'parallel importers' in French law for 'unfair competition' and the question of the exclusive distribution agreement's validity under Article 85 was raised. The European Court decided against the agreement to the extent that its aim of securing absolute territorial protection for Consten against parallel imports partitioned the Common Market along national frontiers. It was argued that the agreement adversely affected the free movement of goods between Member States and distorted competition within the Common Market by giving rise to different prices for the same goods in the different Member States.

As Article 85 competition law developed, in large part on the basis of the *Grundig* decision, it became clear that exclusive distribution agreements between a supplier and a distributor in another Member State were normally exempt under Article 85(3), so long as they did not provide for absolute territorial protection for the distributor against imports. Since 1967 the position has been covered by an EC *legislative* system which, since 1999, enables the parties to draft agreements which allow them in effect to *self-certify* exemption by avoiding certain prohibited 'black list' provisions (including distribution protection) contrary to the free movement of goods across borders and the whole concept of a Common Market. Enormous administrative costs should in this way be greatly reduced.

The European Commission and Court of Justice have also been called upon to rule on the position under Article 81 (formerly 85) of a similar business operation designed to facilitate the distribution of a supplier's products *within a single Member State* rather than across frontiers. These agreements would appear not to meet the requirement that trade *between* Member States must not be affected. Several cases have concerned

Belgian 'brewery contracts' in which only the distributor is burdened with restrictions on their trading activities.

In the UK, a parallel development has occurred as the courts, in a number of cases since 1966, have applied the common law doctrine of restraint of trade to similar agreements concerning national distribution of petrol by oil companies through 'tied' distributional outlets. The common law was resorted to because these agreements were exempted from the provisions of the Restrictive Trade Practices Act 1956. Section 8(3) of that Act stated that agreements for the supply of goods in which the only restrictions are those accepted by the party acquiring the goods are exempt from registration and scrutiny by the Restrictive Practices Court (and see now the 1976 Act).

'Solus' petrol agreements in which the garage or filling station operator agrees not to sell the products of competing oil companies fit this description. There are clear economic advantages for both parties under such agreements. In a market dominated by a handful of suppliers, 'tying' contracts of a fixed duration enables oil companies to achieve continuity of sales through their established outlets. Moreover, distributors gain access to loans for site development offered at favourable rates by their suppliers and they receive rebates on the wholesale price of petrol. From the nature of the business it is obvious that garage proprietors will not sell petrol outside their 'territory', and a network of 'solus' agreements gives oil companies absolute territorial protection as regards their control of a percentage of tied national market outlets. In addition, if, as was the case for UK retail petrol, over 90% of the outlets were tied in the 1960s and it was difficult to obtain planning permission for new sites, it could be argued that these barriers to entry into the market had an anti-competitive effect. In EC terms this tended to separate the UK market or any other Member State market where similar conditions prevailed from the rest of the Community. This point has not been tested specifically in the courts, although guidance on the matter has been gradually forthcoming from Europe, particularly from the Belgian brewery cases and an EC regulation of 1983, both of which are discussed below.

The leading national case on 'solus' petrol agreements was decided before the UK joined the Common Market. In *Esso Petroleum Co Ltd v Harper's Garage (Stourport) Ltd* (1968), Harper owned two garages, A and B, both subject to 'solus' agreements with Esso. Under the garage A agreement, Harper agreed to purchase his total requirements of petrol from Esso and from no other source for four years and five months. He received a rebate from Esso on all petrol purchased. For garage B a similar undertaking was accepted, but the agreement was for 21 years. This was because the tie was part of a package deal under which, in return for a loan of £7,000, Harper mortgaged garage B to Esso, and the loan was to be repaid over 21 years and not earlier. After a time, Harper began selling another type of petrol and when sued by Esso he pleaded that both agreements were in unreasonable restraint of trade and therefore void.

The House of Lords held that the 'solus' agreements were caught by the restraint of trade doctrine. They argued that they were therefore both *prima facie* void and required to be justified on the basis of their reasonableness (i) as between the parties and (ii) as regards the public interest. The four year tie on garage A was found to be reasonable and therefore binding, but the 21 year tie on garage B was unreasonable and therefore void. It was felt that the restrictions placed on distributors by such agreements should be no wider than was reasonably necessary to protect the legitimate interests of suppliers in facilitating distribution and ensuring continuity of sales over a number of years. However, it was held that there was no added advantage except protection from competition in a 21 year tie as opposed to a five year tie. Whether the restraint is reasonable depends on the circumstances of each case, in particular upon the length of the tie. The maximum, renewable, period was generally felt at the time to be no more than five years, as recommended by the Monopolies Commission in its Report on the Supply of Petrol in 1965, and no UK case law, statutory revision or administrative action since then has disturbed this assumption.

It has rightly been said, however, that the public interest protected in such cases is narrowly conceived and shows the limitations of judicial intervention in this field. No attempt was made to ensure that petrol suppliers competed with each other; the effect was merely to allow a particular distributor to opt out of his bargain where the length of tie exceeds five years. The court was fortunate in having the Monopolies Commission's analysis of the market in question to hand in this case. In a similar situation, the House of Lords apparently felt that brewers' tied-house agreements were not subject to the restraint of trade doctrine for reasons that have not been squarely placed before the English courts in modern times.

'Brewery contracts' have, however, been the object of the attention of the European Court of Justice in the context of Article 81 (formerly 85) of the EC Treaty and the case law makes an interesting comparison with that of the English courts in the petrol cases. In *Brasserie de Haecht v Wilkin Janssen* (1967), the plaintiff brewery made business loans to the defendant café proprietors who agreed to obtain their beer and other beverages exclusively from the plaintiffs. When the café began selling another brewery's products, de Haecht sought to stop this breach of the agreement. In the Belgian court, the defendants claimed that the 'brewery contract' was prohibited under Article 85 and was therefore unenforceable against them. Although the agreement was between two Belgian undertakings and any effect on inter-Member State trade would appear to be insignificant and excusable, it was argued that such agreements must be viewed in their overall context. Approximately half such Belgian distributors were bound by exclusive purchasing contracts and the cumulative effect, it was argued for Wilken, was to present a substantial barrier to foreign undertakings seeking to penetrate the Belgian market. So, for example, German brewers would be restricted or prevented from selling in Belgium in the same way as the Italian oil company AGIP was prevented from establishing itself in the UK petrol market where 90% of outlets were tied. In *de Haecht* this general argument was the basis of the contention that the individual agreement was, as a consequence of its economic and legal context, caught by Article 85 and therefore unenforceable against Wilken.

The Belgian court requested a preliminary ruling from the European Court of Justice as to whether this argument was applicable. The Court in Luxembourg ruled that while exclusive purchasing contracts do not *per se* infringe Article 85, they may do so: 'The existence of similar contracts is a circumstance which, together with other circumstances, can as a whole create the economic and legal context within which the contract must be weighed.' The Belgian court was saved from the need, following the ECJ's ruling, to conduct an in-depth inquiry into the national brewery sector by the EC Commission, which carried out its own investigation. A later case, *Concordia Brewery* (1977), made it clear that national 'solus' contracts of the tied-house variety would normally be exempt from Article 85.

In 1983, the Commission issued a regulation relating to both 'service-station agreements' and 'beer supply agreements'. Briefly, such agreements were exempt from

Article 85 unless one of two situations applied: first, in the case of petrol, if the tie was for more than 10 years. However, if the purchaser/distributor was the supplier's tenant, the tie might be imposed for the duration of the period in which the purchaser/distributor 'operated the premises'. Secondly, in the case of beer, if the tie was again for more than 10 years. If the tie covered beer and other drinks, the maximum allowable tie was five years, and in either case the tenancy proviso similarly applied. The new regulatory system introduced in 1999, referred to above, which covers virtually all distribution systems, applies to exclusive purchasing agreements of the petrol and brewery type and now makes no separate special provision for them.

Although there are many other national and international factors that have a bearing on the level of competition and the pricing structure in the UK retail petrol trade and brewing sector, an examination of 'solus' agreements brings together consideration of the common law doctrine of restraint of trade and the competition policy of the EC. For decades, the English courts were preoccupied with entrepreneurial freedom of contract and the consequential right of parties to restrain trade in the furtherance of their own particular interests. In adopting this approach they effectively disqualified themselves from examining the economic, social and political complexities of the public's interest in outlawing business practices of the kind discussed in this section. Or perhaps the judges believed that Adam Smith's 'invisible hand' was busy converting the parties' interests into the interests of the public at large? Consideration of the public interest in the context of monopolies and restrictive business practices is now almost entirely in the hands of such bodies as the EC Commission, the Office of Fair Trading and the Monopolies and Mergers Commission. Regulation cannot ensure competition but it does attempt to secure the required preconditions in a way which has not been possible through development of the common law.

RESTRAINT OF TRADE: SALE OF A BUSINESS AND EMPLOYMENT CONTRACTS

Although the common law doctrine of restraint of trade has failed to meet the challenge of many restrictive trading agreements discussed above, it continues to operate, as it has done since the 16th century, in other fields. Although all contracts are to some extent in restraint of trade, the courts have attempted to find a dividing line between normal commercial relations between parties which should not be covered by the doctrine and situations which should be. Most of the cases which have been subject to regulation are those which concern a contractual clause which prevents a person from working in a certain line of business or profession or restricts their practice to limitations of time and geographical area. The cases usually concern one of two types of contract: first, *contracts for the sale of a business or practice* in which the *buyer* restrains the seller from setting up in immediate competition with them and drawing away customers or clients from the business being sold; secondly, *contracts of employment*, in which an *employer* restrains their employee from competing with them by setting up their own business or moving to a rival firm. These cases are not as economically significant as those discussed earlier but are nonetheless worthy of consideration.

Such clauses are presumed to be void and unenforceable at common law and are only enforceable if the court considers them to be *reasonable*. The reasonableness of a clause is, according to Lord Macnaghten's re-statement of the law in *Nordenfelt v Maxim Nordenfelt Guns and Ammunition Co Ltd* (1894), to be assessed by reference to both the interests of the parties concerned and the public interest. As concerns the parties, the question is essentially one of personal freedom and fairness. In an employment case, it has been argued that it is difficult to see how any restraint in itself can ever be advantageous to the employee. The true meaning of the proposition that the restraint must be in the interests of both parties is that the clause is not a covenant against mere competition but is a covenant directed to securing a reasonable protection of the business interest of the employer, and in the circumstances is not unjust to the employee.

It would seem then that the party imposing the restraint must not be seeking *merely* to protect themselves from ordinary business competition but must be aiming to safeguard, in a manner which is no more than reasonably necessary, a legitimate *business interest* of a proprietary nature. This might, for instance, include the goodwill of the business bought, such as its standing, reputation and established custom, or trade secrets, confidential information and customer connections in the case of employees who leave their jobs. In ex-employee cases, it is considered reasonable for the employer to protect trade secrets and confidential information to which the employee had access and knowledge, even though this to some extent prevents the ex-employee from using skill and knowledge of their own which they utilised during their former employment. This means the employer can protect their customers or clientele to the extent that the employee's former position, say as a sales representative, enabled them to gain sufficient influence over the customers to attract them later to the new firm.

As between the parties, reasonable protection of the business interest involved usually raises questions relating to the *scope* of the restraint, its *geographical area* and its *duration*. First, a restraint must remain within the scope of, and the activities relating to, the interest which merits protection. For example, it cannot cover future situations such as those who become customers of the firm *after* the employee leaves. So, for instance, a restraint in a tailor's contract against working as a milliner or hatter was found to be unenforceable: *Attwood v Lamont* (1920). Moreover, a covenant by an employee drafted with the intention of protecting not only that company's business but also that of a subsidiary company with which the employee had no connection is again an unreasonable restraint. An employer can restrain their employee from working in competition in the *area* from which the employer's customers or clients come, but in some cases a more precise and selective 'solicitation covenant', against soliciting the employer's customers or clients, is all that is reasonably required: *Gledhow Autoparts Ltd v Delaney* (1965). In any event, an 'area covenant' must not be drawn wider than is necessary to protect the employer's interest, nor should it cover products or processes with which the employer has no real connection or interest (see *Commercial Plastics Ltd v Vincent* (1965)).

The question of what is reasonable in terms of the length of time of a restraint depends very much, as in all these matters, on the facts of the individual case. Generally speaking, long restraints are only appropriate where a business's custom or clientele is of a long-standing, stable nature, such as the relationship between solicitor and client, but not where it is of a fluctuating or passing nature. The relative bargaining strength of the parties has often been a factor in assessing fairness or reasonableness as between the parties. So, for instance, the courts might look differently upon a case involving an employee with no union backing from a case where union backing was significant. They have also, in some cases, looked at the adequacy of the consideration flowing from the party imposing the restraint: *Schroeder Music Publishing Co Ltd v Macaulay* (1974).

As we have argued above, judicial inquiries into the relationship between the operation of a restraint and the public interest have rarely played a part in the reasoning displayed in judgments. If, as Lord Atkinson said in 1916, a balance is to be struck between liberty to trade and freedom of contract, it is probable that the nearer the parties are to equality of bargaining strength, the more likely the court will take them to be the best judges of their interest and, on this basis at least, will refrain from interfering with the restraint. The public's interest is taken to be in securing the liberty of the subject, not in general economic utility or 'effective competition' as it is under the statutory scheme of regulation. However, the difficulty with this view is that the requirement of public interest adds nothing to the requirement that the restraint be reasonable in the interests of the parties. It would seem then that the two limbs of the traditional formula for assessing restraints as laid down by Lord Macnaghten are then simply tautologous.

CASE LAW ILLUSTRATIONS

In this final section of the chapter, we attempt to look at the application of these general principles in three particular areas.

(1)   Business transfer restraints

In *Nordenfelt v Maxim Nordenfelt Guns and Ammunition Co Ltd* (1894), Nordenfelt, an armaments manufacturer, sold his business to a company for £287,500 under a contract which restrained his future business activities. Later, this company became Maxim Nordenfelt Ltd and it engaged Nordenfelt as managing director. Under this contract, which contained a similar restraint, Nordenfelt agreed not to compete in the armaments business or in 'any business competing or liable to compete in any way with that for the time being carried on by the company' anywhere in the world for a period of 25 years. The House of Lords held that, apart from the words quoted above, the restraint was valid. The business sold by Nordenfelt was an armaments firm with worldwide interests but the part referring to 'any business competing or liable to compete' was clearly wider than reasonably necessary to protect the proprietary interest that the company had bought. The court was able to sever these words from the restraint and enforce the remainder. The decision reflects a number of considerations discussed above. First, the parties had relatively equal bargaining strength. Secondly, a buyer of goodwill can more easily restrain a seller's future activities than can an employer restrain an employee's future use of his skill and knowledge which is partly his own and partly acquired.

An employer must also show 'an exceptional proprietary interest' in the thing being restrained such as when trade secrets are involved. So, in *British Reinforced Concrete Engineering Co Ltd v Schelff* (1921), BRC manufactured and sold BRC road reinforcements throughout the UK. Schelff sold but did not manufacture 'Loop' reinforcements in any part of the UK. Schelff sold his business to BRC and covenanted that, for a certain period, he would not carry on a business or act as employee 'of any person concerned or interested in' the manufacture or sale of road reinforcements anywhere in the UK. Schelff subsequently entered the employment of a road reinforcement company and BRC sued. It was held by the court that the clause was too wide as it would have prevented Schelff from becoming an employee of a company holding shares in a road reinforcement company. It was also too wide in *area* and as regards *activities* covered, Schelff's firm not having manufactured reinforcements.

Contracts for the sale of a business which contain a 'non-competition' clause extending beyond the UK are also subject to scrutiny under Article 81 (formerly 85) EC. In the German *Reuter/BASF* (1976) case, the EC Commission adopted a similar approach to that taken by the common law. In that case Reuter, the seller, complained about an eight year restraint which restricted him from engaging in research and manufacturing in his field and from divulging know-how to any third party. The Commission decided that where a sale involves goodwill and know-how, a 'non-competition' clause is allowable provided it is necessary 'to secure to the buyer the transfer of the *full* value of the transferred undertaking' and does not 'exceed what is necessary for such preservation'. However, the restraint would be caught and declared void under para (2) of Article 85(2), if it was excessive as regards (a) the *interest* to be protected, such as goodwill and know-how; (b) the *area* covered; and (c) its *duration*. The *Reuter* restraint was considered too wide because it extended to non-commercial research and at more than five years was too long. It restricted competition and reduced inter-Member State trade. In a later Dutch case, *Nutricia* (1984), the court reasoned that if only goodwill is sold, the period of the restraint should not normally exceed two years, but if know-how is also transferred, the maximum period should be in the region of four years.

(2) Employer-employee restraints

Similar considerations have arisen in the context of employer-employee restraints. In *Commercial Plastics Ltd v Vincent* (1965), Commercial Plastics manufactured thin PVC calendered plastic sheeting for adhesive tape. Technical difficulties had been met and £200,000 spent on research, with precautions being taken to ensure the secrecy of new discoveries in this rapidly expanding field. Commercial Plastics' main competitors were all UK firms and the vast bulk of their sales were in the UK. Vincent was employed as research and development co-ordinator and his contract contained a clause stating that he was 'not to seek employment with any of our competitors in the PVC calendering field for at least one year after leaving'. Vincent left and joined a UK competitor within the period. Commercial Plastics sued for an injunction to restrain Vincent from taking up this employment. It was held that Commercial Plastics had an interest, which could be protected, in confidential coded information to which Vincent had regularly had access. This was the case even if it was impossible for him to remember its detailed nature. However, it was also argued that the clause was too wide by extending to the whole calendering field and not merely to adhesive tape. Moreover, being worldwide, it was wider than necessary to protect Commercial Plastics against their actual competitors. The clause was, as a result, considered unreasonable and therefore unenforceable.

Kores Manufacturing Co Ltd v Kolok Manufacturing Co Ltd (1959) raised the question of an indirect restraint by which Kores and Kolok, who manufactured similar products, agreed that neither would employ any employee who had been employed by the other over the preceding five years. In this action against Kolok for breach of the agreement, it was held that there were trade secrets which merited protection but that the covenant was too wide. This was because it covered all employees whether they knew trade secrets or not, and it was too long in its duration. A so-called attempt to 'protect labour supplies' was in fact an indiscriminate attempt to prevent workers moving to higher paid jobs, and to do indirectly what could not be done by direct covenant with individual employees. It was argued that public policy cannot allow third parties to restrict by contract a person's freedom to work for whom he will.

(3)   Restraints on professional sportsmen and women and entertainers

A series of cases involving sportspeople and the entertainment business have attracted much more publicity in the press. In *Eastham v Newcastle United Football Club Ltd and Others* (1964), Eastham, a top-class footballer, had a contract with the first defendants, but wished to move to another club. However, under the then current rules of the Football Association and the Football League, a 'retain and transfer' system operated under which a player 'retained' by his club at the end of the football season was prevented from joining another club unless he obtained the consent of the retaining club. Eastham sought a declaration (the only remedy available) against the Newcastle club, the Football Association and the Football League that the 'retain and transfer' system was in unreasonable restraint of trade. As in the *Mogul* case discussed above, he had no contract with the second and third defendants. However, Wilberforce J could find no legitimate interest worthy of protection in this case. The system was, it was claimed, designed to prevent rich clubs poaching the best players from small clubs. But the system was considered to be in restraint of trade. The court used its jurisdiction to grant a declaratory judgment, not only against the employer who was in contractual relationship with the employee, but also against the association of employers whose rules or regulations place an unjustifiable restraint on his liberty of employment.

Although the declaration in *Eastham* did not require the defendants to take any action, the Football Association and the Football League did alter the transfer system as a result (see also the cricket case of *Greig v Insole* (1978)). Moreover, the European Court of Justice was asked for a preliminary ruling by a Belgian court in Case C-415/93 *Union Royale Belge des Sociétés de Football Association v Bosman* (1996) regarding national and transnational football transfer rules laid down by the various football associations concerned. Bosman, whose contract had expired, was effectively prevented from moving to another club by insistence on a substantial transfer fee. The Court ruled that the regulations breached Article 48 EC on the right of workers to free movement between Member States. The effect of the ruling is to enable 'out of contract' players to move on a 'free transfer', either within a Member State or across EU frontiers.

The final case is important as regards the application of the restraint doctrine to a contract in which there was a patent inequality of bargaining power. It demonstrates that in cases involving significant inequalities, the courts are more likely to be generous towards the restrained party. The case is also of interest because of the emphasis the House of Lords laid on the 'public interest' element of the doctrine. In *Schroeder Music Publishing Co Ltd v Macaulay* (1974), Macaulay, a young and unknown writer of pop songs, signed SMP's standard form contract, under the terms of which he assigned to SMP the world copyright in any compositions produced by him for five years. SMP did not undertake to use his work to advantage but if they did they would pay him royalties on the returns. If the royalties reached a total of £5,000, the contract was automatically extended for a further five years. SMP could terminate the agreement by giving a month's notice but there was no provision for termination by Macaulay. Their Lordships held that such an agreement was covered by the restraint of trade doctrine and the agreement in question was unreasonable since its terms combined a total commitment by Macaulay with an almost complete lack of obligation on the part of SMP. As a result, Macaulay, who had achieved considerable success, was able to escape from the contract (see also *Silverstone Records and Mountfield* (1993) and *Barclays Bank plc v Caplan* (1998)).

SEVERANCE

As a general rule, the presence of an unreasonable, void and unenforceable restraint within a contract does not affect the validity of the rest of the agreement. In addition, as we have seen in the *Nordenfelt* case, the court has the power to sever the 'bad' parts of a restraint clause from the 'good' and enforce only the latter. For such *severance* to operate, it would seem that it must be possible to construe the restraint as being divisible into a number of separate and independent parts. Cutting out, or putting a 'blue pencil' through, the unreasonable parts must leave the undertaking substantially the same in character as when originally framed by the parties. The effect of severance should be that it is merely reduced to reasonable proportions. Alternatively, where the restraint cannot properly be seen as falling into distinct parts, its 'indivisibility' means that it can only be rendered reasonable by amendment rather than severance. The task of rewriting the parties' agreement is one that the courts say they will not undertake.

There are a number of cases where these tests or principles of construction have produced decisions that are difficult to reconcile (see, for instance, *Attwood v Lamont* (1920) and *Goldsoll v Goldman* (1915)). Several sources suggest that the courts have been influenced by the relative power of the parties. So, for instance, a very oppressive clause will not be reduced in its extent but merely declared void or severance will not be readily applied to employee restraints where bargaining strength does not approximate to equality (*Attwood*). Moreover, with business sale restraints, the courts seem more concerned that the purchaser should get what they have paid for. This means that in cases involving material *and* intangible assets (goodwill), the courts are more ready to tailor a restraint and enforce it against the seller.

CONCLUDING REMARKS

The development of the doctrine of restraint of trade demonstrates how far the courts have come from a model of contract underpinned by the notion of *laissez-faire*. Even the most hardened supporters of free trade have come to see that unmitigated adherence to the principle of freedom of contract can lead, somewhat ironically, to a restricted market where it allows power and control to concentrate in the hands of the few. But the issue of what constitutes an *appropriate* level of regulation of the market is far from simple. Indeed, it is one of the most hotly contested political issues of the day. In the wake of a series of political experiments in different regulatory models the area has also become one which is of intense interest to academics. The cases discussed in this chapter may seem extremely remote from the life of a law student who has yet to enter business or engage in a career, but they raise fundamental issues for democratic societies. Moreover, it is in the area of contract law, the archetypal form of private law, in which the dilemmas about the extent to which the courts or legislature should constrain the contracting parties' ability to determine the contents of a contract have been discussed. In many ways, those cases involving inequality of bargaining power are at the easiest end of the spectrum. By far the most difficult cases to resolve are those where the parties are of roughly equal strength but are attempting to distort the market in some way. Here the issue becomes what constitutes an acceptable distortion and what is unacceptable. Since the answer to such a question will undoubtedly differ according to the political leanings of the reader, it is no wonder that this is an area in which the judiciary is shy of heading.

REFERENCES AND FURTHER READING

Bryan, M 'Restraint of trade: back to a basic analysis' (1980) JBL 326.

Davies, F 'Post-employment restraints: some recent developments' (1982) JBL 490.

Furmston, M (2001) *Cheshire, Fifoot and Furmston's Law of Contract*, 14th edn, London: Butterworths, Chapter 12(1)(3) 'Contracts in restraint of trade'.

Hacker, R 'Exclusive distribution agreements and EEC Law I and II' (1978) NLJ, 14 September, p 907 and 12 October, p 1005.

Heydon, J (1971) *The Restraint of Trade Doctrine*, London: Butterworths.

Macneil, I (1968) *Contracts, Instruments for Social Co-operation, East Africa: Text, Cases, Materials*, South Hackensack, NJ: FB Rothman.

Whish, R (2003) *Competition Law*, 5th edn, London: LexisNexis UK, Chapter 2 'Common Law' (and see also the coverage of exclusive distribution agreements and 'solus' agreements).

Wyatt, D 'Restraint of trade, tied houses and "solus" agreements' (1974) NLJ, 14 March, p 243.

QUESTIONS

(1) 'By far the most serious failure of the classical model of contract was its inability to offer any contribution to the problems raised by monopolies and restrictive agreements': Atiyah. Discuss.

(2) In order to ensure that its petrol and allied products will be sold exclusively in certain garages and filling stations, Finesse Petroleum Co Ltd includes 'ties' to that effect for a period of six years in the mortgages, leases and supply agreements it has with these retail outlets. A competing oil company, NIOC Ltd, offers Brown, the owner of one of the garages, an interest-free loan of £30,000 if he will break his 'tie' with Finesse and commence exclusive selling of its products. Brown, who urgently needs money for site development, is keen to accept NIOC's offer. Explain to Brown the legal developments in this field since 1968 as they relate to his position.

(3) Carefully examine the decision in *Shell (UK) Ltd v Lostock Garage Ltd* (1977) and be prepared to discuss the issues raised and the answers provided by the Court of Appeal.

(4) (a) What was the nature of the 'public interest' in the *Nordenfelt* case?

    (b) Edward purchased the Royal Hotel from George in August 1994. As a condition of purchase George covenanted that he would not 'for a period of two years from the date of transfer of ownership engage, either directly or indirectly, in the business of hotelier or restaurateur within 10 miles of the Royal Hotel'. Edward has now heard a rumour that George is going to put his money into a guest house eight miles from the hotel.

    Six months ago Edward engaged Charles as a trainee barman to work in the cocktail bar of the hotel. This bar, which serves a wide range of unusual cocktails, is very popular with members of the general public as well as the hotel guests and those dining at the hotel's restaurant. On entering Edward's employ, Charles agreed that he would not 'work as a barman in any hotel, restaurant, club or public house within two miles for a period of one year' after the termination of his employment. Charles' cousin, who owns a local public house, has offered him a job.

    Advise Edward as to whether he can enforce the restraints against George and Charles.

PART SIX:

WHAT HAPPENS WHEN THINGS GO WRONG?

CHAPTER 18

BREACH OF CONTRACT

INTRODUCTION

So far in this book we have focused on how contracts are made and performed. We have looked at how the courts and legislature have sought to regulate what is included within the contract and excluded from it. In this final substantive section we will look at the issue of what happens when things go wrong. We will consider what constitutes a breach of contract and the remedies which flow from this. In the chapter on dispute resolution we will review the different methods and processes of dispute resolution which the parties can invoke when they need the help of a third party to resolve their disagreement.

Before we go on to discuss these matters in some detail, it is important to stress that if you have read all the chapters which precede this one, then you already know something about breach of contract. A claim that one party is in breach is the trigger for a judgment and none of the many cases reviewed in earlier chapters would have even been considered by the courts unless one party had made this allegation. The issue before the court in each contractual claim is whether or not the behaviour of the party in breach is significant enough to allow remedies to flow from it. Clearly, this issue cannot be looked at in isolation. In order to assess whether the behaviour was unacceptable, the court needs to understand the nature of the agreement between the parties. It is for this reason that an action for breach so often involves the courts in a consideration of whether a contract was formed in the first place, how different terms should be interpreted and the obligations they impose, whether variations to the contract have complied with the appropriate formalities or whether liability for the behaviour complained of has actually been excluded.

We have seen in earlier chapters that contract planning often covers four main issues: the definition of performances, the effect of defective performance, the effect of contingencies and the use of legal sanctions. Cases which come before the courts are those where the parties' planning and co-operation have broken down completely. But it is important to remember that many of the same cases are resolved by bilateral settlement negotiations between the parties. The empirical studies visited in Chapter 4 provide us with a salutary reminder of the limitations of law. It is within this context that we must study breach and the tensions the cases reveal between the need to balance the parties' understanding of the contract, the normative frameworks which define what constitutes good practice in a particular industry and the need to impose external standards of fairness on the parties.

JUDICIAL APPROACHES TO BREACH OF CONTRACT

When looking at terms in the context of breach, the courts' approach has been to introduce a hierarchy between two different types of term. Terms which describe performances are considered to be of primary or substantive nature and indicate what the contractual obligations are and how they will be fulfilled. In addition, they also imply or express the required quality of performance. Clauses in a contract which relate to defective performance, contingencies and sanctions are taken to be of a secondary or procedural nature. These might include clauses to the effect that 'if there is a strike then …' or 'the parties agree to arbitrate any dispute arising …'. (For a discussion of primary and secondary rights in the context of breach, see Lord Diplock in *Photo Production Ltd v Securicor Transport Ltd* (1980).)

When the contractual relationship fails and they bring their dispute to the courts, the role of the law is to clear up the mess caused by breach. In the main, the law achieves this goal by ordering compensatory payments (damages) to be made to aggrieved parties. In some circumstances, a right to terminate the contract is also recognised. The operation of this right to terminate the contract in the face of what a party considers to be a breach by the other can give rise to a problem. For example, Multigaze Cinema agrees to pay Yada for the performance of certain services. In the early days of performance, Yada fails in Multigaze's judgment to match up to the terms of his obligations. Can Multigaze dispense with Yada's services? When has Multigaze a right to terminate the contract? If Multigaze terminates when no such right is available, it is clear that they are liable to an action or counter claim by Yada.

The English courts approach these questions concerning the right to terminate in two ways, *which may or may not give the same answer in a given case*. The first, perhaps longer-standing approach is what is known as *term-based*. In this instance, the right to terminate is related to the nature of the term 'broken'. A distinction is made between major and minor terms. The first, known as conditions, trigger a right to terminate and claim damages if breached. In the case of lesser terms, known as warranties, breach does not allow for termination but only a claim for damages. From the mass of case law in this area, a condition has been variously described as an 'essential' term or one that 'goes to the root of the contract' and the breach of which is 'fairly considered by the other party as a substantial failure to perform the contract at all'. By way of contrast, the Sale of Goods Act 1893 defined a warranty as a term which is 'merely collateral to the main purpose of the contract'. In short, essential or major terms allow for termination, minor terms do not. Terms which are conditions *or* warranties depending on the consequences flowing from their breach have been variously described but are best known as *innominate*. This literally means that they have no name.

This appears to be a very straightforward approach but the question remains: how precisely does a court, a businessperson, or their legal adviser go about making the distinction between the major and the minor terms in a given contract? Terms do not usually specify how they might be classified. The answer given by lawyers is that one must construe or interpret the contract *as at the time it was made* and infer from it the possible intention of the parties. In 1893 Lord Justice Bowen said that it was necessary to look at the contract in the light of the surrounding circumstances and make up one's mind whether the intention of the parties would best be carried out by treating the provision as a warranty or as a condition. This is as far as the courts have got in laying down guidelines for the predication or evaluation of terms and it is clear that there is some degree of obscurity about how this approach to breach operates in practice.

In *Behn v Burness* (1863), it was agreed by a charterparty dated 19 October 1860 that the plaintiff's ship, 'now in the port of Amsterdam … and ready for the voyage, should, with all possible dispatch, proceed to Newport', where the defendant would load it with coal for Hong Kong. At that time, however, the vessel was, in fact, detained by bad weather at Niewdiep, 62 miles from Amsterdam, where it finally arrived on 23 October. When the vessel reached Newport, the charterer who had by then presumably made alternative arrangements, refused to load his coal and repudiated the contract. He was sued for wrongful termination by the shipowner. It was held that the repudiation was justified as Behn was in breach of an essential term which was the clause stating the 'whereabouts of the vessel' at the time of agreement. As Williams J stated:

> Now the place of the ship at the date of the contract, where the ship is in foreign parts and is chartered to come to England, may be the only datum on which the charterer can found his calculations of the time of the ship's arriving at the port of loading ... A statement is more or less important in proportion as the object of the contract more or less depends upon it. For most charters, considering winds, markets and dependent contracts, the time of a ship's arrival to load is an essential fact, for the interest of the charterer. In the ordinary course of charters in general it would be so: the evidence for the [charterer] shows it to be actually so in this case.

To summarise, the 'whereabouts of the vessel' clause was a condition which had been broken by the plaintiff and this meant that the defendant was justified in terminating the contract.

This decision and other cases involving the breach of similar 'essential' terms in regular commercial use led to the understanding that such terms were always to be regarded as conditions. The 'once a condition, always a condition' result was applauded. It was seen as introducing a strong element of certainty into business contracts with the consequences of breaking such terms being readily apparent from the case law. Later, this development was reinforced in certain statutes. As we have seen, certain obligations of a seller of goods, such as the 'satisfactory quality' of those goods and their fitness for a particular purpose, are implied conditions by reason of the Sale of Goods Act 1893. Breach of such an obligation gives the buyer a right to reject the goods as a matter of statute law. We have therefore reached a point where the breach of an essential term gives a right to terminate the contract and some terms are always to be classified as conditions on the basis of precedent or statutory authority.

However, an unsatisfactory feature of this position is revealed by the decision in *Arcos Ltd v Ronaasen & Son* (1933). In this case, a quantity of timber staves, described in the contract as being ½ inch thick, was bought for the purpose of making cement barrels. Most of the staves delivered were 9/16 inch thick. Although the discrepancy in no way impaired their suitability for the contract purpose, it was held that the buyer might nevertheless reject the timber. The seller was in breach of the implied condition, to be found in s 13 of the Sale of Goods Act 1893, that the goods delivered must correspond to the contract description. The fact that the buyer's motive in rejecting the goods was to allow himself the chance to buy elsewhere in a falling market did not affect the reasoning of the judges. However, the case clearly illustrates that breach of an 'essential' term can give a right to terminate even though performance is only marginally defective, the consequences for the 'injured' party are only slight and they are abusing the right to terminate. The situation has been rectified in part by a 1994 amendment to the Sale of Goods Act 1979 as regards sellers of goods who are dealing with buyers who are not dealing as consumers. The Act requires that if the seller's breach concerning description, satisfactory quality or fitness for purpose is so slight that it would be unreasonable for the buyer to reject the goods, the breach is not to be treated as a breach of condition but may be treated as a breach of warranty.

In 1962, the whole question of terms and breach was reopened in the case of *Hong Kong Fir Shipping Co Ltd v Kawasaki Kisen Kaisha Ltd*, where the 'term-based' approach outlined above was seriously challenged. In the leading judgment of the Court of Appeal, Diplock LJ stated that what was critical was not the nature of the term broken but the nature of the event arising from the breach. He argued that if the consequences for the injured party were sufficiently serious, then they should be entitled to terminate the contract. If they were not so serious, then they should only be able to claim damages. Diplock defined a sufficiently serious breach as one which would deprive the victim of the breach of substantially the whole benefit which it was intended that they should have obtained.

The facts of the case were that Kawasaki chartered a vessel from Hong Kong Fir for 24 months. The ship developed engine trouble and was laid up for repairs for 20 weeks out of the first seven months of the contract. Although it was made seaworthy at the end of that period, the charterers terminated the contract. It transpired that the main reason why Kawasaki did this was that freight rates had fallen dramatically and they could charter another vessel at a much lower rate. The owners Hong Kong Fir claimed damages for wrongful repudiation. The court held that Hong Kong Fir's breach of the seaworthiness clause had not given rise to consequences serious enough for Kawasaki to terminate. Amongst other things, the charterparty still had a further 17 of the original 24 months to run. As a result, it was determined that Kawasaki were only entitled to claim damages and Hong Kong Fir won the case.

On the basis of this 'seriousness of consequences' approach, the seaworthiness clause in this case only amounted to a warranty. However, had the court found the consequences of its breach to be such as to deprive Kawasaki of substantially the whole benefit from the contract, termination would have been justified and the clause would therefore have had the status of a condition. Diplock LJ put it this way:

> There are, however, many contractual undertakings of a complex character which cannot be categorised as being 'conditions' or 'warranties' ... of such undertakings all that can be predicated is that some breaches will and others will not give rise to an event which will deprive the party not in default of substantially the whole benefit which it was intended that he should obtain from the contract; and the legal consequences of the breach of such an undertaking, unless provided for expressly in the contract, depend upon the nature of the event to which the breach gives rise and do not follow automatically from a prior classification of the undertaking as a 'condition' or a 'warranty'.

He went on to argue that 'the emphasis in the earlier cases ... upon the breach by one party of his contractual undertakings ... tended to obscure the fact that it was really the event resulting from the breach which relieved the other party of further performance of his obligations'.

This approach to the problem of classifying terms is not necessarily as new as Diplock suggested. In another of 'the earlier cases', *Bettini v Gye* (1876), the court was at pains to look at the contract and the circumstances to see 'whether the particular stipulation goes to the root of the matter, so that a failure to perform it would render the performance of the rest of the contract by the [plaintiff] a thing different in substance from what the defendant has stipulated for'. The court speculated at some length as to what the effect of the plaintiff's breach would have been had not the defendant, in this case wrongfully, terminated the contract. It would therefore appear that before the 'once a condition, always a condition' case law development, the remedy available might depend to some extent on the effect of the breach rather than solely on 'a prior classification' of the term broken. Citing other 19th century cases, Treitel (2002) endorses this point, speaking of an original 'application of a general, open-textured rule under which the extent of the injured party's remedies depended on the seriousness of the breach' (see also *Aerial Advertising Co v Bachelors Peas Ltd* (1938)). The majority of breach cases of this kind since the *Hong Kong Fir* decision have been decided according to the 'seriousness of consequences' approach, although in *The Mihalis Angelos* (1971), a majority of the Court of Appeal reverted to the 'once a condition, always a condition' approach in connection with a common clause relating to a charterparty.

Subsequent cases have had to address the issue of whether the parties are at liberty to determine what constitutes a condition and the nature of judicial discretion in this field. In *Schuler AG v Wickman Machine Tool Sales Ltd* (1974), the parties had themselves stipulated that a certain clause in their agreement was a condition. In that case, Schuler, a German company, made panel presses used mainly by car manufacturers. By a written agreement, they appointed Wickman as English agents and distributors for their products. One of the clauses of the contract, the only one to use the word 'condition', provided that it should 'be a condition of this agreement that' Wickman should send representatives to visit six very important customers once a week. Wickman were in breach of this clause but Schuler did not at that time seek to end the contract and it was held that these breaches had been waived. Later, Wickman were guilty of some very minor breaches of the clause and Schuler terminated the agreement. On appeal from the arbitrator, Mocatta J held that the use of the word 'condition' meant that Schuler could terminate if there was any breach of that term, however slight and however long ago, provided only that it had not been waived.

Following further appeals, the House of Lords held that the parties could not have intended the agreement to mean that a failure by Wickman to make one out of a possible 1,400 visits could entail an immediate right to terminate the distributorship. Lord Wilberforce dissented in strong terms. The clause was a condition. It was wrong to assume:

> ... that both parties to this contract adopted a standard of easygoing tolerance rather than one of aggressive, insistent punctuality and efficiency. This is not an assumption I am prepared to make, nor do I think myself entitled to impose the former standard upon the parties if their words indicate, as they plainly do, the latter.

The effect of this decision is that Schuler were in breach, having wrongfully repudiated. These points were also considered by Edmund-Davies LJ in the Court of Appeal who was also troubled by the tensions between party autonomy and judicial discretion:

> Is it a sufficient indication of the contracting parties' intention as to the grave manner in which the breach of one of their agreed terms is capable of being treated that they have described it as a 'condition'? Other expressions may be insufficient – to take but one example, the undertaking of an opera singer to be in London 'without fail' at least six days before the commencement of his engagement was held by Blackburn J in *Bettini v Gye* to give rise only to ... compensation in damages. But if a term is described as a 'condition', is that enough of itself to make clear what the innocent party's rights are if it be breached?

It is now clear that the common law allows the parties to a contract to indicate expressly the consequences to be attached to any particular breach. However, it may be that they cannot do this by merely pinning the labels 'condition' or 'warranty' to their clauses. They must also state the effect with sufficient clarity. In default of such indication, it is probably for the court to decide the legal result of a breach.

More recently still, the matter was considered in *Cehave NV v Bremer Handelsgesellschaft mbH* (1976). In this case, the Court of Appeal held that breach of a stipulation in a cif contract that goods were 'shipped in good condition' did not entitle the buyer to reject the goods unless the extent of the breach went to the root of the contract. The facts were that part of a £100,000 shipment of citrus pulp pellets was not in good condition and the buyers purported to reject the whole consignment. It was found that the provision as to shipment in good condition was an 'intermediate term', the breach of which in this case did not justify the buyer's termination of the contract. His proper remedy was in damages for the amount by which the value of the goods was reduced by their damaged condition.

By 1976 then it appeared that the 'seriousness of consequences' approach would, by weight of recent authority, push the 'term-based' solution into relative obscurity. Only in *The Mihalis Angelos* had the Court of Appeal regarded the interests of certainty, as established through a line of precedents, as paramount. In that case, Megaw LJ stressed that:

> One of the important elements of the law is predictability. At any rate in commercial law there are obvious and substantial advantages in having, where possible, a firm and definite rule for a particular class of legal relationships ... It is surely much better both for shipowners and charterers (and incidentally for their advisers) when a contractual obligation of this nature is under consideration – and still more when they are faced with the necessity of an urgent decision as to the effects of a suspected breach of it – to be able to say categorically: 'If a breach is proved, then the charterer can put an end to the contract.'

The argument that the 'seriousness of consequences' approach dilutes commercial certainty is often raised, but certainty in business is an elusive concept. Upon what data does a businessperson make the decision to 'throw up' a contract? A number of factors may affect their decision. What is the state of the market? What alternative ways of proceeding are available? What advice does he or she ask for and receive? Do they want to deal with this party again? Is a dispute or litigation likely to attract unwelcome publicity? If he or she is wrong, will the other party sue? What are the relative costs? Is paying damages less expensive than keeping the contract alive?

In 1976, a further clue as to the way the law would develop was seemingly given in the House of Lords by Lord Wilberforce. He was of the opinion that some of the earlier cases were 'excessively technical and due for fresh examination'. He continued:

> The general law of contract has developed along much more rational lines in attending to the nature and gravity of a breach or departure than in accepting rigid categories which do or do not automatically give a right to rescind, and if the choice were between extending cases under the Sale of Goods Act 1893 into other fields, or allowing more modern doctrine to infect those cases, my preference would be clear.

Nevertheless, in 1981, in *Bunge Corp v Tradax Export SA*, the House of Lords reached a decision which, in line with *The Mihalis Angelos*, re-emphasised the requirements of commercial certainty. The facts of this case were that Tradax agreed to sell 15,000 tons of soya bean meal to Bunge. The first shipment was to be delivered in June, beginning on a day chosen by the buyers. The buyers were to give at least 15 days' notice of the ship's readiness to load. The notice was given four days late and Tradax alleged that this breach allowed them to terminate the contract as regards the June shipment. They argued that the clause as to notice was a *condition, any breach* of which justified termination. It was held, rejecting Bunge's claim that the term was 'innominate', that this time stipulation in a mercantile agreement was 'of the essence' and was indeed a condition in the sense alleged.

It would seem then that confusion continues about where the balance lies between the 'term-based' approach which emphasises certainty and the *Hong Kong Fir* approach which emphasises flexibility. However, a close analysis of the case suggests that the following terms will be found to be conditions without recourse to the question of the seriousness of the consequences of the breach:

(i)   Statutorily implied conditions since *Arcos* can now be avoided following the 1994 amendment of the Sale of Goods Act 1979.

(ii) A term which has to be performed by one party as a condition precedent to the ability of the other party to perform another term. This might, for instance, include notice to enable loading to commence on time, as in *Bunge*. The key factor here would appear to be the strict need for *co-operation* between the parties as without it the contract will not work.

(iii) Other mercantile terms well-established as conditions by precedent.

(iv) Terms clearly and reasonably designated as conditions by the parties themselves in the contract: see also *Lombard North Central plc v Butterworth* (1987).

However, the law is far from settled and debate amongst the judiciary reveals a series of different concerns which may conflict with each other. Of these, perhaps the greatest tension exists between the view that the parties are in the best position to define the seriousness of a breach and the proposition that the terms of a contract should only be enforced where a breach is important enough to disrupt performance in a serious way. Alongside an emphasis on party autonomy and an emphasis on the paper deal, some members of the judiciary are clearly concerned that their intervention is *proportionate* to the harm caused. To do otherwise might be to allow the parties to avoid a contract when there has only been a technical breach which does not go to the heart of the agreement. We have already learnt in Chapter 4 that many technical breaches are often ignored by the parties to business agreements on a day-to-day basis where the overall purpose of the contract is still attainable. Approaches to these issues raise much more fundamental questions about the role of law and the judiciary in contract. It is suggested that those who adopt an overly formalistic approach to breach are in danger of ignoring the implicit underpinnings of business agreements by allowing technical breaches to justify avoidance of a contract that has become uncomfortable to one of the parties.

FUNDAMENTAL BREACH

From the mid-1950s onwards, a series of cases threw up a new category of breach known as fundamental breach which can be understood as the opposite of technical breach. A fundamental breach is one which has disastrous consequences for the innocent party. In other words, this means that when the performance promised is compared with actual performance, they were deprived of all, or substantially all, they had bargained for. The key to fundamental breach lay in the fact that it was only encountered in exclusion clause cases. The reason for this was that it was created as a judicial device to defeat clauses as wide-ranging and unfair as one which protected the defendant company in *L'Estrange v Graucob* (1934). In this case, the exclusion clause was in 'regrettably small print', in 'a part of the document where it easily escaped notice' and printed on brown paper. It read: 'any express or implied condition, statement or warranty, statutory or otherwise not stated herein is hereby excluded.'

Those in favour of promoting the idea of fundamental breach argued that if the court was able to find what was called a 'radical departure' from the contemplated performance, as opposed to a serious misperformance of an agreed obligation, then a doctrine of fundamental breach could deny a supplier the protection of a clause which excluded liability for breach. The difficulty came in distinguishing fundamental breach which warranted such special measures from other types of breach.

In one case, *Karsales (Harrow) Ltd v Wallis* (1956), it was held that there was a fundamental breach where the agreement had been about the sale of a car in good running order which would not go *at all* when delivered. In that case, Wallis inspected and drove a secondhand Buick in excellent condition. He made arrangements to acquire it on hire purchase under an agreement that excluded liability for breach of conditions and warranties. The car was later towed to his house at night. Many parts had been replaced by old and defective ones. When Wallis refused to pay instalments for the car, he was sued! The court held that the breach was 'fundamental', Karsales could not rely on the exclusion clause and Wallis had a complete defence.

The doctrine of fundamental breach was brought to bear not only in supply of goods cases but also in those relating to the provision of services and work and materials. However, a major legal controversy arose as to the way in which it operated. Some judges, notably Lord Denning, considered it to be a rule of law with the effect that once a fundamental breach was found, the clause, *no matter how it was worded, automatically* failed to protect its user from liability. Other judges laid down that the doctrine of fundamental breach operated as a rule of construction which required the judges to exercise discretion. This meant that the exclusion clause was not automatically extinguished by the breach but stood to be read or construed in the light of the breach, even though it was rarely if ever taken to have been intended by the parties to be applicable to a fundamental breach.

In reality, the willingness of the court to find a fundamental breach meant that an unfair exclusion clause would have been defeated whichever approach was used. However, the controversy was more than a storm in a legal tea cup and the distinction between the two approaches is important because it is only the rule of construction approach which accords with the long-established general rules relating to breach of contract. These rules lay down that a party faced by a serious breach, such as a breach of condition, has, as we have discussed, a *right* to treat the contract as at an end. In other words, they have an election: they may terminate and sue for damages or they may affirm the contract but nevertheless sue for damages. They may even ignore or waive the breach as seen in *Schuler v Wickman* above. It follows that before a serious breach situation can give rise to termination of the contract, the injured party must, expressly or impliedly, elect to bring the contract to an end as regards unperformed primary obligations. The breach may be of such a nature that the question of election is made redundant. This means that in practical terms further performance is impossible.

The rule of law approach to fundamental breach distorted these rules by claiming that such a breach automatically deprived the wrongdoer of the benefit of his exclusion clause, the contract in which it was to be found having ceased to exist. After several differences of legal opinion, it is now settled, following the decision of the House of Lords in *Photo Production Ltd v Securicor Transport Ltd* and the passing of the Unfair Contract Terms Act 1977. To the extent that the concept of fundamental breach remains, the injured party's rights are the same as for other serious breach situations, so they include, for example, the right to elect to terminate or to affirm. To the extent that exclusion clauses are not invalidated by the 1977 Act, the question of whether they provide protection for suppliers of goods or services is one of *construction* of the clause and the contract containing it.

CONCLUDING REMARKS

In this chapter we have, once again, seen tensions emerge between judicial intervention and respect for the preferences of the parties. Whilst some have sought to introduce a sense of proportion into the consideration of the gravity of breach, others have been concerned to respect the parties' prescriptions as to what constitutes a sufficiently serious chasm to warrant the ending of a contract. Although these matters might appear to only be relevant at the end of the contractual relationship, for lawyers they are matters which need clarifying from the outset if planning of risks and benefits is to be clearly thought out in advance. In reality, the cases suggest that the parties are not always that clear at the offset of the contractual relationship about how things will work out in the event of a breach. For some, this suggests a lack of business acumen, for others a reduction of costs. Planning can be expensive in a business community where the emphasis may be on quick turnaround and subsequent deals.

REFERENCES AND FURTHER READING

Adams, J and Brownsword, R 'Contractual indemnity clauses' (1982) JBL 200.

Adams, J and Brownsword, R (2000) *Understanding Contract Law*, 3rd edn, London: Sweet & Maxwell.

Bojczuk, W 'When is a condition not a condition?' (1987) JBL 353.

Brownsword, R 'Retrieving reasons, retrieving rationality? A new look at the right to withdraw for breach of contract' (1992) 5 Journal of Contract Law 83.

Devlin, Lord 'The treatment of breach of contract' (1966) CLJ 192.

Greig, D 'Condition – or warranty?' (1973) 89 LQR 93.

Reynolds, F 'Discharge of contract by breach' (1981) 97 LQR 541.

Treitel, G (2002) *The Law of Contract*, 11th edn, London: Sweet & Maxwell.

Weir, T 'The buyer's right to reject defective goods' (1976) CLJ 33.

QUESTIONS

(1) Can you think of any situations in 'The Sad Tale of Angie and Georgie' in which the legal right to terminate a contract may well be of no practical significance?

(2) Appraise critically the following statements:

   (a) 'In penalising wickedness the *Hong Kong* rule rewards the incompetent; like other moralism it operates unfairly.'

   (b) 'When the right to reject depended on the nature of the term in the contract which was broken, the innocent party simply had to go to the filing cabinet, consult the contractual document and then decide whether the term broken was a very serious one or not.'

   (c) 'Many people put forward their contractor's breach as a ground of release when they actually want to quit for wholly different, and legally inadequate, reasons, such as a movement in market or exchange rate, or a change in their own requirements or resources. This may be good business, but it seems a poor show' (Weir, 1976).

(3) 'For the most part, the relationships between the classification and the consequential approaches, their underlying principles, and the contractual ideologies are quite clear. The proportionality and bad faith principles are consumer-welfarist, and are currently served by the consequential approach. The certainty principle and the principle of sanctity of contract are market-individualist, and are better served by the classification approach': Adams and Brownsword, *Understanding Contract Law* (2000). Discuss.

CHAPTER 19

REMEDIES

INTRODUCTION

In this book we have laid emphasis on the things lawyers need to be aware of when planning contracts. Lawyers are most often in the news in connection with high profile and high value litigation. Because of this we may lose sight of the fact that a large number of lawyers devote their time solely to transactional matters, the essence of which is advising their clients on the most appropriate structure of a proposed transaction, understanding and clarifying their client's commercial objectives in connection with that transaction and translating into an agreed form of contract the terms of business agreed between the parties. Part of the lawyer's role will be to ensure that, so far as is possible, there are built into the contract adequate safeguards for their client in the event things later go wrong in that business relationship. The lawyer's objective will be to ensure that, in the event such difficulties do arise, the client will have a sufficient armoury of legal arguments and remedies to enable them to deal with problems in the most commercially sensible way. It is therefore in this context that we need to understand the necessary overlap between prudent commercial planning by the lawyer and client and a proper appreciation of legal remedies.

It is only by understanding the legal nature of breach and the available legal remedies that parties can seek to make express provision for particular situations that may arise so as to avoid or at least limit the potential for full-scale litigation. If you look at the examples of standard form contracts included in this volume you will see that lawyers go beyond specifying what constitutes performance to plan for changes in circumstance which might make performance difficult and how disputes which arise should be managed. When a contract is broken, the first thing a businessman will ask once they have exhausted self-help remedies is 'what are my legal rights?'.

A well-structured contract will have addressed this at a number of levels. First, the draftsman may have been able to anticipate the possibility of particular circumstances arising and may have included a specific remedy or mechanism for addressing the problem. One obvious example of this is a 'cure notice' procedure by which the party not in default delivers to the defaulting party a notice specifying the particular breaches complained of and requiring the defaulting party to remedy those breaches within a specified period. As we mention later in this chapter, it is also open to the parties to agree and include in the contract a specified financial penalty in the event of a particular breach occurring.

Secondly, and assuming that the contract provides no clear answer to the particular breach of which complaint is made, the contract may provide an escalation procedure by which the parties are required to adopt a number of dispute resolution procedures aimed at securing a speedy settlement of the dispute at modest cost. We deal with such procedures in the next chapter. The final approach is the use of contractual provisions concerned with exclusion and limitation of liability, liquidated damages and termination procedures. It is this raft of provisions that, in combination with an analysis of legal remedies, will provide the foundations for a party's negotiating stance, whether those negotiations take place as part of an informal dispute resolution procedure or at the door of the court. For this reason, it is essential for both client and adviser to understand how the courts approach the issue of remedies. Whilst commercial factors often take precedent over legal doctrine and process, it is clear from empirical studies of contractual disputes that when negotiating a settlement after breach the parties bargain 'in the shadow' of the law. Disputants can and do use the 'bargaining chips' created by a legal precedent to bolster their position and add credibility to a claim that their position would be upheld by a court. The *threat* of litigation when used judiciously is, of itself, a powerful tool in the armoury of the lawyer. Likewise, a proper understanding of the weaknesses in a party's position can inform that party's risk and cost analysis and thus perhaps facilitate an early settlement on commercially realistic terms. Whether or not litigation is used, it is important to know what remedies might be available. The answer is not always easy or satisfactory, but an analysis of legal remedies is the framework within which the parties have to work in moving towards a resolution of the dispute by one means or another.

There are three principal remedies for a breach of contract. These are specific performance, termination and damages. It will be seen that each of these respond to the different needs of those who are the victims of breach. In some circumstances, what the injured party will want most is to bring the contractual relationship to an end and move on. This is a particularly attractive option where there has been a complete breakdown in trust or it makes better business sense to find another supplier. In other cases, the injured party might want to insist on performance of contractual obligations. This situation might arise where the party in breach is a specialist, is supplying a rare commodity or has agreed to perform a service at a low cost. In each of these examples termination is not appropriate because the contract is special in some way and cannot easily be replicated. In a third scenario, the injured party may need to be compensated for financial losses which have been suffered as a result of the breach. In the remainder of this chapter we will go on to consider how the three principal remedies available for breach of contract address these various needs.

There is one further approach that may be adopted in appropriate circumstances in place of, or in addition to, damages. This is a claim in restitution. This may arise, for example, where the party in breach has wholly failed to perform its part of the contract. If a seller agrees to deliver goods to a buyer for which the buyer has paid in advance and the seller then fails to deliver, they must restore what they have gained to the buyer. A restitutionary claim may also arise where the party in breach has, as a result of the breach, obtained an unjust benefit which they would not otherwise have had. This topic has received recent judicial attention and, along with restitutionary claims in the event of a partial failure of consideration, is a fast developing area of law.

SPECIFIC PERFORMANCE

By an order for specific performance, the court directs one of the parties to perform its obligations under the contract in accordance with the terms of that contract. Such a remedy may appear to be a very natural one in response to breach of an obligation freely entered into by the party in breach. However, in English law the remedy of specific performance is rarely granted. This is because it is generally unrealistic to speak of compelling performance in cases where a party is refusing to perform, has so managed their affairs as to put performance beyond its capabilities, or has broken the contract in a serious way. As a result, specific performance tends to be granted only where it is economically realistic to do so and damages are considered to be an inadequate remedy. For example, the remedy will not be granted for contracts for the sale of goods which are readily available in the market, but it will be granted where the contractual subject matter is land, property or other things which fall within the concept of 'commercial uniqueness'.

In *Perry & Co v British Railways Board* (1980), during the steel strike of 1980, Perry obtained an order that the Railways Board deliver a quantity of steel owned by him. The Railways Board, frightened of strike action, had refused to allow it to be moved. In this case, it was said that damages might be an inadequate remedy because they would be 'a poor consolation if the failure of supplies forces a trader to lay off staff and disappoint his customers'. At the time of *Perry*, steel was very difficult to obtain, as was petrol during the 1973 shortage. Thus, in *Sky Petroleum Ltd v VIP Petroleum Ltd* (1974), Sky, who had contracted to take all their petrol from VIP, were granted an interim injunction to stop VIP withholding supplies. This amounted to temporary specific performance of a contract for the sale of goods for which, although there were normally alternative sources of supply, the market had failed.

Traditionally, the courts have also refused specifically to enforce a contract under which one party is bound by *continuous duties*, the due performance of which might require constant supervision by the court. However, in some such cases, specific performance has been ordered and it has been suggested that the difficulty of supervision is sometimes exaggerated. There are various devices that the court could adopt to overcome such difficulty, such as appointing a receiver and manager, and there are several judicial statements in recent cases to suggest that 'constant supervision' is no longer a bar to specific performance but merely a factor to be taken into account. There has, in recent years, been some indication of an increased willingness by the courts to sanction the use of the remedy, although some doubt has been cast on this change in attitude by the case of *Co-operative Insurance Society Ltd v Argyll Stores (Holdings) Ltd* (1998). However, the decision of the House of Lords in that case has itself been subject to criticism. As things stand, the standard question 'are damages an adequate remedy?' might be rewritten to allow for consideration of whether it is just, in all the circumstances, that a claimant should be confined to a remedy in damages.

TERMINATION OF THE CONTRACT

Depending upon the nature of the contractual term breached and the consequences of the breach, the innocent party may, in addition to a claim in damages, be entitled to take the further step of terminating the contract. The right to do so may arise under the contract or as a matter of general law. Termination is not a straightforward remedy for the businessperson who will need to think through the legal and commercial consequences of termination very carefully before deciding whether to adopt this remedy. Having made the decision to terminate, implementation of that decision must in many cases be undertaken with great care if the situation is not to be made even worse. As a first step, the innocent party and their lawyer will need to check the contract carefully to see if it contains express provision for early termination in the event of a breach. Such provisions may restrict or impose conditions upon the right to terminate or may provide a contractual procedure for termination that will need to be implemented in tandem with other rights. If a contractual provision for termination appears to be the safest route, there may be procedures such as service of a cure notice that will need to be followed to make the termination effective. A failure to do so may expose the innocent party to an argument by the defaulting party that the termination is ineffective.

If more than one legal basis for termination is available, the innocent party will need to consider which option is the safest in terms of minimising the risk of a claim by the defaulting party that the termination is invalid. Even an apparently clear provision in a contract giving a right to terminate may not be all it seems. In the case of *Rice v Great Yarmouth Borough Council* (2000), a council sought to exercise a right of termination by reason of a contractor's various breaches of a contract for the provision of leisure management and grounds maintenance services. The right of termination for breach was expressed in the following very wide terms:

> ... if the contractor ... commits a breach of any of its obligations under the contract ... the council may ... terminate the contractor's employment under the contract by notice in writing having immediate effect ...

However, the Court of Appeal found that only a repudiatory breach or an accumulation of breaches that as a whole could properly be described as repudiatory could justify termination. The breaches relied upon by the council were found to be insufficiently serious.

A further factor to consider where more than one basis for termination exists is the extent to which the particular facts relied upon may impact upon the level of damages that the innocent party is able to recover following termination. For example, if the act giving rise to a contractual right to terminate relied upon by the party not in breach is not sufficient to constitute a repudiatory breach on the part of the defaulting party, damages may be limited to losses arising as a result of that particular breach but not loss of the bargain or expectation damages in relation to future performance (see *Financings Ltd v Baldock* (1963) and *Lombard North Central plc v Butterworth* (1987)).

A decision to terminate also has to be properly communicated to the party in breach. The right to terminate may be lost if, in the meantime, the innocent party demonstrates an intention to continue with the contract. This might be the case, for example, if they place an order for additional services or make an advance payment of charges due under the contract. If the innocent party gets it wrong and purports to terminate in circumstances where, as a matter of law, it was not entitled to do so, the party in breach may be able to treat such 'wrongful' termination as a basis upon which it can then legitimately terminate the contract. Such a situation might arise, for example, where the consequences of the breach were not sufficiently serious to warrant termination by the innocent party. This was the position in *Anglo Group plc v Winther Browne & Co Ltd* (2001) in which Winther Browne by means of a third-party leasing agreement purchased a computer system from a supplier. Winther Browne defaulted on payments due and the leasing company sued, claiming that they had repudiated the contract. Winther Browne claimed that there were defects in the system and counter claimed for loss of profits and wasted salaries. The court found that contracts for the design and installation of computer systems required parties actively to co-operate with each other. Implied into the contract was a term requiring Winther

Browne to communicate its needs clearly to the supplier and that the parties work together to resolve problems. The defects in the system had not been proven to constitute fundamental breaches of contract entitling Winther Browne to repudiate the contract. The supplier had performed substantially what it had contracted to do and Winther Browne had not fully co-operated in helping to resolve problems that had arisen.

Where an ineffective termination by the innocent party enables the defaulting party to terminate, the end result (termination of the contract) is clearly the same. However, there may be very serious financial consequences for the innocent party. If the party in breach is struggling to meet its obligations or can only do so on an uneconomic basis, it may like nothing better than for the innocent party to terminate in circumstances where it may not have been entitled to do so. Not only will the defaulting party have escaped future performance under the contract, but it may also have a claim against the innocent party for damages for wrongful termination. Even the opportunity for the defaulting party to raise such an argument will enhance its position in any subsequent negotiations for settlement that may take place.

These matters are intended to illustrate the many legal difficulties that may beset a company thinking of exercising a right of termination, but of course, in reality, it will also have to deal with the many commercial issues that may arise. If it terminates a contract for the supply of manufacturing parts, will it be able to find an alternative supplier at a competitive price; will it be able to honour its contracts with a third party for the supply of the finished item? As mentioned below, it may well have a remedy in damages in relation to such problems, but this may be of little comfort to it in the short term or in the context of its reputation in the marketplace. As a result of these various factors, even where a right of termination exists, it is for many businessmen a remedy of last resort. It is in this context that the remedy of damages assumes an even greater importance since it may in practice be the only remedy sought by the innocent party.

DAMAGES

A breach of contract gives the innocent party the right to claim damages to compensate it for any loss caused by the breach. This is subject only, in general, to restrictions imposed by any exclusion or limitation of liability provisions contained in the contract. By the mid-19th century, damages had come to be regarded as the acceptable form of 'insurance' against the risk of default by a contracting party. Operating within the context of a market economy, the basic aim of the law was to ensure that a party was compensated for loss for which a financial value could be found. However, the judiciary was also concerned to see that the 'engines of industry' were slowed as little as possible by breach situations. As a result, it gave weight to a requirement that the injured party could only terminate a contract following a serious breach and, if it did, so it had a duty to mitigate its loss.

The injured party's 'duty' to mitigate the loss means that it will not be compensated for loss which it could have avoided by taking reasonable steps: see Viscount Haldane LC in *British Westinghouse Electric and Manufacturing Co Ltd v Underground Electric Railways Co of London Ltd* (1912). So, for example, where a seller fails to deliver goods, the buyer must immediately or within a reasonable time go into the market and secure substitute equivalent goods. Its damages will then be assessed on the basis of the difference, if any, between the contract price and the market price. The buyer cannot delay at a time of a rising market. An early illustration of the market price rule arose in the case of *Gainsford v Carroll* (1824). That case concerned a seller who failed to deliver a quantity of bacon as agreed. It was held that the buyer, having terminated the contract, ought to have gone into the market at once for a replacement supply. As he had failed to do this, he could not recover damages in respect of the increase in the market price after that time. He could only recover damages equal to the difference between the contract price and the market price at the date of the breach. As the law developed, freedom and sanctity of contract demanded that contracts be enforced not so much by the law compelling adherence to contracts but by placing before a party the choice of either performing its obligations or compensating the other party for the loss which arose as a result of the breach.

The nature of loss or damage

The statement that the injured party may recover damages for the loss sustained as a result of the breach obscures as much as it reveals. In fact, we have it on judicial authority that the law relating to damages is 'a branch of the law in which one is less guided by authority laying down definite principles than in almost any other matter one can consider'. Since 1925 when this statement was made, the law of damages has moved no nearer to 'definite principles'. One matter that lawyers have sought to have clarified is the *kind* of damage or loss for which the injured party is entitled to recover compensation.

The traditional approach to this question is to say that the law protects the *expectations created by the contract*. Damages are therefore awarded to put the injured party, so far as money can do it, in the same position as if the contract had been properly performed (see the judgment of Parke J in *Robinson v Harman* (1848)). The injured party is entitled to damages for the loss of its bargain so that its expectations arising from the contract are protected. An alternative view, which is being increasingly applied, is that some situations require that if the injured party is to obtain adequate compensation, it is necessary to put it back in the position in which it would have been in had the contract *never been made*. This is referred to as *reliance damages*, where the intention is to put the innocent party into the position it would have been in if it had not entered into the contract at all. It will be remembered from the chapter on misrepresentation that this is a standard which has traditionally been associated with tortious remedies rather than contractual ones. In broad terms, damages calculated on this basis comprise the wasted expenditure incurred *in reliance on the contract*. This is not limited to expenditure incurred after the contract was concluded. The innocent party can also claim expenditure incurred before the contract was entered into, provided it was within the reasonable contemplation of the parties that it would be likely to be wasted as a result of the other party's breach. We will return to this subject later.

The two approaches mentioned above are illustrated in diagrammatic form below.

Figure 19.1: Expectation and reliance damages

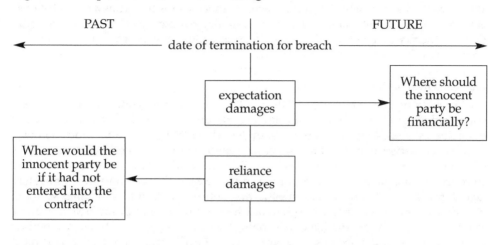

Expectation damages

An award of damages to compensate the injured party for loss of the benefit they would have secured had the contract been properly performed may require a relatively straightforward calculation of lost profits in the case of non-delivery of goods for resale. In other cases, such as where there has been defective delivery of some sort, the position may not be so simple. Broadly speaking there are two ways of measuring expectation damages. First, they may be measured by reference to the cost of cure of the defective performance. Secondly, they may be assessed by reference to the reduced value of what has been 'delivered'. In some cases, the two different approaches will produce the same result; in others, the results will be different and the view a court will take as to the correct measure of loss will depend very much on the individual circumstances of the case. The distinction between the two is very well-illustrated in a case concerning a swimming pool. In *Ruxley Electronics and Construction Ltd v Forsyth* (1996), builders were asked to build a swimming pool. The agreed depth was to be seven feet six inches but when the builders completed the swimming pool it was only six feet deep. There was nothing else wrong with it. The impact on the value of the pool was assessed at nil. The cost of correcting the breach, which was only possible by demolishing the pool and building a new one, was £21,560. In considering the question of which of the two approaches to measurement of damages was the correct one, the House of Lords held that it would not be reasonable for the owner of the pool to recover the cost of cure damages because the cost of carrying out the corrective work was out of all proportion to the benefit that he would obtain. In their view, the correct measure was the diminution in value, even in a case where such value was nil. A finding by the original trial judge that the pool owner was entitled to damages for 'loss of amenity' (the disappointment experienced in not getting a pool of the dimensions specified) of £2,500 was allowed to stand.

The same principles will apply whether the claim is a large or a small one. For example, in *Sabir v Tiny Computers* (1999), Mr Sabir purchased a computer from Tiny Computers but sought to reject it seven months later on the basis that it was crashing more often than was acceptable. He brought an action against Tiny for damages for breach of contract. Even though it was found that an upgrade from Windows 95 to Windows 98 that Mr Sabir had undertaken without consulting Tiny had contributed 50% to the problem, Mr Sabir was held to be entitled to damages for loss occasioned by faults in the machine not attributable to the upgraded software. The modest award of damages of £670 was made up of the cost of telephone calls between Mr Sabir and Tiny, compensation for loss of use, diminution in value of the computer and reimbursement of the cost of repair.

The case of *Pegler v Wang* (2000) involved much larger financial claims. This concerned a dispute in relation to a contract between Wang and Pegler, a manufacturer of engineers' and plumbers' brassware, under which Wang was to provide computer hardware, software and related services designed to improve Pegler's business efficiency. The total price agreed was £1,198,130 plus £235,000 each year for three years to cover maintenance. Wang's performance was extremely poor and they ultimately abandoned the contract. Pegler served formal notice of breach and required Wang to remedy its various breaches, but Wang took no steps to comply. Pegler treated Wang's failure to do so as a repudiation of the contract which it relied on to bring the contract to an end. In tandem it exercised a contractual right of termination. Pegler used third parties to provide the services it needed and issued proceedings against Wang claiming damages of nearly £23 million. Pegler eventually admitted liability and the trial of the claim was principally concerned with examination of the damages claimed. Pegler was ultimately awarded £9 million. The heads of loss included lost sales, lost opportunity to increase margins, lost opportunity to make staff cost savings, the cost of replacement systems and consultancy services, lost opportunity to reduce finished stock held, the ability to negotiate improved purchasing terms and wasted management time.

Reliance damages

It has already been indicated that, in certain circumstances, an alternative approach to assessment of damages, namely the reliance model, may be adopted. If expectation damages are claimed, the claimant will be expected to give satisfactory evidence of the value of its expectations. If this is not possible, a reliance claim may be appropriate. *Anglia Television Ltd v Reed* (1972) concerned a case in which an actor failed to honour his contract with a TV company to appear in a film. The company was unable to find a substitute and the film was never made. It could not say what its profits on the project would have been and chose instead to make a wasted expenditure claim. The judge found that the TV company was entitled to recover wasted expenditure on fees paid to the director, designer and stage manager both *before* and after the contract had been entered into on the basis that the actor must have known perfectly well that such expenditure was likely to be incurred and would be wasted if he broke his contract.

A further example of this approach is the case of *Salvage Association v CAP Financial Services Ltd* (1995), which concerned a contract for the development of new accounting software. When it became clear that the supplier would fail to sort out serious problems in the system in time to meet an agreed deadline for completion of the project, the customer exercised a right of termination and engaged another company to design a replacement system from scratch. It succeeded in recovering from the supplier £291,388 paid under the two development and implementation contracts entered into with the supplier. In addition, it recovered £231,866 wasted expenditure (made up of payments made to a bureau facility for use of terminal time, wasted computer stationery, payment to consultants and payments to an independent third party in connection with testing) and £139,672 wasted management time that could have been put to productive use in connection with other activities.

Reliance damages may be appropriate in relation to certain types of contract that require major 'up front' expenditure. It is, however, important to distinguish between costs incurred in connection with the project which may have been entirely wasted and costs that have provided some value. For example, work undertaken may relate to steps that will not need to be undertaken again, such as where the contract is put out to tender a second time. In addition, what the claiming party cannot do is use the reliance measure of loss in an attempt to escape the consequences of a poor commercial bargain. This proviso is illustrated by the case of *C and P Haulage Co Ltd v Middleton* (1983) where the plaintiff had been granted a licence to occupy premises for renewable periods of six months. Despite the fact that the contract provided that fixtures were not to be removed at the end of the licence, the plaintiff carried out a number of improvements to the property to enable him to carry out his work. The owner of the property acted in breach of contract by evicting the plaintiff from the property 10 weeks prior to the end of the six month period. The plaintiff was able to work from home during that 10 week period and therefore suffered no loss of business. He did, however, bring a claim for the cost of the improvements. The court held that this was not recoverable because the loss flowed not from the breach but from the fact that he had entered into a contract under which he had agreed not to remove fixtures at the end of the term. Even if there had not been a wrongful eviction, the loss would still have been suffered because of the terms agreed. For a review of the cases on reliance loss, see *CCC Films (London) Ltd v Impact Quadrant Films Ltd* (1985). A further factor to bear in mind is that the claimant will not be entitled to any element of double recovery. They cannot, for example, claim both the cost of raw materials and the loss of profits on sale of the finished goods that they had expected to sell to the party in breach.

Remoteness of loss

A breach of contract may initiate a course of events which results in loss to the claimant, but the law will not necessarily hold the defendant liable for all the loss that flows from the breach. It may regard part of the loss as being too remote. In support of this position it has been argued that 'in the varied web of affairs the law must abstract some consequences as relevant, not perhaps on grounds of pure logic, but simply for practical reasons'. The principal justification for not permitting recovery of all loss is that if this were to be permitted, the risk of entering into a contract might be considered so great that parties might be discouraged from doing so or, even in the event that they were prepared to proceed, that they would do so only on very onerous terms. The remoteness rule places a limit on damages, as does the rule on mitigation referred to below.

The basic test of remoteness, laid down in *Hadley v Baxendale* (1854), is whether the loss was within the reasonable contemplation of the parties. That case involved a flour mill which was driven by a steam engine. The engine came to a standstill owing to a broken crankshaft and the owner of the mill had to send the shaft to the makers as a pattern for a new one. The makers, in breach of contract, delayed delivery of the new shaft which the mill owner did not receive until five days after he would otherwise have done. The mill being idle during this period, the owner claimed for loss of profits occasioned by the delay. It was found by Baron Alderson that:

> Where two parties have made a contract which one of them has broken, the damages ... should be such as may fairly and reasonably be considered either arising naturally, ie according to the usual course of things, from such breach of contract itself, or such as may reasonably be supposed to have been in the contemplation of both parties, at the time they made the contract, as the probable result of the breach.

It was held that the stoppage did not arise in 'the usual course of things' but was the result of special circumstances, namely the fact that the mill owner had only one crankshaft. This was not considered to be within the reasonable contemplation of the carrier at the time the contract was made. The maker of the shaft was therefore not liable for the loss of profits; he was only liable for nominal damages.

It is important to note that everyone is assumed *to know* the usual course of things and to know the consequences of breach in such circumstances. Knowledge of special circumstances, however, must be shown to be actual knowledge in order to attract liability for special loss. In *Hadley*, the miller's special circumstances militated against the application of the first limb of the remoteness rule and his failure to communicate his lack of a spare crankshaft to the carrier meant that he was not covered by the second limb either. It has been said of this case that the court implied that the optimal mill owner would not allow himself to be caught without a spare. Avoidable consequences must be avoided by those with power to avoid them. It would distort the market system to allow an offender against this principle to cast his losses upon another party, since a market system required the penalties for bad planning of enterprise to fall upon those who planned badly. Alternatively, it may be said that the court considered it to be unfair to impose such a wide liability for damages upon a carrier unless he was aware of the circumstances and had the opportunity to settle special terms.

As a result of *Hadley*, a party looking for compensation must now seek to bring its claim to compensation within one of the two limbs of the test mentioned in that case. The first possibility is that the loss occurred 'naturally'. The proper meaning of 'naturally' is something that has been expressed in the cases in many different ways. For example, it has been described as being 'in the usual course of events', 'a serious possibility' or 'a real danger'. In the case of *Koufos v Czarnikow* (1969), sugar merchants chartered a ship to carry some sugar from Constanza to Basrah. In breach of contract, the shipowner made a number of detours along the way which resulted in the sugar arriving at its destination nine days later than would otherwise have been the case. During that nine day period the price of sugar on the Basrah market had fallen and the merchant therefore achieved a lower price on sale. The court found that it must have been within the common contemplation of both parties that if there was a delay in delivery, it was 'not unlikely' that there would be a decline in the price of the goods during that period. In other words, it was a natural consequence.

The second possibility is that the claimant must demonstrate that the loss was within the reasonable contemplation of the parties at the time the contract was made. The notion of reasonable contemplation has also caused problems of interpretation. Words such as 'loss', 'reasonable contemplation' and 'communication' are capable of manipulation, and in the modern business world it may more readily be assumed than was the case when *Hadley* was decided that a party has a fair knowledge of another's operations and techniques. This is not always true, however, as is well-illustrated by the case of *Balfour Beatty v Scottish Power plc* (1994). Balfour Beatty had entered into a contract with the local electricity board for the supply of electricity to a concrete batching plant used in connection with the construction of an aqueduct. The electricity company was not aware that the construction work required a continuous pour of concrete and, in breach of contract, the supply of electricity was interrupted. As a result, a substantial part of the construction had to be demolished and rebuilt. The court found that the electricity company could not be expected to be aware of construction manufacturing processes, such as the need for continuous pour, and, as a result, the damage suffered as a result of the failure in supply could not be said to have been within the reasonable contemplation of the company.

It is also true that a party cannot be expected to know details of the other party's business strategy unless this has been clearly communicated to them. *Amstrad plc v Seagate Technology Inc* (1998) concerned a contract between Amstrad, a major manufacturer and supplier of IBM-compatible personal computers aimed at the lower end of the market, and Seagate, which at the time was the biggest manufacturer of hard disk drives for such computers. Amstrad decided to launch a new range of upmarket models, with enhanced disk drives. It bought 56,000 hard disk drives from Seagate for the new range at a cost of $17 million. The launch of the new range was unsuccessful largely because of major problems with the disk drives that meant users were unable to retrieve data. Amstrad was found to be entitled to receive damages for lost and delayed sales of the new range and for wasted costs but was not entitled to recover any damages for loss of sales of a successor range of personal computers planned by Amstrad because such losses were not within the reasonable contemplation of the parties at the time the contract was made. The more information a party possesses regarding the risks attached to contract performance, the better opportunity it has to modify its terms. Actual knowledge of 'special circumstances' might, for example, lead or enable a party to increase its price, exclude the risk or insure against its occurrence.

The case of *Victoria Laundry (Windsor) Ltd v Newman Industries Ltd* (1949) is often used to illustrate the distinction between losses that flow naturally from the breach and those which must be categorised as 'special' losses. In that case, the defaulting party, an engineering company, had agreed to immediate delivery of a boiler to the plaintiff, a laundry business. The defendant did not know that the boiler was needed to extend the business. The boiler was delivered five months late and the plaintiff sued for loss of profits. The court found that the plaintiff was entitled to compensation for loss of normal profits which were an entirely natural consequence of late delivery. The court did not accept that the plaintiff should be entitled to recover losses under especially lucrative contracts that it had just entered into with the government which it could not perform without the new boiler. The defendant did not know about these contracts and the loss was not within the reasonable contemplation of the parties. It has been suggested, however, that the law should not ignore the extent of the loss if it is to achieve appropriate restrictions on recovery. In a commercial contract the *kind* of loss will nearly always be within the contemplation of the parties. For example, in the *Victoria Laundry* case, the loss under the normal contracts and under the lucrative contracts was the same in nature. It was only the amount of profit under the lucrative contracts that was exceptional and it could be argued that it is legitimate to distinguish between ordinary and exceptional losses in relation to both direct and consequential losses.

Non-pecuniary loss: disappointment and distress

Other factors have operated in recent years to widen the scope of loss in the context of damages for breach of contract. It has for many years been clear that where a breach causes personal injury, an award of damages can go beyond pure economic loss and take account of pain and suffering. This was the case in *Godley v Perry* (1960), in which Godley bought a catapult which broke and as a result lost an eye. More significantly, inroads have been made into the old rule that contract damages could not be awarded for injured feelings. In part, this has come about as a result of similar developments in negligence cases and the growth of consumer protection. In *Jarvis v Swan's Tours Ltd* (1973), Jarvis booked a winter holiday in the Alps with Swan's tours, whose brochure listed many attractions. The holiday fell far short of Jarvis' expectations and in the second week he was the sole visitor. On appeal on the issue of damages, the award was increased from £32 to £125. The court decided that 'damages can be given for the disappointment, the distress, the upset and frustration caused by the breach'. Similarly, in *Farley v Skinner* (2002) the House of Lords upheld an award of £10,000 for non-pecuniary losses to the purchaser of a house near an airport who had asked their surveyor to investigate whether the house would be affected by aircraft noise. The purchaser had gone ahead with the transaction on the basis of the surveyor's assurance that the property was unlikely to be affected. It was held by the court that the award of damages was justified either because a major or important part of the contract was to 'give pleasure, relaxation or peace of mind' or as compensation for 'inconvenience and discomfort'.

Liquidated damages

In the opening section of this chapter we referred to the planning function of lawyers and it is to this point that we now return. Detailed planning of a contractual relationship can allow the parties to avoid costly disputes and litigation should a breach occur. One means at their disposal is the inclusion in the agreement of a clause providing for a fixed or calculable sum to be paid on the occurrence of an anticipated possible breach. For example, a building contract may provide that 'the contractor shall pay the building owner £500 per week or part thereof for delay in completion of the works'. Such a clause usually indicates the parties' willingness to avoid litigation over questions such as remoteness of loss and assessment of damages when the fact of non-compliance with the contract is not in dispute. However, the party in default may resist the operation of the clause and plead that it is an unenforceable *penalty*. If the court decides that the sum fixed is a 'genuine pre-estimate' of the actual loss likely to be suffered by the injured party in the event of the specified breach, then it is recoverable, whatever the actual loss. In these cases, the sum due is known as 'liquidated damages'. These can be compared with 'unliquidated damages' of the nature discussed above which can only be quantified by the court after a breach has occurred.

A liquidated damages clause must be distinguished from both a limitation of liability clause and a penalty, neither of which are genuine pre-estimates of loss. The objective of a limitation of liability clause is to place an upper limit on the amount of damages recoverable by one or both parties. The limit agreed often has little connection to the possible losses that may be suffered as a result of a breach of contract. It is very much determined by commercial expediency and the relative bargaining strength of each party, limited only by the restrictions imposed by the Unfair Contract Terms Act 1977. This is not to deny that a liquidated damages clause may in practice limit liability where actual loss exceeds the agreed figure, but its object is to benefit both parties by avoiding litigation on the matter. The essence of such a clause is that the stipulated figure can be seen as a genuine pre-estimate of loss: 'It is essential that the sum assessed should be reasonable in relation to the damage anticipated and to all known facts, even though precise calculation is not possible.'

If the sum fixed is obviously 'extravagant and unconscionable in comparison with the greatest loss which the injured party could suffer as a result of the breach', then it is viewed by the courts as a penalty. Such a sum is not recoverable, although the injured party can recover on the basis of unliquidated damages for actual loss. When distinguishing between a penalty and a liquidated damages clause, the vital factor is the reasonableness of the amount. The use of either term by the parties in the contract is *not* in itself conclusive.

The basis of the law relating to liquidated damages was laid down by Lord Dunedin in *Dunlop Pneumatic Tyre Co Ltd v New Garage and Motor Co Ltd* (1915). More recently in *Robophone Facilities Ltd v Blank* (1966), Blank agreed to rent one of Robophone's telephone answering machines for seven years at £17 11s per quarter. A clause in the agreement stated that if it was terminated for any reason, Blank was to pay Robophone 'all rentals accrued due and also by way of liquidated or agreed damages a sum equal to 50% of the total of the rentals which would thereafter have become payable'. Blank cancelled the agreement before the machine was installed. It was held that Robophone could recover agreed damages of £245 11s. Since Robophone's facilities for supplying the machines exceeded and were likely to continue to exceed the demand, they were entitled to recover their loss of profit.

CONCLUDING REMARKS

In this chapter we have looked at the remedies available to parties who believe they have suffered from a breach of contract. The overlap with the law of tort has become apparent as we have given consideration to the different methods for compensating those who have suffered loss. These issues are important because whether or not an injured party decides to pursue their grievance in the courts the law will undoubtedly have a part to play in the framing of a dispute. But to put the whole matter in perspective it is clear that self-help remedies will often be resorted to before the injured party considers litigation. Self-help remedies have a number of economic advantages. They are cheaper, informal and quick. In the everyday world of business, they may also produce a powerful incentive to perform. Complaints and threats to reputation, the holding of the other party's belongings and realisation of a 'security' all pose a considerable risk to those who claim legitimate breach or hope that an illegitimate breach will not be actioned because of the financial consequences. These factors provide an important backdrop to our consideration of formal remedies and will continue to be relevant as we move on to a consideration of whether or not litigation is the appropriate dispute resolution mechanism.

REFERENCES AND FURTHER READING

Barton, J 'The economic basis of damages for breach of contract' (1972) 1 Journal of Legal Studies 277.

Burrows, A 'Mental distress damages in contract – a decade of change' (1984) LMCLQ 119.

Burrows, A 'Specific performance at the crossroads' (1984) 4 Legal Studies 102.

Burrows, A (1993) *The Law of Restitution*, London: Butterworths.

Burrows, A (1994) *Remedies for Torts and Breach of Contract*, London: Butterworths.

Carter, J (1995) 'Suspending contract performance for breach' in Beatson, J and Danzig, R, '*Hadley v Baxendale*: a study in the industrialization of the law' (1975) 4 Journal of Legal Studies 249.

Friedmann, D (eds) *Good Faith and Fault in Contract Law*, Oxford: Clarendon.

Harris, D, Campbell, D and Halson, R (2002) *Remedies in Contract and Tort*, 2nd edn, London: LexisNexis Butterworths.

Law Commission (1983) *Law of Contract: Pecuniary Restitution on Breach of Contract*, Report No 121, London: Law Commission.

Opeskin, B 'Damages for breach of contract terminated under express terms' (1990) 107 LQR 293.

Owen, M 'Some aspects of the recovery of reliance damages in the law of contract' (1984) 4 Oxford Journal of Legal Studies 393.

Tillotson, J 'The Portuguese bank note case: legal, economic and financial approaches to the measure of damages in contract' (1994) 68 Australian Law Journal 93.

QUESTIONS

(1) Angie and Georgie are clearly in a mess! Imagine that you have set up a series of meetings between Angie and Georgie and the following people:

(a) Mister C;

(b) Chelsea;

(c) Orange Peril plc;

(d) Wacky Machine Company and Ned;

(e) Dipti;

(f) Marcus;

(g) Monkish Soup Company;

(h) Claude;

(i) Kirsteen;

(j) St Ives Bank; and

(k) the multi-storey car park.

What do you think they need to ask for in each of these meetings to improve their situation? Are the other parties in a position to provide what they want? How much of what they want can be translated into claims for specific performance or damages?

(2) How many actions for breach of contract can you identify in 'The Sad Tale of Angie and Georgie'? How would you advise Angie and Georgie to proceed as (a) a lawyer, and (b) a friend?

(3) Draw up a schedule of damages that you think Angie and Georgie could claim.

CHAPTER 20

DISPUTE RESOLUTION

INTRODUCTION

People in the business community today do not have any enthusiasm for litigation. Although, at first glance, recourse to the courts appears to be the obvious means by which a party to a contract seeks to enforce its contractual rights in the event of default or non-compliance by the other party, in practice, a whole host of factors may militate against the commencement of litigation as a means of securing enforcement of such rights. In this chapter we consider the various ways in which the parties to a contract might go about resolving their dispute. In an introductory text of this kind it is not possible to describe the full range of dispute resolution techniques employed by parties in conflict about a contract. As a result, some processes, such as early neutral evaluation and the mini trial, can only be mentioned in passing. What we are able to do is focus on the three forms of dispute resolution most discussed in legal circles: litigation, arbitration and mediation.

DISTASTE FOR LITIGATION

During the course of studying for your law degree you will spend thousands of hours reading the judgments of our superior courts. Legal education is renowned for its court-centric approach and this is inevitable given the emphasis placed on doctrine in subjects such as contract. However, most research on disputes demonstrates that cases which are litigated, let alone reach the Court of Appeal, are unusual and atypical. There are a number of reasons for this. Perhaps most importantly, the pursuit of litigation can involve an immense commitment of resources, both in legal costs and management time. For the commercial party, even if the claim is successful, not all of the costs can be recovered and time spent by personnel in protracted preparation and hearings might be better spent devoted to its business.

An additional factor is that the delay involved in obtaining a judgment on the dispute may have significant adverse financial and commercial consequences. Even having obtained a judgment, the defaulting party may have insufficient assets to satisfy it. There are also the uncertainties associated with litigation. Whatever the rights and wrongs of the case, there may be insufficient evidence to support a claim and the fear of 'litigation risk' is ever-present. However strong the case, you may have the misfortune to meet the wrong judge on the wrong day from whom you receive a perverse decision or one less likely to favour your interests. For private individuals, these same factors come into play but are exacerbated by the often small amounts involved in consumer disputes and the distress caused by involvement in stressful and unfamiliar litigation procedures. These various factors have led many researchers to suggest that many disputants react to a grievance by 'lumping it' and cutting their losses.

Research demonstrates that trading organisations have become larger in size but fewer in number, with the result that not only are there fewer potential litigants but that there is a greater inclination to compromise disputes. Large organisations will only litigate a dispute if the amount at stake is much larger or the principle involved is much more important than the trading concerns of the past would have tolerated without a contest. The shifting of the risk of loss to insurance companies may also be a factor here, bearing in mind that such risk-bearers may pursue their subrogated rights through the courts.

The costs and the 'win or lose' nature of litigation have also led the business community, from the late-19th century onwards, more and more towards *increased self-regulation* as regards contractual disputes. Various techniques have been adopted by the business community in order to avoid entering the litigation arena. Many of these techniques arise at the drafting stage of a contract. At the mid to high value end of commercial transactions, contracts have become increasingly more sophisticated as lawyers seek to tighten up wording, thereby avoiding ambiguity and reducing the scope for dispute. One party may be able to impose its 'tried and tested' standard form of agreement but most contracts now contain carefully drafted exclusion and limitation of liability provisions, geared to risk management. In addition, liquidated damages provisions which regulate the amount of compensation to be paid on occurrence of some possible future specified breach are commonplace. If potential recovery under the contract is capped, the potential for early settlement is much greater.

Another recently relevant development is the adoption in commercial contracts of escalation procedures designed to contain and encourage settlement of disputes at an early stage by means of referral and discussion between senior management on both sides. Such provisions will generally provide for representatives on both sides to engage in negotiations within a specified time period of a dispute having arisen. If discussions fail, the matter is referred to senior management, perhaps in the form of a mini trial and if that is unsuccessful, then to mediation. Only if all of these various processes fail will the parties resort to litigation or other form of adjudication.

The ability to exploit market pressures is another significant factor in influencing how a dispute is handled. The growth of the corporate giant and the commercial bargaining power it wields in the context of a dispute with a business partner are factors that should not be underestimated. In the public sector arena the power to remove the other party from an approved panel of suppliers may facilitate a settlement. At a more general level, negotiation in one form or another is something that has never gone out of fashion. An ongoing business relationship or need can very often provide the context within which a commercial settlement is possible. The relative strength of each party's legal position will be a factor in the negotiations but not always a determinative one.

The conclusion to be drawn from all of the above factors is that in making a decision as to whether or not to pursue a legal claim following a breach of contract, the matters the aggrieved party will need to discuss with its lawyer go far beyond the strength of its legal position. Figure 20.1 summarises the most important of these considerations.

Whilst not exhaustive, Figure 20.1 illustrates that in the real world, the application of contractual principles cannot be determinative of how a breach of contract is resolved. This is so because in a dispute situation it is only by some form of adjudicatory process, such as litigation, that these principles will be applied and

Figure 20.1: Deciding whether to make a legal claim

The strength of the legal case	Is there sufficient documentary and oral evidence to establish the facts necessary to support the claim? Will the witnesses of fact make credible witnesses? How will they stand up to cross-examination? Are relevant witnesses still employed? If they have moved on will they be willing/interested in assisting in preparation of the case?
	Will it be possible to obtain the expert evidence necessary to support technical points needed to prove the claim?
	If successful in establishing the facts relied upon, what is the percentage chance of success of the legal arguments succeeding?
Financial factors	What is the value of the claim compared to the legal costs involved in pursuing it?
	What is the value of the management time that will be involved in preparation of the legal case? Can we afford to divert this time away from our business?
	What percentage of legal costs can be recovered from the other party in the event the claim is successful? What is the likely amount of legal costs that will be payable to the other party in the event that the claim is unsuccessful? Is insurance cover available in relation to costs exposure? If so, what is the amount of the premium payable?
Commercial factors	Are we likely to want to do business with this party again?
	Will our reputation in the marketplace be damaged by pursuing a claim?
	Will litigation attract adverse or unwanted publicity?
	Will an adverse decision by the court produce a binding precedent that may have 'knock-on' consequences in relation to other contracts on similar terms?
	What are our commercial objectives in relation to the claim? Can we achieve these by other means or perhaps more quickly/cheaply by using some other form of dispute resolution process?
Other	Litigation risk – whatever the apparent strength of the claim it is impossible to predict with certainty the decision the judge will make.
	Litigation is a destructive and stressful process. Do we have sufficient resources and commitment?

enforced. In light of the various factors mentioned above it should not be assumed that the prosecution of such proceedings is possible or even desirable in a large number of cases.

To the extent that an aggrieved party concludes that it *does* wish to pursue a claim, it must next give consideration to the best means of doing so. As explained in the opening paragraphs of this chapter, the natural inclination of most businesspeople will be to look for a quicker and cheaper form of dispute resolution than that offered by the courts, although in some circumstances the litigation process may still offer real advantages over other forms of procedures. We will now turn to consider the various forms of dispute resolution process available in today's market, what is involved in those processes and the factors that may influence a party in deciding whether to adopt a particular procedure.

DISPUTE RESOLUTION PROCEDURES

A significant development in recent years, brought about by a combination of private enterprise, government intervention and industry pressure, has been the overhaul of civil court procedures that has gone some way to meeting concerns about the court process. These changes have occurred in tandem with an increase in the range of dispute resolution procedures available to parties with the result that the emphasis in modern dispute resolution is on selection of the best process to achieve a favourable outcome by the most efficient means. As already discussed, this is not the same thing as securing proper application of contractual principles in order to prove a good legal case. For most businesspeople, a favourable outcome is defined in terms of commercial objective and financial cost.

The range of dispute resolution procedures now available to parties seeking to enforce their rights is huge. The principal ones are described below. Before looking at these, however, it is very important to understand the distinction between mandatory and voluntary procedures. The former, often generically referred to as adjudication, involve a neutral third party imposing an outcome on the parties. By way of contrast, voluntary procedures are aimed at bringing the parties to an agreement on how the dispute is to be resolved. In general terms, in the case of mandatory procedures, a party has no choice but to participate and to submit to the decision made. In the case of litigation this is because, subject to certain limitations, an aggrieved party always has the right to take its claim to the court and the court will nearly always have the necessary authority over the defending party to compel it to submit to its authority. In the case of other mandatory procedures, such as arbitration, the basis of the tribunal's power will be the parties' prior agreement to submit a dispute to that tribunal for determination. Thus, in these cases, the process is mandatory because there is a binding contract to deal with the dispute in this way. Mandatory procedures necessarily involve the appointment of an independent third party charged with determining the 'correct' legal position on the matters in dispute between the parties. Subject to any right of appeal that may exist, such decision is binding on the parties, that is, in general terms they have no choice but to accept the decision. If the losing party fails to comply with the decision, the successful party will be entitled to look to the court to assist in enforcement.

Voluntary procedures are much more flexible and enable parties to keep their options open while exploring the possibility of compromise. As a general rule, voluntary procedures are conducted on a without prejudice basis, that is, communications between the parties and documents created for the purposes of the procedure cannot be relied upon by the other party at a later date should the matter not be resolved. If at the end of a voluntary procedure the parties are unable to reach terms of settlement which each feels that it can accept, each party is free to walk away from the process without having prejudiced its legal position in any way.

A further important distinction lies in the nature of the remedy that may be achieved through each of these two categories of process. Where a dispute is referred for mandatory or binding determination to a third party acting in a judicial or quasi-judicial capacity, the role of the parties to the dispute is strictly limited. They have no control over the outcome of the process: that aspect is determined by the third party. The necessary corollary of this is that the third party, charged with such responsibility, is confined to adjudicating upon the specific issues referred to them and in strict accordance with the legal merits and rights of the parties. Many voluntary procedures, on the other hand, involve active participation by the parties in the formulation of an agreed outcome, the form of which often embraces matters not at all connected with the claims in dispute but which may enable a business solution to be achieved. It is this flexibility, inherent in many forms of voluntary process, that enables businesspeople to do what they do best – cut a deal. The non-binding procedures mentioned below (mediation, mini trial and early neutral evaluation (ENE)) are just a few of the many on offer in today's dispute resolution market. There are many variations and the forms of process available are increasing as businesspeople and their lawyers become more imaginative in their approach to dispute resolution.

NEW APPROACHES TO DISPUTE RESOLUTION

Litigation

Where resort to binding determination by a third party cannot be avoided, litigation remains the last port of call for a significant number of parties. Litigation is probably the form of adjudication that you are most familiar with. In common with other forms of adjudication it involves a neutral third party listening to the opposing arguments of two disputants and, on the basis of the evidence presented, determining which of the two arguments is the more convincing. It follows that adjudication produces a winner and a loser and that, in this country at least, the approach to the preservation of evidence is an adversarial one. It is also important to stress that adjudication is undertaken by someone with the authority to *impose* a decision upon the parties.

The landscape of court-based adjudication is, however, significantly different to how it was 10 or even five years ago. This is because of the radical changes made to civil litigation as a result of the Woolf Reforms. The aims of his review of the civil justice system, entitled *Access to Justice* (commissioned in 1994), were to improve access to justice, reduce the cost of litigation, reduce the complexity of the existing rules, modernise terminology and remove unnecessary distinctions of practice and procedure. In short, to address the 'key problems facing civil justice – cost, delay and complexity'. After extensive consultation, Lord Woolf published his *Final Report* and Draft Civil Procedure Rules in July 1996. The draft Rules were subsequently amended by the Rules Committee of the Lord Chancellor's Department and new Civil Procedure Rules (CPR) were published in January 1999. They apply to all proceedings in the county court, High Court and Court of Appeal and became law on 26 April 1999.

In his *Final Report* of July 1996, Lord Woolf identified a number of principles which a justice system should meet. These included the need to offer appropriate procedures at reasonable cost, to deal with cases with reasonable speed, to be fair in the way it treated litigants and to be effective, adequately resourced and organised. The key to how the aims of the Woolf Reforms were intended to be achieved is contained in the most important rule of all, Rule 1, which sets out the 'overriding objective' of the CPR.

This states that 'these Rules are a new procedural code with the overriding objective of enabling the court to deal with cases justly'.

Dealing with a case justly is defined to include, so far as practicable, a number of objectives. The first of these is to ensure that the parties are on an equal footing. This is an extremely important concept in the application of civil justice. All too often in court proceedings it is the party with the 'deepest pockets' and the least pressing need who is best able to exploit court procedures to its advantage. For example, they may insist that the case requires a number of experts in different disciplines, all of whom will cost a great deal of money and delay a trial date by some months, or they may argue that they are entitled to extensive and costly disclosure of documents from an impecunious opponent. Formal recognition of the need to adopt procedures that help to eradicate the uneven nature of the litigation playing field is an important development. It mirrors to an extent the efforts made by judges to address imbalances in bargaining power between the parties in case law dealing with substantive law issues.

Other objectives in 'dealing with a case justly' are to save expense, to deal with a case in ways that are proportionate to the amount of money involved, to the importance of the case, to the complexity of the issues and to the financial position of each party. Finally, the reforms were concerned to ensure that a case is dealt with expeditiously and fairly. These are important tools. For example, the concept of proportionality has been adopted into the Court Rules in relation to assessment of costs. This is the procedure by which a party, in whose favour a court has made an order for payment of costs by the other party, has the amount of those costs assessed by a specialist costs judge. In determining the amount of costs that will be allowed, the costs judge will, in appropriate cases, consider issues of proportionality.

The scope of the overriding objective as described marks an important acknowledgment that the attainment of a 'Rolls-Royce' consideration of evidence and analysis of legal merits, at whatever costs and over whatever period, is not necessarily what most litigants seek. Whilst claims must continue to be dealt with justly, there is a recognition that expedition and reasonable cost are the context within which the claim should be administered. Whilst some might attack this approach as achieving less than the high standard of justice traditionally associated with the English courts, it should be borne in mind that a correct legal decision on the basis of facts and evidence as established in the case does not necessarily reflect justice nor is it typical. Establishing facts and expert evidence is an expensive process and the party that has unlimited resources to invest in such preparation has an enormous advantage over its opponent. In addition, it is doubtful that the quality of legal precedent in relation to questions of law, of itself valuable to society in general, has been compromised. For the most part, the adoption of expedited or more cost-effective procedures relates to evidence rather than legal argument and the quality of such argument and judicial decision in relation to legal issues therefore remains undiminished. We will mention below the encouragement now given to parties to reach a negotiated settlement and thus avoid a trial, but it is the increased settlement of claims that poses the greater threat to development of legal precedent.

Application of the overriding objective by the court is mandatory. It is also mandatory for the parties to help the court in furthering the objective. To an extent, these two requirements have resulted in a sea change in the manner in which litigation is conducted. Certainly, if the culture encouraged by the CPR was to be adopted wholeheartedly by all those involved in the litigation process, the manipulation of procedures by a party to its own advantage, irrespective of the merits of the case and questions of cost, would be substantially diminished. However, in reality, it remains an inescapable truth that parties with deep pockets, assisted by able lawyers, can exert considerable procedural and commercial pressure within the litigation landscape and that, however far the reforms may have improved procedures, litigation remains very much a process of last resort.

That said, the achievements of the reforms should not be underestimated and many of the changes introduced have made a significant impact on the approach adopted by parties in formulating claims, managing costs and seeking an early resolution of their claims, often outside the court process. This is evidenced by the significant reduction in the number of claims issued in the courts over the period since the introduction of the CPR. In the Queen's Bench Division of the High Court, the number of claims issued fell from 21,237 in 1998/1999 to 8,470 in 1999/2000. Key elements of the reforms which have led to this change in approach are discussed in the sections which follow.

Pre-action conduct

With effect from 1 April 2003, the CPR impose on all parties to a dispute an obligation to comply with pre-action procedures aimed at avoiding the premature commencement of litigation and encouraging an informed dialogue that may lead to a settlement of the claim. The pre-action procedures require the party making the claim to deliver to the prospective defendant a letter of claim and supporting documents giving sufficient detail to enable the defendant to understand and investigate the claim, identify any additional documents required from the defendant and indicate that the claimant is prepared to enter into mediation or some other form of alternative dispute resolution (ADR). The defendant must respond to the letter of claim within a reasonable time, indicating that the claim is not accepted or confirming that all or part of the claim is admitted, in which case the response should set out proposals for settlement. The defendant must also send with the response all essential documents upon which it relies and indicate whether it is prepared to enter into mediation or some other form of ADR. Thus, in relation to a breach of contract claim, the claimant will be required to indicate with reasonable detail the terms of the contract upon which it relies, the breaches it says have been committed by the defendant and the nature and amount of its financial loss. This then gives the defendant an opportunity to assess at an early stage whether there is substance in the claims made by the claimant and, if it does not accept the validity of all or any of the claims, to respond to the claimant explaining in detail why this is so.

In this way, the parties ought to be in a relatively good position to assess the strengths and weaknesses in their position and to decide whether a claim or defence is likely to succeed. An early 'reality check' can be extremely effective in facilitating meaningful negotiations or some form of ADR process that may avoid the need for the claim to be taken any further. The objective is to compel a party to be completely 'upfront' about the nature of its claim or defence so as to enable that claim or defence to be tested by the other party at a much earlier stage in the proceedings than has traditionally been the case. This enables parties to re-evaluate the strength of their position in the context both of encouraging settlement discussions and, equally important, discouraging the prosecution of claims which have been demonstrated by the other party to be flawed. In denying the other party the benefits of this process, a party who refuses to comply with pre-action procedures may have encouraged or engaged in litigation that could have been avoided had the procedures been properly implemented. Parties who do not comply with the procedures risk potentially heavy financial sanctions should the dispute later go to court. The range of powers that the court may exercise includes the power to order the defaulting party to pay all or part of the costs of the case, in an appropriate case, on an indemnity basis, and penalising the defaulting party through varying or disapplying the normal rules of interest awarded on costs and monetary awards from which it would otherwise benefit.

Allocation

Defended claims are allocated to one of three tracks: the small claims track, the fast and the multi-track. The objective of such allocation is to ensure that every claim is dealt with by the fastest and most cost-effective procedure appropriate. The small claims track is the normal track for any claim which has a financial value of less than £5,000 and is exclusive to the county court. This will be the track appropriate for most small contractual claims: for example, the sale of faulty consumer goods or a dispute about the quality of minor building works. In small claims, special procedures apply to simplify the steps needed to prepare for trial, there are limits on recoverable costs and the hearing itself is less formal than in the other two tracks: for example, strict rules of evidence do not apply. Claims allocated to the small claims track are generally given time estimates for trial of between one and three hours. The fast track is an innovation brought about by the Woolf Reforms and is the normal track for claims valued between £5,000 and £15,000. The fast track is intended as a limited procedure designed to take to trial within a short but reasonable timescale straightforward claims that do not require the more complex procedures of the multi-track and that can be dealt with by a trial lasting not more than one day. The multi-track is for the more complex, high-value claims that it is not appropriate to deal with in one of the other two tracks.

Case management

A fundamental change recommended by Lord Woolf was for judges to manage the conduct of a case rather than for the parties and/or their lawyers to do so. His *Interim Report* stated that:

> Without effective judicial control ... the adversarial process is likely to encourage an adversarial culture and to degenerate into an environment in which the litigation process is too often seen as a battlefield where no rules apply. In this environment, questions of expense, delay, compromise and fairness may have only a low priority. The consequence is that expense is often excessive, disproportionate and unpredictable; and delay is frequently unreasonable.

It is now the court, rather than the parties, that dictates the procedure and timetable to be adopted, thus facilitating practical implementation of the principles laid down in the overriding objective. The court rules contain a list of 12 factors which go to make up effective case management. These include encouraging the parties to co-operate with each other in the conduct of proceedings, deciding the order in which issues are to be resolved, considering whether the cost of taking a particular step justifies the cost of taking it and fixing timetables or otherwise controlling the progress of the case.

The objective of the provisions introduced by the Woolf Reforms is to encourage a much more interventionist approach on the part of the judiciary. In the past, the role of judges in relation to preparation for trial was responsive rather than pro-active. Although at a relatively early stage in the action a timetable and list of agreed steps providing, for example, for disclosure of documents, the preparation of statements of witnesses of fact and experts' reports, etc, would be laid down by the court, if the parties subsequently agreed to vary the timetable, this was very much a matter for them and the court would not interfere. Trial dates were not fixed until very late in the process and there was therefore very little pressure upon the parties to work to the original timetable. Deadlines would slip by weeks and sometimes months in relation to several of the steps agreed to be taken.

Not only did this delay a trial and therefore resolution of the dispute, but it also greatly increased the amount of time for which lawyers were working on the case and therefore the amount of their fees. In addition, since in many cases parties did not give serious consideration to engaging in negotiations until the door of the court, the possibility of a resolution by this means was also postponed. Under the CPR the judge will now take a more pro-active role in managing the case. The judge will be looking to see that the most time and cost-effective procedures are adopted and should look to the parties to justify any proposed departure from these. Trial dates are fixed at a much earlier stage which increases the pressure on parties to get on with preparation of the case and makes it much more difficult to accommodate any adjustment to the timetable.

Alternative (or appropriate) dispute resolution

The courts now actively promote the use of ADR procedures as a means of resolving claims without the need for a trial. For example, pre-action protocols require those thinking of litigating their dispute to indicate whether they are prepared to participate in such procedures. In addition, active case management by the courts in the post-Woolf environment has meant that the parties are now encouraged to use ADR procedures if the court considers it appropriate. The allocation questionnaire, completed by the parties and used to assist the court in determining the most appropriate claims track, also contains provision for a party to request proceedings to be delayed (stayed) while the parties try to settle the dispute by ADR. Perhaps most significantly, in appropriate cases, the court's powers in relation to costs enable it to penalise a party that has adopted an unreasonable position in refusing the use of ADR. The need for such sanctions arises as a result of the reluctance of some parties and their advisers to participate in, or even consider the use of, mediation or another form of ADR. The reasons for such reluctance are varied, ranging from an unwillingness on the part of lawyers to engage in a process with which they have no familiarity or confidence, to a level of animosity between the parties that causes them to refuse to even consider any form of out-of-court negotiation. In introducing sanctions for failure to consider ADR, the court makes it essential for lawyers to discuss with their clients the possibility of ADR and to ensure that their clients understand the possible costs consequences if such an approach is not at least explored.

The possible imposition of costs sanctions raises to the question of what constitutes unreasonable conduct. How far does a party have to go in order to establish that they have acted reasonably? Do they have to accept an offer of mediation in all cases even if they believe that the process will be a complete waste of time? This issue has been considered by the courts in a number of recent cases. In *Dunnett v Railtrack plc* (2002), the Court of Appeal penalised Railtrack, which had succeeded in defending an appeal brought by Dunnett and as a result would normally expect to recover its costs. Instead, the court decided to make no order for costs which meant that Railtrack had to pay the costs of bringing the action. The basis for the court's decision was Railtrack's rejection prior to the appeal proceedings of an offer by Dunnett at the suggestion of the lower court to take the dispute to mediation. The court indicated that if a party rejected ADR out of hand when it had been suggested by the court, it would suffer the consequences when the question of costs came to be decided. The court emphasised that the parties themselves also had a duty to consider whether ADR was a possible remedy. The court decided that the fact that Railtrack had made an offer of settlement to compromise the action prior to the appeal being heard was irrelevant. The later case of *Hurst v Leeming* (2003) gave further guidance as to acceptable reasons for refusing ADR. It was held that the already high costs of the case, the serious nature of the other party's allegations, or one party's subjective view of the merits of the other's cases were not valid reasons to reject ADR. A reasoned conclusion that there was no real prospect of success in a mediation was a valid reason for refusal but the hurdle to overcome in relying on this ground is high.

Two recent cases have, however, emphasised that a refusal to mediate is not fatal. In *Valentine v Allen* (2003), Valentine argued that Allen should not be entitled to the costs of successfully resisting his appeal in the usual way because Allen had rejected two separate offers of mediation. The Court of Appeal pointed out that before the hearing of the appeal, Allen had made without prejudice offers of settlement which were reasonable and generous. The parties had met to discuss settlement and the respondents' solicitors had entered into considerable correspondence in an effort to try to settle the appeal, even offering a further 'round the table' meeting. The Court of Appeal held that the respondents had acted reasonably and it was not appropriate to deny Allen his costs. In *Corenso (UK) Ltd v Burnden Group plc* (2003), the judge found that neither party could be blamed for a failure to mediate. Various methods of ADR had been suggested, negotiations had been attempted and it was clear that the parties were prepared to attempt to resolve the matter without going to court. The judge emphasised that a party's obligation is to attempt to resolve the dispute by using ADR, of which mediation is only one form. Mediation would only be appropriate in some cases and, so long as the parties had shown a genuine and constructive willingness to try to settle the dispute, a party would not be penalised because it had not agreed to go along with a particular form of ADR proposed by the other side. The lesson to be drawn from these cases is that the obligation to consider ADR is not an inflexible one and that each case must be carefully considered on its individual facts. That said, it is a brave litigant who will now dismiss an offer of ADR out of hand.

The Woolf Reforms have sought to encourage the use of ADR yet, in truth, alternatives to litigation in the form of private dispute resolution procedures have existed and been used extensively for many years by the business community. Until recent years, however, these have for the most part taken the form of binding procedures in which an independent third party considers the dispute as presented to them by the parties and makes a decision which is then enforceable against them. Arbitration and expert determination are examples of such procedures and are often the norm for resolving disputes in certain industry sectors. For example, arbitration is often used to resolve reinsurance disputes and commercial leases frequently incorporate an expert determination procedure in relation to disagreements arising on rent review. Provision for these methods of dispute resolution traditionally appeared in the body of the underlying contract to which the dispute related. A more recent development is the use of mediation in the commercial sphere. This process has been extensively adopted in other fields such as family law and neighbourhood disputes for a number of years and, although clear evidence of their growing use in business disputes has been seen for some time, it is the Woolf Reforms that have given added impetus to the adoption of these methods.

DIFFERENT TYPES OF DISPUTE RESOLUTION

Expert determination

An expert determination is where parties agree to refer a dispute to a neutral third party with a particular technical expertise who will apply that knowledge when *adjudicating* the matters in dispute. The exercise is very often done on paper without a hearing. Each party will provide the expert with written submissions setting out its case and supported by relevant documents. There may be an opportunity for each party to reply to the submissions made by his opponent and the expert will then make their decision. With some limited exceptions, the decision of the expert is final and binding. There is no appeal.

The advantages of the process are that because of the procedure adopted, the cost and, perhaps more importantly, the delay involved can be significantly less than most other forms of binding dispute resolution. An expert determination may be appropriate where a dispute is concerned solely with a technical issue. For example, did work performed by an IT contractor comply with a technical specification or has a financial calculation been undertaken correctly? In these circumstances, expert determination by an engineer or accountant may be by far the best route for parties to adopt. A third party expert will be familiar with industry norms and practices and can thereby bring useful background knowledge to the dispute that will aid speedy and cost-effective resolution. Expert determination is routinely used in certain industry sectors. For example, it is commonly used to determine a revised rent on implementation of a rent review clause in a commercial lease. It is also used in certain types of agreement, such as completion accounts in a share sale agreement.

Arbitration is one of the most popular forms of expert determination. Indeed, it is so common that many have argued that it is no longer an 'alternative' for dispute resolution. Arbitration is a private adjudicatory process by which parties appoint a third party to make a binding determination in relation to matters in dispute between them. The parties are free to select arbitrator, venue and any procedural rules to be applied. An agreement to arbitrate disputes may be included in the parties' contract in the form of an arbitration clause. Alternatively, it may be entered into after a dispute has arisen as a submission agreement. An arbitration agreement is itself a contract and subject to the same rules as to validity, construction and enforceability as other contracts. For example, if a particular issue in dispute between the parties does not fall within the description of matters referred to arbitration, the arbitrator will have no power to deal with it even if requested to do so by one of the parties. In very general terms, an arbitrator is master of the procedure adopted in the arbitration subject to any procedures that may have been agreed by the parties or mandatory requirements of the law of the place where the arbitration is conducted.

Commentators have identified a number of advantages of arbitration over litigation. Of these, finality and speed have been shown to be particularly important in the commercial sector. In broad terms, parties are free to opt out of any right of appeal against the arbitrator's determination and, even where they do not agree to do so, in most jurisdictions the grounds for appeal to the local courts will be extremely limited. In this way, the process meets the needs of business people to achieve certainty of outcome at the earliest date possible and thus allow them to move on in their business. Various business decisions may be held up while a company waits to find out whether it will be found liable to pay a substantial capital sum, or if it has the right to sell products on to a third party. A further factor is that the cost of taking a dispute through various levels of appeal can be substantial. As a consequence, the parties' businesses may be deprived of much-needed resources. However, the benefits of finality naturally carry a cost. The advantage of having no right of appeal is not one that will necessarily be recognised by the losing party to the dispute. In very general terms, when the parties have appointed a robust arbitrator, a determination may be obtained in a much shorter timeframe than would be the case were the dispute to be litigated.

Arbitration also has the advantage of being a private dispute process and under most systems of law is a more confidential procedure than litigation. The proceedings are held in private and under English law there is an implied obligation on both parties not to disclose events in the arbitration room or to use for their own purpose documents prepared for the arbitration process or provided by the other party as part of a general disclosure of documents. It may be commercially desirable for the dispute to remain confidential for a variety of reasons. One of the parties may be seeking to expand their business and may feel that publicity about the dispute may damage the market's perception of it, or the dispute may relate to sensitive technical information or business strategies that the parties prefer should remain confidential.

The parties to an arbitration also have a much greater degree of control over the choice of arbitrator than the parties to litigation will have over the selection of a judge hearing a case. It is possible to specify in the arbitration agreement appropriate qualifications which an arbitrator appointed under the contract should have and these can be tailored to meet the particular type of dispute or issues arising. So, for instance, contractual disputes concerning issues of foreign law may result in the appointment of a panel of arbitrators of whom one has a legal qualification in that jurisdiction. The arbitration process also allows for greater procedural flexibility than may be the case in relation to many court processes and procedures can be tailored to the particular needs of the dispute.

The amount of international trade has increased enormously in the last few decades. In an ideal world, when parties from different jurisdictions negotiate a dispute resolution provision in a contract, their objective will be to find a form of provision with which they both feel comfortable. For many parties, the first choice will be litigation before their home courts but this leaves the other party at risk of feeling they are at a disadvantage. In such situations, it is possible that the suggestion by the weaker party of arbitration in a neutral venue is something that the parties are prepared to consider. Although the arbitration will take place in a jurisdiction foreign to the parties, the experience will at least be mutual. In addition, the parties will have the comfort of being involved in the choice of arbitrator and can therefore select someone in whom they have confidence and trust rather than relying on the judgment of an unknown foreign judge.

Another key benefit relates to enforcement. While important steps have been taken over the last few decades in relation to international agreements governing reciprocal enforcement of foreign court-based judgments on harmonised terms, the position is still rather patchy at a global level although there are some very good regional regimes. Examples include the Brussels and Lugano Conventions relating to Europe. Most trading nations are parties to the New York Convention on the Recognition and Enforcement of Arbitration Awards 1958 which provides a global regime for enforcement of arbitration awards in States other than the one in which the award was made. The principle underlying the convention is that an award made in any State will be recognised and enforced by any other State which is a party to the Convention, provided that the award satisfies certain basic conditions. The formalities required for obtaining the recognition and enforcement of Convention awards are relatively straightforward and the Convention does not permit any review on the merits of an award to which it applies.

Arbitration also has a number of disadvantages. Somewhat surprisingly, the cost of arbitration can be significantly higher than litigation. The parties will have to pay the arbitrator's fees and expenses unlike in litigation where a judge comes free. The parties will also have to provide a suite of rooms for the hearing, together with appropriate support services such as transcription and secretarial services. If there is a panel of three arbitrators and a lengthy hearing in a foreign venue, these may be considerable.

Prior to 1979, the Arbitration Acts of 1950 and 1975 provided numerous opportunities for recalcitrant parties to seek judicial intervention in the arbitration proceedings and to attack the arbitrator's award once published. As well as the disruption and costs that this caused to the arbitration process, in relation to international arbitration, there was evidence that it was beginning to deter parties from agreeing to London as a venue for international arbitration, with adverse economic consequences for the city. There was a degree of frustration amongst many users and practitioners that what was intended to work as an efficient and speedy process was becoming subject to the same disadvantages of delay and inflexibility in procedures that were sometimes perceived to exist in litigation. Many expressed concerns that it was beginning to mirror litigation rather than provide a meaningful alternative.

The Arbitration Act 1979 implemented a number of recommendations made by a Departmental Advisory Committee chaired by Lord Donaldson which severely restricted the scope for challenge to an award. Despite these important changes which went a substantial way to meeting the concerns referred to above, the position of English arbitration was still unsatisfactory because there was a substantial body of common law relating to English arbitration practice which was entirely inaccessible to all but English specialist arbitration practitioners. In addition, there remained scope for judicial intervention where the arbitration proceedings failed to run smoothly.

These problems were addressed in the Arbitration Act 1996 which sets out in one piece of legislation, accessible to English and foreign lawyers alike, the provisions of English arbitration law. Significantly, the legislation made clear that the role of the court was recognised as being a support role rather than a supervisory one. Its powers were to be confined to specific statutory powers, principally designed to protect the integrity of the arbitration process; for example, the power to remove an arbitrator who is not impartial. The Act specifically states that the parties should be free to agree how their disputes are resolved, subject only to such safeguards as are necessary in the public interest. Moreover, it also clearly sets out procedures that will come into play in the arbitration in the event that the parties have failed to reach express agreement on various elements of the process. These provisions serve to confirm and enhance the autonomy and effectiveness of the arbitration process. The 1996 Act is generally regarded as a success story in terms of safeguarding London as an international arbitration centre both in terms of reputation and in economic terms. International arbitration is an industry in its own right involving as it does a large pool of professional arbitrators, institutional bodies, trade organisations and specialist lawyers and other professionals, all of whom have a vested interest in ensuring that London arbitration meets the needs and expectations of business users and practitioners.

Mediation

The use of mediation to resolve commercial disputes has increased significantly in recent years and, in response to the changes introduced by the Civil Procedure Rules, the Chartered Institute of Arbitrators is involved in a number of mediation schemes, and large-scale consumer mediation schemes have also been set up by companies such as Norwich Union. The increasing importance of mediation in the commercial sphere has also been signalled by the creation of the City Disputes Panel which handles disputes in the financial services industry and claims to have dealt with cases involving a total value in dispute exceeding $4,000 million. More recently, a preference for mediation schemes has also been demonstrated by the British Marine Federation, the British Institute of Architectural Technologists and the Baltic and International Maritime Council. The Centre for Effective Dispute Resolution (CEDR), one of the country's largest mediation providers, claims that in the 12 months between April 1999 and March 2000 they experienced a 141% increase in the number of commercial disputes referred to them. In the following year, the organisation arranged 467 commercial mediations, of which commercial contract disputes accounted for 31% of cases, some of which involved damages of between $1.1 million and $8 million.

In March 2001, the then Lord Chancellor's Department (LCD) announced that all government departments should seek to avoid litigation by using mediation and a year later the Office of Government Commerce published a dispute resolution guide for all those involved in the drafting of UK procurement contracts. At a European level, the European Commission's Green Paper on developing commercial mediation in the EU was also published and adopted in 2002 and it is anticipated by mediation providers that by the end of 2004 the Member States of the United Nations Commission on International Trade Law will have voted to adopt a model law of international commercial conciliation encouraging those countries with no mediation provision to use it as a basis for reform. The Insurance Mediation Directive of 2002 also supports this trend and seeks to ensure a high degree of professionalism and competence amongst intermediaries in insurance disputes.

Mediation is a private process in which the parties to a dispute, with authority to reach a binding settlement, come together for an agreed period, often a single day. With the assistance of a neutral mediator, they attempt to reach a resolution of their dispute. In a commercial setting, they are often accompanied by their lawyers, although this is less common in other spheres. If terms are agreed, a settlement agreement is drawn up and signed there and then. The process is a consensual one in the sense that the parties have chosen to mediate and have not been forced into the process in the same way they might be forced into litigation in the event of the other party exercising the right to issue court proceedings. If the parties cannot reach agreement they are free to revert to what other form of process they think appropriate. All of the discussions and negotiations that take place during a mediation remain confidential and may not be disclosed to a judge or arbitrator who may later have to deal with the dispute.

In general terms there are two forms of mediation, although there are an increasing number of variations: facilitative mediation in which the mediator assists the parties to formulate a settlement, and evaluative mediation in which the mediator may assist the process by giving a non-binding third party view of the merits of the particular issues between the parties. It is possible for parties to agree to mediation-arbitration in which case the mediator, in the event the parties are unable to reach a settlement, will change role to become an arbitrator and in that capacity will then make a binding decision on the merits.

A mediator will adopt a much less interventionist role than a judge. In contrast to adjudication, the role of the mediator is to encourage the parties to reach a result that best suits their needs rather than imposing one upon them. The mediation process usually opens with a joint meeting of the parties and mediator at which each party is given an opportunity to make a statement about its position but there is considerable flexibility about how the process can be organised. Frequently, the meeting will then break up into two camps or 'caucuses' and the mediator will embark upon a form of shuttle diplomacy, moving from party to party, trying to narrow issues, play 'devil's advocate' and assist the parties in identifying some common objectives. There are, however, no hard and fast rules about how the process should work. The essence of mediation is that it should be as responsive as possible to the needs of the parties and the particular dispute.

Mediation can be of considerable value in relation to commercial disputes, particularly where the number of companies operating in the particular industry sector is small or where the contractual relationship between the parties is a long-term one. In these circumstances it is, for obvious reasons, in both parties' interests to find a solution that will enable them to continue working together. This factor itself can assist the mediator in trying to establish some common ground upon which a settlement can be reached. They will often try to explore with the parties factors outside the dispute itself to see if there are commercial matters not directly connected with the dispute but which may assist the parties in reaching a commercial compromise acceptable on both sides. For example, if the dispute concerns a question of whether one party is due an additional payment in relation to work undertaken, a settlement in which the amount paid is significantly less than that claimed but the paying party will also commit itself to placing an order for additional work may well be acceptable to both parties and may allow the parties to preserve the relationship more or less intact.

Mediation clauses in commercial agreements are now extremely common. Central government has made clear that where the other party agrees, they should be included in most public sector contracts. Even if the contract does not contain a mediation clause, commercial entities have in recent years become much more receptive to the idea of mediation. Its attractions for the businessperson are clear. In addition to the obvious savings in costs, it enables them to exercise some degree of control over the outcome of the dispute, it avoids the considerable waste of management time involved in the litigation or arbitration process and can salvage a valuable business relationship. Lawyers, no doubt responding to the requirements of the new post-Woolf litigation environment referred to above, are now much more likely to advise their clients to try mediation and this has been a significant factor in extending the practice of mediation to embrace commercial disputes.

Where parties have already embarked upon litigation, mediation can often serve as a valuable opportunity to undertake a 'reality check' on their position. Most legal advisers will ensure that when the mediation takes place, their client has detailed information on the key factors that should inform their approach to settlement. These will almost certainly include details of legal costs incurred to date and legal costs likely to be incurred in taking the dispute to trial. A second important factor will be an analysis of possible outcomes at trial and net financial consequences in relation to each. The percentage chance of success and net financial outcome are matters to which most businesspeople will readily relate and in the context of which they can make informed decisions in relation to their negotiating position in the mediation.

Figure 20.2: Analysis of litigation factors prior to mediation

key factors	
costs incurred to date	£20,000
additional costs likely to be incurred to date of trial	£50,000
total costs likely to be incurred by the other side in taking the matter to trial (some guidance on this can be gleaned from the forecast of costs which each party is obliged to file with the court)	£80,000
percentage chance of success in litigation	70%
value of claim	£200,000
possible scenarios	
success at trial: 1 recover amount claimed (£200,000) 2 obtain an order for costs resulting in a recovery, following an assessment of costs by the court, of approximately 60–70% of actual costs incurred (£45,500)	net outcome: receive £175,500
lose at trial: 1 recover nothing 2 bear 100% of own costs (£70,000) 3 subject to an order for payment of costs to the other side resulting in a payment out of approximately 60–70% of opponent's actual costs (£52,000)	net outcome: pay out £122,000

Figure 20.2 illustrates the sort of cost/benefit/risk analysis that a party, with the assistance of its lawyers, will be undertaking in preparation for and during a mediation. In the example given, the percentage chance of success is, in litigation terms, high and a party in this position may well feel relatively comfortable in taking the claim to trial should a mediation fail to produce a satisfactory outcome. However,

even in a case as strong as this, the 25% possibility of a nil recovery and payment of an opponent's costs in the order of £50,000 is something that will cause pause for thought. Clearly, were the percentage chance of success to be significantly lower, the incentive to find a solution in the mediation will be that much greater. In complex cases, such analyses are not always straightforward. There may be several different issues or claims in the case with different risk–cost factors attached to each. The range of permutations may be considerable and the lawyer will have to focus in on the most likely scenarios in order to determine a negotiating strategy with their client. However, if properly advised, both parties will be approaching the mediation in this way and one of the goals of the mediator will be to find a position where for each party the risk/benefit of proceeding to trial is less attractive than the proposal on the table in the mediation.

CONCLUDING REMARKS

The key development in relation to State policy as regards dispute resolution is the effort to devolve power for management of disputes to the parties. Disputes which previously would have plodded through the litigation system are now more commonly referred to 'facilitators' such as mediators and there are many new incentives to work towards bilateral management of disputes. Although this may result in fewer cases on which to challenge existing case law and doctrine, there is an obvious advantage to the parties. In the business sector, there has long been a desire to manage disputes more effectively and thus avoid the trials and tribulations of litigation. The net result of this is that, where used appropriately, dispute resolution procedures can become almost an extension of routine business activity as parties seek to renegotiate their position on the basis of familiar commercial factors such as risk and cost. In this way, litigation becomes much more accessible to business people and is no longer the great mystery it might once have seemed. The role of the lawyer will be as much to assist clients in finding the most appropriate form of dispute resolution process as to advise on the legal merits of the case.

Our consideration of mediation also leads us back to some of the key themes introduced at the beginning of the book and referred to throughout. Mediators are far from alone in arguing for a relational and contextualised understanding of contracts. Reformulation of traditional contract models is an imperative for a variety of modern-day scholars of a critical, feminist or socio-legal bent. Researchers in these traditions have identified a number of ways in which the judiciary has failed to understand, or respond to, the needs of contracting parties, especially those involved in long-term relationships and we have argued that the law of contract is facing something of a legitimation crisis as a result. A succession of empirical studies have demonstrated that formal law is frequently ignored or circumvented by contracting parties because of its inability to reflect the needs of the contracting parties and nuances of their relationship. For some, formal law has become more or less irrelevant to the performance of long-term contracts because of its reliance on individual self-interest and economic rationality at the cost of more widely accepted notions of common interest and flexibility, such as those espoused by many feminist writers.

This state of affairs has led academics to call for the architects of the law and legal system to devise doctrines and processes which give adequate expression to relationships guided by the knowledge acquired about their empirical character. It could be argued that these concerns have begun to be addressed in the post-Woolf environment. In common with many mediators, modern contract theorists are much more likely than their forebears to advocate a return to models of contract that address communication between embodied subjects whose desires and needs develop and change over time. They have argued that modern contractual relationships are better understood as involving long-term bonds, concern about reputation, interdependence, co-operation, morality and even altruistic desires.

REFERENCES AND FURTHER READING

Abel, R (1982) 'The contradictions of informal justice' in Able, R (ed), *The Politics of Informal Justice*, London: Academic Press, pp 267–320.

Brown, H and Marriot, A (2002) *ADR Principles and Practice*, London: Sweet & Maxwell.

Campbell, D (2002) 'Forbearance, alternative dispute resolution and settlement' in Collins, H (2003) *The Law of Contract*, London: LexisNexis Butterworths.

Galanter, M 'Worlds of deals: using negotiations teach about legal process' (1984) 34 *Journal of Legal Education* 268.

Genn, H (1998) *Final Report to the Lord Chancellor on the County Court Pilot Scheme*, London: Lord Chancellor's Department.

Genn, H (1999) *Paths to Justice*, Oxford: Hart Publishing.

Grillo, T 'The mediation alternative: process dangers for women' (1991) 100(2) Yale Law Journal 1900–91.

Harris, D, Campbell, D and Halson, R (2002) *Remedies in Contract and Tort*, 2nd edn, London: LexisNexis Butterworths.

Mulcahy, L (2005) 'Bargaining in the shadow of the flaws? The feminisation of dispute resolution' in Mulcahy, L and Wheeler, S (eds), *Feminist Perspectives on Contract Law*, London: Cavendish Publishing.

Palmer, M and Roberts, S (1998) *Dispute Processes: ADR and the Primary Forms of Decision Making*, London: Butterworths.

Woolf, Lord (1994) *Access to Justice: Interim Report*, London: HMSO.

Woolf, Lord (1996) *Access to Justice: Final Report*, London: HMSO.

QUESTIONS

(1) Look back at each of the disputes that Angie and Georgie have become embroiled in and identify which of the following dispute procedures is most likely to help them achieve what they want:

   (a) bilateral negotiation;

   (b) mediation;

   (c) arbitration;

   (d) court-based adjudication.

   Give reasons for your response.

(2) Can you find out how much each of the processes named in question (1) might cost? What costs other than lawyers' fees and third party fees could you include in your list?

(3) Can you fill in the checklist in Figure 20.2 in relation to Angie and Georgie's dispute with Orange Peril plc? Is your conclusion that they should mediate or not?

(4) Appraise critically the argument that the Woolf Reforms of the civil litigation system pose a threat to the development of the common law.

(5) Can you discover 10 reasons why commercial arbitration is preferable to litigation in the field of international commerce?

INDEX